Sunset

Easy Basics for International Cooking

BY THE EDITORS OF SUNSET BOOKS AND SUNSET MAGAZINE

One great cook book calls for another. Sunset's EASY BASICS FOR GOOD COOKING has proved such a success that, by popular demand, we continue its theme of illustrated cooking technique in this new companion volume. In addition to bringing you more than 375 recipes from over 60 countries, cultures, and regions of the world, this book is replete with full details on technique, supported by 236 step-by-step color photographs taken in Sunset's test kitchens. All recipes were selected not only for their regional interest, but also for their excellence of flavor and ease of preparation. They include well-known classics and national specialties, as well as new and delectable discoveries —all to be enjoyed at your table.

Lane Publishing Co. • Menlo Park, California

Coordinating Editor
Cornelia Fogle

Research & Text
Elaine R. Woodard
Janeth Johnson Nix
Joan Griffiths

Contributing Editor
Susan Warton

Special Consultant
Jerry Anne Di Vecchio
Home Economics Editor
Sunset Magazine

Design
Joe di Chiarro

Photography
Darrow M. Watt

Photo Editor
Lynne B. Morrall

Illustrations
Sally Shimizu

Best of the world's cuisines...

Ethnic cooking is anything but foreign to Sunset. For dozens of years, we have researched and published exciting recipes from all over the world. Most recently, our *Chinese Cook Book, Country French Cooking, International Vegetarian Cook Book, Italian Cook Book, Mexican Cook Book,* and *Oriental Cook Book* have all met with widespread appreciation and acclaim.

Now, in this volume, we invite you to our grandest banquet yet—celebrating the best of more than sixty of the world's cuisines, and deliciously revealing what makes these cuisines special, often world-famous. At the same time, our recipes illustrate and explain the many cooking techniques shared around the globe.

Spiced with local color, and detailed in technique, the recipes in this book come from the cooking traditions of the following lands and cultures: Argentina, the Armenian heritage, Australia, Austria, Belgium, Brazil, Canada, the Caribbean, Chile, China, Colombia, Cuba, Czechoslovakia, Denmark, Ecuador, El Salvador, England, Ethiopia, Finland, France, Germany, Ghana, Greece, Hungary, India, Indonesia, Ireland, Israel, Italy, Jamaica, Japan, the Jewish heritage, Korea, Lebanon, Malaysia, Mexico, the Middle East, Morocco, Nepal, the Netherlands, Nicaragua, Norway, Pakistan, the Philippines, Poland, Portugal, Russia, Samoan Islands, Saudi Arabia, Scotland, South Africa, Spain, Sri Lanka, Sweden, Switzerland, Tahiti, Thailand, Turkey, the United States, Vietnam, Wales, the West Indies, and Yugoslavia.

Our special thanks to Rebecca La Brum for her thorough and sensitive editing of the manuscript. For their generosity in sharing props for use in photographs, we thank The Abacus, Agapanthus, Allied Arts Traditional Gift Shop, Best of All Worlds, Biordi Art Imports, Brass International, Brown's, House of Today, Menlo Park Hardware Co., Mikado Japanese Imports, Nak's Oriental Market, S. Christian of Copenhagen, Taylor & Ng, William Ober Co., Williams Cutlery, Williams-Sonoma Kitchenware, and Wisnom Hardware.

Cover photograph: From the Spanish province of Valencia comes the classic Paella (page 154), a one-dish feast that combines shellfish, chicken, sausages, and vegetables in golden, spicy rice. Cover photograph by Michael Lamotte. Food styling by Amy Nathan. Cover design by Williams and Ziller Design.

Editor, Sunset Books: David E. Clark

First Printing September 1984

CONTENTS

SPECIAL FEATURES

WELCOME!

Welcome to the big, wide, good-tasting world of international cooking. Welcome to Thailand, France, Turkey, Ghana, Sweden, Ecuador, Pakistan, and dozens of other countries along the way. Welcome to their kitchens, traditions, and glorious regional seasonings, and to their time-honored artistry and wisdom with local ingredients.

Reinforcing that welcome in the most practical way are 48 step-by-step cooking lessons, photographed in color and offering techniques that will serve as your passport to great cooking from any quarter of the globe.

Like a cooking school tour of the world's cuisines, this book can guide you to delicious adventures with such classic favorites as Japanese Teriyaki Beef, Greek Moussaka, Swiss Cheese Fondue, and German Black Forest Cherry Cake.

But any good tour must wander off the beaten path if intriguing discoveries are to be made. And this book opens up an abundance of culinary marvels just now being discovered by American cooks: Morocco's *Bastilla*, Indonesia's *Gado Gado*, India's *Tandoori* Chicken, Holland's *Stamppot*, Hungary's *Langos*, and the Philippines' Chicken & Pork *Adobo*, to name just a few.

Each recipe, whether well or little known, was carefully selected, repeatedly tested, and occasionally adapted to meet Sunset's high standards. Our first consideration, naturally, was excellence of flavor—authentic, yet acceptable to American tastes (for example, we slightly toned down the fierce heat of Indian curry seasonings). Next, we sought to foil any frustrations in the ingredients

lists by applying these criteria: To the extent it was possible, we called for ingredients that can easily be found in good supermarkets around the country. But where this standard seemed inapplicable, we suggested substitute ingredients or gave a recipe for preparing your own (Hoisin-style Sauce, for example, or Chinese five-spice or chili oil).

We streamlined the recipes to eliminate any traditional procedures that today's cook might consider too time-consuming and laborious. Purchased fila dough wraps up our marvelous Austrian Strudel Meat Roll, and ready-to-use egg roll skins make classic Italian Cannelloni a breeze.

Finally, as the step-by-step photographs reveal, this book has been organized primarily to teach technique—using a different magnificent dish for each lesson. We start you off with some basic background information, plus a glossary of foreign ingredients, and an exciting collection of menus for inspired entertaining.

Try international cooking with family, too. You'll find that a little touch of Tokyo or Mazatlán, Genoa or Budapest, brings delight to simple weeknight dining—whether in a full ethnic meal, a menu of mixed cuisines, or a single, spectacular salad or dessert.

No matter how much cooking—or traveling— background you have, adventures await when you use this book as your deluxe guided tour of the world's cuisines. Welcome aboard ... for fun, great flavor, and a whole world of new cooking expertise.

Useful kitchen equipment

Metal spatulas

Wooden spoons

Rubber spatulas

Ice cream scoop

Wire whisks

Mixing bowls

Bulb baster

Utility spoon

Slotted spoon

Ladle

Bottle opener

Can opener

Kitchen scissors

2-tined kitchen fork

Poultry shears

Wide metal spatula

Mallet

Tongs

Nonmetal spatula

Meat thermometers

Spaghetti rake

Vegetable peeler

Oriental wire skimmer

Vegetable steamer

Strainer

Garlic press

Mortar and pestle

Grater

Colander

Sifter

Funnel

Nutmeg grater

Rolling pin

Pastry bag and tips

Pastry brushes

Pastry blender

Cooky cutters

Cooky press and plates

RANGE-TOP ACCESSORIES

ROASTING & BAKING ACCESSORIES

BROILING & GRILLING ACCESSORIES

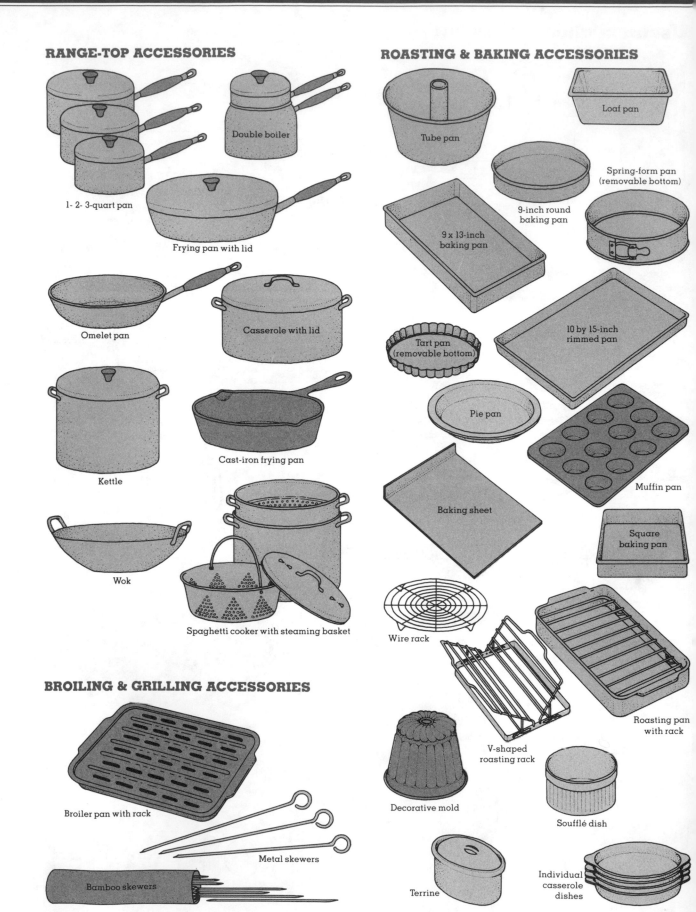

1- 2- 3-quart pan

Double boiler

Frying pan with lid

Omelet pan

Casserole with lid

Kettle

Cast-iron frying pan

Wok

Spaghetti cooker with steaming basket

Tube pan

Loaf pan

Spring-form pan
(removable bottom)

9-inch round
baking pan

9 x 13-inch
baking pan

Tart pan
(removable bottom)

10 by 15-inch
rimmed pan

Pie pan

Muffin pan

Baking sheet

Square
baking pan

Wire rack

Decorative mold

V-shaped
roasting rack

Roasting pan
with rack

Soufflé dish

Terrine

Individual
casserole
dishes

Broiler pan with rack

Metal skewers

Bamboo skewers

Knives: The basic cutting tools

Many otherwise well-equipped kitchens lack a set of good knives—possibly because the cook hasn't yet discovered how expertly a really good knife performs.

A knife's performance depends on the quality of its steel and the excellence of its "grind" (cutting edge). To take and hold a keen edge, a blade must be made of steel with a high carbon content. Carbon content determines the hardness of a blade—and hardness is essential for a sharp edge.

A carbon steel knife, therefore, would seem to be the best choice, but there's one disadvantage—this material tends to turn dark, and it will rust if you don't dry it immediately after each washing. Stainless steel, a combination of carbon steel and chromium, has noncorrosive properties, so it stays shiny. But most stainless steel has a low carbon content and won't keep a sharp edge. You can find high carbon stainless, which takes a good edge, but it's more difficult to sharpen.

The pros and cons of carbon and stainless balance each other fairly well—you'll probably put as much effort into keeping a carbon steel knife clean and rust-free as you would into keeping a stainless steel knife sharp, and if frequently sharpened, the stainless will probably give just as good a cutting edge as the carbon.

Chrome-plated knives look like stainless steel knives, but they don't give anything like the same service. In time, the chromium finish wears off, and the edge is likely to rust.

Test for quality. Usually a knife's cost is directly related to its quality, but there are other tests besides price. Grip the handle to be sure the knife is well balanced, with the center of gravity near the handle (especially important in large knives). Look for a "full tang"—an extension of the blade that runs the full length of the handle. This extension may not be visible, but three rivets in the handle usually indicate a full tang (watch out for knives with fake rivets hiding a tang of only 2 inches or so). The best knives taper from heel to tip, and from the top of the blade to the cutting edge. The bolster protects the grip hand from the blade.

Proper care of knives. Keep your knives in their own protected place—not in a miscellany drawer where edges will be dulled by knocking against other tools. Hang them on a magnetic rack or keep them in a grooved wooden knife block. To preserve their handles, never soak knives in dishwater, and absolutely never subject them to a dishwasher. The water may dry and warp wooden handles, causing the tang to loosen. The best way to care for knives is simply to wash them quickly and dry them immediately. It's perfectly safe to scour carbon knives with abrasives—this actually helps keep them sharp.

Basic knives. Listed below are eight knife types that can handle virtually any kitchen cutting job you're likely to encounter: **paring knife,** for peeling, seeding, and pitting; **utility knife,** for slicing tomatoes and fruit; **boning knife,** for boning meat, fish, and chicken; **slicing knife,** for thinly slicing large cuts of meat; **butcher knife,** for cutting up raw meat and poultry and large foods like watermelon; **French knife,** for chopping and mincing vegetables and for many other uses; **serrated knife,** for cutting bread and baked goods such as angel food cakes; and flexible-bladed **filleting knife,** for boning and skinning fish.

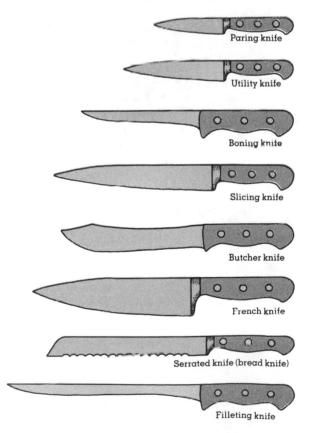

Paring knife

Utility knife

Boning knife

Slicing knife

Butcher knife

French knife

Serrated knife (bread knife)

Filleting knife

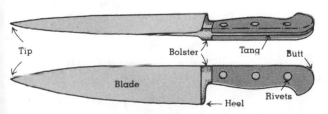

Tip

Bolster

Tang

Butt

Blade

Heel

Rivets

Menu-making around the globe

For imaginative entertaining as well as tempting family fare, let international cooking guide you. Using the recipes in this book, you'll be able to devise dozens of appealing menus; let the samples we offer here serve as a springboard for your meal-planning creativity. Mix and match different cuisines, as in our International Buffet; or focus on the cooking of just one country or region of the world, as in our Mexican Fiesta and Southeast Asian Barbecue.

When you compose a menu, keep convenience in mind—choose just one or two dishes requiring last-minute attention, and complete the meal with "make-aheads."

Mexican Fiesta

(Serves four)

When you enjoy this festive meal, you're sampling a cuisine with a long history. Corn, chiles, avocados, and tomatoes—all so typical of modern Mexican cooking—have been used since the days of the Aztecs and Mayans. Other popular ingredients have a somewhat briefer tradition; pork and the wheat used in breads and tortillas are 16th-century Spanish contributions.

You can prepare the Gazpacho, Chimichangas, Flan, and Teacakes the day before serving.

Mexican Tomato Gazpacho (page 29)
Pounded Pork & Chili Chops (page 84)
or
Pork Chimichangas (page 66) with
Guacamole (page 16) and Sour Cream
Acapulco Corn Medley (page 168)
Sangría, Beer, or Iced tea
Flan (page 207) or Papaya Halves with Lime Wedges
Teacakes (page 197)
Coffee or Tea

Spanish Tapas Party

(Serves eight to ten)

Spain's dining schedule runs comfortably late: the main meal is served at 2 or 3 in the afternoon, and dinner's at 10 o'clock. But there's a meal of sorts in the early evening, too; that's the time to visit a *tasca* (pub) and enjoy a glass of sherry and an array of tasty *tapas* (appetizers).

All these tapas are finger foods that can be made ahead and refrigerated; remove from the refrigerator about an hour before party time (you may want to reheat the meat). Cut the omelet into bite-size pieces before serving, then set out the food buffet style.

Broiled Small Pork Chops
Sliced Cooked Sausages
Marinated Clams or Mussels (page 21)
Marinated Vegetable Medley (page 137)
Potato Omelet (page 56)
Cubes of Jack Cheese   Spanish Olives
Potato Chips
An Assortment of Sherry Wines

Southeast Asian Barbecue

(Serves eight to ten)

Let this tempting outdoor banquet introduce you to the cooking of Southeast Asia. Our menu includes recipes from three of the region's countries: Indonesia, Thailand, and Malaysia.

The sweet-sour vegetable medley and the spicy peanut dipping sauce (for pork, raw vegetables, and shrimp chips) can be made a day ahead. You can fry the shrimp chips ahead, too; stored airtight, they'll stay crisp for a day or two.

At party time, let guests cook their own pork strips on a small tabletop grill while one person tends to the succulent barbecued poultry.

Grilled Pork (double recipe; page 87)
Assorted Raw Vegetables
Peanut Sauce (double recipe; page 143)
Shrimp Chips
Bangkok-style Barbecued Birds (page 104)
Festive Yellow Rice (double recipe; page 156)
Sesame-topped Vegetables (page 168)
Sliced Mangoes over Ice Cream
Coffee or Tea

Quick European Dinner

(Serves four)

If you time the cooking right, you can have this dinner on the table in about 40 minutes. Make the coffee sauce for the Belgian sundaes the night before. Start the Hungarian rice dish 40 minutes before dinner; when it's almost done, slip the Italian-style sole into the oven. Broil the French herbed tomatoes last of all.

Roman Sole (page 121)
Rice with Mushrooms & Peas (page 152)
Basil Tomatoes (half recipe; page 167)
Crusty Rolls   Butter
White Wine
Coffee Cream Sundaes (page 214)
Coffee or Tea

International Buffet

(Serves twelve)

The delicious parade of recipes below offers an unforgettable feast of international flavors. Everything can be made in advance. Choose two or three kinds of turnovers for the party; assemble them up to a week ahead, then freeze uncooked. Thaw in the refrigerator for 24 hours before baking; serve hot or at room temperature.

Carry out the international theme by identifying each dish with a tiny flag of its country (buy flags at a novelty store).

Marinated Beets & Onions (page 137)
Italian Marinated Mushrooms (page 137)
Fresh Fruit Salad
Marinated Potato Salad (double recipe; page 44)
Spicy Beef Turnovers (page 73),
Cornish Pasties (page 73),
Piroshkis (page 74), or Chicken Empanadas (page 74)
Wine or Beer
Lemon Yogurt Cake (page 204)
Coffee or Tea

Cook-at-the-table Dinner

(Serves four)

Here's a cozy, informal dinner. Diners cook their own servings of meat and vegetables Japanese-style in the communal pot, then sip the flavorful cooking broth from individual bowls. Mexican Flan and Chinese cookies bring the meal to a sweetly satisfying close.

Shabu Shabu (page 98)   Steamed Rice
Flan (page 207) or Zabaglione (page 207)
Almond Cookies (page 200)   Fortune Cookies
Green Tea (page 217)

European Brunch

(Serves six)

There's a pleasing balance of light and hearty dishes here. Make the Danish apple cake the day before your brunch, or bake it while you make the Russian pie filling. Wait until just before serving to fry the ham.

Fresh Fruit Compote or Fresh Berry Soup (page 210)
Cheese & Mushroom Pie (page 60)
Pan-fried Ham   Cherry Tomatoes
Apple Cake (page 204)
Coffee or Tea

Elegant Italian Dinner

(Serves two)

Share this superb dinner with someone very special. Make the coffee ice a few days ahead; prepare melon or oysters, salad, and dressing several hours before dinner, then refrigerate each separately (remove dressing from the refrigerator an hour before serving). You can even boil the noodles a few hours ahead; rinse them under cold running water after cooking, then reheat with butter just before serving.

Melon Crescents (page 25)
or
Oysters on the Half Shell (page 25)
Italian Bread   Butter
Veal with Peppers (page 89)   Buttered Noodles
Tossed Green Salad with Vinaigrette Dressing
Champagne or Wine
Caffè Granita (page 216)

Spring Luncheon

(Serves four to six)

Fresh asparagus, tiny shrimp, and plump strawberries highlight this easy luncheon menu. You can prepare the salad and its citrus dressing hours ahead, then toss just before serving. Make the cookies up to a month in advance and store them in the freezer.

Sicilian Green Salad (page 41)
Bread Sticks   Butter
Spring Green Noodles & Shrimp (page 145)
Fruity White Wine or Iced Tea
Fresh Strawberries
Assorted Swedish Butter Cookies (page 199)
Coffee or Tea

Middle Eastern Picnic

(Serves four)

Find a shady spot, spread out a blanket, and dine like the nomadic Bedouins of the Middle East. Everything can be served at room temperature. Pieces of pocket bread serve to scoop up the hummus and beans; lettuce leaves are handy dippers for the salad.

Hummus (page 17)
Lemon Pinto Beans (page 157)
Pocket Bread (page 185 or purchased)
Eggplant & Tomato Salad (page 45)
Romaine Lettuce Leaves
Lemony Broiled Chicken (page 105)
Fresh Fruits and Nuts

Glossary of cooking terms

Acid water: Water to which vinegar or lemon juice has been added; used to prevent discoloration and darkening of certain foods.

Al dente: Italian term used to describe pasta cooked until tender but still slightly firm to the bite.

Bake: To cook, covered or uncovered, by dry heat (usually in an oven). When applied to meats and poultry cooked uncovered, the process is called roasting.

Baste: To brush or spoon pan drippings, other fat, or a liquid mixture over food as it cooks, to keep the surface moist and add flavor.

Batter: A semiliquid mixture (containing flour and other ingredients) that can be dropped from a spoon or poured.

Beat: To stir or mix rapidly, adding air with a quick, even, circular motion to make a mixture smooth, light, or fluffy. When using a spoon or wire whisk, lift mixture up and over with each stroke.

Blend: To thoroughly combine two or more ingredients.

Boil: To cook liquid rapidly so that bubbles constantly rise and break on the surface. To cook food in boiling liquid.

Bone: To remove bones from meat, poultry, or fish.

Braise: To cook slowly in liquid in a covered kettle or casserole. Food may or may not be browned first in a small amount of fat.

Bread: To coat with bread or cracker crumbs before cooking, usually after first dipping food into egg or other liquid so crumbs will adhere.

Broil: To cook below direct heat in the broiler of an electric or gas range.

Broth: Liquid in which meat, poultry, fish, vegetables, or a combination of these has been cooked.

Brown: To cook in a small amount of fat until browned on all sides, giving food an appetizing color and, in meats, sealing in natural juices.

Butterfly: To cut a piece of meat, fish, or poultry in half horizontally, leaving one side attached.

Caramelize: To melt sugar over low heat, without scorching or burning, until it turns golden brown and develops characteristic caramel flavor. To cook onions until sweet and golden.

Chop: To cut food into small pieces.

Coagulate: To thicken into a curd or thick jelly.

Coat: To cover a food with a surface layer of another ingredient, such as beaten egg or flour, by sprinkling, dipping, or rolling.

Coat a spoon: Stage reached by a thickened liquid mixture when it leaves a thin film on the back of a metal spoon.

Condiment: A sauce, relish, or additional ingredient used to season food at the table.

Core: To remove the center of a fruit or vegetable.

Cream: To beat with a spoon or an electric mixer until soft, smooth, and creamy, as in blending butter and sugar.

Cube: To cut into small cubes (about ½ to 1 inch). In meats, to tenderize by pounding with a special tool (usually a mallet) that imprints a small checkered pattern on the surface, breaking tough muscle fibers to increase tenderness.

Curdled: Separated into a liquid containing small solid particles (caused by overcooking or too much heat or agitation).

Cut in: To distribute solid fat into dry ingredients with a pastry blender (or 2 knives, used scissor-fashion) until particles are desired size.

Dash: A very small amount, less than ⅛ teaspoon.

Deep-fry: To cook immersed in hot fat, in a large, deep, heavy pan.

Degrease: To skim fat from surface of a liquid.

Dice: To cut into very small pieces (about ⅛ to ¼ inch).

Dollop: A large spoonful of a mixture, such as whipped cream or sour cream; usually placed on individual servings of a finished dish to enhance both flavor and appearance.

Dot: To scatter bits of an ingredient, such as butter, over surface of food.

Dough: A thick, pliable mixture of flour and liquid ingredients, firm enough to be kneaded or shaped with the hands.

Drippings: Melted fat and juices given off by meat and poultry during cooking.

Drizzle: To pour melted fat, sugar syrup, or other liquid in a fine stream, making a zigzag pattern over food surface.

Dust: To sprinkle lightly with powdered sugar or flour. (Shake off excess after dusting meats, poultry, or fish with flour.)

To flour-dust pans, first spread a small amount of solid shortening over pan bottom and sides; then sprinkle with flour. Shake pan to coat greased surfaces. Invert pan over sink; tap sharply to remove excess flour.

Entrée: The main dish of a meal.

Fat: Generic term for butter, margarine, lard, solid vegetable shortening; also the rendered drippings of meat or poultry.

Fillet: A piece of meat or fish that is naturally boneless or has had all bones removed.

Flake: To lightly break into small, thin pieces.

Flan: A baked custard with a liquid caramel topping.

Flour-dust: See Dust.

Floweret: A small flower, one of a cluster of composite flowers, as in broccoli or cauliflower.

Flute: To make decorative indentations around edge of pastry; to cut indentations into a vegetable or fruit (see page 142).

Fold in: To gently combine a light, delicate, aerated substance (such as whipped cream or beaten egg whites) with a heavier mixture, using an over-and-under motion.

Forcemeat: Finely chopped, seasoned meat, served separately or used as a stuffing.

Freeze: To chill rapidly at 0° until solid.

Garnish: To decorate a completed dish, making it more attractive.

Gel: To congeal, becoming firm enough to retain shape of container.

Glaze: To coat with smooth mixture, giving food a sheen.

Grate: To rub solid food against a metal object that has sharp-edged holes, reducing food to thin shreds.

Grease: To rub fat or oil on surface of utensil to prevent food from sticking.

Grill: To cook on a rack over direct heat—gas, electricity, or charcoal; to broil on a grill.

Grind: To reduce nuts, dry bread, chocolate, or other food to crumbs or powder by crushing, pounding, or whirling in a food processor or blender. To finely chop meat, poultry, or fish in a food chopper.

Julienne: Matchstick pieces of vegetables, fruits, or cooked meats.

Knead: To work dough with hands in a fold-and-press motion.

Line: To cover inside or bottom of baking dish or pan with foil, parchment paper, wax paper, or crumbs.

Marinade: A seasoned liquid (usually containing acid such as vinegar or wine) in which food soaks. Marinating helps to tenderize meats, enhances flavor of all foods.

Marinate: To soak in a marinade.

Mash: To crush to a pulpy, soft mixture.

Mask: To cover completely with a sauce, aspic, mayonnaise, or cream.

Mince: To cut or chop into very fine particles.

Mousse: A sweet or savory dish, often stabilized with gelatin or eggs, molded and generally served cold.

Pan-broil: To cook, uncovered, in an ungreased or lightly greased frying pan, pouring off fat as it accumulates. Sometimes pan is salted or rubbed with a piece of fat from meat.

Pan-fry: To cook in a frying pan in a small amount of fat. See page 88

Parboil: To boil until partially cooked.

Pare: To remove outer skin.

Pâté: A mixture of one or more chopped meats or puréed vegetables, served chilled as an hors d'oeuvre. Some pâtés are baked; others are not.

Peel: To strip, cut off, or pull away skin or rind; the colored outer layer of citrus.

Pit: To remove seed from whole fruits such as apricots, avocados, or cherries.

Poach: To cook gently in a simmering liquid, so that food retains its shape.

Pot roast: To cook a large piece of meat by braising; also, meat cooked by this method.

Precook: To cook food partially or completely before final cooking or reheating.

Preheat: To heat oven or griddle to desired temperature before beginning to cook (done when temperature is critical or cooking time is short).

Punch down: To deflate a risen yeast dough by pushing it down with fist to expel air.

Purée: To sieve in a food mill or whirl in a food processor or blender into a smooth, thick mixture.

Reduce: To decrease quantity and concentrate the flavor of a liquid by rapid boiling in an uncovered pan.

Refresh: To plunge a food that is hot from cooking into cold water, halting the cooking process.

Render: To free fat from animal tissue by heating.

Roast: To cook meat or poultry, uncovered, by dry heat (usually in an oven); also, a cut of meat cooked by this method.

Salad oil: Vegetable oil.

Scald: To heat milk to just below the boiling point (bubbles form slowly and burst before reaching the surface).

Score: To cut shallow grooves or slits through outer layer of food to increase tenderness, to prevent edge fat of meat from curling, or to make

decorative top before roasting certain meats.

Sear: To brown meat briefly over high heat to seal in juices.

Shortening, solid: A white, solid fat made from refined vegetable oil that has been partially hydrogenated, chilled, and whipped.

Shred: To cut or grate into thin strips.

Simmer: To cook in liquid over low heat just below the boiling point (bubbles form slowly and burst before reaching the surface).

Skim: To remove fat or foam from the surface of a liquid with a spoon or bulb baster.

Stabilize: To hold together to prevent from breaking down or curdling. A stabilizer is a substance which keeps fat and water evenly combined (in an emulsion).

Steam: To cook in steam, on a rack or in a steaming basket, in a covered pan above boiling water.

Stew: To cook food slowly in simmering liquid in a covered pot.

Stir: To mix ingredients (without beating) using a spoon or whisk in a broad, circular motion.

Stir-fry: To cook sliced food quickly in a small amount of fat over high heat, stirring constantly.

Sweat: To cook chunks of meat, covered, until the natural juices are released.

Texture: The structural quality of a food—roughness, smoothness, graininess, or creaminess.

Toss: To mix lightly and rapidly by lifting and turning ingredients with 2 forks or spoons.

Vinaigrette dressing: A mixture of oil, an acid (lemon juice or vinegar), and seasonings, shaken or stirred together until emulsified.

Whip: To beat rapidly with a wire whisk or electric mixer, incorporating air to lighten a mixture and increase its volume.

Whisk: To beat with a wire whisk until blended and smooth.

Yeast: See pages 183 and 191.

Zest: Thin, colored outer layer of citrus peel.

Glossary of international ingredients

Asiago: Nutty-tasting Italian grating cheese made from cow's milk.

Baguette: French bread shaped like a long stick and slashed across the top. Length averages 24 inches, weight ½ pound.

Bean curd (tofu): Bland, custardlike product made from soybeans, used in Asian cooking. Fresh bean curd, packed in water in plastic tubs, comes in soft, medium-firm (regular), and firm consistencies. Quite bland on its own, bean curd readily absorbs the flavors of other foods. Rinse packaged curd after opening; then cover with cold water and keep in the refrigerator.

Bean threads: Thin, near-transparent strands made from ground mung beans. Used in Asian cooking. Soaked and heated through, they have a slippery texture; dropped into hot oil (see page 51), they puff up crisp.

Bûcheron: Soft, mild, rich French cheese made from goat's milk.

Bulgur (quick-cooking cracked wheat): Wheat berries that have been crushed, steamed, dried, and ground. A staple in Middle Eastern cooking.

Caper: Flower bud of a low shrub native to Mediterranean countries, pickled and used as a seasoning.

Chicken fat (*schmaltz*): Rendered chicken fat (homemade or purchased in jars), used in Jewish cooking.

Chili oil: Hot, orange red, chili-flavored oil used sparingly in Asian cooking as seasoning and table condiment.

Chorizo: Highly seasoned, chili-spiked Mexican and Spanish sausage.

Chutney: Relish of fruits or vegetables and spices, used as a condiment for Indian dishes.

Cornichons: Tiny French gherkins pickled in vinegar, traditionally served with terrines and meat pâtés.

Couscous: A grain product derived from steamed semolina (coarsely milled hard wheat), used in North African cooking.

Fermented black beans: Small black beans, preserved in salt, used in small amounts to flavor Chinese sauces.

Feta: Sharp, salty cheese used in Greek and Balkan cooking. Cured and stored in brine, it's sometimes called "pickled cheese."

Fila: Tissue-thin pastry used in Middle Eastern and North African sweet and savory pastries (see page 18 for tips on working with fila).

Fish sauce: Thin, salty, brownish gray sauce; all-purpose seasoning in Southeast Asia. You may see it labeled as fish soy or fish's gravy. Thai and Filipino fish sauces are much milder than those used in Vietnam and Burma.

Garam masala: Mixture of ground spices added to Indian dishes during cooking or at the table (see page 111).

Ginger: See page 116.

Gjetost: Faintly sweet Scandinavian cheese made from caramelized goat's milk.

Hoisin sauce: Spicy, slightly sweet soybean-based sauce used as seasoning and table condiment in Chinese cooking. (See page 143 for an easy-to-make substitute.)

Kasha: Toasted buckwheat kernels (groats). A staple grain in Russia.

Kielbasa: Polish smoked pork sausage; needs no further cooking.

Knackwurst: Short, thick, German-style pork sausage, sometimes seasoned with garlic.

Linguisa: Spicy Portuguese sausage seasoned with ground red pepper (cayenne) and paprika. Available in links and as bulk sausage.

Mirin: Sweet Japanese rice wine used in cooking.

Montrachet: Pleasantly tangy, creamy French cheese made from goat's milk.

Napa cabbage (Chinese cabbage): Sweet, mild-tasting cabbage, similar in shape to romaine lettuce, used throughout the Orient and Southeast Asia.

Orange flower water: Fragrant, concentrated nonalcoholic flavoring, popular in Middle Eastern and North African cooking (see page 211).

Oriental mushrooms: Brownish-black dried mushrooms. Soak in warm water before using; after soaking, mushrooms have a mild flavor and firm, succulent texture.

Oyster sauce: Thick, brown, bottled sauce with rich, subtle oyster flavor. Used as seasoning in Chinese cooking.

Prosciutto: Dry-cured Italian ham that can be eaten without further cooking. Slice thinly for best flavor.

Rice sticks: Thin noodles made from rice flour; used in Chinese and Southeast Asian soups and stir-fries. Soak before using, or cook in broth. Rice sticks may also be deep-fried to make a puffy, crunchy garnish.

Sake: Japanese rice wine used as a beverage and in cooking.

Sesame oil: Golden brown, aromatic oil pressed from toasted sesame seeds; used as seasoning in Chinese, Japanese, and Korean cooking. Since it's strong, it's used in very small quantities.

Shiitake mushrooms: Large, deep brown mushrooms with thick caps; used in Japanese and Chinese cooking. (If you can't find fresh shiitake, use regular mushrooms.)

Snow peas (also called edible-pod peas, sugar peas, and Chinese pea pods): Flat, crisp, bright green pods with tiny peas inside. Used in Asian cooking, especially in stir-fries.

Soba: Slender Japanese buckwheat noodles, usually sold dried.

Soy sauce: Dark, savory, salty sauce made from soybeans; most versatile and frequently used seasoning in Asian cooking. Imported soy is definitely the best; saltiness varies from brand to brand.

Tahini: Paste made from pulverized sesame seeds, used throughout the Middle East. Oil floats to top, so stir to reblend before measuring out.

Tomatillo: Relative of husk tomato with distinctive acid flavor. Used in Mexican soups, sauces.

EMERGENCY SUBSTITUTIONS

It's always best to use the exact ingredients called for in a recipe. But if you don't have a particular ingredient on hand, look below for a substitute that will give satisfactory results. We recommend that you avoid making more than one substitution in a single recipe.

Ingredient		Substitution
1	cup cake flour	1 cup all-purpose flour minus 2 tablespoons; or all-purpose flour sifted 3 times, then measured to make 1 cup
1	teaspoon baking powder	¼ teaspoon baking soda plus ½ teaspoon cream of tartar
1	tablespoon cornstarch (used for thickening)	2 tablespoons all-purpose flour
1	cup buttermilk or sour milk	1 tablespoon white (distilled) vinegar or lemon juice plus 1 cup milk, allowed to stand for 5 minutes
1	cup milk	½ cup evaporated milk plus ½ cup water, or ⅓ cup instant nonfat dry milk stirred into 1 cup water
1	cup coconut milk	1 cup whipping cream plus ½ teaspoon each coconut extract and granulated sugar
1	cup corn syrup (except for making candy)	1 cup granulated sugar plus ¼ cup liquid*
1	cup honey	1¼ cups granulated sugar plus ¼ cup liquid*
2	egg yolks (used for thickening in custards)	1 whole egg
1	square (1 oz.) unsweetened chocolate	3 tablespoons unsweetened cocoa plus 1 tablespoon butter or margarine, melted
1	cup regular-strength chicken or beef broth	1 chicken or beef bouillon cube plus 1 cup hot water
1	can (1 lb.) tomatoes	2½ cups chopped, peeled fresh tomatoes, simmered for about 10 minutes
1	cup catsup or tomato based chili sauce	1 can (8 oz.) tomato sauce plus ½ cup granulated sugar and 2 tablespoons white (distilled) vinegar
1	anchovy fillet	½ teaspoon anchovy paste
¼	cup minced fresh onion	1 tablespoon instant minced onion (let stand in liquid as directed)
2	tablespoons minced fresh parsley	1 tablespoon dehydrated parsley flakes
½	teaspoon grated fresh ginger	¼ teaspoon ground ginger
1	dried whole hot red chile (1 to 2 inches long)	½ to 1 teaspoon crushed red pepper
1	teaspoon dry mustard (in wet mixtures)	1 tablespoon prepared mustard
1	teaspoon Chinese five-spice	¼ teaspoon each crushed anise seeds, ground cinnamon, ground cloves, and ground ginger
1	teaspoon fines herbes	¼ teaspoon each thyme leaves, oregano leaves, sage leaves, and dry rosemary
1	teaspoon Italian herb seasoning	¼ teaspoon each thyme leaves, marjoram leaves, oregano leaves, and dry basil
¼	teaspoon chili oil	¼ teaspoon salad oil plus ⅛ teaspoon ground red pepper (cayenne)
1	tablespoon sesame oil	1½ teaspoons sesame seeds toasted in ½ teaspoon salad oil
	Hoisin sauce	see page 143
½	cup rice vinegar	⅓ cup white (distilled) vinegar plus 3 tablespoons water, seasoned to taste with salt
½	cup seasoned rice vinegar	⅓ cup white (distilled) vinegar plus 3 tablespoons each water and sugar, seasoned to taste with salt

*Use the same liquid called for in recipe. Equivalence is based on how product functions in recipe, not on sweetness.

APPETIZERS & FIRST COURSES

From Russia's *zakuski* to Hawaii's *pupus* to France's *hors d'oeuvres*, appetizers abound the world around. In some countries, they're offered in stunning collections—Italian *antipasto*, Middle Eastern *meza*, and Swedish *smörgåsbord* are a few examples.

Choosing the very best appetizers from such an array was as hard (but just as much fun) as selecting only a few chocolates from a five-pound box of candy—especially when we included in our survey knife-and-fork appetizers to serve at the table as first courses. We hope you enjoy the final, flavorsome sampling as much as we have.

A world of choices

When it comes to appetizers, almost anything goes: possibilities range from simple to sophisticated, familiar to exotic.

Is speedy simplicity what you have in mind? Serve blanched asparagus marinated in a light sesame dressing, or whip up a creamy crab dip and offer raw vegetables as scoopers.

Are you in the mood for something a bit more elegant and complex? Flaky fila-wrapped pastries stuffed with a savory filling may be just what you have in mind. Or try baked chicken wings redolent of coconut and curry, or a smooth, shell pink dip flavored with carp roe. Whatever your mood, whatever the occasion, you'll find the right appetizer here.

Narrowing the field

When you choose appetizers, you'll want to make sure that your selections suit the size and style of your party.

At a stand-up cocktail party, for example, guests will find finger foods easiest to eat; these are easy to pass around, too. If you prefer to let guests help themselves from an array of tidbits, it's thoughtful to provide small plates and forks. Do whatever will make your guests comfortable, but be sure that the choice and arrangement of food lets you enjoy the party, too.

As far as quantity goes, again let the type of occasion be your guide. Before a sit-down meal, offer just one or two choice appetizers. But if the gathering doesn't include a dinner, your guests will appreciate a variety of hot and cold appetizers, filling enough to compose a small meal.

Beyond these guidelines, there are no hard and fast rules for selecting appetizers—anything that fits the rest of the meal will fill the bill. Of course, you may well want to open an ethnic meal with an appetizer from the same region. But feel free to mix cuisines; if a starter from another area suits your menu perfectly, don't hesitate to serve it.

Dips & spreads

For small groups or large, dips and spreads are a busy cook's dream. Fast to whip up, they're also easy to serve, and most can be made a day ahead.

Sturdy crackers and breads in variety are good accompaniments for thick spreads (be sure to provide butter knives for spreading). Crisp raw vegetables pair perfectly with dips—and since these scoopers are low in calories, they're sure to delight weightwatchers.

Most vegetables make good dippers. Possibilities include whole radishes, button mushrooms, green onions, snow peas, cherry tomatoes, and asparagus spears; Belgian endive leaves; carrots, zucchini, and cucumbers (cut into sticks); turnips, rutabagas, fennel, sunchokes, red and green peppers, and daikon (cut into slices); and broccoli and cauliflower flowerets.

You can give yourself a head start by cutting the vegetables a day ahead. Wrap cut vegetables in dampened paper towels, then enclose in plastic bags and refrigerate until party time.

Dilled Shrimp Mousse

Sweden

Especially elegant when made in a fish-shaped mold, this creamy pink mousse pairs two Scandinavian favorites: dill weed and tender shrimp.

- 1 **envelope unflavored gelatin**
- ¾ **cup tomato juice**
- ½ **pint (1 cup) sour cream**
- ¼ **teaspoon Worcestershire**
- 1 **tablespoon lemon juice**
- 1½ **teaspoons dill weed**
- ¼ **pound small cooked shrimp, chopped**
  Parsley sprigs
  Thinly sliced French rolls, crackers, or Belgian endive leaves

Sprinkle gelatin over tomato juice in a small pan; let stand for 5 minutes to soften. Place pan over low heat and stir until gelatin is dissolved. Remove from heat and let cool to room temperature.

In a bowl, combine sour cream, Worcestershire, lemon juice, dill weed, and gelatin mixture. Beat with a wire whisk or rotary beater until well blended. Stir in shrimp. Pour mixture into a 2½ to 3-cup mold; cover and refrigerate until completely set (at least 4 hours).

Unmold onto a plate (see page 42); garnish with parsley. Spread on rolls. Makes 2½ cups.

Pacific Crab Dip

United States

Cream cheese, crabmeat, and savory seasonings make a tempting dip for crisp raw vegetables.

- 1 **large package (8 oz.) cream cheese, softened**
- ¼ **cup sour cream**
- 1 **tablespoon lemon juice**
- 3 **tablespoons thinly sliced green onions (including tops)**
- 1 **small clove garlic, minced or pressed**
- 1 **tablespoon milk**
- ½ **pound crabmeat, flaked**
  Salt
- 2 **tablespoons slivered almonds, toasted (page 87)**
  Assorted raw vegetables

Beat cream cheese and sour cream until fluffy. Stir in lemon juice, onions, garlic, milk, and crabmeat; season to taste with salt. Cover and refrigerate for 2 to 4 hours to blend flavors.

Spoon into a serving dish and top with almonds; bring to room temperature to serve. Scoop up with vegetable dippers. Makes about 2 cups.

Fish Roe Dip

Greece

Red caviar, the key ingredient in Greek *taramosalata*, is available in delicatessens and imported food shops.

- 4 **slices white bread, crusts removed**
- 1 **small onion, grated**
- 1 **jar (4 oz.) red caviar (such as carp roe or red whitefish caviar) or 1 tube (about 3.3 oz.) red smoked carp roe paste**
- ¼ **cup lemon juice**
- ½ **cup each olive oil and salad oil**
  Crusty bread cubes and raw vegetables

Soak white bread in water to cover for 5 minutes; squeeze dry. In a food processor or blender, whirl bread, onion, caviar, and lemon juice until smooth. With motor running, gradually add oil—a few drops at a time at first, then increasing to a slow, steady stream. Transfer to a serving bowl; cover and refrigerate for at least 2 hours. Scoop up with crusty bread and vegetables. Makes 2 cups.

...Dips & spreads

Guacamole

Mexico

Study in complementary contrasts: Mexico's famous guacamole, a blissful blend of mellow, buttery-smooth avocado and spicy-hot seasonings.

- 1 **large ripe avocado**
- 1 **tablespoon lemon or lime juice**
- 1 **to 2 tablespoons finely minced onion or green onion (including top)**
- 2 **to 3 teaspoons minced fresh cilantro (coriander) or ¼ teaspoon ground coriander**
- 1 **to 2 tablespoons canned diced green chiles, or liquid hot pepper seasoning to taste**
  Salt
  Tortilla chips or assorted raw vegetables

Cut avocado in half and remove pit; with a spoon, scoop pulp into a bowl. Coarsely mash pulp with a fork, gradually blending in lemon juice. Stir in onion, cilantro, and chiles; season to taste with salt. Serve at once, or cover and refrigerate for up to 2 hours. Serve with chips or vegetables for scooping. Makes about 1 cup.

Liptauer Cheese Spread

Hungary

Lively liptauer cheese originated in Hungary—but today, this paprika-sparked spread is enjoyed all over central Europe. Offer our zippy liptauer with crisp pickles and a basket of rye bread.

- 2 **large packages (8 oz. *each*) cream cheese, softened**
- 4 **tablespoons butter or margarine, softened**
- 1 **tablespoon milk**
- 2 **cloves garlic, minced or pressed**
- 2 **teaspoons Dijon mustard**
- ½ **teaspoon anchovy paste**
- 1 **teaspoon sweet Hungarian paprika or regular paprika**
- 1 **teaspoon caraway seeds**
  Small butter lettuce cups
  Garnishes: Crumbled cooked bacon, capers (drained well), and sliced dill pickle
  Thinly sliced rye or pumpernickel bread

In a food processor, whirl cream cheese, butter, milk, garlic, mustard, anchovy paste, and paprika until smoothly blended (or beat with an electric mixer). Stir in caraway seeds; cover and re-

frigerate for at least 8 hours. To serve, mound cheese on a plate. Surround with lettuce cups, then fill cups with bacon, capers, and pickle. Spread cheese on bread; top with garnishes. Makes about 2¼ cups.

Eggplant Dip

Saudi Arabia

Tempting *baba ghannouj* is wonderful alongside *shish kebab* and irresistible as an appetizer.

- 1 **large eggplant, unpeeled**
- 1 **medium-size onion, unpeeled**
- ¼ **cup tahini (sesame-seed paste)**
- 3 **tablespoons lemon juice**
- 1 **large clove garlic, cut into thirds**
  Salt
  Garnishes (optional): Chopped parsley, chopped green pepper, or pomegranate seeds
  Pocket bread, cut into small wedges, or thinly sliced French bread

Pierce eggplant and onion in several places to let steam escape. Place both in a rimmed baking pan. Bake in a 400° oven, uncovered, for 50 minutes to 1 hour or until eggplant is very soft. Rinse cooked vegetables under cold running water to cool them; then drain, peel, dice, and place in a food processor or blender. Add tahini, lemon juice, and garlic. Whirl until smooth; season to taste with salt. Let cool. Serve at once, or cover and refrigerate until needed (serve at room temperature).

Mound dip on a plate; garnish with parsley, if desired. Scoop up with pocket bread or spread on French bread. Makes about 2 cups.

Layered Cheese Torta

Italy

In Lombardy, this colorfully layered *torta* is made with *mascarpone*, a rich, fresh cheese that's hard to find in the United States. We've used cream cheese and butter in its place—and come up with a torta just as luscious as the Italian original.

- **Filling & topping (recipes follow)**
- 1 **large package (8 oz.) cream cheese, softened**
- 1 **cup (½ lb.) unsalted butter, softened**
  Thinly sliced baguettes or crackers

Prepare choice of filling; set aside.

With an electric mixer, beat cream cheese and butter until well blended. Cut two 12-inch squares of cheesecloth; moisten with water, wring dry, and lay out flat, one atop the other. Smoothly line a 3-cup straight-sided plain mold (such as a small loaf pan, terrine, charlotte mold, or clean flowerpot) with cheesecloth, draping excess over rim of mold.

Set topping in mold bottom. With a rubber spatula, add ¼ of the cheese, covering topping and spreading to make an even layer. Cover with ⅓ of the filling, spreading it evenly to sides of mold. Repeat until mold is filled, finishing with cheese.

Fold ends of cheesecloth over torta; press down lightly with your hands to compact. Refrigerate until torta feels firm when pressed (about 1 hour). Grasp ends of cheesecloth and lift torta from mold; invert on a serving dish and gently pull off cheesecloth. Serve at once, or wrap airtight and refrigerate for up to 5 days. Offer as a spread for baguettes. Makes about 12 servings.

Pesto filling & topping. In a blender or food processor, whirl to a paste 1¼ cups lightly packed **fresh basil leaves,** ½ cup grated **Parmesan cheese,** and 2½ tablespoons **olive oil.** Stir in 2 tablespoons **pine nuts.** For topping, use a **fresh basil sprig.** Put sprig in mold bottom if serving within 2 days; otherwise, set atop torta after unmolding.

Smoked salmon filling & topping. With a knife, finely chop ¼ pound **smoked salmon.** Put 1 or 2 thin **lemon slices** in bottom of mold for topping.

Mushroom Caviar

Russia

Probably first made with wild mushrooms, this "peasant's caviar" makes a savory start for a Russian meal.

> 3 **tablespoons butter or margarine**
> 3 **tablespoons salad oil**
> 1 **large onion, finely chopped**
> 1 **pound mushrooms, finely chopped**
> ¼ **cup lemon juice**
> 3 **tablespoons dry sherry**
> ¼ **teaspoon** *each* **salt and thyme leaves**
>   **Pepper**
> 1 **green onion (including top), thinly sliced**
>   **Thinly sliced rye bread or toast**

Heat butter and oil in a wide frying pan over medium heat. Add chopped onion and cook, stirring occasionally, until soft but not browned (about 10 minutes). Add mushrooms and lemon juice; increase heat to medium-high and cook, stirring, until mushrooms are soft and have released their liquid. Add sherry, salt and thyme; season to taste with pepper. Continue to cook and stir until almost all liquid has evaporated. Spoon into a shallow serving dish. Let cool to room temperature; then garnish with green onion and serve as a spread for bread. Makes about 1⅓ cups.

Hummus

Lebanon

Throughout the Middle East, you'll find countless variations of *hummus,* a simple mixture of puréed garbanzo beans (often called chick peas) and sesame-seed paste. This version comes from Lebanon.

> 1 **can (15 oz.) garbanzo beans**
> ¼ **cup tahini (sesame-seed paste)**
> 3 **tablespoons lemon juice**
> 1 **large clove garlic, cut into thirds**
> ¼ **teaspoon ground cumin**
>   **Salt and pepper**
>   **Garnishes (optional): Chopped parsley or olive oil**
>   **Pocket bread, cut into small wedges, or sesame crackers**

Drain garbanzos, reserving liquid and 3 or 4 whole beans. Place remaining garbanzos in a food processor or blender. Add tahini, lemon juice, garlic, cumin, and ¼ cup of the garbanzo liquid. Whirl until mixture is smooth and the consistency of sour cream, adding more liquid as needed. Season to taste with salt and pepper.

Spread hummus on a rimmed plate; garnish with reserved whole beans and, if desired, parsley. Or, if you wish, make several indentations in hummus by pressing with the back of a spoon; fill hollows with oil. Scoop up hummus with pocket bread or spread on crackers. Makes about 1½ cups.

Fila-wrapped & baked appetizers

When it's party time, cooks in the Middle East think first of fila—a tissue-thin dough that's the base for dozens of pastries, both savory and sweet. Available in imported food shops, Middle Eastern markets, and many supermarkets, fila is sold ready to use, fresh or frozen, in 1-pound packages. (You may see it labeled as filo, fillo, phyllo, or strudel leaves.) For easier handling, let fresh or thawed frozen fila stand at room temperature, unopened, for an hour or so before using. (To thaw frozen fila, let it stand overnight in the refrigerator, still in the unopened package.)

Despite its fragile appearance, fila isn't too tricky to work with—it withstands a fair amount of handling. The thin sheets do dry out quickly when exposed to air, though, so be sure to keep any sheets you aren't using covered with plastic wrap or a barely damp towel until you need them.

If you open packaged fila and find that the dough has cracked around the edges, simply cut off the cracked portions and use the trimmed sheets. And if your fila tears when it's folded, just overlap the edges of the tear or patch the crack with a moistened scrap of dough.

Place any unused fila in a plastic bag; close tightly and store in the refrigerator for up to 2 weeks, in the freezer for up to 6 months.

Cheese Rolls

Greece   (Pictured on facing page)

For the neatest slices, cut Greek *bourekakia* with a serrated knife (the flaky crusts shatter easily).

> 8 ounces feta cheese, crumbled (about 2 cups)
> 1 small package (3 oz.) cream cheese, softened
> 1 cup (8 oz.) ricotta cheese
> 2 eggs
> 2 tablespoons all-purpose flour
> ½ teaspoon ground nutmeg
> ¼ teaspoon white pepper
> ¼ cup chopped parsley
> 24 sheets fila
> About 1 cup (½ lb.) butter or margarine, melted

In a food processor, whirl feta cheese, cream cheese, ricotta, eggs, flour, nutmeg, pepper, and parsley until smoothly blended (or beat with an electric mixer).

Make each cheese roll as shown in photos 1 and 2 on facing page, using ⅓ to ½ cup filling and

3 sheets fila for each roll. Place filled rolls, seam side down, in ungreased shallow rimmed baking pans. Brush tops with butter. At this point, you may cover with plastic wrap and refrigerate until next day. For longer storage (up to 3 months), freeze rolls until firm; then transfer to plastic bags and return to freezer.

Bake in a 375° oven, uncovered, for about 15 minutes (25 minutes if frozen) or until puffed and golden brown. Let cool slightly, then cut into 1½-inch pieces. Makes 8 rolls (about 4 dozen appetizers).

Meat-filled Triangles

Lebanon   (Pictured on facing page)

Just a pound of meat fills dozens of *sambusik*: plump, flaky fila triangles stuffed with a spicy lamb and onion mixture.

> 2 tablespoons butter or margarine
> 1 small onion, finely chopped
> 1 pound lean ground lamb or lean ground beef
> ½ teaspoon *each* ground allspice and salt
>   Dash *each* of pepper and ground cinnamon
> ¼ cup pine nuts
> 24 sheets fila
>   About 1 cup (½ lb.) butter or margarine, melted

Melt the 2 tablespoons butter in a wide frying pan over medium-high heat; add onion and cook until soft. Crumble in lamb and cook, stirring, until browned. Add allspice, salt, pepper, cinnamon, and pine nuts. Cook for 2 minutes. Remove from heat; let cool.

Cut each fila sheet crosswise into 5 strips, each about 3 by 12 inches; cover with plastic wrap. Make each triangle as shown in photos 3, 4, and 5 on facing page. Place triangles, seam side down, in ungreased shallow rimmed baking pans. At this point, you may cover with plastic wrap and refrigerate until next day. For longer storage (up to 3 months), freeze until firm; then transfer to plastic bags and return to freezer.

Bake in a 375° oven, uncovered, for about 15 minutes (25 minutes if frozen) or until puffed and golden brown. Makes about 3 dozen appetizers.

Two ways to wrap fila (Recipes on facing page)

1 *To make each cheese roll,* stack 3 sheets of fila on a towel, brushing top of each layer with melted butter. Spoon a ribbon of filling along one side, 1 inch from edge.

2 Fold edge over filling, then fold in ends. Using towel to help you lift, roll up loosely, jelly roll fashion. Wet edge of fila with water and press gently to seal.

3 *To make triangles,* cut each fila sheet crosswise into 5 equal strips, each about 3 by 12 inches. Stack 2 strips, streaking butter over each one. Cover unused fila with plastic wrap to prevent drying.

4 Place a rounded teaspoon of meat filling on one end of fila strip. Fold over one corner to make a triangle.

5 Fold triangle over again on itself. Continue folding from side to side, as if you were folding a flag. (You can wrap cheese filling in this fashion too.)

6 Hot, crisp fila-wrapped appetizers, garnished with mint leaves, set the mood for an elegant Middle Eastern feast.

Marinated appetizers

No need to leave your guests for long to put the finishing touches on these tempting tidbits. You prepare them hours in advance, letting them soak up flavor as they marinate in the refrigerator; at party time, your appetizer is ready for serving or last-minute cooking.

Rumaki

Japan/United States–Hawaii

Rumaki need little introduction: these bacon-wrapped treats have been American favorites for years. Credit for the savory creations goes to cooks in Hawaii's large Japanese community.

> ¾ **pound chicken livers**
> ½ **pound bacon**
> 1 **can (8 oz.) whole water chestnuts, drained well**
> ½ **cup soy sauce**
> 1 **small clove garlic, minced or pressed**
> 1 **small dried whole hot red chile, crushed**
> 6 **thin slices fresh ginger**

Cut chicken livers in half; rinse and pat dry. Cut each bacon strip in half crosswise. Fold each piece of liver around a water chestnut; then wrap with bacon and fasten with a wooden pick.

In a bowl, stir together soy, garlic, chile, and ginger. Add chicken liver bundles; cover and refrigerate, turning occasionally, for at least 3 hours or until next day.

Place rumaki on a broiler pan or on a rack in a shallow baking pan. Broil 6 inches below heat, turning once, until bacon is crisp (about 7 minutes *total*). Makes about 1½ dozen appetizers.

Pickled Salmon

Sweden

This is just one of the ways Swedes prepare salmon taken from their icy waters.

> 1 **cup white (distilled) vinegar**
>   **Water**
> ¾ **cup sugar**
> 1 **pound salmon steaks or fillets, *each* about 1 inch thick**
> 1 **large onion**
> 16 **whole allspice**
> ½ **teaspoon dill weed**

Place vinegar, 1 cup water, and sugar in a pan; bring to a boil over high heat. Let cool.

Place salmon in a wide frying pan and add cold water to barely cover. Cut ⅔ of the onion into thin slices, separate rings, and set aside. Chop remaining onion; add to salmon, along with 6 of the allspice. Place over high heat; cook, uncovered, until small bubbles form around pan edges. Reduce heat to low, cover, and simmer until fish tests done (8 to 10 minutes; see page 120). Transfer fish to a plate and let cool; discard poaching liquid.

Break fish into bite-size pieces, discarding skin and bones. Place in a shallow bowl. Top with onion rings, then sprinkle with dill weed and remaining 10 allspice.

Pour vinegar mixture over fish. Cover and refrigerate for at least 4 hours or up to 3 days. To serve, lift fish and onion rings from pickling mixture and arrange on a platter. Makes 8 servings.

Marinated Beef Cubes

Korea

Though we've toned down the fiery Korean seasonings a bit, these tender morsels of beef still serve up plenty of gingery, peppery flavor.

> 1 **tablespoon sesame seeds, toasted (page 99)**
> ¼ **cup soy sauce**
> 2 **to 3 teaspoons minced fresh ginger**
> 3 **cloves garlic, minced or pressed**
> 1 **teaspoon *each* sugar and vinegar**
> 2 **green onions (including tops), thinly sliced**
> ¼ **to ½ teaspoon ground red pepper (cayenne)**
> 1½ **pounds boneless beef sirloin, top round, or boneless chuck, cut into ¾-inch cubes**
>   **About 5 tablespoons salad oil**

In a bowl, combine sesame seeds, soy, ginger, garlic, sugar, vinegar, onions, pepper, beef, and 1 tablespoon of the oil. Stir to coat meat thoroughly. Cover and refrigerate for at least 2 hours or until next day.

Heat 2 tablespoons of the oil in a wide frying pan over high heat. Add half the meat and stir-fry until browned on the outside but still pink within (about 2 minutes). Serve hot, with wooden picks for spearing. Repeat with remaining meat, adding remaining oil as needed. Makes about 4 dozen appetizers.

Coconut Curried Chicken Wings

Indonesia

A double dose of coconut gives crunchy baked chicken wings the flavor of Southeast Asia. You start by marinating the wings in coconut milk, then roll them in a curry-spiked coconut-crumb coating before baking.

 2 **dozen chicken wings (about 5 lbs.)**
 1 **cup canned or thawed frozen coconut milk, or 1 cup whipping cream mixed with ½ teaspoon coconut extract**
 1½ **cups fine dry bread crumbs**
 4 **teaspoons curry powder**
 3 **tablespoons sweetened flaked coconut**
 6 **tablespoons butter or margarine, melted**
 2 **cloves garlic, minced or pressed**

Cut chicken wings apart at both joints; reserve tips for other uses. Pour coconut milk into a large bowl; add wings and stir well. Cover and refrigerate for at least 2 hours or until next day.

On a piece of wax paper, combine crumbs, curry powder, and coconut. Stir chicken to moisten; then lift out, one piece at a time, and roll in crumb mixture to coat completely. Place pieces slightly apart on greased 10 by 15-inch rimmed baking pans.

Combine butter and garlic; drizzle over chicken. Bake in a 375° oven, uncovered, for about 45 minutes or until well browned and crisp. Serve hot. Makes 4 dozen appetizers.

Marinated Clams or Mussels

Spain

These succulent marinated shellfish might well appear in a collection of *tapas* (page 8)—small snacks both hot and cold, typically enjoyed alongside a glass of sherry. (For tips on cleaning mussels, see page 132.)

 3 **dozen small hard-shell clams or mussels, scrubbed well**
 Boiling water
 2 **tablespoons *each* olive oil and lemon juice**
 1 **tablespoon chopped fresh cilantro (coriander)**
 1 **clove garlic, minced or pressed**
 2 **green onions (including tops), finely chopped**
 Salt, pepper, and liquid hot pepper seasoning

Arrange half the clams in a wide frying pan. Pour in boiling water to a depth of about ½ inch. Cover and simmer over medium heat until shells open (8 to 12 minutes). As their shells open, remove clams from pan and set them aside to cool. Discard any unopened shells. Repeat with remaining clams.

With a fork, remove clams from shells and place in a bowl. Break shells apart; save half of each for serving and discard remaining pieces. Cover shells and refrigerate.

In a bowl, combine oil, lemon juice, cilantro, garlic, and onions. Pour over clams. Season to taste with salt, pepper, and hot pepper seasoning. Cover and refrigerate for up to 24 hours.

Lift clams from marinade and set one in each shell; arrange on a platter. Spoon any remaining marinade over clams. To eat, hold shell to mouth and tip in the contents. Makes 3 dozen appetizers.

Sesame Marinated Vegetables

China

What's on a Chinese "cold plate"? A varied array of appetizing tidbits, all served chilled or at room temperature. These marinated lightly cooked vegetables are a typical cold plate offering, as is Cold Spiced Cabbage (page 136).

 1 **pound carrots or asparagus or ½ pound snow peas**
 1 **tablespoon *each* soy sauce and white (distilled) vinegar**
 2 **teaspoons sugar**
 ¼ **teaspoon salt**
 1 **teaspoon sesame oil**

Cut carrots diagonally into ⅛-inch-thick slices. Or snap off and discard tough ends of asparagus and cut stalks diagonally into 1½-inch slices; or snap off ends of peas and remove strings.

In a 2 to 3-quart pan, bring 2 inches water to a boil. Add vegetable and boil, uncovered, until tender-crisp to bite (about 4 minutes for carrots, 1½ minutes for asparagus or peas). Drain, rinse under cold running water, and drain again.

Place soy, vinegar, sugar, salt, and oil in a plastic bag. Place drained vegetable in bag; seal. Refrigerate, turning occasionally, for at least 1 hour or up to 8 hours.

Arrange vegetable on a serving plate; spoon marinade over top. Makes 8 servings.

Making Filipino Lumpia (Recipe on facing page)

1 Paint lumpia batter on ungreased griddle in 2 firm strokes. Work quickly. If wrapper has holes, discard it and start again. (We've allowed enough batter for a few throwaways.)

2 In seconds, wrapper dries on top and curls at edges; adjust heat so it cooks without burning. Lift cooked wrapper from griddle. (Wrapper size may vary at first as you practice.)

3 Think of wrapper as a baseball diamond. Place a spoonful of filling at home plate; use 1 to 2 tablespoons, depending on size of wrapper.

4 Roll home plate to pitcher's mound to enclose filling. Fold in first and third bases. Brush edges with egg to seal; roll to second base.

5 Tissue-thin lumpia wrappers cook at lower oil temperature than sturdier egg roll skins. Cook 4 or 5 lumpia at a time; lift out and drain on paper towels.

6 Any party seems like a Filipino *fiesta* when you start with crisp, delicate Lumpia. Offer zingy sweet and sour sauce for dipping.

Wrapped & deep-fried appetizers

Easy to eat out of hand, deep-fried appetizers make delicious surprise packages to pass at parties. For more information on deep-frying techniques and equipment, see page 127.

Lumpia

Philippines   (Pictured on facing page)

The Filipino snacks called *lumpia* are close kin to China's egg roll. To make these flavorful treats, you enclose a simple filling in a delicate wrapper, then fry the bundle in oil until it's golden.

We tell you how to make lumpia wrappers, but you can also buy them in Filipino and Chinese markets. Purchased wrappers are convenient to use, but be warned—separating the paper-thin layers demands a fair amount of patience.

Egg roll skins can be used as wrappers, too. These are thicker than our homemade lumpia wrappers, so they don't produce quite as delicate a crust after frying.

      Sweet & sour sauce (recipe follows)
      **About 2 dozen lumpia wrappers (recipe follows)
      or egg roll skins**
  4 Oriental dried mushrooms
  ¾ pound lean ground pork
  1 medium-size onion, chopped
  3 cloves garlic, minced or pressed
  ⅓ pound medium-size raw shrimp, shelled, deveined, and chopped
  ⅓ cup water chestnuts, chopped
  1 tablespoon soy sauce
  1 egg, lightly beaten
    Salad oil

Prepare sweet & sour sauce; set aside. Also prepare lumpia wrappers and set aside.

Soak mushrooms in warm water to cover for 30 minutes, then drain. Cut off and discard stems; finely chop caps. Crumble pork into a wide frying pan. Add onion and garlic and cook over medium-high heat, stirring, until meat is browned (about 6 minutes). Add shrimp, mushrooms, and water chestnuts and cook for 2 minutes. Stir in soy. Let cool; then discard excess pan juices.

Fill and fold lumpia as shown in photos 3 and 4 on facing page, moistening wrapper edges with egg to seal. (At this point, you may cover and refrigerate for up to 8 hours.)

Into a 2 to 3-quart pan, pour oil to a depth of 1½ inches and heat to 340° on a deep-frying ther-

mometer. (If using egg roll skins, heat to 360°.) Add 4 or 5 lumpia; cook, turning as needed, until golden brown (2 to 3 minutes). Remove with a slotted spoon and drain on paper towels; keep warm in a 200° oven. Repeat with remaining lumpia. Serve with sweet & sour sauce. Makes 2 dozen lumpia.

Sweet & sour sauce. In a 2-quart pan, combine ½ cup each **water** and **sugar,** ¼ cup **cider vinegar,** 1 tablespoon each **cornstarch** and **catsup,** 1 clove **garlic** (minced or pressed), and ¼ to ½ teaspoon **crushed red pepper.** Stir until cornstarch is dissolved. Place over medium heat and cook, stirring constantly, until sauce boils and thickens slightly. Let cool to room temperature. Makes about 1 cup.

Lumpia wrappers. In a bowl, place 1½ cups **all-purpose flour.** Add 1½ cups plus 3 tablespoons **water;** stir until smooth. Let stand for 30 minutes.

Heat an ungreased griddle or wide frying pan with a nonstick finish over medium-high heat. Using a new 4-inch-wide paintbrush, brush batter in a 6 to 7-inch-long strip on griddle. Immediately paint a second strip parallel to the first, overlapping edges slightly. As soon as batter appears dry and edges begin to curl (about 15 seconds), lift wrapper from pan and let cool. Repeat with remaining batter (to stack cooked wrappers, separate with wax paper). Makes about 2 dozen wrappers.

CHINESE EGG ROLLS

Follow directions for **Lumpia,** but use 1 package (1 lb.) **egg roll skins** in place of lumpia wrappers. For the filling, heat 2 tablespoons **salad oil** in a wide frying pan over high heat. Add 1 large **onion,** chopped; 1 cup thinly sliced **celery;** 1 clove **garlic,** minced or pressed; 1 teaspoon minced **fresh ginger;** 1 pound **cooked ham,** cut into matchstick pieces; ½ cup sliced **bamboo shoots,** cut into matchstick pieces; and 2 cups finely shredded **cabbage.** Stir-fry until vegetables are tender-crisp to bite (about 3 minutes). Combine 1 tablespoon **cornstarch,** ½ teaspoon **salt,** 2 teaspoons **soy sauce,** and 1 tablespoon **dry sherry.** Add to pan and cook until sauce thickens. Let cool.

Fill, fold, and cook egg roll skins as directed for **Lumpia,** heating oil to 360° on a deep-frying thermometer. Cut cooked egg rolls in half; serve with **sweet & sour sauce.** Makes 2 dozen egg rolls.

First courses

Long a tradition in Europe, first courses are less often served in the United States. But they bring both elegance and enhanced enjoyment to any small dinner party, formal or casual. Presenting guests with extra delight to both eye and palate, first courses also extend the pleasures of the table a few minutes longer.

In this section, we offer a selection of traditional European first courses. But you might also serve a simple appetizer, a salad, or a small portion of meat or fish.

Caponata

Italy

Russia's "vegetarian caviar" (page 17) is based on mushrooms; Italy's version is made with eggplant. Try it both as a first course and as an appetizer spread (it's wonderful on crisp plain crackers).

> ½ **cup olive oil or salad oil**
> 1 **large eggplant (1¼ to 1½ lbs.), cut into ¾-inch cubes**
> 1½ **cups sliced celery**
> 1 **large onion, chopped**
> 3 **cloves garlic, minced or pressed**
> ¼ **cup tomato paste**
> 1 **cup water**
> 2 **teaspoons sugar**
> ¼ **cup red wine vinegar**
> 1 **cup sliced ripe olives**
> 2 **tablespoons capers, drained well**
> ½ **cup chopped pimentos**
> **Lettuce cups**
> ½ **cup pine nuts**

Heat oil in a wide frying pan over medium heat. Add eggplant; cover and cook until eggplant begins to sweat (about 5 minutes). Uncover and continue to cook, stirring often, until eggplant is browned (about 5 more minutes). Stir in celery, onion, and garlic; cook until onion is soft.

In a bowl, stir together tomato paste, water, sugar, and vinegar; stir into eggplant mixture. Cook, stirring often, until mixture thickens and eggplant is very soft (about 10 minutes). Remove from heat and stir in olives, capers, and pimentos. Let cool; then cover and refrigerate for up to 2 days.

To serve, bring to room temperature; then spoon into lettuce cups and garnish with pine nuts. Makes 6 to 8 servings.

Pears with Goat Cheese

Switzerland

Tangy goat cheese perfectly enhances the juicy sweetness of ripe pears.

> **Dijon vinaigrette (recipe follows)**
> 3 **medium-size ripe pears, unpeeled**
> **About 1 teaspoon lemon juice**
> 4 **ounces goat cheese (such as bûcheron or Montrachet), or Parmesan or Romano cheese**
> **Freshly ground pepper**
> **Parsley sprigs**

Prepare Dijon vinaigrette; set aside. Cut pears in half lengthwise; core. Cut a wedge-shaped piece, 2 inches long and ¾ inch wide at the base, from blossom end of each pear half. Eat wedges or discard. Brush cut surfaces with lemon juice.

Cut cheese into 6 equal triangles and stuff into wedge-shaped spaces in pears. Place each pear half on a salad plate and drizzle with Dijon vinaigrette; sprinkle with pepper and garnish with parsley. Makes 6 servings.

Dijon vinaigrette. In a jar, combine ½ cup **olive oil** or salad oil, 3 tablespoons **lemon juice,** and 1 tablespoon *each* **Dijon mustard** and finely chopped **shallots** or red onion. Shake to blend well; then season to taste with **salt.**

Smoked Salmon Pâté

France

For a first course in the elegant style of *nouvelle cuisine*, present each portion of pâté with a border of cucumber slices and a trio of garnishes.

> 3 **ounces smoked salmon or lox, coarsely chopped**
> 1 **egg yolk**
> 1½ **tablespoons lemon juice**
> 3 **tablespoons salad oil**
> 1 **cucumber, thinly sliced**
> **Watercress sprigs**
> **Red onion slivers**
> **Lemon wedges**

In a food processor or blender, whirl salmon, egg yolk, and lemon juice until puréed. With motor running, add oil in a slow, steady stream, whirling until smoothly blended. Cover and refrigerate until thickened (at least 1 hour or until next day).

Arrange about ¼ of the cucumber in an attractive pattern on each of 4 salad plates, overlapping slices slightly. Mound a spoonful of pâté near cucumber. Garnish each plate with watercress, onion, and a lemon wedge. Makes 4 servings.

Florentine Pâté

Italy

In most of Italy, *crostini* means bread served as a first course. But if you ask for *crostini* in Florence, you'll be treated to this resplendent pâté.

    ½ cup olive oil or salad oil
    1 each large onion, celery stalk, and carrot,
       finely chopped
    1 pound chicken livers or calf's liver
    4 tablespoons butter or margarine
    6 anchovy fillets, chopped
    2 tablespoons finely chopped capers
       Pepper
       Chopped parsley, whole capers, and tiny sour
       pickles or cornichons
       Thinly sliced French rolls or toast

Heat oil in a wide frying pan over medium heat. Add onion, celery, and carrot; cook, stirring occasionally, until vegetables are soft but not browned (about 15 minutes). Meanwhile, cut chicken livers in half (or trim and discard membrane from calf's liver, then cut liver into ½-inch chunks). Add livers to vegetables and continue cooking until livers are no longer pink when slashed (5 to 7 minutes). Add butter and stir until melted; then add anchovies and chopped capers.

In a food processor or blender, whirl mixture to make a coarse purée. Season to taste with pepper.

Serve pâté warm or cold, mounded on small individual plates and garnished with parsley, whole capers, and pickles. Offer rolls alongside. Makes about 8 servings.

Liverwurst & Smoked Tongue Pâté

Germany

Layers of smoked tongue, liver sausage, and green onions make a simple pâté that's very rich and very good. You'll need to have the tongue sliced paper thin at the meat market.

    1 pound smooth-textured liver sausage
       (liverwurst or braunschweiger), softened
    ¾ cup (¼ lb. plus 4 tablespoons) butter, softened
    1 pound smoked tongue, sliced paper thin
    ¾ cup thinly sliced green onions (including tops)
       Small sweet gherkins or dill pickles
       Thinly sliced rye bread or French bread
       German-style or Dijon mustard

Discard casing from sausage. Whirl sausage with butter in a food processor until smooth (or beat with an electric mixer). Line bottom and sides of a 4½ by 8-inch loaf pan with 2 layers of tongue slices, overlapping them to cover pan completely; allow ends to hang over rim. Spread ⅛ of sausage on top of tongue. Sprinkle with some of the onions.

Repeat layers until all ingredients have been used, pressing down as you work to form a firm loaf. Use tongue as top layer; fold in ends of tongue. Cover and refrigerate until firm (until next day or for up to 4 days).

Slip a knife between loaf and pan edges; invert pan to release loaf. Cut loaf into ½-inch-thick slices. Serve with gherkins, bread, and mustard. Makes 12 to 16 servings.

QUICK AND EASY OPENERS

Some of the most appealing first courses you can offer are ready to eat when purchased and require only the briefest preparation—you just slice, garnish, or add appropriate accompaniments.

Melon crescents. Perfectly ripe melon makes an elegant meal starter. Choose **cantaloupe, honeydew, Crenshaw, casaba,** or **Persian melon.** Allow 1 melon slice per serving; serve plain or accompany with **lemon wedges** or a few thin slices of **prosciutto.**

Smoked salmon. Garnish sliced **smoked salmon** with thin slivers of **onion, capers** (drained), and **lemon wedges;** serve with **toast** and **butter.**

Oysters on the half shell. Accompany plates of fresh **oysters** with **prepared horseradish, lemon wedges,** and **cocktail sauce.** Allow 4 to 6 oysters per serving.

...First courses

Terrine of Pork, Veal & Ham

France   (Pictured on facing page)

In culinary language, the word "terrine" refers both to a glorious French meat loaf (served cold) and to the straight-sided dish in which it's baked.

- ¼ **pound cooked ham, cut ¼ inch thick**
- ¼ **pound boneless veal (cut from leg), cut ¼ inch thick**
- 1 **small onion, sliced**
- 3 **tablespoons brandy**
- 1¼ **teaspoons thyme leaves**
- ¾ **teaspoon ground allspice**
- 6 **strips bacon**
- ½ **pound pork fat, cut into ½-inch cubes**
- 1 **pound *each* lean ground pork and ground veal**
- 2 **tablespoons chopped parsley**
- 2 **eggs, lightly beaten**
- ⅓ **cup half-and-half (light cream)**
- 2 **teaspoons salt**
- ¼ **teaspoon pepper**
- 2 **bay leaves**
- 8 **to 12 whole black peppers**

Cut ham and the ¼ pound veal into ¼-inch-wide strips. In a bowl, combine meat, onion, brandy, and ¼ teaspoon *each* of the thyme and allspice. Let stand for 15 minutes.

Place bacon in a pan, add water to cover, and bring to a boil over high heat. Reduce heat and simmer, uncovered, for 10 minutes; drain.

Using a food processor or a food chopper fitted with a fine blade, finely chop pork fat; place in a large bowl. Remove onion from marinated meat mixture and finely chop; add to fat. Drain brandy from marinated meat and add to fat. Then add ground pork, the ground veal, parsley, eggs, half-and-half, salt, pepper, and remaining 1 teaspoon thyme and ½ teaspoon allspice. Mix well. Whirl in food processor to make a smooth forcemeat (or put through food chopper again).

Arrange 3 of the bacon strips lengthwise on bottom of a 6-cup straight-sided baking dish (oval or rectangular) or a 5 by 9-inch loaf pan. Spread ⅓ of the forcemeat in dish; arrange half the veal and ham strips lengthwise atop meat. Repeat, using half the remaining forcemeat and all remaining meat strips. Evenly spread remaining forcemeat over top; cover with remaining 3 bacon strips. Place bay leaves and whole peppers on top.

Cover dish tightly with foil and set in a larger pan or dish at least 2 inches deep. Pour in scalding water to a depth of 1 inch. Bake in a 350° oven for 1 hour and 45 minutes or until juices run clear (slash in center to test). Remove from water bath.

Uncover and let cool briefly. Place baking dish in a pan; then place a piece of foil-wrapped cardboard directly atop meat in dish. Place a weight on top of cardboard. Refrigerate for at least 8 hours or up to 1 week.

To unmold, immerse dish up to rim in very hot water until exterior fat begins to melt. Invert onto a board. Scrape off fat and meat jelly; turn terrine right side up and remove whole peppers and bay leaves. Cut into slices. Makes 10 to 12 servings.

Country Terrine

France

For an elegant light supper, just partner a slice or two of terrine with French bread and a green salad.

- 2 **tablespoons butter or margarine**
- 1 **small onion, finely chopped**
- 3 **tablespoons brandy**
- ¼ **pound prosciutto**
- ½ **pound *each* chicken livers, lean ground pork, and ground veal**
- 2 **eggs, lightly beaten**
- ⅓ **cup half-and-half (light cream)**
- 1½ **teaspoons salt**
- ½ **teaspoon thyme leaves**
- ¼ **teaspoon ground allspice**
- ⅛ **teaspoon pepper**
- 2 **bay leaves**
- 6 **whole black peppers**

Melt butter in a small frying pan over medium heat. Add onion and cook, stirring, until soft. Pour in brandy; boil until liquid is reduced by half.

Using a food processor or a food chopper fitted with a fine blade, finely chop prosciutto, livers, and onion mixture; place in a bowl. Add pork, veal, eggs, half-and-half, salt, thyme, allspice, and pepper. Mix well. Whirl in food processor until smooth (or put through food chopper again).

Pack mixture in a 6-cup straight-sided baking dish (oval or rectangular) or a 5 by 9-inch loaf pan. Place bay leaves and whole peppers on top. Cover, bake, weight, refrigerate, and serve as directed for Terrine of Pork, Veal & Ham. Makes 10 to 12 servings.

Assembling a savory French terrine (Recipe on facing page)

1 After lining bottom of dish with bacon, add ⅓ of pork-veal forcemeat and spread to edges. Top with ham and veal strips. Continue to layer forcemeat and meat strips, finishing with forcemeat.

2 Place 3 bacon strips atop assembled terrine. Arrange bay leaves and whole peppers on top.

3 Cover dish tightly with foil. Set in a 2-inch-deep baking pan; pour in scalding water to a depth of 1 inch.

4 Cover baked terrine with foil-wrapped cardboard and refrigerate. To compact meat and flatten top curve, weight with canned goods during chilling.

5 Serve terrine sliced and garnished with watercress. Pair with crusty bread, sour pickles, and mustard for an elegant buffet first course.

SOUPS

Homemade soup, light or hearty—what warmer welcome could you offer a guest? A delicate soup begins a meal on a gracious note; a sturdy potage makes a heartwarming main course in chilly weather.

Around the world, soup is popular with diners —from France's cool, velvety Vichyssoise to Hungary's chunky, meaty Goulash Soup. One reason for this popularity is clear: soup is always easy on the cook. Even soups that require hours of simmering demand little attention while they bubble. And since the flavor of such "slow" soups improves after a few hours' resting time, you can make them ahead, then reheat just before serving.

Serving soups

Soups invite a rich variety of presentation. They offer you the opportunity to use your most decorative utensils and serving dishes—to emphasize the festive nature of the meal or the foreign origin of the menu.

Take an imaginative look about your kitchen. The classic soup server is a lidded tureen—but any handsome pot, bowl, or casserole of appropriate size will do just as well. And pitchers make practical and unusual dispensers for smooth, pourable soups.

When you choose containers for individual servings, apply the same creativity—don't feel limited to bowls. Sip hot soups from cups or mugs; offer chilled ones in your prettiest glasses or stemware. Soufflé cups, ramekins, and deep bowls are ideal for thin soups that cool quickly; wide, shallow soup plates suit thick, heat-retaining soups.

Condiments add creative pleasure not only to soup making, but also to soup tasting. For easy selection, set them on a lazy Susan placed in the center of the table. Or present each in its own small container—try using custard cups or Oriental teacups or rice bowls.

Creating your own soups

If you're a cook who likes to experiment with recipes, you'll find that soup offers an ideal outlet for your adventurous spirit. Unlike more precise types of cooking—cake baking, for example—soup making is by nature inexact and open to innovation. Throughout the world, there are probably as many versions of any given soup as there are cooks simmering it! Keep this in mind as you look over the recipes in this chapter. Then, when you stir up one of our enticing soups, feel free to adjust the recipe according to your tastes, what you have on hand, and what looks best at the market.

Remember, too, that it's easy to transform a light soup into one that's more robust. Just stir in cooked meat, poultry, or a handful or two of fresh vegetables a few minutes before serving. In many countries, the same basic soup is served in light or hearty variations simply depending on what ingredients are handy to the cook.

Light soups

As worthy co-stars beside a salad or sandwich, or as savory starters to stimulate the palate before the entrée arrives, light soups bring delicious satisfaction to lunch or supper. (In some countries, light soups even appear at breakfast.)

Many such soups begin with beef or chicken broth; you can make it yourself (page 33) or use canned broth. Enrich this simple base with eggs, cream, cheese, meat, seafood, vegetables, or some combination of these. In many countries, condiments are passed at the table to embellish each portion.

Chilled Seafood Potpourri

United States

Wherever there's great seafood, there are great seafood recipes. Here's one from America's Pacific coast: a creamy, tangy shellfish soup.

> 2 **green onions (including tops), thinly sliced**
> 2 **tablespoons minced green pepper**
> 1 **cup peeled, diced cucumber**
> 1 **teaspoon *each* dry tarragon and Dijon mustard**
> 2¼ **teaspoons sugar**
> 2 **teaspoons Worcestershire**
> **Dash of liquid hot pepper seasoning**
> 6 **cups buttermilk**
> ⅔ **cup milk**
> **About 1 cup flaked crabmeat**
> **About 1½ cups small cooked shrimp**
> **Salt and white pepper**

In a large bowl, combine onions (reserve some of the tops for garnish), green pepper, cucumber, tarragon, mustard, sugar, Worcestershire, and hot pepper seasoning. Stir in buttermilk and milk. Stir crabmeat and shrimp into milk mixture; season soup to taste with salt and pepper. Cover and refrigerate for at least 4 hours or until next day.

Just before serving, stir well and garnish with reserved onion tops. Makes about 10½ cups.

Gazpacho Cream with Condiments

El Salvador

Because it's made with cream, El Salvador's gazpacho is milder than its Mexican counterpart (at right). A topping of chopped fresh vegetables adds color and crunch to each serving.

> 2 **cans (14½ oz. *each*) regular-strength chicken broth or 3½ cups homemade chicken broth (page 33)**
> 2 **cans (10 oz. *each*) chile-seasoned tomato cocktail**
> ½ **cup half-and-half (light cream)**
> **Condiments: About ⅔ cup *each* shredded carrot, seeded and chopped cucumber, chopped green pepper, thinly sliced green onions (including tops), and seeded, chopped tomato**

In a pitcher, combine broth, tomato cocktail, and half-and-half. Cover and refrigerate for at least 4 hours or until next day.

Place carrot, cucumber, green pepper, onions, and tomato in separate bowls. Stir broth mixture well, then pour into soup bowls. Pass vegetables at the table. Makes 6½ to 7 cups.

MEXICAN TOMATO GAZPACHO

Follow directions for **Gazpacho Cream with Condiments,** but omit half-and-half; instead, add 3 medium-size **tomatoes,** peeled and chopped; 1 tablespoon **red wine vinegar;** ½ teaspoon **oregano leaves;** and 1½ tablespoons **olive oil** or salad oil.

Omit carrot and tomato from condiments. Instead, use 2 **avocados,** pitted, peeled, and chopped, 1 cup chopped **fresh cilantro** (coriander), and 2 **limes,** cut into wedges.

Avgolemono

Greece

Avgolemono refers not only to this tangy egg-thickened broth, but also to a basic Greek sauce that tops everything from fish to vegetables.

> 4 **cups regular-strength chicken broth**
> 4 **eggs**
> ¼ **cup lemon juice**
> **Lemon slices**

Pour broth into a 3-quart pan; bring to a boil over medium heat. Meanwhile, in a bowl, beat eggs until light and foamy; then beat in lemon juice. Pour a small amount (about 1 cup) of the hot broth into egg mixture, beating constantly.

Reduce heat to low; slowly pour egg-broth mixture back into pan, beating constantly. Cook, stirring, until soup is thickened. Pour into cups; garnish with lemon slices. Makes about 4½ cups.

Preparing creamy Maritata Soup (Recipe on facing page)

1 In a 4 to 5-quart kettle, bring beef or chicken broth to a boil. Break vermicelli into short lengths; drop into broth.

2 Beat butter, egg yolks, and cheese together with a wire whisk; slowly add cream and beat until blended.

3 Remove about 1 cup bubbling broth; slowly pour broth into egg mixture, beating constantly.

4 Pour warmed egg-broth mixture back into kettle, beating constantly; continue to beat until soup thickens slightly.

5 Rich with egg and cheese, this creamy, velvety soup makes an elegant dinner party opener.

..Light soups

Maritata Soup

Italy   (Pictured on facing page)

This elegant soup illustrates a perfect marriage of simple flavors—and that explains its name (*maritata* means "married" in Italian).

>   3   cans (14½ oz. *each*) regular-strength beef or chicken broth or 5½ cups homemade broth (page 33)
>   2   ounces vermicelli
>   ½   cup (¼ lb.) unsalted butter, softened
>   1   cup (4 to 5 oz.) freshly grated Parmesan cheese
>   4   egg yolks
>   ½   pint (1 cup) whipping cream
>   Ground nutmeg (optional)

Pour broth into a 4 to 5-quart kettle and bring to a boil over high heat. Break vermicelli into short lengths and add to boiling broth. Reduce heat to medium and simmer, uncovered, until pasta is *al dente* (3 to 5 minutes).

Meanwhile, in a bowl, beat butter, cheese, and egg yolks until well blended; gradually beat in cream. Slowly pour a small amount (about 1 cup) of the hot broth into egg mixture, beating constantly; then pour all into kettle, beating constantly. Ladle into individual bowls. If desired, dust each serving with nutmeg. Makes about 7 cups.

Vichyssoise

France

Delicate, velvety vichyssoise is a chilled purée of potatoes and leeks. Try it for a hot-weather lunch or supper.

>   3   cans (14½ oz. *each*) regular-strength chicken broth or 5½ cups homemade chicken broth (page 33)
>   4   cups sliced leeks (white part only)
>   3   cups peeled, diced thin-skinned potatoes
>   ½   pint (1 cup) whipping cream
>   3   tablespoons dry vermouth or dry sherry
>   Salt and white pepper
>   Chopped chives

Pour broth into a 4-quart pan; add leeks and potatoes. Bring to a boil over high heat; then cover, reduce heat, and simmer until vegetables are tender when pierced (about 20 minutes).

In a blender or food processor, whirl mixture, a portion at a time, until puréed. Stir in cream and vermouth. Season to taste with salt and pepper. Cover and refrigerate for at least 6 hours or until next day. Stir well; pour chilled soup into bowls and sprinkle with chives. Makes about 10 cups.

Lobster Soup

Philippines

This mild soup showcases a popular Asian cooking practice: beaten eggs are swirled in hot broth to form decorative, tasty golden strands.

>   2   tablespoons butter or margarine
>   1   frozen rock lobster tail (about 8 oz.), thawed and cut in half lengthwise
>   1   large can (49½ oz.) regular-strength chicken broth or 6 cups homemade chicken broth (page 33)
>   1   cup broken vermicelli or small egg noodles
>   1   small zucchini, thinly sliced
>   2   eggs
>   Salt and pepper
>   Hot cooked rice (optional)

In a 3-quart pan over medium heat, melt butter; add lobster, cut side down, and cook for 1 minute. Pour in broth, increase heat to high, and bring to a boil. Lift lobster from broth with a slotted spoon and set aside.

Stir pasta and zucchini into broth; then reduce heat and simmer, uncovered, until pasta is *al dente* (3 to 5 minutes).

Meanwhile, remove lobster meat from shell and cut into chunks. In a bowl, beat eggs lightly. Return lobster meat to soup; slowly pour in eggs, stirring constantly until they form long threads. Season to taste with salt and pepper. Ladle soup into bowls; if desired, add a spoonful of rice to each serving. Makes 9 to 10 cups.

CHINESE EGG DROP SOUP

Follow directions for **Lobster Soup,** but omit lobster and butter. Add 2 teaspoons *each* **dry sherry** and **soy sauce** to broth. In place of vermicelli and zucchini, use 1 bunch **watercress,** tough stems discarded and long sprigs broken in half, or 2 cups coarsely shredded spinach. Cook for just 2 minutes before adding eggs. Makes about 6 cups.

...Light soups

Beet & Cabbage Soup

Finland

This bright Finnish soup is a "kissing cousin" of Russia's *borscht*—and a perfect partner for Russian Piroshkis (page 74).

> 3 cans (14½ oz. each) regular-strength beef broth, or 5 cups homemade beef broth (facing page)
> 1 small head cabbage (about 1¼ lbs.), shredded
> 1 tablespoon lemon juice
> 3 large beets, peeled and shredded
> ⅛ teaspoon each caraway seeds and pepper
> Sour cream
> Lemon slices

Pour broth into a 4 to 5-quart kettle and bring to a boil over high heat. Add cabbage, lemon juice, beets, caraway seeds, and pepper. Cover, reduce heat, and simmer until cabbage is tender to bite (about 15 minutes). Ladle into individual bowls; top each serving with a dollop of sour cream and 1 or 2 lemon slices. Makes about 8 cups.

Leek Soup with Cheese

Netherlands

Leeks lend a subtle oniony flavor to soups in Holland and neighboring countries. Shredded Edam or Gouda cheese enriches each serving of this creamy Dutch treat.

> 4 medium-size leeks (about 1 lb. *total*)
> ¾ cup all-purpose flour
> 8 cups regular-strength beef broth
> 1 cup milk
> ⅛ teaspoon each pepper and ground mace
> ¼ cup whipping cream
> 4 cups (1 lb.) shredded Edam or Gouda cheese

Discard tough outer leaves from leeks. Split lengthwise; rinse well, then thinly slice crosswise.

Place flour in a 5 to 6-quart kettle; blend in broth, a little at a time. Stir in milk, pepper, and mace. Bring to a boil over high heat, stirring constantly; then reduce heat and simmer, uncovered, for 10 minutes, stirring occasionally. Add cream and leeks; continue to simmer, stirring occasionally, until leeks are tender to bite (about 10 more minutes). Pass cheese at the table. Makes 3 quarts.

Sausage & Kale Soup

Portugal

Sausages and greens are a favorite combination in much of Europe. Here, spicy linguisa and kale pair up to make a zesty, bright green soup.

> 1 large can (49½ oz.) regular-strength chicken broth or 6 cups homemade chicken broth (facing page)
> 3 large white thin-skinned potatoes, peeled and cut into ½-inch cubes
> ½ pound linguisa sausage
> 2 pounds kale, spinach, or chard
> Pepper

Pour broth into a 5-quart kettle and bring to a boil over high heat. Add potatoes; cover, reduce heat, and boil gently until very tender when pierced (about 35 minutes).

In a 3-quart pan, bring 1 inch water to a boil over high heat. Add sausage; cover, reduce heat, and simmer for 15 minutes. Drain. Remove casings; cut meat into ½-inch slices and set aside. Discard tough stems from kale. Cut leaves into shreds and add to broth mixture; then cover and simmer until tender to bite (about 10 minutes).

In a blender or food processor, whirl soup, a portion at a time, until greens are coarsely chopped. Return to kettle and add sausage; heat for 10 more minutes. Season to taste with pepper. Makes about 10 cups.

Fried Egg & Pork Soup

Thailand

In America, ham-and-eggs is a breakfast classic. But in Thailand, eggs and pork come to the dinner table—in soups like this, for example.

> 4 eggs
> 3 tablespoons salad oil
> 1 pound lean boneless pork, cut into ⅛ by 1 by 2-inch strips
> 4 cloves garlic, minced or pressed
> ⅛ teaspoon pepper
> 1 large can (49½ oz.) regular-strength chicken broth or 6 cups homemade chicken broth (facing page)
> 1 teaspoon each sugar and vinegar
> ½ teaspoon soy sauce
> ¾ cup sliced green onions (including tops)

In a bowl, lightly beat eggs. Heat 1 tablespoon of the oil in a wide frying pan over high heat. Pour in eggs all at once; as they begin to set, lift cooked portion to let liquid run underneath. When eggs are set and lightly browned on bottom, turn over and cook until lightly browned on other side. Turn out of pan; cut into ½-inch-wide, 2-inch-long strips. Set aside.

In a bowl, combine pork, garlic, and pepper. Heat 1 more tablespoon oil in pan over high heat; add half the pork mixture and cook, stirring, until lightly browned (about 3 minutes). Remove from pan and set aside. Repeat with remaining 1 tablespoon oil and remaining pork mixture.

Place broth, sugar, vinegar, and soy in a 5 to 6-quart kettle; bring to a boil over high heat. Add eggs, pork, and onions and cook just until pork is heated through (1 to 2 minutes). Makes about 8 cups.

Garlic Soup

Spain

A poached egg in steaming chicken broth, topped with crunchy garlic croutons—that's Spanish *sopa de ajo.*

- 4 **slices firm-textured white bread, crusts removed**
- 2 **tablespoons butter or margarine**
- 3 **cloves garlic, minced or pressed**
- 2 **cans (14½ oz. each) regular-strength chicken broth or 3½ cups homemade chicken broth (recipe at right)**
- 1 **bay leaf**
- 1 **teaspoon lemon juice**
- 4 **eggs**
  Finely chopped parsley or coarsely chopped fresh cilantro (coriander)

Cut bread into ½-inch cubes. In a wide frying pan over medium heat, melt butter; add garlic and bread cubes and cook, stirring often, until bread is lightly browned. Remove from pan and set aside.

Pour broth into pan; add bay leaf and lemon juice. Bring to a simmer over medium heat. Break eggs, one at a time, into a saucer; carefully slip each into hot broth and cook until whites are set but yolks are still runny (3 to 4 minutes). Transfer eggs to 4 individual bowls; ladle broth over top and sprinkle with croutons and parsley. Makes 4 servings.

PREPARING HOMEMADE BROTH

Though canned regular-strength broth is excellent, it's easy and economical to make broth from scratch (it takes only a few hours). Your kitchen will smell marvelous while the broth simmers; and when it's done, you'll have enough richly flavored base for several kettlefuls of soup.

Homemade broth freezes beautifully. Store it in containers that hold enough for a full recipe of soup. Or freeze it in ice cube trays; then release the cubes and store them in freezer bags, ready to use whenever you need a small amount of broth.

Besides improving soups, broths give full, rich flavor to stews, gravies, and sauces.

Homemade beef broth. Place 4 pounds cut-up **beef and veal shanks** (or all beef shanks) in a roasting pan. Bake in a 450° oven, uncovered, for 20 to 25 minutes or until browned. Transfer meat to a 6 to 8-quart kettle. Add 1 cup **water** to roasting pan, and stir to scrape up browned bits; then pour into kettle along with 11 more cups **water.** Add 2 **carrots,** cut into chunks; 2 medium-size **onions,** quartered; 2 stalks **celery,** cut into pieces; 1 **bay leaf;** 2 cloves **garlic;** 2 **whole cloves;** 6 **whole black peppers;** and ¼ teaspoon **thyme leaves.** Bring to a boil; then cover, reduce heat, and simmer until meat falls from bones (about 2½ hours).

Let broth cool; then pour it through a wire strainer and discard meat, vegetables, and seasonings. Cover and refrigerate for up to 4 days. To freeze, lift off and discard fat (see page 35); transfer broth to freezer containers, leaving about ½ to 1 inch head space. Cover and freeze for up to 6 months. Makes about 3 quarts.

Homemade chicken broth. Follow directions for **homemade beef broth,** substituting 5 pounds **chicken backs, necks, and wings,** for beef and veal shanks. Omit garlic and whole cloves. Do not oven-roast chicken parts; instead, place them directly in kettle with 12 cups **water,** vegetables, and seasonings. Then proceed with recipe.

Hearty soups

Hearty soups from around the world are worthy of the starring role at family dinners and informal parties. Bright with vegetables and thick with meat, poultry, or fish, these soups are rib-sticking fare. To complete the meal, you need add only a crisp salad and good crusty bread. If you serve dessert, choose a simple sweet—ice cream or fresh fruit, perhaps.

Goulash Soup

Hungary

Originally, the thick, meaty soup or stew called *gulyás* was cooked over an open fire by Hungarian cowboys (in fact, the word *gulyás* means "cowboy").

  2 **tablespoons salad oil**
  3 **pounds boneless beef chuck, cubed**
  2 **tablespoons butter or margarine**
  2 **large onions, chopped**
  1 **clove garlic, minced or pressed**
  1 **tablespoon sweet Hungarian paprika or regular paprika**
  5 **cups water**
  1 **large green pepper, seeded and cut into strips**
  1 **teaspoon caraway seeds**
  2 **tomatoes, peeled, seeded, and chopped**
  1 **small dried whole hot red chile, crushed (optional)**
  2 **large white thin-skinned potatoes, peeled and cut into eighths**
     Salt and pepper

Heat oil in a 5-quart kettle over medium-high heat. Add beef, about ¼ at a time, and cook until browned on all sides. Remove to a plate.

Discard drippings from kettle. Add butter; reduce heat to medium, then add onions and garlic and cook until onions are soft. Blend in paprika. Return meat (and any juices collected on plate) to kettle. Then add water, green pepper, caraway seeds, tomatoes, and chile (if used).

Bring to a boil; then cover, reduce heat, and simmer until meat is tender when pierced—about 2 hours. (At this point, you may let cool, then cover and refrigerate until next day.)

Skim (or lift off) and discard fat from soup. Bring soup to a boil over high heat. Add potatoes; cover, reduce heat, and simmer until potatoes are tender when pierced (20 to 30 minutes). Season to taste with salt and pepper. Makes about 3 quarts.

Cock-a-leekie Soup

Wales   (Pictured on facing page)

Welsh cooks prepare leeks in dozens of tasty ways—it's no wonder the leek is the national emblem of Wales! Here, leeks and chicken team up in a richly flavored soup.

  1 **large frying chicken (about 4 lbs.), cut up**
  2 **large cans (49½ oz. *each*) regular-strength chicken broth or 3 quarts homemade chicken broth (page 33)**
  2 **large carrots, cut into chunks**
  1 **large onion, quartered**
  2 **stalks celery (including tops), sliced**
  3 **parsley sprigs**
  3 **whole black peppers**
  1 **cup pearl barley**
  8 **medium-size leeks (about 2 lbs. *total*)**
  1 **large russet potato, peeled and shredded**
  1 **cup half-and-half (light cream)**
     Salt and pepper
     Chopped parsley

Reserve chicken giblets for other uses. Pull off and discard large lumps of fat; then rinse chicken and place in a 6 to 8-quart kettle. Add broth, carrots, onion, celery, parsley sprigs, and whole peppers. Bring to a boil over high heat; cover, reduce heat, and simmer until chicken is very tender when pierced (about 1¼ hours).

Let chicken cool for about 1 hour, then lift from broth. Remove and discard skin and bones; cut meat into bite-size pieces.

Pour broth through a wire strainer or colander; discard vegetables and peppers. Let cool; then cover and refrigerate broth and chicken separately until next day.

Lift off and discard fat from broth. Bring broth to a boil over high heat; stir in barley. Cover, reduce heat, and simmer for 20 minutes.

Meanwhile, trim and discard ends and tops from leeks, leaving about 1½ inches of green leaves. Discard tough outer leaves. Split leeks lengthwise; rinse well, then thinly slice crosswise. Add leeks and potato to broth and simmer, uncovered, stirring occasionally, until vegetables and barley are tender to bite (about 15 minutes).

Add chicken; then stir in half-in-half and heat until steaming. Season to taste with salt and pepper. Pour into a soup tureen and sprinkle with chopped parsley. Makes about 5 quarts.

Making hearty Cock-a-leekie Soup (Recipe on facing page)

1 Simmer meaty chicken parts with vegetables until tender. Let cool; remove chicken and strain broth. Then cover and refrigerate meat and broth separately until next day.

2 Using a large spoon, lift off solidified fat from chilled broth. Bring broth to a boil; then add barley.

3 Meanwhile, trim root ends and tops from leeks. Split leeks lengthwise; rinse well, thinly slice crosswise, and add to soup.

4 Ladle hot and hearty soup, brimming with tender chicken, barley, and vegetables, into wide soup plates.

...Hearty soups

Chicken & Potato Soup

Colombia

Bogotá's *ajiaco* contains two kinds of potatoes—russets, mashed to thicken the broth, and thin-skinned potatoes, cut into chunks. But that's just the beginning; corn on the cob and chicken pieces also enrich this knife-and-fork soup. Assorted condiments, sprinkled atop individual servings, add a tasty finishing touch.

    1 **frying chicken (3 to 3½ lbs.), cut up**
    2 **large onions, cut into chunks**
    4 **medium-size russet potatoes, peeled and cubed**
    6 **cups water**
    6 **chicken bouillon cubes**
    1 **bay leaf**
    1 **teaspoon ground cumin**
    3 **medium-size thin-skinned potatoes, peeled and halved**
    3 **to 4 ears corn on the cob, cut crosswise into 1½-inch slices**
      Salt and pepper
      Condiments (directions follow)

Reserve chicken giblets for other uses. Pull off and discard large lumps of fat; then rinse chicken and place in an 8-quart kettle. Add onions, russet potatoes, water, bouillon cubes, bay leaf, and cumin. Bring to a boil over high heat; cover, reduce heat, and simmer until meat near thighbone is no longer pink when slashed (about 50 minutes).

Lift out chicken pieces; set aside. Pour broth through a colander and reserve cooked vegetables. Return about 3 cups of the broth to kettle; add thin-skinned potatoes. Bring to a boil over high heat; cover, reduce heat, and simmer for 15 minutes. Add corn; cover and cook until potatoes are tender when pierced (about 5 more minutes).

Meanwhile, remove bay leaf from reserved cooked vegetables. In a blender or food processor, whirl vegetables, a portion at a time, with remaining broth until smooth. Remove meat from chicken wings, back, and neck; discard skin and bones. Leave breast halves, legs, and thighs whole. Stir puréed vegetables, whole chicken pieces, and boned chicken into kettle. Season to taste with salt and pepper; heat through.

Ladle broth, 1 whole chicken piece, 1 potato half, and 1 or 2 pieces corn into each of 6 wide soup plates. Pass condiments to spoon into individual portions. Makes 6 servings.

Condiments. Offer each of the following in a small serving dish: about ½ cup **capers,** drained well; 2 **avocados,** pitted, peeled, and sliced; about 1 cup **sour cream;** 3 or 4 **hard-cooked eggs,** chopped; ½ cup coarsely chopped **fresh cilantro** (coriander); and **prepared taco sauce** or salsa.

Fish & Potato Selyanka

Finland

Though Finland gained independence from Russia in 1917, Russian influence is still apparent in Finnish cooking. Sturdy *selyanka* combines the best of both culinary traditions.

    2 **pounds halibut, shark, or swordfish steaks**
    1 **large can (49½ oz.) regular-strength chicken broth or 6 cups homemade chicken broth (page 33)**
    1 **pound thin-skinned potatoes, peeled and cut into ½-inch cubes**
    1 **large yellow onion, finely chopped**
      Dill weed
    6 **tablespoons butter or margarine, melted**
    1 **medium-size mild red onion, chopped**
      Salt and pepper

Place fish in a 5-quart kettle; add broth. Bring to a boil over medium-high heat; then cover, reduce heat, and simmer just until fish tests done (about 5 minutes; see page 120). Set aside for at least 20 minutes; or let cool completely, then cover and refrigerate for up to 8 hours. Lift out fish with a slotted spoon. Remove and discard skin and bones, then cut fish into bite-size chunks.

Return kettle with broth to high heat; add potatoes, yellow onion, and 1 teaspoon dill weed. Bring to a boil; cover, reduce heat, and boil gently until potatoes are tender when pierced (about 15 minutes). Add fish and heat through.

Ladle soup into bowls; let diners season their soup with butter, red onion, salt and pepper, and additional dill weed. Makes about 3 quarts.

Lamb & Sausage Soup

France

Every bit as hearty as Germany's bean and sausage soup (facing page), this thick French potage makes delectable use of two kinds of meat and a variety of popular vegetables.

About 3 pounds lamb shoulder or lamb
shanks, cracked

1 pound kielbasa (Polish sausage), cut into
½-inch slices

1 large clove garlic, minced or pressed

2 large onions, chopped

1 bay leaf

6 chicken bouillon cubes
Hot water

¾ teaspoon thyme leaves

2 cups fresh peas or 1 package (10 oz.) frozen
peas, thawed

1 can (14 oz.) artichoke hearts in water, drained
well and quartered

1 can (15 oz.) baby corn, drained well
Salt and pepper

Place lamb, fat side down, in a 6 to 8-quart kettle;
cook over medium-high heat, turning as needed,
until well browned on all sides. Lift out and set
aside. Add sausage, garlic, and onions to drippings; cook until onion is soft.

Return lamb to kettle. Add bay leaf, bouillon
cubes, and 6 cups hot water. Bring to a boil; then
cover, reduce heat, and simmer until lamb is
tender when pierced (about 1½ hours).

Discard bay leaf. Lift out lamb; when it's cool
enough to handle, discard bones and fat and tear
meat into bite-size pieces. Return meat to simmering broth. Add 6 more cups hot water, thyme,
peas, artichokes, and corn; cover and simmer until flavors are blended (about 10 minutes). Season
to taste with salt and pepper. If made ahead, let
cool; then cover and refrigerate for up to 5 days.

Skim (or lift off) and discard fat from soup (and
reheat refrigerated soup). Ladle into individual
bowls. Makes 4 to 4½ quarts.

Mosel Valley Bean & Sausage Soup

Germany

A vegetable-rich broth chock-full of spicy sausage
makes a robust Rhineland meal in the tastiest
European tradition. Offer a crisp salad and warm
Slavic Farmer's Bread (page 184) alongside.

4 strips bacon, cut crosswise into ½-inch pieces

2 medium-size onions, chopped

1 large can (49½ oz.) regular-strength chicken
broth or 6 cups homemade chicken broth
(page 33)

4 medium-size thin-skinned potatoes, peeled
and cut into ½-inch cubes

2 medium-size carrots, thinly sliced

¼ cup chopped parsley

1 teaspoon dill weed

½ teaspoon marjoram leaves

¼ teaspoon white pepper

1 pound smoked bratwurst, kielbasa (Polish
sausage), or frankfurters, thinly sliced

1 pound green beans, ends removed, cut into
1-inch lengths

Place bacon in a 5 to 6-quart kettle over medium
heat; cook, stirring occasionally, until lightly
browned. Spoon off and discard all but 1 tablespoon drippings. Add onions and cook, stirring
often, until soft. Stir in broth, potatoes, carrots,
parsley, dill weed, marjoram, and pepper. Bring
to a boil; then cover, reduce heat, and simmer until potatoes are very tender when pierced (about
35 minutes).

Using a slotted spoon, lift out about half the
vegetables and set aside. Slightly mash remaining vegetables into broth to thicken soup. Return
reserved vegetables to kettle; add sausage and
beans. Bring to a boil over high heat; then reduce
heat and boil gently, uncovered, until beans are
tender to bite (about 15 minutes). Makes about
4 quarts.

FREEZING HOMEMADE SOUPS

You can store most hearty soups in the
freezer for up to 6 months; homemade broth
freezes beautifully, too (see page 33). After
reheating, the soup will still have bright,
fresh flavor; green vegetables may become
drab in color, though, and shellfish will
toughen.

Before you freeze any soup, be aware of
a few do's and don'ts. Omit potatoes from
soups you plan to freeze; freezing alters
their texture, making them mushy and
mealy. Cook potatoes in the soup when
you're reheating it, or add freshly cooked
potatoes just before serving.

Let soup cool completely before freezing. Skim and discard any fat; then pour
soup into containers that hold the amounts
you plan to heat and serve at one time. Liq-
uids expand upon freezing, so be sure to
leave about an inch of space beneath container lids.

Easy Meatball Soup from Mexico (Recipe on facing page)

1 Quickly shape the ground beef mixture into 1½-inch balls and drop into bubbling broth.

2 With a large spoon, skim off fat and foam as they accumulate on surface of broth. Add carrots, rice, and cilantro; simmer until tender.

3 Stack rinsed spinach leaves. With a sharp knife, cut leaves crosswise into thin shreds.

4 Embellish colorful Meatball Soup with a squeeze of lime and a sprig or two of cilantro.

.Hearty soups

Meatball Soup

Mexico   (Pictured on facing page)

Need an easy, crowd-pleasing menu? *Sopa de albondigas* offers a fiesta of flavor for little effort. Accompany the soup with warm, soft corn tortillas and refreshing Orange Salad (page 47). For dessert, continue the Mexican theme with delicate Flan (page 207).

- 1½ **pounds lean ground beef**
- ¼ **cup all-purpose flour**
- 2 **eggs**
- 1 **large can (49½ oz.) regular-strength chicken broth or 6 cups homemade chicken broth (page 33)**
- 3 **cans (10½ oz. *each*) condensed consommé**
- 1 **teaspoon oregano leaves**
- 2 **medium-size onions, chopped**
- 1 **large dried whole ancho or pasilla chile, seeded and crumbled, or 1 small dried whole hot red chile, seeded**
- 6 **medium-size carrots, very thinly sliced**
- ¼ **cup long-grain white rice**
- ⅓ **cup chopped fresh cilantro (coriander)**
- ¾ **pound spinach**
  Fresh cilantro (coriander) sprigs
- 2 **or 3 limes, cut into wedges**

In a bowl, combine beef, flour, eggs, and ½ cup of the broth. Pour remaining broth into an 8-quart kettle; add consommé, oregano, onions, and chile. Bring to a boil over high heat; then reduce heat to low. Quickly shape beef mixture into 1½-inch balls, dropping them into broth as you shape them. Simmer meatballs, uncovered, for 5 minutes, spooning off any fat and foam from surface of broth. Add carrots, rice, and chopped cilantro; simmer, uncovered, until carrots and rice are tender to bite (about 20 minutes).

Discard spinach stems; rinse leaves well, then cut crosswise into thin shreds. Add spinach to soup and cook, uncovered, for 5 minutes. Discard whole chile (if used). Ladle into wide soup plates or bowls; pass cilantro sprigs for garnish and lime wedges to squeeze into individual portions. Makes about 5½ quarts.

Lamb-stuffed Meatball Soup

Armenian heritage

Only a cuisine that has long looked to lamb as a dietary mainstay could create such elegant morsels as the *kufta* that go into this soup. To make the savory meatballs, you enclose portions of seasoned lamb filling in "shells" of uncooked ground lamb. After poaching the filled shells in simmering broth, you serve the soup with cool yogurt— another Armenian staple.

- ¾ **pound lean ground lamb**
- 1 **small onion, finely chopped**
- 2 **tablespoons lemon juice**
- 2 **teaspoons paprika**
- ½ **teaspoon ground red pepper (cayenne)**
- ½ **cup finely chopped parsley**
  Salt and pepper
  Lamb shells (recipe follows)
- 8 **cups regular-strength chicken broth**
  Parsley sprigs
  Plain yogurt

Finely crumble lamb into a wide frying pan over medium-high heat. Add onion and cook, stirring, for 5 minutes. Add lemon juice, paprika, and red pepper; continue to cook, stirring, until meat is no longer pink (about 10 more minutes). Remove from heat; mix in chopped parsley and season to taste with salt and pepper. Let cool.

Prepare lamb shells. With moistened hands, firmly pat each lamb shell portion into a round patty about 4 inches in diameter. Spoon about 1 tablespoon of the cooked mixture into center of each; then bring edges together and pinch to seal. Pat smooth. Set meatballs on a wax-paper-lined baking sheet. (At this point, you may cover and refrigerate until next day.)

Pour broth into a 5 to 6-quart kettle and bring to a boil over high heat. Reduce heat to low; add meatballs. Cover and simmer until shell is firm throughout (about 10 minutes—cut to test).

Serve meatballs in broth; or lift out of broth and serve as an entrée, offering clear broth as a first course. Garnish with parsley sprigs; pass yogurt to spoon over individual portions. Makes 8 servings.

Lamb shells. Using an electric mixer, smoothly blend 2¼ pounds **lean ground lamb** with ¾ cup **whole wheat flour.** Divide into 24 equal pieces.

SALADS

The English word "salad" derives from Latin *salata*—literally, "salted"—and the original salad was nothing more than raw fresh herbs or other edible plants sprinkled with salt. Today, though, the ingredient list is much longer and more varied. Greens are still popular, but a salad can also contain fruits, raw or cooked vegetables, meats, eggs, cheese, and pasta—to name a few! Dressings, too, have evolved far beyond the original sprinkling of salt; sweet or tangy, clear or creamy, they're available in wide variety.

This chapter takes you on a refreshing tour of the salad-making world, sampling some of the best recipes from such places as France, Hungary, China, Morocco, Italy, Thailand, Germany, India, Mexico, and the United States' Hawaii.

At what point in the meal should you serve salad? In the United States, it's often presented as a light first course to whet the appetite. In France, the opposite order holds—a crisp salad follows the entrée, cleansing the palate before dessert. Some salads (marinated vegetables, for example) are delightful served alongside the entrée. And if the salad is hearty enough, it can stand alone as the meal's main event.

Green salads

Crisp, fresh greens topped with flavorful dressings are popular the world around. Here's a small sampling—all delicious, and all easy to make.

Rouge et Noir Salad

France

Arranged on a bed of watercress, red cherry tomatoes and shiny black ripe olives create a striking scene, as delicious to view as to taste. (The tangy lemon mayonnaise tastes wonderful with cold boiled artichokes, too.)

   2 **bunches watercress**
   ¾ **pound mushrooms, thinly sliced**
   1 **can (3½ oz.) pitted ripe olives, drained well**
   18 **cherry tomatoes, halved**
     Lemon mayonnaise (recipe follows)

Discard tough stems from watercress; then break cress into 2-inch lengths. Rinse and pat dry. In a large bowl, combine watercress, mushrooms, olives, and tomatoes; cover and refrigerate for 2 to 4 hours. Prepare lemon mayonnaise; pass at the table to spoon over individual portions. Makes 6 servings.

Lemon mayonnaise. In a blender or food processor, combine 1 **egg yolk,** ¼ cup **lemon juice,** ½ teaspoon each **salt** and **ground nutmeg,** and ⅛ teaspoon **white pepper;** whirl until well blended. With motor running, gradually add ½ cup **salad oil**—a few drops at a time at first, increasing to a slow, steady stream as mixture begins to thicken. Spoon into a serving dish; cover and refrigerate for up to 2 weeks.

Apple & Cabbage Slaw

Germany

Apples and cabbage are both German favorites; both show up in this crisp, caraway-flavored slaw.

- ⅓ cup *each* sour cream and mayonnaise
- 2 tablespoons *each* German-style mustard, sugar, and white wine vinegar
- 1 tablespoon caraway seeds
- 6 cups finely shredded cabbage
- ½ cup thinly sliced green onions (including tops)
- 2 red-skinned apples, cored and diced

In a small bowl, stir together sour cream, mayonnaise, mustard, sugar, vinegar, and caraway seeds. Cover and refrigerate for at least 1 hour to blend flavors. Place cabbage, onions, and apples in a serving bowl; pour dressing over all and toss lightly to coat. Makes 6 servings.

Sicilian Green Salad

Italy

If you like the sweet, tangy taste of citrus fruit, you'll enjoy this Sicilian salad.

- 1 head romaine, rinsed and patted dry
- 2 oranges, peeled, white membranes removed
- 1 can (2¼ oz.) sliced ripe olives, drained well
- ¼ cup orange juice
- 2 teaspoons red wine vinegar
- ½ teaspoon salt
- ¼ teaspoon paprika
- ¼ cup olive oil or salad oil

Tear romaine into bite-size pieces and place in a large bowl. Thinly slice oranges crosswise; place oranges and olives atop romaine. In a jar, combine orange juice, vinegar, salt, paprika, and oil; shake to blend well. Pour over salad and toss lightly to coat. Makes 6 servings.

Spinach Salad

Greece

For a light, lovely feast full of Mediterranean flavor, augment this salad with hard-cooked eggs and *dolmas*—rice-stuffed grape leaves, sold in cans or jars at imported food shops.

- ¾ to 1 pound spinach
- 1 small mild white or red onion, thinly sliced and separated into rings
- 1 green pepper, seeded and cut into thin rings
- 1 small cucumber, thinly sliced
- 1 large tomato, cut into 12 wedges
  Dried cured olives or sliced ripe olives
- 3 ounces feta cheese, crumbled (about ¾ cup)
- 5 tablespoons olive oil or salad oil
- 5 tablespoons lemon juice
- 1 teaspoon *each* oregano leaves and dry mustard
  Salt
  Freshly ground pepper

Remove and discard tough spinach stems; rinse leaves and pat dry. Tear leaves into bite-size pieces and arrange on 6 individual plates. Top each with onion, green pepper, cucumber, tomato, a few olives, and cheese.

In a jar, combine oil, lemon juice, oregano, and mustard; shake to blend well. Season dressing to taste with salt and pepper; then drizzle over each salad. Makes 6 servings.

Sprout & Cress Salad

China

The Chinese rarely serve salads—but here's a delicious exception. This cool, crunchy tangle of watercress and bean sprouts is a welcome accompaniment to any meal.

- ¾ pound bean sprouts
- 1 bunch watercress
- 2 tablespoons soy sauce
- 1 tablespoon *each* white (distilled) vinegar and sesame oil
- 1 teaspoon sugar

Half-fill a 5 to 6-quart kettle with water and bring to a boil over high heat. Drop in bean sprouts; cook for 30 seconds. Drain, rinse under cold running water, and drain again. Discard tough stems from watercress; break cress into 2-inch lengths. Rinse and pat dry. Cover watercress and sprouts and refrigerate separately until cold.

Stir together soy, vinegar, oil, and sugar in a small bowl. Drain bean sprouts again; then combine with watercress and dressing. Toss until vegetables are well coated. Makes 4 servings.

Molded salads

Shimmering molded salads bring welcome refreshment on hot summer days. They do take time to set, so you'll need to make them well before serving; then, at mealtime, you need only unmold your creation and collect the compliments.

Broccoli & Egg Aspic

France   (Pictured on facing page)

Here's a nutritious jewel of a salad, an example of French appreciation of gelatin in a cool, summery refreshment. Make sure that each layer is set before pouring on the next one.

>   About 1 pound broccoli
>   Water
> 1 envelope unflavored gelatin
> 1 can (14½ oz.) regular-strength chicken broth or
>   1¾ cups homemade chicken broth (page 33)
> 6 cold hard-cooked eggs
> ⅓ cup each mayonnaise and thinly sliced green
>   onions (including tops)
> 2 tablespoons Dijon mustard

Lightly oil a deep 1-quart baking dish or soufflé dish; set aside. Cut off broccoli flowerets; peel stalks and cut into pieces.

In a wide frying pan, bring 1 inch water to a boil over high heat. Add broccoli. When water returns to a boil, cover pan, reduce heat, and simmer just until broccoli is tender when pierced (about 7 minutes). Drain; plunge into a large quantity of cold water, drain again, and set aside.

Sprinkle gelatin over ½ cup cold water in a small pan; let stand for 5 minutes to soften. Place pan over low heat and stir until gelatin is dissolved. Remove from heat and stir in broth. Let cool to room temperature, then pour about ¼ cup into prepared dish. Refrigerate until set.

Thinly slice 1 of the eggs. Arrange 4 center slices (reserve remaining slices) and 4 or 5 broccoli flowerets atop set gelatin. Slowly add ½ cup gelatin, pouring it through a funnel. Refrigerate until firm. Also refrigerate remaining gelatin separately until syrupy and slightly thickened.

Meanwhile, chop reserved egg slices, remaining 5 eggs, and remaining broccoli; place in a bowl. Stir in mayonnaise, onions, and mustard. Add remaining gelatin; blend well, then pour into dish and smooth out. Cover and refrigerate until firm (at least 4 hours). Unmold as directed at right; cut into wedges. Makes 6 servings.

Molded Gazpacho

Spain

Some warm day, try the famous Spanish and Mexican soup in a bright new guise—as a cool, crunchy molded salad.

> 2   envelopes unflavored gelatin
> 1   cup cold water
> 2½ cups tomato juice
> 1   can (6 oz.) tomato paste
> ½   cup white wine vinegar
>   About 3 tablespoons lemon juice
> 1½ teaspoons dry basil
> 1   avocado
> ½   cup each finely chopped green pepper and
>   peeled cucumber
> ¼   cup chopped green onions (including tops)

Sprinkle gelatin over water in a small pan; let stand for 5 minutes to soften. Stir in 1 cup of the tomato juice. Place pan over low heat and stir until gelatin is dissolved. Remove from heat and stir in remaining 1½ cups tomato juice, tomato paste, vinegar, 3 tablespoons of the lemon juice, and basil. Refrigerate until syrupy and slightly thickened.

Halve and pit avocado. Sprinkle one half with lemon juice, then cover and refrigerate. Peel and finely dice remaining avocado half and stir into tomato mixture along with green pepper, cucumber and onions. Pour into a 6-cup mold; cover and refrigerate until firm (at least 4 hours). Unmold onto a serving plate as directed below. Peel and slice reserved avocado half; arrange around salad. Makes 6 servings.

HOW TO UNMOLD GELATIN SALADS

Just before serving, immerse mold up to its rim in a container of hot tap water for 5 to 7 seconds. Quickly wipe mold dry with a towel; then cover it with a cold, wet plate of wider diameter. Hold plate and mold together and quickly invert them. Gently shake mold to loosen salad; lift off mold. If salad doesn't slide out, run a knife around mold edge; immerse in hot tap water for another 5 to 7 seconds (be careful—if mold is immersed too long, gelatin may melt).

Making Broccoli & Egg Aspic (Recipe on facing page)

1 Place egg slices and broccoli flowerets in a decorative pattern atop first layer of set gelatin.

2 To avoid disturbing the decorative pattern and to prevent egg slices from breaking apart, slowly pour liquid gelatin through a funnel to make an even layer.

3 Chilled gelatin should be the consistency of unbeaten egg whites: syrupy and slightly thickened. Stir into egg mixture. Before pouring into dish, make sure first 2 gelatin layers are set.

4 To unmold, immerse to rim in hot tap water. Cover mold with a cold, wet plate that's wider than mold. (Wetting plate allows you to center salad once mold is removed.) Hold plate and mold together.

5 Quickly invert—salad shimmies down to plate. If salad sticks to mold, dip into hot tap water again, but be careful not to melt gelatin. Center salad on plate; blot off excess water.

6 Surrounded with watercress sprigs and rolls of cooked ham, Broccoli & Egg Aspic makes a delightful warm-weather entrée. Croissants round out the meal.

Marinated vegetable salads

Marinated vegetables are especially popular in the hot and arid countries of the Middle East—but they're common in just about every other region of the world, too, from Southeast Asia to eastern Europe. Across the globe, the basic method of preparation is the same: You marinate raw or cooked vegetables in a vinaigrette-type dressing for several hours to blend flavors, then serve the mixture at room temperature, alongside the entrée.

Tomato-Onion Salad

India

A Mexican cook might call this a cool, minty version of Tomato Salsa (page 138). You'll call it an extra-refreshing accompaniment to hot, spicy entrées of any nationality.

    5 large tomatoes, peeled, seeded, and diced
       (about 5 cups)
    1 cup finely chopped onion
    ⅓ cup minced fresh mint or 2 tablespoons dry
       mint
    3 tablespoons lemon juice
       Salt and pepper

In a bowl, combine tomatoes, onion, mint, and lemon juice; cover and refrigerate for at least 2 hours. Remove from refrigerator 1 hour before serving; season with salt and pepper. Makes 8 servings.

Marinated Cucumbers

Thailand

When you need a refreshing salad, try these chilled cucumber slices in a sweet-tart marinade.

    ⅓ cup white (distilled) vinegar
    ¼ cup *each* sugar and water
    ¼ teaspoon salt
    1 large cucumber (about 1 lb.), peeled and
       thinly sliced

In a small pan, combine vinegar, sugar, water, and salt. Bring to a boil over high heat; then remove from heat and let cool to room temperature. Place cucumber in a serving bowl; pour in marinade and stir to coat. Cover and refrigerate for at least 2 hours. Remove from refrigerator 1 hour before serving; drain. Makes 4 servings.

Carrot Salad

Morocco

Ten cloves of garlic? That's right—but don't be alarmed. Brief simmering tames their pungency.

    10 cloves garlic, unpeeled
     2 pounds carrots
     ¼ cup olive oil or salad oil
     3 tablespoons lemon juice
     1 tablespoon paprika
     ½ teaspoon ground cumin
     ⅛ teaspoon ground red pepper (cayenne)
     ½ cup chopped parsley
        Salt

Drop garlic into a small pan of rapidly boiling water. Boil, uncovered, until tender when pierced (about 3 minutes for ¼-inch-thick cloves, 10 minutes for 1-inch-thick cloves). Drain and let cool. Pinch cloves so garlic slips out of skins; discard skins. Slice garlic lengthwise into very thin slivers and set aside.

Cut carrots into 2-inch lengths, then into julienne strips. In a wide frying pan, bring 1 inch water to a boil over high heat; add carrots. Bring to a boil again; cook, uncovered, just until carrots are tender when pierced (1 to 2 minutes). Drain, rinse under cold running water, and drain again.

In a bowl, stir together oil, lemon juice, paprika, cumin, pepper, parsley, and garlic; stir in carrots. Season to taste with salt. Let stand at room temperature for 1 hour to blend flavors, or cover and refrigerate for up to 1 week. Serve at room temperature. Makes 8 to 10 servings.

Marinated Potato Salad

Germany

Take along a taste of Germany on your next picnic —potatoes bathed in a bold mustard marinade.

    2¼ pounds thin-skinned potatoes
     ¼ cup *each* finely chopped parsley and green
        onions (including tops)
     1 beef bouillon cube dissolved in ½ cup boiling
        water
     ¼ cup salad oil
     ½ teaspoon *each* salt, pepper, and sugar
     ¼ teaspoon dill weed
     2 tablespoons German-style mustard
     3 tablespoons white wine vinegar

Arrange potatoes on a steaming rack; steam over boiling water, covered, until tender when pierced (about 20 minutes). When potatoes are cool enough to handle, peel them; then cut into ½-inch cubes. Place in a bowl and stir in parsley and onions.

In a bowl, combine bouillon liquid, oil, salt, pepper, sugar, dill weed, mustard, and vinegar; stir until well blended. Pour over potato mixture and stir to coat. Cover and let stand at room temperature for at least 1 hour before serving. Makes 6 servings.

Green Pepper Salad

Hungary

How do you make a sweet pepper even sweeter? Roasting is one good answer to that question—and the proof is in this mellow Hungarian salad.

- 3 **large green peppers, roasted (directions follow)**
- 2 **large tomatoes, peeled, seeded, and cubed**
- 1 **small mild red onion, thinly sliced and separated into rings**
- 3 **tablespoons white wine vinegar**
- 1 **teaspoon sugar**
- ¼ **cup olive oil or salad oil**
  Salt and pepper

Prepare roasted peppers; cut into ½ to 1-inch-wide strips and place in a bowl. Add tomatoes and onion. In a jar, combine vinegar, sugar, and oil; shake to blend, then pour over pepper mixture and stir well. Season to taste with salt and pepper. Cover and refrigerate for at least 4 hours or up to 2 days. Bring to room temperature before serving. Makes 4 to 6 servings.

Roasted peppers. Set **whole peppers** in a shallow pan; broil about 1 inch below heat, turning frequently with tongs, until well blistered and charred on all sides. Place peppers in a plastic bag, close bag tightly, and let peppers sweat for 15 to 20 minutes to loosen skins. Peel off and discard skins.

Eggplant & Tomato Salad

Lebanon

Middle Eastern favorites get together for a wonderfully fresh-tasting salad. Try this minty eggplant-and-tomato mélange alongside Lemony Broiled Chicken (page 105).

- 2 **medium-size eggplants (1¾ to 2 lbs. *total*)**
- ⅓ **cup olive oil**
- 2 **large tomatoes, peeled, seeded, and cubed**
- ¼ **cup *each* finely chopped parsley and fresh mint**
- ¾ **cup sliced green onions (including tops)**
- 3 **tablespoons *each* lemon juice and olive oil**
- 1 **small clove garlic, minced or pressed**
  Salt
  Lettuce leaves

Peel eggplants and cut into 1-inch-thick slices. Brush cut surfaces with the ⅓ cup oil and arrange in a single layer on a rimmed baking sheet. Broil 6 inches below heat until lightly browned and soft but not mushy (about 10 minutes). Turn and broil until other side is browned (about 10 more minutes); then let cool. Cut into cubes and place in a bowl. Add tomatoes, parsley, mint and onions.

In a small bowl, combine lemon juice, the 3 tablespoons oil, and garlic; blend well, then pour over eggplant mixture and stir to coat. Season to taste with salt. Cover and let stand at room temperature for 1 hour to blend flavors. To serve, mound on a lettuce-lined plate. Makes 4 to 6 servings.

Preparing fruit for Tropical Fruit Salad (Recipe on facing page)

1 Cut pineapple lengthwise just to one side of crown, slicing off about ⅓ of pineapple. With a curved knife, cut around inside of fruit, leaving a ¼-inch shell.

2 With a straight knife held at a 45° angle to pineapple, cut out fruit in wedge-shaped pieces, slicing through core and fruit (not through shell). Trim and discard core from each wedge.

3 Cut papaya in half lengthwise. Scoop out seeds and reserve 1 tablespoon. Peel off skin with a paring knife; cut fruit into bite-size pieces.

4 Stand mango on one edge. Cut fleshy "cheeks" away from sides of center pit. Peel tough skin from each "cheek" with a paring knife; then cut fruit into bite-size pieces.

5 Piled high in a pineapple boat, Tropical Fruit Salad takes center stage. To carry out the tropical theme, offer papaya-seed dressing in a seashell server.

Fresh fruit salads

Cool, juicy, and naturally sweet, fresh fruit salads are perfect partners for spicy-hot main dishes from any country. We offer two—both as pretty to look at as they're delicious to eat.

Orange Salad

Mexico

Sweet oranges and mild red onion slices mingle in Mexico's colorful *ensalada de naranjas*.

> 5 **large oranges, peeled, white membranes removed**
> 1 **mild red or white onion, thinly sliced**
> ⅓ **cup salad oil**
> ¼ **cup white wine vinegar**
> 1 **teaspoon sugar**
> ¼ **teaspoon chili powder**
> **Lettuce leaves**

Cut oranges crosswise into thin slices; arrange alternately with onion slices in a large salad bowl. In a jar, combine oil, vinegar, sugar, and chili powder; shake to blend well, then pour over salad. Cover and refrigerate for at least 2 hours. Toss gently; serve on lettuce leaves. Makes 8 servings.

Tropical Fruit Salad

United States-Hawaii   (Pictured on facing page)

Need a dramatic centerpiece for a summertime buffet? Try our pineapple "boat," piled high and temptingly with luscious fruit. The sweet tropical flavor comes from its cargo of Hawaiian papaya, banana, pineapple, and mango chunks.

> ½ **cup coarsely shredded coconut**
> 1 **large pineapple (3½ to 4 lbs.)**
> 1 **papaya**
> 1 **large mango**
> 1 **large banana**
> 1 **cup hulled, halved strawberries**
> **Papaya-seed dressing (recipe follows)**

Spread coconut in a shallow pan and toast in a 350° oven for 3 to 5 minutes or until light brown; set aside.

With a sharp knife, slice pineapple lengthwise just to one side of crown, cutting off about ⅓ of pineapple. Reserve cut-off piece. With a grapefruit knife, cut around fruit in remaining pineapple, leaving a ¼-inch-thick shell. Insert a straight knife through core at a 45° angle; then, making sure not to cut through shell, cut out a wedge-shaped piece. Cut out remaining fruit in 3 more wedges. Trim and discard core from wedges; cut wedges into bite-size pieces and place in a bowl. Cut out fruit from reserved pineapple, cut into bite-size pieces, and add to bowl. Cover pineapple shell and refrigerate until serving time.

Cut papaya in half lengthwise. Scoop out seeds; reserve 1 tablespoon for dressing and discard remainder. Peel papaya halves. Cut fruit into bite-size pieces and add to pineapple in bowl.

Stand mango on one edge. With a sharp knife, cut flesh away from each side of pit (see illustrations below). Peel tough skin from flesh with a paring knife, then cut flesh into bite-size pieces and add to papaya.

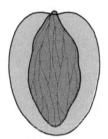 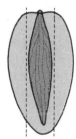

Cut banana into ¼-inch-thick slices; add to mango along with strawberries. Toss fruit lightly. Prepare papaya-seed dressing and refrigerate separately for at least 1 hour.

Spoon fruit into pineapple shell and sprinkle with coconut. (Or simply serve fruit from bowl.) Pass dressing at the table to spoon over individual servings. Makes 4 to 6 servings.

Papaya-seed dressing. In a food processor or blender, combine ¼ cup **white wine vinegar;** 1 tablespoon each **papaya seeds,** minced **onion,** and **honey;** ¼ teaspoon **salt;** and ⅛ teaspoon **dry mustard.** Whirl until seeds look like coarsely ground pepper. Gradually pour in ¼ cup **salad oil** in a slow, steady stream; whirl until dressing is well blended and slightly thickened. Makes about 1 cup.

Hearty salads

If light, leisurely dining is what you have in mind, these salads are for you—just take your pick from our choice international array. Whatever your selection, you'll be satisfied: these are all high in protein, including lots of meat, seafood, eggs, or cheese. To complete the meal, you need add only crusty bread, fresh fruit, and a cool beverage. (If you wish, prepare the salad makings in advance, then assemble just before serving.)

Shrimp Salad

Brazil

From the seaport of Salvador (Bahia), on Brazil's east coast, comes this unusual combination of shrimp and vegetables in a tangy lime dressing.

> Lime dressing (recipe follows)
> 1 to 1½ pounds medium-size raw shrimp, shelled, deveined, and cooked (directions at right); or 3 cups cubed cold cooked chicken
> 1 medium-size green pepper, seeded and cut into thin strips
> 2 stalks celery, cut crosswise into ¼-inch slices
> ½ cup sliced green onions (including tops)
> ¼ cup finely chopped fresh cilantro (coriander)
> 4 to 6 cups torn spinach leaves
> 4 medium-size green-tipped bananas
> 2 limes, cut into wedges
> ½ cup chopped salted peanuts or unsweetened shredded coconut

Prepare lime dressing. In a medium-size bowl, combine shrimp, green pepper, celery, onions, and cilantro; pour in dressing and stir to coat. Cover and refrigerate for at least 2 hours to blend flavors. Remove from refrigerator 1 hour before serving.

To serve, arrange spinach on 4 individual plates. Stir shrimp mixture; then mound about ¼ of it on each plate. Cut bananas diagonally into 1-inch slices and sprinkle with juice from 2 of the lime wedges. Arrange bananas and remaining lime wedges around shrimp mixture; sprinkle with peanuts. Makes 4 servings.

Lime dressing. In a jar, combine 1 teaspoon *each* grated **lime peel, crushed red pepper,** and **ground cumin;** ¼ cup **lime juice;** 1 tablespoon **sugar;** and ⅓ cup **salad oil.** Shake to blend well.

Cheese & Wurst Salad

Germany

Sausages, Swiss cheese, and mild, crisp onions combine with a piquant mustard dressing in this robustly flavored salad.

> 4 knackwurst (about 1¼ lbs. *total*)
> 4 ounces Swiss cheese
> ½ cup *each* thinly sliced celery, diced sweet pickles, and diced green pepper
> 2 small red onions, thinly sliced and separated into rings
> 2 hard-cooked eggs, sliced
> Mustard dressing (recipe follows)

Place sausages in a wide frying pan and pour in enough water to cover. Bring to a boil over high heat; then cover, reduce heat, and simmer for 10 minutes. Remove from water and let cool; peel off and discard casings, if desired.

Slice meat and cheese into 3-inch-long julienne strips. In a salad bowl, combine celery, pickles, and green pepper. Top with meat, cheese, onions, and eggs. Cover and refrigerate for 2 hours. Meanwhile, prepare dressing; cover and refrigerate. At serving time, combine dressing and salad; toss to coat. Makes 4 to 6 servings.

Mustard dressing. In a bowl, combine ½ cup *each* **sour cream** and **mayonnaise,** 3 tablespoons **German-style mustard** or Dijon mustard, and 1 tablespoon *each* **prepared horseradish** and **cider vinegar.** Stir to blend.

HOW TO COOK RAW SHRIMP

Raw shrimp are easiest to clean if you shell and devein them before cooking. To devein a shelled shrimp, just make a shallow cut down back of shrimp; then rinse out the sand vein.

Pour 4 cups **water** into a deep pot; add 1 tablespoon **salt,** 2 tablespoons **lemon juice,** 1 **onion,** sliced, and 1 **bay leaf.** Bring to a boil over high heat. Add 1 to 2 pounds **raw deveined shrimp;** reduce heat and simmer, uncovered, until shrimp turn pink (4 to 6 minutes—don't overcook). Drain at once. Serve hot; or cool, cover, and refrigerate.

Gado Gado

Indonesia

Indonesians enjoy numerous versions of *gado gado*, a composition of cold vegetables (both raw and lightly cooked) topped with a warm, spicy peanut dressing. Our rendition includes plenty of shrimp, making it substantial enough for a luncheon or supper entrée. You can alter the choice of vegetables to suit your taste and the season; sliced cooked potatoes, broccoli flowerets, and zucchini rounds are all good substitutes for the selections we suggest below.

  ½ **pound green beans, ends removed, cut into 1-inch pieces**
      Boiling salted water
  ¾ **pound spinach**
  ⅓ **pound bean sprouts**
      Peanut dressing (recipe at right)
  1 **cucumber, very thinly sliced**
  3 **cups shredded lettuce or cabbage (or a combination)**
  1 **pound medium-size raw shrimp, shelled, deveined, and cooked (directions at left)**
  4 **medium-size tomatoes, cut into wedges**
  2 **hard-cooked eggs, quartered**
      Lemon wedges

Cook beans in 1 inch boiling salted water in a medium-size pan, covered, just until tender-crisp to bite (4 to 7 minutes). Drain, rinse under cold running water, and drain again. Discard wilted spinach leaves and tough stems; rinse well in cold water. Place spinach (with water that clings to leaves) in a pan. Cook over medium heat, covered, just until wilted (about 2 minutes); drain.

Plunge bean sprouts into a kettle of boiling water for 30 seconds; drain, rinse under cold running water, and drain again. (Or use sprouts raw.) Cover beans, spinach, and sprouts and refrigerate separately for at least 2 hours or until next day.

Just before serving, prepare peanut dressing. Arrange cucumber slices around outside edge of 4 large salad plates. Cover center of each plate with lettuce. Sprinkle beans and bean sprouts over lettuce. Arrange spinach in a circle in center of each plate; top with shrimp. Arrange tomatoes and eggs around edge of each plate.

At the table, pass dressing to spoon over individual servings and lemon wedges to squeeze on top. Makes 4 servings.

Peanut dressing. Heat 1 tablespoon **salad oil** in a small pan over medium heat. Add ½ small **onion,** chopped, and 2 large cloves **garlic,** minced or pressed. Cook until golden, stirring occasionally. Stir in ½ cup *each* **boiling water** and **crunchy peanut butter,** 1 teaspoon **brown sugar,** ⅛ to ¼ teaspoon **liquid hot pepper seasoning,** 1 tablespoon **lemon juice,** and 1½ teaspoons grated **fresh ginger.** Blend well.

Reduce heat to low and cook, stirring constantly, until mixture is smooth and slightly thickened. Remove from heat and pour into a serving bowl. Serve slightly warm or at room temperature (dressing stiffens if chilled).

Vermicelli Salad

Italy

Good Italian flavors blend harmoniously in this pasta salad—*delizioso* both to see and to taste.

  8 **ounces vermicelli or spaghetti**
      Boiling salted water
  1 **jar (6 oz.) marinated artichoke hearts**
  ⅓ **cup olive oil or salad oil**
  2 **tablespoons white wine vinegar**
  1 **teaspoon *each* oregano leaves and dry basil**
  ¼ **teaspoon *each* dry rosemary and pepper**
  2 **cloves garlic, minced or pressed**
1½ **teaspoons dry mustard**
  1 **medium-size carrot, diced**
  1 **small zucchini, diced**
  1 **package (3 oz.) sliced salami, cut into julienne strips**
  2 **cups (8 oz.) shredded mozzarella cheese**
  ⅓ **cup grated Parmesan cheese**
      Lettuce leaves

Following package directions, cook vermicelli in a large kettle of boiling salted water until *al dente.* Drain, rinse under cold running water, and drain again.

Drain marinade from artichoke hearts into a large bowl; chop hearts and set aside. To marinade, add oil, vinegar, oregano, basil, rosemary, pepper, garlic, mustard, and vermicelli. Stir to coat pasta thoroughly. Add carrot, zucchini, salami, mozzarella, Parmesan, and artichoke hearts; stir well.

Line a platter with lettuce; spoon salad into center. Serve at room temperature. Makes 6 servings.

...Hearty salads

Oriental Chicken Salad

China   (Pictured on facing page)

Nippy fresh cilantro makes this salad zesty; peanuts and sesame seeds add a nutty flavor. The delicate crunch comes from deep-fried bean threads—thin, translucent noodles available in Asian markets and well-stocked supermarkets.

Bean threads are packaged in tight bundles that are messy to separate; the noodles shatter into fragments when broken. To avoid this problem, place bundles in a paper bag; then pull them apart, in the bag, into small sections. You can cook them ahead, but don't add to the salad until just before serving (they soften quickly).

    ¼ cup all-purpose flour
    ½ teaspoon *each* Chinese five-spice and salt
      Dash of pepper
    2 *each* chicken breast halves and thighs
    3 ounces bean threads
      Salad oil
      Dressing (recipe follows)
    4 cups finely shredded iceberg lettuce
    3 green onions (including tops), thinly sliced
    1 large bunch fresh cilantro (coriander), washed, stemmed, drained, and finely chopped *Note:* If fresh cilantro is unavailable, add 1 tablespoon dry cilantro leaves or ½ teaspoon ground coriander to dressing.
    ½ cup sesame seeds, toasted (page 99)
    1 cup coarsely chopped salted peanuts

Place flour, five-spice, salt, and pepper on a large plate; stir together. Dredge chicken in flour mixture until well coated on all sides; then shake off excess flour. Set chicken aside.

Break bean threads into sections (see recipe introduction); reserve a few for testing oil temperature. Pour oil into wok or wide pan to a depth of 1½ inches and heat to 375° on a deep-frying thermometer. Test oil by dropping in one bean thread; if it expands immediately, oil is ready.

Drop a handful of bean threads into oil. As they puff and expand, push them down into oil with a wire skimmer or slotted spoon; then turn over entire mass. When bean threads stop crackling (about 30 seconds), remove them with a skimmer and drain on paper towels. Repeat until all are cooked. After cooking each batch, skim and discard any bits of bean threads from oil. (At this point, you may let them cool completely, then package airtight and store at room temperature until next day.)

Before cooking chicken, test oil temperature with a bean thread. Then add chicken and cook, turning as needed, until well browned (about 10 minutes for breasts, 12 minutes for thighs). Drain on paper towels; set aside and let cool.

Meanwhile, prepare dressing. Cut chicken and skin off bones, then cut into bite-size pieces. (At this point, you may cover chicken and dressing and refrigerate separately until next day.)

Place lettuce in a large bowl; top with onions, cilantro, and chicken. Sprinkle with sesame seeds and peanuts. Stir dressing, then drizzle over salad and toss. Add bean threads, lightly crushing some of them with your hands; toss lightly. Serve immediately. Makes 4 servings.

Dressing. In a small bowl, combine ¾ teaspoon **dry mustard,** 1 teaspoon *each* **sugar** and grated **lemon peel,** 1 tablespoon *each* **soy sauce** and **lemon juice,** and ¼ cup **salad oil.** Stir well.

Marinated Beef Salad

Mexico

All over the world, leftovers have inspired the creation of marvelous recipes. Here's how a Mexican cook serves up yesterday's beef.

    4 cups thin strips cooked lean beef
    1 large onion, thinly sliced
    2 tablespoons *each* drained capers and minced parsley
    ¼ cup red wine vinegar
    ½ cup olive oil or salad oil
    1 teaspoon *each* oregano leaves and prepared mustard
    ½ teaspoon salt
    1 avocado
    1 large tomato, cut into wedges
      Pitted ripe olives

Place beef in a 9 by 13-inch dish; top with onion, then with capers and parsley. In a jar, combine vinegar, oil, oregano, mustard, and salt; shake to blend well, then pour over meat. Cover and refrigerate for at least 3 hours to blend flavors. Remove from refrigerator 1 hour before serving.

Mound beef mixture on a platter. Pit, peel, and slice avocado; arrange avocado, tomato, and olives around beef. Makes 4 servings.

Making Oriental Chicken Salad (Recipe on facing page)

1 To test temperature of oil, drop 1 bean thread into pan—it should expand at once. When oil is ready, drop in bean threads, a handful at a time.

2 As soon as bean threads hit hot oil, they start to expand. To ensure even cooking, push them down into oil with a wire skimmer or slotted spoon; then turn entire mass over and press down into oil.

3 Cook chicken in same pan of oil (test oil temperature with a bean thread before adding chicken). Cook chicken until well browned on all sides; drain.

4 Chicken cuts most easily when still slightly warm. Anchor chicken with fork; then cut meat and skin off bones. Chicken and bean threads can be prepared a day in advance.

5 Accompanied with fresh fruit and tea, Oriental Chicken Salad makes a satisfying meal. Dressing softens crisp bean threads quickly, so serve salad immediately after tossing.

EGG & CHEESE ENTRÉES

In the United States, we buy them by the dozen, packed in cartons of styrofoam or cardboard. In rural Korea, they're sold by tens, nestled in a bed of straw. And in Ireland, Greece, and countless other countries, you can purchase them just one at a time, from farmer or street vendor.

The subject, of course, is the egg—probably the most universal everyday food in the world, and certainly one of the most versatile. If you think that scrambled, sunny side up, and soft-cooked just about exhaust the egg's possibilities, let our collection of entrées convince you otherwise. *All recipes in this book are based on large eggs.*

As you look through our egg entrées, you'll notice that many contain cheese—sometimes stirred into a dish before cooking, sometimes sprinkled atop at the last. And in fact, these two foods are popular partners in many lands. But cheese easily plays a starring role, too—as in Cheese Fondue, Cheese Curry, and the other choice entrées on page 60 to 63.

Eggs in a sauce

In these entrées, simply cooked eggs—poached, hard-cooked, or fried—get a touch of glamor from flavorful sauces.

Tomatoes & Eggs with Mushrooms

Italy

The hot, bright colors of this simple dish inspired its name—*uova in purgatorio* ("eggs in purgatory"). It's a good choice for a Mediterranean brunch, perhaps accompanied with fresh figs, buttered toast, and cups of *caffè latte*.

> 3 or 4 large tomatoes, peeled
> 3 tablespoons butter or olive oil
> 1 pound mushrooms, thinly sliced
> 6 to 8 eggs
> Salt and pepper
> ¾ cup shredded jack cheese
> Chopped parsley

Cut tomatoes into cubes and let drain in a colander for several minutes. Meanwhile, melt butter in a wide frying pan over high heat. Add mushrooms; cook, stirring, until liquid has evaporated. Add tomatoes and stir until heated through.

With a spoon, make 6 to 8 indentations in tomato mixture; break 1 egg into each. Sprinkle with salt, pepper, and cheese. Cover, reduce heat to low, and cook until eggs are set to your liking. Garnish with parsley. Makes 3 or 4 servings.

Eggs with Sweet Onions & Peas

Portugal

Explorers and traders introduced Europe to the fragrant Eastern spices that enhance this dish.

> 2 **tablespoons butter or margarine**
> 2 **medium-size onions, cut in half, then thinly sliced**
> 1 **clove garlic, minced or pressed**
> 2 **tablespoons tomato paste**
> ¼ **teaspoon** *each* **ground cumin and ground cinnamon**
> ⅛ **teaspoon ground allspice**
> 3 **cups water**
> 1 **teaspoon** *each* **vinegar and salt**
> **Pepper**
> 1 **cup frozen peas, thawed**
> 6 **to 8 hard-cooked eggs, thickly sliced**
> 3 **or 4 hot boiled potatoes**

Melt butter in a wide frying pan over medium heat. Add onions and cook for 10 minutes, stirring occasionally; then add garlic. Cook until onions are soft and golden (about 10 more minutes). Stir in tomato paste, cumin, cinnamon, allspice, water, vinegar, and salt; season to taste with pepper.

Bring to a boil; then reduce heat and simmer, uncovered, for 10 minutes. Add peas and simmer until sauce is slightly thickened (about 10 more minutes). Gently stir in eggs and heat through. Serve over potatoes. Makes 3 or 4 servings.

Simmered Pork & Eggs

Thailand

Thailand has a sizable Chinese population, so it's no surprise that much Thai cookery features favorite Chinese seasonings—such as five-spice, the fragrant blend that flavors this lively dish.

> **About 2½ pounds lean boneless pork, cut into 1-inch cubes**
> 6 **tablespoons soy sauce**
> 2 **tablespoons sugar**
> 2 **teaspoons Chinese five-spice**
> 4 **cloves garlic, minced or pressed**
> 2 **tablespoons salad oil**
> ¾ **cup water**
> 6 **hard-cooked eggs, shelled**
> **Fresh cilantro (coriander) sprigs**

In a bowl, combine pork, 2 tablespoons of the soy, sugar, five-spice, and garlic. Heat oil in a 5 to 6-quart kettle over high heat. Add meat mixture and cook, turning as needed, until lightly browned (about 7 minutes). Add water and remaining 4 tablespoons soy. Lower eggs into sauce; cover, reduce heat, and simmer gently for 25 minutes. Turn eggs over. Continue to simmer until meat is tender when pierced (about 20 more minutes).

With a slotted spoon, lift eggs from sauce; set aside. Transfer meat to a platter. Slice eggs in half and arrange around meat. Skim off and discard fat from sauce; pour over meat. Garnish with cilantro. Makes 6 to 8 servings.

Egg-topped Potato Cakes

Ecuador

Thrifty cooks everywhere appreciate eggs, peanuts, and potatoes. Here, the trio stack up splendidly in Ecuador's savory *llapingachos*.

> 3 **tablespoons butter or margarine**
> 2 **large onions, chopped**
> ¼ **cup creamy or crunchy peanut butter**
> ½ **cup regular-strength beef broth, heated**
> **Whipped potato cakes (recipe follows)**
> 4 **eggs, softly fried or poached**
> **Chopped salted peanuts**

Melt butter in a wide frying pan over medium heat. Add onions and cook, stirring often, until very soft and golden (20 to 30 minutes). Reduce heat and blend in peanut butter and broth.

Prepare whipped potato cakes; place each one on a plate and top with an egg. Pass warm peanut sauce to spoon over individual servings and peanuts to sprinkle on top. Makes 4 servings.

Whipped potato cakes. In a bowl, combine 2 to 2½ cups cold **mashed potatoes,** 2 tablespoons chopped **parsley,** and 2 **green onions** (including tops), finely chopped. Add 1 **egg yolk** and stir to blend well. Cut 1 ounce **jack cheese** into 4 rectangles, each about ½ inch thick. Divide potato mixture into 4 portions; shape each portion around a piece of cheese, forming a 1-inch-thick cake. Lightly coat each cake with **yellow cornmeal.**

Melt 3 tablespoons **butter** or margarine in a wide frying pan over medium heat. Add potato cakes; cook until browned on both sides.

Cooking a French omelet (Recipe on facing page)

1 Beat eggs just until whites and yolks are mixed. Then pour all at once into hot, foamy butter.

2 Once in pan, eggs should set at edges almost immediately. Look for bubbles in eggs: this tells you moisture is evaporating and your omelet will be light and fluffy.

3 Push cooked portion aside to allow uncooked eggs to flow underneath. Shake pan often to keep eggs moving freely.

4 Fill omelet when eggs are half set but still moist. Slip filled half of omelet onto plate; then flip pan over so omelet folds onto itself.

5 An omelet makes a great meal in minutes. This omelet gets its French flavor from a filling of basil and blue-veined cheese.

Omelets

The word is French, but don't let that fool you. Omelets are served throughout the world, recognized by good cooks as versatile dishes that are as delicious as they're quick to prepare.

An omelet has just two basic components: beaten eggs and seasoning. Change the seasoning or cooking fat, and you give an omelet a new ethnic identity; fold a filling inside it, top it, or add extra ingredients to the beaten eggs, and you change the identity again.

French-style omelets are speediest to prepare, but all these omelets go from kitchen to table quickly. Any one is a perfect entrée for days when you're short on time or energy.

Cheese & Basil Omelet

France   (Pictured on facing page)

This classic French creation cooks in a flash, so have its cheese-and-basil filling ready before you begin. (If you're cooking for more than one person, it's easiest to cook individual omelets in succession, rather than trying to make a larger omelet in a larger pan.)

> 2 or 3 eggs
> 1 tablespoon water
> Dash each of salt and pepper
> 1 tablespoon butter or margarine
> 1 to 1½ tablespoons crumbled blue-veined cheese
> 2 teaspoons chopped fresh basil leaves or ¼ teaspoon dry basil

Break eggs into a bowl and add water, salt, and pepper. Beat with a fork just until yolks and whites are mixed.

In a 7 to 8-inch omelet pan with a nonstick finish, melt butter over medium-high heat. When butter is foamy, pour in egg mixture all at once. As edges begin to set (almost immediately), push cooked portion aside to allow uncooked eggs to flow underneath. Shake pan often to keep eggs moving freely.

When eggs are about half set but still moist, sprinkle with cheese and basil. Continue to cook, shaking pan gently, until eggs are set on the bottom but still moist on top.

Hold pan over a serving plate; then shake pan so half of omelet slips out onto plate. Quickly flip pan over so omelet folds onto itself. Makes 1 serving.

MEXICAN OMELET

Follow directions for **Cheese & Basil Omelet,** but substitute 1 tablespoon *each* **canned diced green chiles** and chopped **green olives** for cheese and basil. Top omelet with **sour cream.**

PORTUGUESE OMELET

For each omelet, crumble 2 ounces **linguisa sausage** into a frying pan and cook over medium heat, stirring, until well browned. Then follow directions for **Cheese & Basil Omelet,** but substitute sausage and 1 tablespoon coarsely chopped **fresh cilantro** (coriander) for cheese and basil.

Chicken Liver Frittata

Italy

Though clearly related to the French omelet, the *frittata* is thicker and firmer, and it's never folded over a filling. Serve this Italian family favorite hot or at room temperature, cut into generous wedges.

> ½ cup sour cream
> 8 eggs
> ½ teaspoon oregano leaves
> ¼ teaspoon ground red pepper (cayenne)
> ½ pound chicken livers
> 1 tablespoon butter or margarine
> ½ cup chopped green onions (including tops)
> ¼ cup grated Parmesan cheese
> Thin tomato wedges

In a bowl, blend sour cream, eggs, oregano, and pepper with a wire whisk. Set aside. Cut chicken livers in half.

In a 10-inch frying pan with a heatproof handle, melt butter over high heat. When butter sizzles, add half the livers and cook, turning, until lightly browned but still very pink in centers (about 30 seconds). Lift out with a slotted spoon and set aside; cook remaining livers.

Reduce heat to low and return all livers to pan. Pour in egg mixture; top with ¼ cup of the onions, then with cheese. Bake in a 350° oven for 8 to 10 minutes or until almost set in center. Top with tomato wedges and remaining ¼ cup onions. Makes 4 servings.

...Omelets

Knackwurst Omelet

Germany

Once again, the omelet changes costume. Knackwurst, cabbage, and potatoes—and a nippy burst of caraway—give this dish a German accent.

> 6 eggs
> ½ teaspoon salt
> ¼ teaspoon pepper
> 4 tablespoons butter or margarine
> 1 or 2 knackwurst, frankfurters, or kielbasa (Polish sausage), thinly sliced
> ¼ cup minced onion
> 1 cup *each* shredded cabbage and diced cooked potato
> ¼ teaspoon caraway seeds

In a bowl, beat eggs with salt and pepper. Set aside. In a wide frying pan with a heatproof handle, melt butter over medium heat. Add sausage and cook until lightly browned. Stir in onion, cabbage, potato, and caraway seeds. Cook, stirring often, until cabbage is limp. Pour eggs over vegetable mixture and cook until almost completely set.

Place pan under broiler; broil 2 to 3 inches below heat until top is set to your liking. Cut into wedges to serve. Makes 4 servings.

Potato Omelet

Spain

Bright with bell pepper and chunky with potato, this big omelet makes a spirited one-dish supper.

> 9 eggs
> ¾ teaspoon salt
> ¼ teaspoon pepper
> 4 strips bacon
> 2 tablespoons olive oil or salad oil
> 1 medium-size onion, finely chopped
> 1 large clove garlic, minced or pressed
> 1 large thin-skinned potato, cooked, peeled, and finely chopped
> 1 *each* medium-size green and red bell pepper, seeded and finely chopped

In a bowl, beat eggs with salt and pepper. Set aside. In a 10-inch frying pan with a heatproof handle, cook bacon over medium heat until crisp. Remove from pan, drain, crumble, and set aside. Discard all but 1 tablespoon drippings.

Pour 1 tablespoon of the oil into pan and place over medium heat. Add onion, garlic, and potato; cook, stirring occasionally, until vegetables are golden. Add bell peppers; cook until peppers are soft and liquid has evaporated. Stir in bacon.

Push vegetable mixture to one side and drizzle remaining 1 tablespoon oil over pan bottom. Redistribute vegetable mixture. Pour in eggs; cook until almost completely set.

Place pan under broiler; broil 2 to 3 inches below heat until top is set and lightly browned. Cut into wedges to serve. Makes 4 to 6 servings.

Country Corn Omelet

United States

This satisfying farm-style omelet is pretty as a picture—golden corn and eggs, deep green chard, and a snowy topping of sour cream.

> 4 strips bacon
> ¼ cup sliced almonds
> About 4 tablespoons butter or margarine
> 1 small onion, chopped
> 1 can (8 oz.) whole kernel corn, drained
> 4 cups lightly packed, coarsely shredded Swiss chard or kale
> 6 to 8 eggs
> ½ cup diced jack cheese
> ⅓ cup sour cream

In a wide frying pan, cook bacon over medium heat until crisp. Remove from pan; drain, crumble, and set aside. Cook almonds in drippings until lightly browned. Remove from pan.

If necessary, add about 1 tablespoon butter to drippings to make ¼ cup fat. Add onion and cook until soft. Stir in corn and heat through. Remove vegetables from pan. Place chard and 1 more tablespoon butter in pan. Cook, stirring, until tender (about 2 minutes); remove from pan.

In a bowl, beat eggs just until blended. Melt 2 more tablespoons butter in pan, then pour in eggs. As eggs begin to set, push set portion aside to allow uncooked eggs to flow underneath. When eggs are set but still moist and creamy on top, remove from heat. Arrange chard over eggs; spoon corn mixture over chard, then sprinkle with cheese and bacon. Mound sour cream in center and garnish with almonds. Present omelet in pan; cut into wedges to serve. Makes 4 servings.

Unsinkable soufflés

Beaten eggs give volume and lightness to these soufflés—but unlike their more delicate French counterpart, they won't begin to sink when you remove them from the oven.

Blintz Brunch Soufflé

Jewish heritage

One of the delights of Jewish cooking is the blintz—a tender egg pancake filled with creamy cheese and topped with fruit. This cherry-sauced brunch treat has the rich, creamy taste of a true blintz—though it's more like a soufflé.

      1 cup (½ lb.) butter or margarine, softened
    ⅓ cup sugar
      6 eggs
   1½ cups sour cream
    ½ cup orange juice
      2 teaspoons baking powder
      1 cup all-purpose flour
      1 large package (8 oz.) cream cheese
      1 pint (2 cups) small curd cottage cheese
      2 egg yolks
      1 tablespoon sugar
      1 teaspoon vanilla
        Cherry sauce (recipe follows)

In a large bowl, cream butter and the ⅓ cup sugar with an electric mixer until light and fluffy. Add eggs one at a time, beating well after each addition; then beat in sour cream, orange juice, and baking powder. Turn mixer to lowest speed and beat in flour. Pour half the batter into a buttered shallow 3-quart (9 by 13-inch) casserole.

Dice cream cheese and mix with cottage cheese, egg yolks, the 1 tablespoon sugar, and vanilla. Drop by spoonfuls evenly over batter in dish (mixture will sink slightly into batter). Gently pour remaining batter over all.

Bake in a 350° oven, uncovered, for about 55 minutes or until puffed in center and golden brown. Serve soufflé immediately, topping each portion with cherry sauce. Makes 8 to 10 servings.

Cherry sauce. In a 2½ to 3-quart pan, combine 2 teaspoons *each* **cornstarch** and **lemon juice,** ¼ cup **sugar,** ½ cup **water,** and 3 cups **pitted sweet cherries** (fresh or frozen unsweetened). Bring to a boil over medium heat, stirring constantly; cook until thickened and clear. Serve warm or cooled.

Chili Cheese Soufflé

Mexico

Here's a chile-spiked Mexican spin-off of France's airy soufflé.

   3½ cups (14 oz.) shredded jack cheese
   3½ cups (14 oz.) shredded sharp Cheddar cheese
      1 large can (7 oz.) diced green chiles
      2 medium-size tomatoes, seeded and chopped
      1 can (2¼ oz.) sliced ripe olives, drained
    ½ cup all-purpose flour
      6 eggs, separated
      1 small can (5¼ oz.) evaporated milk
    ½ teaspoon *each* salt and oregano leaves
    ¼ teaspoon *each* ground cumin and pepper
    ¼ teaspoon cream of tartar

In a bowl, combine jack cheese, Cheddar cheese, chiles, tomatoes, olives, and 2 tablespoons of the flour. Stir until blended. Transfer mixture to a well-greased shallow 3-quart (9 by 13-inch) casserole.

In a small bowl, beat egg yolks. Alternately add remaining 6 tablespoons flour and milk. Stir in salt, oregano, cumin, and pepper.

In a large bowl, beat egg whites with cream of tartar until stiff, moist peaks form. Fold in yolk mixture; then spoon over cheese mixture in casserole. Bake in a 300° oven for 1 hour or until top is golden brown and firm to touch. Let stand for 15 minutes before serving. Makes 10 to 12 servings.

HOW TO MAKE EGG SHREDS

Every cuisine has its typical garnishes. Western cooks rely on parsley; in Asia, egg shreds are a common choice. To make them, beat 2 **eggs** with a pinch of **salt.** Heat a 7 to 8-inch omelet pan with a nonstick finish over medium heat. When pan is hot, brush with ¼ teaspoon **salad oil.** Pour in ⅓ of the eggs; swirl pan to cover entire bottom. When egg sheet is lightly browned on the bottom and set on top (45 seconds to 1 minute), flip it over and cook for 5 more seconds. Slide out of pan; let cool. Repeat with remaining eggs to make 2 more sheets, brushing pan with ¼ teaspoon salad oil each time. Let sheets cool; then cut in half, stack, and cut crosswise into ⅛-inch-wide shreds. Refrigerate for up to 3 days.

Egg wrappers

These whimsical little packages perfectly illustrate the Asian cook's flair for devising dishes that please the eye as well as the palate. Almost all the preparation can be completed in advance; only the final steaming need be done at the last minute.

Golden Egg Bundles

Korea   (Pictured on facing page)

Serve these dainty and delectable bundles as an imaginative first course—or as a golden addition to almost any Oriental menu.

> 5   **eggs**
> 2   **tablespoons water**
> 1½   **tablespoons salad oil**
>   **Cooking sauce (recipe follows)**
> ½   **pound lean ground pork**
> 1   **small onion, finely chopped**
> 2   **cloves garlic, minced or pressed**
> 1   **teaspoon minced fresh ginger**
> ½   **teaspoon ground coriander**
> 2   **cups finely shredded spinach leaves**
> 2   **teaspoons sesame seeds, toasted (page 99)**
>   **Salt and ground red pepper (cayenne)**
> 6   **whole spinach leaves with long stems**

In a bowl, beat eggs with water; pour through a fine sieve. Heat a frying pan with a nonstick finish, measuring 8 inches across the bottom (10 inches across top), over medium heat. When pan is hot, brush with ¼ teaspoon of the oil. Pour in ¼ cup of the egg mixture; then quickly tilt pan so egg covers bottom. Cook just until egg is set and looks dry on top (45 seconds to 1 minute). Turn over and cook for 5 seconds, then turn out onto paper towels. Repeat with remaining egg mixture, making 5 more wrappers.

Prepare cooking sauce and set aside.

Heat remaining 1 tablespoon oil in a wide frying pan over medium heat. Crumble in pork and cook until browned; discard all but 2 tablespoons drippings. Add onion, garlic, ginger, and coriander. Cook, stirring, until onion is soft. Stir in shredded spinach; cook just until wilted (about 30 seconds). Add cooking sauce and cook, stirring, until mixture boils and thickens. Add sesame seeds. Season to taste with salt and pepper. Let cool.

In another pan, bring 1½ inches water to a boil over high heat. Submerge whole spinach leaves and cook just until leaves are wilted and stems are pliable (about 30 seconds). Lift out, rinse with cold water, and drain.

Place ⅙ of the filling in center of each wrapper. Gently gather up edges of wrapper around filling. Carefully wind a wilted spinach leaf around each bundle and tie to secure.

Place bundles on a shallow plate that will fit on a rack inside a deep frying pan, steamer, or wok. Drape with a piece of wax paper. Pour water into pan to a depth of about 1 inch; then cover pan and bring water to a boil. Steam bundles just until heated through (3 to 5 minutes). Makes 6 servings.

Cooking sauce. In a bowl, blend 2 tablespoons **dry sherry,** 1 tablespoon **cornstarch,** 1½ tablespoons **soy sauce,** 1 teaspoon *each* **sugar** and **vinegar,** a dash of **ground red pepper** (cayenne), and ⅓ cup **water.**

SZECHWAN FISH ROLLS

Following directions for **Golden Egg Bundles,** prepare 6 egg wrappers—but use 7 eggs and cook wrappers in a 12-inch frying pan with a nonstick finish, using about ⅓ cup of the egg mixture for each wrapper. Cut each into 4 wedges.

In a bowl, combine 1 pound boneless **sole fillets,** cut into ¼ by 1-inch pieces; 1 **green onion** (including top), chopped; 1 tablespoon minced **fresh ginger;** ⅛ teaspoon **white pepper;** ½ teaspoon **salt;** 2 tablespoons **salad oil;** and 1 tablespoon *each* **sesame oil, dry sherry,** and **cornstarch.** Stir in 1 **egg white,** lightly beaten. Lightly beat 1 **egg yolk.**

Place 1 tablespoon of the fish mixture in center of 1 egg wedge; dot corners with egg yolk. Starting at wide end, roll up wedge ⅓ of the way; then tuck sides in around filling and continue to roll toward point of wedge. Repeat to fill remaining egg wedges. Arrange rolls in 2 greased 9-inch pie pans.

In a pan, combine 1½ cups **regular-strength chicken broth,** 1½ tablespoons *each* **dry sherry** and **sesame oil,** 1 tablespoon **cornstarch** mixed with 1 tablespoon **water,** and a dash of **white pepper.** Cook over high heat, stirring, until sauce boils and thickens. Season to taste with **salt.** Stir in ½ cup sliced **green onions** (including tops).

Drape wax paper over rolls in pans and steam as for **Golden Egg Bundles,** increasing time to 10 minutes. (If steaming rolls in 2 batches, cover first batch with foil and keep warm in a 200° oven while steaming second batch.) Serve with warm sauce. Makes 24 rolls.

Making Golden Egg Bundles (Recipe on facing page)

1 Pour egg mixture into hot pan, then tilt pan so egg coats pan bottom. When top of wrapper looks dry, lift up, turn over and cook for 5 seconds.

2 To make each bundle, spoon filling in center of a cooled wrapper. Gently gather wrapper around filling.

3 Wind a blanched spinach leaf around bundle and tie in a knot. Spinach is tender, so tie knot loosely; if you pull too hard, leaf will tear.

4 This golden pouch holds a "treasure" of spicy pork and spinach filling. Serve as part of an Oriental dinner or as the first course of a special meal.

Cheese entrées

Legend has it that the first cheese was made by accident. An Arab, preparing for a desert crossing, filled his drinking pouch—one made from an animal's stomach—with milk. But when he stopped to drink, he found not milk but flavorful curds in the pouch. The combination of desert heat and rennin, an enzyme found in the stomach lining of young animals, had coagulated the milk.

Whatever its beginnings, cheese has long played a central role in the diet of people raising milk-giving animals. Modern cheese makers produce marvelous cheeses of every texture and flavor—creamy to crumbly, mild to pungent. Here, we focus on some very special cheese entrées, suitable for family meals and company dinners alike.

Cheese & Mushroom Pie

Russia

Mushrooms, yogurt, and the nip of horseradish add a little Russian flavor to this tasty quiche.

>   9-inch unbaked pastry shell, 1½ inches deep
> 1   tablespoon butter or margarine
> 1   small onion, chopped
> ¼   pound mushrooms, sliced
> ½   teaspoon thyme leaves
> 1   cup (4 oz.) shredded Swiss cheese
> 3   eggs
> ½   pint (1 cup) plain yogurt
> 2   tablespoons all-purpose flour
> ½   teaspoon prepared horseradish
> ¼   teaspoon *each* salt and dry mustard
>   Paprika

Preheat oven to 450°; prick pastry shell, then bake for 7 to 10 minutes or until lightly browned. Let cool.

Melt butter in a wide frying pan over medium heat. Add onion and mushrooms and cook until onion is soft; then stir in thyme. Let cool.

Sprinkle cheese over bottom of pastry shell; top with mushroom mixture. In a bowl, lightly beat eggs. Add yogurt, flour, horseradish, salt, and mustard; stir until well blended. Pour over mushroom layer. Sprinkle with paprika.

Bake in a 375° oven for 40 to 45 minutes or until filling is puffy and browned, and a knife inserted just off center comes out clean. Let stand on a wire rack for 10 minutes before serving. Makes 6 servings.

Cheese Curry

India

Creamy-textured *paneer* is a soft cheese that Indian cooks prepare in minutes, simply by coagulating boiling milk with lemon juice. In this unusual curry, cubes of mildly tangy paneer provide a delicious foil for a boldly seasoned sauce.

Served over rice and topped with cashews, the curry makes an authentic entrée for an Indian-style meal. Round out the menu with a cooling cucumber salad, Tomato-Lemon Chutney (page 137), and chewy Chapaties (page 177).

> 1¼   cups pressed paneer (recipe follows), cut into ½-inch cubes
> 1½   cups whey from paneer or 1½ cups water
> 1   tablespoon butter or margarine
> 1   tablespoon salad oil
> 1   large onion, finely chopped
> 4   large cloves garlic, minced or pressed
> 2   teaspoons minced fresh ginger
> 2   medium-size tomatoes, peeled, seeded, and chopped
> 1   teaspoon *each* cumin seeds, ground coriander, and turmeric
> ¼ to ½   teaspoon ground red pepper (cayenne)
> ¼   teaspoon fennel seeds, crushed
> 1   tablespoon chopped fresh cilantro (coriander)
>   Salt
>   Hot cooked rice
>   Cashews, coarsely chopped

Prepare paneer, reserving 1½ cups whey. Set paneer and whey aside.

Heat butter and oil in a wide frying pan over medium-high heat. Add onion, garlic, and ginger; cook, stirring occasionally, until onion is lightly browned (about 10 minutes). Add tomatoes, cumin seeds, coriander, turmeric, pepper, and fennel seeds. Cook, stirring, until tomatoes no longer hold their shape (about 10 minutes).

Stir in whey. Bring to a boil over high heat; boil, stirring, for 3 minutes. Stir in cilantro; season to taste with salt. Cover, reduce heat, and simmer until slightly thickened (about 20 minutes). Gently stir in paneer. Cover and cook until paneer is heated through. Serve over rice; top with cashews. Makes 4 servings.

Paneer. In a deep, heavy 6 to 8-quart kettle, combine 8 cups **whole milk** and, if desired, ½ teaspoon **salt.** Bring to a boil over medium-high heat, stirring occasionally (15 to 20 minutes). (Milk at bottom of kettle may become scorched, but this will not affect cheese.) Stir in ⅓ cup **lemon juice;** curd will separate from whey quickly. Continue to boil for 2 more minutes without stirring (milk will froth); then remove from heat.

Line a colander with cheesecloth that has been dipped in cold water and wrung dry. Cloth should be large enough to hang over sides of colander. Set colander in a large bowl; pour milk mixture into colander and let cheese stand until most of whey has drained into bowl (about 5 minutes). Scrape curds toward center.

To press cheese, fold cheesecloth securely over cheese to enclose, then invert onto a 10 by 15-inch rimmed baking pan. Place a 4 to 5-quart kettle filled with water on wrapped cheese; let stand for about 30 minutes. Lift off kettle, unwrap cheese, and discard drained liquid. Wrap cheese airtight and refrigerate for up to 2 weeks. Makes 1¼ cups.

Artichoke & Ricotta Wedges

Italy

Creamy cousin of our own cottage cheese, Italian ricotta gives smooth balance to this hearty crustless quiche.

> 1 jar (6 oz.) marinated artichoke hearts
> 4 eggs
> ¼ cup all-purpose flour
> ½ teaspoon baking powder
> ¼ teaspoon pepper
> 1 cup (8 oz.) ricotta cheese
> 2½ cups (10 oz.) shredded jack cheese

Drain marinade from artichokes into a large bowl. Cut artichokes into ½-inch pieces.

To marinade in bowl, add eggs, flour, baking powder, and pepper. Mix with a rotary beater until blended. Stir in artichokes, ricotta cheese, and 2 cups of the jack cheese. Pour into a well-greased 9-inch round cake pan. Sprinkle remaining ½ cup jack cheese over top.

Bake in a 350° oven for about 40 minutes or until top is lightly browned and center feels firm when gently pressed. Let stand on a wire rack for 15 minutes before serving. (Or let cool to room temperature.) Cut into wedges to serve. Makes 6 servings.

Cheese Enchiladas

Mexico

Enchiladas certainly bear some resemblance to the filled and rolled crêpes of France—and they're easily as enticing. Mild cheese filling, zesty sauce, and do-ahead preparation make these enchiladas a favorite with cooks and diners alike.

> **Cheese filling (recipe follows)**
> **Salad oil**
> 1 **dozen corn tortillas**
> 1 **can (7 oz.) green chile salsa**
> 2 **cups (8 oz.) shredded mild Cheddar cheese**
> **Garnishes: About 1 cup shredded iceberg lettuce; 2 medium-size tomatoes, thinly sliced; 3 green onions (including tops), thinly sliced**

Prepare cheese filling; set aside.

Into a small frying pan, pour salad oil to a depth of ¼ inch and heat over medium heat. When oil is hot, dip in 1 tortilla; cook just until limp and beginning to blister (only a few seconds). *Do not fry until firm or crisp.* Remove with tongs and drain briefly. Repeat with remaining 11 tortillas, adding more oil as needed.

Pour ⅓ of the salsa into a 9 by 13-inch baking dish. Spoon about ⅓ cup filling down center of each tortilla; roll to enclose. Arrange tortillas in dish, seam side down. Cover with remaining salsa and sprinkle evenly with shredded cheese. (At this point, you may cover and refrigerate until next day.)

Bake in a 375° oven, uncovered, for 20 minutes or until bubbly (cook for 30 minutes if refrigerated, keeping covered for first 15 minutes). Garnish enchiladas with lettuce, tomatoes, and onions. Makes 6 servings.

Cheese filling. In a bowl, combine 1½ pints (3 cups) **large curd cottage cheese,** 1 cup (4 oz.) shredded **mild Cheddar cheese,** 1½ cups sliced **green onions** (including tops), and ¼ teaspoon **oregano leaves.**

Preparing Swiss Cheese Fondue (Recipe on facing page)

1 Shred cheeses. Emmenthaler (with large holes) provides mild, nutlike flavor. Fuller-flavored Gruyère melts well, gives fondue a satiny texture.

2 Toss cheeses with cornstarch and mustard; add pepper and nutmeg. Cornstarch helps to thicken fondue and prevent it from separating.

3 When wine mixture bubbles, add cheese mixture, a handful at a time. After adding each batch, stir in figure-eight pattern until cheese is melted and mixture is smooth.

4 Bring fondue just to a simmer; stir in kirsch, if desired. Again bring just to a simmer—if heat is too high, fondue may separate.

5 Spear a chunk of crusty bread and dip in. Swirl bread in fondue—but don't lose it! (The Swiss say, "First loser pays for the works.")

..Cheese entrées

Cheese Fondue

Switzerland   (Pictured on facing page)

Switzerland's famous fondue is a hot cheese dip that takes its name from the French verb *fondre* ("to melt"). Fondue has counterparts in many other cuisines, and it's easy to see why. In addition to tasting marvelous, fondue is quick to prepare—and because it's served in a communal pot, it gets a party off to a cozy, informal start.

The secret to making a smooth fondue is to keep the heat just low enough during both cooking and serving. If the heat is too low, the cheese will not melt smoothly—but if it's too high, the cheese becomes stringy.

A traditional fondue pot of heavy metal or heat-resistant earthenware is ideal for one-step cooking and serving. But you can make fondue in any heavy metal 2 to 3-quart pan, then transfer it to a chafing dish over an alcohol burner or to a casserole on an electric warmer.

>   2 **cups (8 oz.) shredded imported Swiss cheese (Emmenthaler)**
>   2 **cups (8 oz.) shredded Swiss Gruyère or Danish Samsoe cheese**
>   1½ **tablespoons cornstarch**
>   1 **teaspoon dry mustard**
>   **Freshly ground black pepper and nutmeg**
>   1 **clove garlic, cut in half**
>   1½ **cups dry white wine**
>   1 **tablespoon lemon juice**
>   2 **tablespoons kirsch (optional)**
>   1 **loaf French bread, cut into bite-size cubes**

In a bowl, toss Swiss and Gruyère cheeses with cornstarch and mustard; season to taste with pepper and nutmeg.

Rub cut sides of garlic over sides and bottom of a fondue pot or 2-quart pan. Discard garlic. Add wine and lemon juice, place over medium heat, and heat until bubbles rise slowly to the surface. Add a handful of the cheese mixture and stir with a wooden spoon until melted. Repeat until all cheese mixture has been added. Adjust heat so fondue is just simmering. If desired, add kirsch, a tablespoon at a time.

If fondue is too thick, add a small amount of warmed (never cold) wine and stir in completely. If fondue separates, mix 1 tablespoon cornstarch, 1 teaspoon lemon juice, and ¼ cup wine; warm slightly and stir into fondue.

Place fondue over heat source and adjust heat so fondue keeps bubbling *slowly*. Offer fondue forks or bamboo skewers to spear bread for dipping. Makes 4 main-dish servings or 12 appetizer servings.

DUTCH GOUDA FONDUE

Prepare **Cheese Fondue,** but substitute 4 cups (1 lb.) shredded **Gouda cheese** for imported Swiss and Swiss Gruyère cheeses.

Chile con Queso

Mexico

Mellow cheddar cheese helps temper the heat of green chiles in this chunky Mexican fondue.

>   3 **tablespoons butter or margarine**
>   1 **medium-size onion, chopped**
>   1 **small can (about 8 oz.) stewed tomatoes**
>   1 **can (4 oz.) diced green chiles**
>   ¼ **teaspoon oregano leaves**
>   4 **cups (1 lb.) shredded Cheddar cheese**
>   **Tortilla chips or French bread cubes**

Melt butter in a wide frying pan over medium heat. Add onion and cook, stirring occasionally, until lightly browned (about 10 minutes). Stir in tomatoes (break up with a spoon) and their liquid, chiles, and oregano. Reduce heat and simmer, uncovered, for 5 minutes. Add cheese, a handful at a time, stirring until cheese is melted and mixture is well blended.

Transfer to a fondue pot or chafing dish and keep warm over heat source. Offer tortilla chips for dipping. Makes about 3 cups.

ITALIAN TOMATO FONDUE

Follow directions for **Chile con Queso,** but cook 1 clove **garlic,** minced or pressed, with onion. Omit chiles and add ½ teaspoon **dry basil** and ⅛ teaspoon **pepper.** In place of Cheddar cheese, use 2 cups (8 oz.) shredded **Longhorn cheese** and ¼ cup grated **Parmesan cheese,** tossed with 1 tablespoon **cornstarch.** Makes about 2 cups.

SANDWICHES

To some, "sandwich" defines just one dish: two slices of bread holding between them a filling of some sort. When it comes to international cookery, though, this definition is too narrow. For one thing, you don't always need two slices of bread to make a sandwich—a Danish open-faced sandwich, for example, uses just one slice of bread as a base for varied toppings.

Many sandwiches don't rely on sliced bread at all—the filling may be enclosed inside a crusty roll, wrapped up in a soft flour tortilla, or stuffed into pocket bread. And sometimes a pastry or yeast-dough wrapper is baked around a savory filling, to make treats such as Cornish Pasties and Lamb and Spinach Turnovers.

Though sandwiches are traditionally lunchtime fare, they're just as delicious for brunch, supper, or a hearty snack. To turn a sandwich meal into an informal feast, you need only add a few accompaniments: soup or salad, a hot or cold beverage, and fresh fruit or other simple dessert.

Best bread choices

Tortillas, pocket breads, sliced bread, rolls—all make superlative sandwich wrappers. Below, we offer a few pointers for choosing breads appropriate for the types of sandwiches in this chapter.

For *grilled sandwiches*, use sturdy, firm-textured bread: white, whole wheat, rye, multigrain, or whatever you like best. Sturdiness is especially important if the sandwich is dipped in

egg before grilling—soft breads become soggy after this treatment, and are likely to break or tear during cooking. (Day-old, slightly dry bread is a good choice for egg-dipped grilled sandwiches, too.)

When you make our *pocket sandwiches*, use pocket breads—puffy, chewy, hollow-centered rounds that are especially popular in the Middle East. Split in half crosswise, they make convenient "envelopes" for hot and cold fillings.

You can make pocket sandwiches with hollowed-out rolls, too, as in Hot Chicken Sandwiches. Be sure the rolls you use are crusty; if they're soft, the filling may soak through them. And be sure to purchase unsliced rolls, so you can make a case that's deep enough to hold a generous amount of filling.

Tortilla sandwiches use tortillas, of course. Made from corn or flour, these round flatbreads are the daily bread of Mexico. We've used flour tortillas in our recipes, since they're easier to fold and roll than those made with corn. They're sold in several sizes; our sandwiches call for medium-size tortillas (8 to 10 inches across).

Choose fresh, soft, slightly thick tortillas; they're less likely to tear when folded. It's also important to use thick fillings, since mixtures that contain too much liquid will cause the tortilla to become soggy. Simmer the spicy meat fillings for our Burritos and Chimichangas until all the liquid has cooked away.

Easy pocket sandwiches

Flavorful fillings are packaged inside "pockets" of bread to make these sandwiches. Quick to assemble and easy to eat, they're ideal for a casual dinner.

Hot Chicken Sandwiches

Italy

Anchovies, garlic, and ripe olives add bursts of *buon gusto* to these crusty sandwiches. For best results, make the piquant chicken filling a day in advance so flavors have a chance to mingle; reheat just before placing in bread cases.

    1 tablespoon butter or margarine
    1 tablespoon olive oil or salad oil
    2 cloves garlic, minced or pressed
    ¼ to ½ teaspoon crushed red pepper
    2 whole chicken breasts (2 lbs. *total*), skinned, boned, split, and cut into ½-inch cubes
    3 tablespoons *each* chopped parsley and chopped drained capers
    3 or 4 anchovy fillets, finely chopped
    1 can (2¼ oz.) sliced ripe olives, drained well
    ½ cup dry white wine
      Salt and pepper
      Garlic butter (recipe follows)
    4 unsliced crusty sandwich rolls

Heat butter and oil in a wide frying pan over medium-high heat. Add garlic, red pepper, and chicken; stir-fry until chicken is lightly browned (2 to 3 minutes). Stir in parsley, capers, anchovies, olives, and wine. Cook, stirring occasionally, until most of liquid has evaporated (5 minutes). Season to taste with salt and pepper.

Prepare garlic butter. Split rolls lengthwise. Tear some of the soft bread out of center of each half; then brush both halves of each roll with garlic butter. Spread about ¼ of the chicken mixture on each roll bottom; cover with roll tops. (At this point, you may wrap rolls in foil and refrigerate until next day.) Place rolls on a baking sheet and bake in a 350° oven, uncovered, for 5 minutes or until crisp. Or bake foil-wrapped refrigerated rolls for 15 minutes, then unwrap and bake for 5 more minutes or until crisp. Makes 4 sandwiches.

Garlic butter. In a small pan, melt ⅓ cup **butter** or margarine with 1 clove **garlic,** minced or pressed.

Pocket Bread Sandwiches

Turkey

Slip succulent Turkish *shish kebab* into halved pocket bread, then add a few onions, a wedge or two of tomato, and a dollop of yogurt ... and you've got a hand-held meal, Middle Eastern style. Make the pocket breads from our recipe (page 185) or buy them at your supermarket.

    ½ cup lemon juice
    ¼ cup olive oil or salad oil
    1 teaspoon *each* chopped fresh cilantro (coriander) and ground cumin
    ½ teaspoon *each* turmeric and black pepper
    ¼ teaspoon crushed red pepper
    2 pounds lean boneless lamb, cut into ¾-inch cubes
    2 large onions, thinly sliced and separated into rings
    6 pocket breads
      Romaine leaves
    3 medium-size tomatoes, cut into thin wedges
      Plain yogurt

In a small bowl, combine lemon juice, oil, cilantro, cumin, turmeric, black pepper, and red pepper. Place lamb and onions in separate bowls. Pour half the marinade over lamb; pour remaining marinade over onions. Cover lamb and onions and refrigerate for 2 to 4 hours, stirring occasionally.

Lift lamb cubes from marinade and drain briefly, reserving marinade. Thread on sturdy metal skewers and place on a lightly greased grill 4 to 6 inches above a solid bed of glowing coals.

Cook, turning and basting with reserved marinade, until lamb is well browned on all sides but still pink in center when slashed (12 to 15 minutes).

Meanwhile, cut pocket breads in half crosswise and wrap tightly in foil. Place at edge of grill (not directly over coals) and warm for about 10 minutes, turning often.

Lift onions from marinade with a slotted spoon and place in a bowl. Stuff each pocket bread half with a romaine leaf (tear in half if large), 5 or 6 lamb cubes, several onion rings, several tomato wedges, and a dollop of yogurt. Makes 6 to 12 servings.

Tortilla sandwiches

Perfect partnership: a mild-tasting flour tortilla wrapped around a spoonful of spicy-hot meat. Here are two examples of that winning combination, both featuring pork fillings pungent with chiles and garlic. Tortillas are available at most supermarkets, but you may want to try making your own (see page 178).

Pork Chimichangas

Mexico   (Pictured on facing page)

A *chimichanga* is a crackling-crisp version of a *burrito* (right). It usually gets its crunch from deep-frying, but we've devised a simple baked version that's every bit as flaky and good.

1 pound lean boneless pork butt, cut into 1½-inch pieces
2 cups water
2 tablespoons white (distilled) vinegar
3 tablespoons canned diced green chiles
1 clove garlic, minced or pressed
¼ teaspoon each ground oregano and ground cumin
Tomato Salsa (page 138)
4 tablespoons butter or margarine
4 medium-size (8 to 10-inch) flour tortillas, homemade (page 178) or purchased
Shredded lettuce
1 to 1½ cups (4 to 6 oz.) shredded jack cheese
Sour cream

Place pork in a wide frying pan or 5-quart kettle; cover and cook over medium heat until juices have been released (about 10 minutes). Uncover; increase heat to high. Cook, stirring often, until liquid has evaporated; continue to cook and stir until meat is browned.

Pour water into kettle; stir to free browned bits. Cover, reduce heat, and simmer until meat is tender when pierced (1 to 1½ hours). Uncover, increase heat to high, and boil until liquid has evaporated. Reduce heat to low. Stir in vinegar, chiles, garlic, oregano, and cumin. Stir to free browned bits; then spoon meat mixture onto a plate. Using 2 forks, shred meat. (At this point, you may cover and refrigerate for up to 2 days; bring to room temperature before using.) Prepare Tomato Salsa; refrigerate until needed.

Preheat oven to 500°. In a small pan, melt butter. Brush butter on both sides of each tortilla, then spoon about ¼ of the meat filling into center of each. Fold sides of tortilla toward center, covering about 1 inch of filling on each side; then fold lower edge of tortilla over filling and roll over once to enclose. Place bundles, seam side down, in a greased 9 by 13-inch baking dish. Drizzle any remaining butter over bundles. Bake for 8 to 10 minutes or until golden and crisp.

Line 4 plates with lettuce; set chimichangas atop lettuce and sprinkle with cheese. Serve with salsa and sour cream. Makes 4 servings.

Spicy Pork Burritos

Mexico

Burritos are a great choice for casual dining—you provide the ingredients, guests do all the assembly.

2½ to 3 pounds lean boneless pork butt, cut into ½-inch cubes
1 tablespoon salad oil
1 can (13 oz.) tomatillos or 1 can (about 1 lb.) tomatoes
1 small can (8 oz.) tomato sauce
½ cup water
2 cloves garlic, minced or pressed
1½ to 3 teaspoons crushed red pepper
1 dozen medium-size (8 to 10-inch) flour tortillas, homemade (page 178) or purchased
1 cup (4 oz.) shredded jack cheese
1 cup guacamole, homemade (page 16) or purchased
Shredded lettuce
Sour cream

Place pork in a rimmed baking pan and drizzle with oil; stir to coat. Bake in a 325° oven for 30 minutes. Drain off and discard juices; stir meat, then bake for 30 more minutes or until meat is slightly crisp. Drain off and discard fat; set meat aside.

Meanwhile, place tomatillos and their liquid in a food processor or blender. Add tomato sauce, water, garlic, and pepper; whirl until blended. Pour into a 5-quart kettle and add meat. Bring to a boil over high heat; then cover, reduce heat, and simmer until meat is tender when pierced (about 30 minutes). Uncover, increase heat to medium-high, and cook, stirring, until sauce is thickened.

Heat tortillas, if desired. Serve meat, cheese, guacamole, lettuce, and sour cream in separate bowls. Place about 3 tablespoons of the meat filling in center of each tortilla; add cheese, guacamole, lettuce, and sour cream, then roll up and eat out of hand. Makes 6 to 12 servings.

Making Pork Chimichangas (Recipe on facing page)

1 After cooking meat briefly in its own juices, uncover kettle and increase heat to boil away juices. Cook meat in the rendered drippings until browned on all sides.

2 Spoon meat and chile mixture onto a plate or small wooden cutting board. Use 2 forks to shred meat into small strands.

3 Spoon ¼ of the meat filling down center of buttered tortilla. Fold sides of tortilla toward center; lap lower edge over filling.

4 Fold tortilla bundle over on itself to enclose filling. Place in a greased baking dish, seam side down; drizzle any remaining butter over bundles.

5 A south-of-the-border specialty, chimichangas make a hearty luncheon fiesta. Accompany with Guacamole (page 16) and a cool glass of sangría.

Grilled sandwiches

From Italy and France to the United States, grilled sandwiches are a favorite choice for a light repast.

Cook as many sandwiches at a time as your frying pan will comfortably hold, using 2 to 3 teaspoons melted butter for each sandwich. Let sandwiches cool briefly before serving—straight out of the pan, they can be hot enough to burn hands and mouth.

Reuben Sandwich

United States

This hot corned beef and sauerkraut sandwich has long been a lunch-time favorite in the United States.

- ½ cup mayonnaise
- 2 tablespoons tomato-based chili sauce
- 1 teaspoon minced green onion
- 8 large slices dark rye bread
- 8 slices (8 oz. *total*) Swiss cheese
- ½ pound cooked corned beef, thinly sliced
- 1 can (1 lb.) sauerkraut, drained well
- ½ pound cooked turkey, thinly sliced
  Butter or margarine

In a bowl, combine mayonnaise, chili sauce, and onion; blend well. Spread mixture over one side of each bread slice. Top each of 4 slices of bread with a slice of cheese. Place ¼ of the corned beef atop each cheese-topped bread slice; then layer each with ¼ of the sauerkraut, ¼ of the turkey, another cheese slice, and one of remaining 4 slices of bread, dressing side down. Press sandwiches lightly to compact them.

Melt butter in a wide frying pan over medium heat. Add sandwiches; cook, turning once, until sandwiches are browned on both sides and cheese begins to melt. Makes 4 sandwiches.

Croque-Monsieur

France

The verb *croquer* means "crunch"—and that's just what you'll hear when you bite into this exquisite sandwich. Serve *croque-monsieur* for lunch, accompanied with a crisp green salad; or cut each sandwich into squares and offer the savory tidbits as a hot hors d'oeuvre.

Prepared mustard
- 4 slices day-old French bread
- 4 ounces sliced cooked ham
- 4 ounces sliced Swiss cheese
- 2 eggs
- ½ cup milk
  Butter or margarine

Spread mustard over 2 slices of the bread; top each with half the ham and half the cheese, then cover each with one of remaining 2 bread slices. In a rimmed plate or pie pan, lightly beat eggs; add milk and beat until well blended. Press each sandwich firmly to hold it together, then dip into egg mixture, turning to coat both sides.

Melt butter in a wide frying pan over medium-high heat. Add sandwiches, cheese side down. Cook, turning once, until sandwiches are browned on both sides and cheese begins to melt. Cut sandwiches in half and serve hot. Makes 2 sandwiches.

Tostas

Italy

These Milanese ham and cheese sandwiches are great for parties—you toast them quickly in a sandwich grill, then let guests add their choice of condiments. *Tostas* can get messy, so provide small plates (to catch drips) and large napkins.

- 4 to 8 ounces sliced fontina or tybo cheese
- 8 to 12 ounces teleme or jack cheese, sliced
- ½ to ¾ pound sliced cooked ham
- ¼ to ½ pound thinly sliced prosciutto (optional)
- 1 large loaf (1 lb.) sliced egg bread, Italian bread, or French bread
  Condiments (suggestions follow)

Have all ingredients assembled and close at hand. To make each tosta, place 1 or 2 slices of each cheese and 1 or 2 slices of meat between 2 slices of bread. Toast sandwiches in an ungreased sandwich grill on medium-high heat or in an ungreased wide frying pan, covered, over medium heat. Cook, turning as needed, until sandwiches are browned on both sides and cheese is melted. Let diners open sandwiches and add their choice of condiments. Makes 6 servings.

Russian dressing. In a small bowl, blend ⅔ cup **mayonnaise** with ¼ cup drained **sweet pickle relish** and 2 tablespoons **tomato-based chili sauce.** Cover and refrigerate until serving time.

Artichokes. Use 2 jars (6 oz. *each*) **marinated artichoke hearts,** drained and cut into thin slices.

Red peppers. Seed and sliver 1 large **red bell pepper.** Heat 2 tablespoons **olive oil** in a small frying pan over medium-high heat. Add pepper; stir-fry until soft. (Or use one 8-ounce jar roasted red peppers.)

Mushrooms. Thinly slice ½ pound **mushrooms.** Heat 2 tablespoons **olive oil** in a medium-size frying pan over medium heat. Add mushrooms and cook until soft; add 2 tablespoons **white wine vinegar** and cook until liquid has evaporated. (Or use one 5-ounce jar marinated mushrooms, drained well and thinly sliced.)

Caponata. Use homemade Caponata (page 24) or 1 can (5 oz.) caponata.

Hot Tuna Sandwiches

United States

Here's a glorified rendition of a popular American lunchbox sandwich, all dressed up for supper.

- ⅔ cup mayonnaise
- 3 tablespoons sweet pickle relish, drained well
- 2 teaspoons prepared mustard
- 1 can (12½ oz.) chunk-style tuna, drained well and flaked
- 1 cup (4 oz.) shredded Cheddar cheese
- ½ cup *each* chopped green onions (including tops) and chopped celery
- 8 slices firm-textured white bread
  Butter or margarine

In a bowl, stir together mayonnaise, relish, and mustard. Add tuna, cheese, onions, and celery; stir until well combined. Spread tuna mixture evenly over 4 slices of bread; top with remaining 4 slices.

Melt butter in a wide frying pan over medium heat. Add sandwiches and cook, turning once, until browned on both sides. Cut in half and serve hot. Makes 4 sandwiches.

OPEN-FACED SANDWICHES

As beautiful to behold as to taste, Danish open-faced sandwiches (*smørrebrød*) are equally good for brunch, lunch, supper, or snacks. You compose each sandwich like a picture, arranging various ingredients to form an attractive design on a bread or cracker background.

Choose one of our sandwiches—or dream up your own recipes, using whatever you have on hand. Starting with cooked meat or fish, assorted cheeses, and raw, cooked, or marinated vegetables, you can devise any number of tempting combinations.

Use firm-textured bread for these sandwiches; pumpernickel, rye, white, and whole wheat are all good choices (toast bread and remove crusts, if you wish). Crisp unsalted cracker bread also makes a suitable base for smørrebrød, as long as it's sturdy enough to hold several layers of ingredients.

One or two smørrebrød are usually sufficient for a serving. Assemble the sandwiches just before serving; eat with knife and fork.

Anchovy, tomato & onion. Spread **butter** or mayonnaise over a slice of **rye bread.** Top with a few thin **tomato** slices, then sprinkle with chopped **green onion** (including top). Cross 2 flat **anchovy fillets,** drained, over onions; sprinkle with chopped **hard-cooked egg.**

Shrimp & cheese. Mix a little **dill weed** into softened **cream cheese.** Spread on a crisp **rye cracker.** Sprinkle with **small cooked shrimp.** Place 4 **cherry tomato halves** atop shrimp, then sprinkle with **lemon juice** and additional dill weed.

Turkey & red cabbage. Spread **butter** over a thin slice of **firm-textured white bread.** Top with overlapping thin slices of **cooked turkey breast.** Place 1 small **lettuce leaf** at one corner; fill lettuce with 2 tablespoons well-drained **canned sweet-sour red cabbage** and a dollop of **sour cream.**

Assembling Lamb & Spinach Turnovers (Recipe on facing page)

1 Shape risen dough into a rectangle; then cut rectangle into quarters with a floured knife. Cut each quarter into 3 equal pieces.

2 To form each piece into a ball, cup it in one hand. Then, with your other hand, pinch dough toward center until a smooth ball forms. Set balls on a floured board, pinched side down.

3 Roll out each ball into a round and place filling in center. Moisten edges of dough; then fold edges toward center in 3 sections and pinch together over filling.

4 Holding dough together in center with one hand, pinch seams together with your other hand. Finished turnover looks like a 3-cornered hat.

5 Golden brown and glossy, Lamb & Spinach Turnovers are a meal in themselves. Accompany with fresh and dried fruits, nuts, and your favorite beverage.

Yeast turnovers

Turnovers are popular with diners in almost every country in the world. To make them, you enclose a filling in some kind of dough—either flaky pastry or yeast-bread dough—then bake the packets until golden.

Here and on page 72, we offer three hearty turnovers, all featuring savory fillings wrapped in a basic yeast dough. (For pastry-wrapped turnovers, see pages 73 and 74.) From Lebanon come three-cornered pastries filled with lamb, spinach, and tangy feta cheese; Germany's offering is a tasty rectangular package stuffed with beef and chopped cabbage. Round Chinese *bow* hold a pork mixture laced with soy and ginger.

For a tempting international luncheon, present all three kinds of turnovers together on a buffet table. Raw vegetable sticks, ripe olives, and pickles make simple and delicious accompaniments.

If you bake turnovers ahead of time, let them cool completely on wire racks; then wrap in foil and refrigerate for up to 3 days (freeze for longer storage). You can serve them at room temperature, if you wish, but they taste best warm. To reheat turnovers, place them (thawed if frozen) on baking sheets, cover with foil, and heat in a 350° oven for about 20 minutes or until heated through.

Lamb & Spinach Turnovers

Lebanon   (Pictured on facing page)

Topped with sesame seeds and stuffed with a spicy, raisin-dotted lamb filling, these Lebanese pastries make a deliciously satisfying lunch or supper.

    Yeast bun dough (recipe at right)
 ½ teaspoon salt
 1 pound lean ground lamb
 1 large onion, chopped
 2 cloves garlic, minced or pressed
 ¾ teaspoon ground allspice
 ½ teaspoon ground cinnamon
 ¼ teaspoon *each* ground cloves and pepper
 1 package (10 oz.) frozen chopped spinach, thawed and squeezed dry
 ½ cup raisins
 1 tablespoon lemon juice
 6 ounces feta cheese, crumbled (about 1½ cups)
 1 egg
 1 tablespoon sesame seeds

Prepare yeast bun dough. While dough is rising, prepare filling: Sprinkle salt into a wide frying pan over medium-high heat. Crumble in lamb. Add onion and garlic; cook, stirring occasionally, until meat is no longer pink and all liquid has evaporated (about 10 minutes). Stir in allspice, cinnamon, cloves, and pepper; cook for 2 more minutes. Remove from heat and stir in spinach, raisins, lemon juice, and cheese. Set aside.

Punch dough down. Turn out onto a lightly floured board and knead for 1 minute. Shape into a rectangle. With a floured knife, cut rectangle into quarters, then cut each quarter into thirds. Shape dough pieces into balls and let stand on a lightly floured board, covered, for about 20 minutes. Roll each ball into a 5½-inch round. In center of each, place ⅓ cup of the meat mixture. Lightly moisten edges of dough with water; then bring up edges in 3 sections, fold toward center, and pinch firmly together over filling.

Place turnovers about 1 inch apart on lightly greased baking sheets. Cover and let rise in a warm place until puffy (30 to 45 minutes). In a small bowl, beat egg lightly, then brush over turnovers. (Don't let egg drip down sides of turnovers onto baking sheet, or baked turnovers will stick to pan.) Sprinkle with sesame seeds.

Bake in a 400° oven for 15 to 17 minutes or until golden brown. Transfer to wire racks and let cool slightly. Makes 12 turnovers.

HOW TO MAKE YEAST BUN DOUGH

Pour 1 cup **warm water** (110°) into a large bowl; sprinkle with 1 package **active dry yeast.** Add 1 teaspoon **sugar** and let stand until bubbly (5 to 12 minutes). Add 1 teaspoon **salt,** ¼ cup **salad oil,** and 2 cups **all-purpose flour;** beat with an electric mixer at medium speed for 5 minutes.

Using a spoon or a heavy-duty mixer, stir in 1¼ cups more **flour** to make a soft dough. Sprinkle about ¼ cup more **flour** on a board; turn out dough and knead until smooth and satiny (about 10 minutes). Transfer to a greased bowl, turn over to grease top, cover, and let rise in a warm place until almost doubled (about 1 hour).

...Yeast turnovers

Pork-filled Buns

China

Savory *bow* are popular teahouse offerings in Guangzhou (Canton). They're traditionally steamed—but many modern-day Chinese cooks bake them, too, to make a round bun that's crisper and less chewy than the steamed version. Our baked *bow* are good warm or cooled.

> **Yeast bun dough (page 71)**
> ¼ cup sugar
> **Cooking sauce (recipe follows)**
> 1½ **pounds lean boneless pork, cut into ½-inch cubes**
> 2 **cloves garlic, minced or pressed**
> ½ **teaspoon grated fresh ginger**
> 2 **tablespoons soy sauce**
> 2 **teaspoons sugar**
> 1 **tablespoon salad oil**
> 1 **large onion, chopped**
> **Melted butter or margarine**

Prepare yeast bun dough, but stir in the ¼ cup sugar with the first addition of flour. While dough is rising, prepare cooking sauce and set aside.

In a bowl, stir together pork, garlic, ginger, soy, and the 2 teaspoons sugar. Heat oil in a wok or wide frying pan over high heat. When oil is hot, add pork mixture and stir-fry until browned (about 5 minutes). Add onion and stir-fry until onion is soft (about 2 minutes). Stir cooking sauce, pour into pan, and cook, stirring, until sauce boils and thickens. Set aside and let cool.

Punch dough down. Turn out onto a lightly floured board and knead for 1 minute. Shape into a rectangle. With a floured knife, cut rectangle into quarters, then cut each quarter into thirds. Shape dough pieces into balls and let stand on a lightly floured board, covered, for about 20 minutes. Roll each ball into a 5-inch round; press edges to make them thinner than rest of round.

Place 2 rounded tablespoonfuls of filling in center of each round. Lightly moisten edges of dough with water; then pull edges up around filling and twist at top to seal. Place buns, sealed side down, about 2 inches apart on lightly greased baking sheets. Cover and let rise in a warm place until puffy (30 to 40 minutes).

Brush tops with butter and bake in a 350° oven for 15 minutes or until golden brown. Transfer to wire racks and let cool slightly. Makes 12 buns.

Cooking sauce. In a bowl, stir together 2 teaspoons **sugar** and 1 tablespoon **cornstarch.** Then stir in 2 tablespoons **soy sauce,** 1 teaspoon **dry sherry,** and ¼ cup **water.**

Beef & Cabbage Turnovers

Germany

Ground beef teams up with cabbage—a favorite German vegetable—in these hearty bundles.

> **Yeast bun dough (page 71)**
> 1 **pound lean ground beef**
> 1 **large onion, chopped**
> 2 **large cloves garlic, minced or pressed**
> 4 **cups coarsely chopped cabbage**
> 1 **beef bouillon cube dissolved in ½ cup hot water**
> ½ **teaspoon oregano leaves**
> ¼ **teaspoon ground cumin**
> **Salt and pepper**
> 1 **egg**

Prepare yeast bun dough. While dough is rising, prepare filling: Crumble beef into a wide frying pan and cook over medium-high heat, stirring, for 2 minutes. Add onion and garlic. Cook, stirring occasionally, for 5 more minutes. Add cabbage, bouillon, oregano, and cumin; stir until blended. Cover, reduce heat, and simmer until cabbage is tender to bite and all liquid has evaporated (about 20 more minutes). Season to taste with salt and pepper; let cool.

Punch dough down. Turn out onto a lightly floured board and knead for 1 minute. Divide in half; cover one half and set aside. Roll other half out to a 12 by 18-inch rectangle; then cut rectangle into six 6-inch squares. Place about ¼ cup filling in center of each square. Lightly moisten edges of each square with water, then bring all 4 corners together in center over filling and pinch seams together to seal. Repeat with rest of dough.

Place turnovers, seam side down, about 2 inches apart on lightly greased baking sheets. Cover and let rise in a warm place until puffy (30 to 45 minutes). In a small bowl, beat egg lightly, then brush over turnovers. (Don't let egg drip down sides of turnovers onto baking sheet.)

Bake in a 400° oven for 15 to 17 minutes or until golden brown. Transfer to wire racks and let cool slightly. Makes 12 turnovers.

Savory pastry turnovers

Start with one basic pastry dough—then add savory fillings to turn out an international array of delectable turnovers. Our egg-enriched pastry is crisp and flaky, but sturdy enough to be eaten out of hand without shattering. (If you substitute margarine for butter, the pastry will be more crumbly.)

Spicy Beef Turnovers

Jamaica

In Jamaica, bakeries and street vendors sell spicy pies like these for snacks and quick, light meals.

     Turnover pastry (recipe at right)
  2 teaspoons curry powder
  2 teaspoons cornstarch
  2 tablespoons dry sherry
  ½ cup regular-strength beef broth
  ½ teaspoon salt
  1 pound lean ground beef
  1 clove garlic, minced or pressed
  1 large tomato, peeled, seeded, and chopped
  ½ cup thinly sliced green onions (including tops)
  ¼ to ½ teaspoon crushed red pepper
  ½ teaspoon thyme leaves

Prepare turnover pastry, but stir curry powder into dry ingredients before cutting in butter and shortening.

Stir together cornstarch, sherry, and broth; set aside. Sprinkle salt into a wide frying pan over medium-high heat. Crumble in beef and cook, stirring, until browned; spoon off and discard excess fat. Add garlic, tomato, onions, pepper, and thyme; cook, stirring, until most of liquid has evaporated. Stir cornstarch mixture, then pour into pan and cook, stirring, until mixture boils and thickens. Set aside and let cool.

Cut pastry dough in half, then cut each half into 4 equal pieces. Shape dough pieces into balls; roll each out on a floured board to a 6-inch round. Lightly moisten edges of dough with water. Place about ⅓ cup of the meat filling on half of each round, spreading it to within ½ inch of edges; then fold other half over to enclose filling. With a fork, press edges together to seal; prick top in several places.

Using a wide spatula, transfer turnovers to an ungreased baking sheet, placing them 1 inch apart. Bake in a 425° oven for 20 to 25 minutes or until browned. Serve warm. Makes 8 turnovers.

HOW TO MAKE TURNOVER PASTRY

In a bowl, stir together 2½ cups **all-purpose flour** and ½ teaspoon **salt**. With a pastry blender or 2 table knives, cut ¼ cup *each* **solid shortening** and **butter** into flour until particles are about the size of small peas. Break 1 **egg** into a glass measure and add enough **water** to make ½ cup; beat lightly.

Stirring flour mixture lightly and quickly with a fork, sprinkle on egg mixture, about 2 tablespoons at a time. Continue stirring until dough forms a ball and almost cleans sides of bowl.

With your hands, gather mixture into a ball; shape into a rectangle, wrap in plastic wrap, and refrigerate for 1 hour.

Cornish Pasties

England

Tin miners in Cornwall often carried a lunch of freshly baked pasties to the mines early in the morning; wrapped in layers of newspaper, the turnovers stayed warm until noon.

     Turnover pastry (recipe above)
  1 pound top round steak, cut about ¼ inch thick, trimmed of fat and minced
  1 small russet potato, finely chopped
  1 large onion, finely chopped
  1 small turnip, peeled and finely chopped
  1 to 1½ teaspoons *each* salt and pepper
  4 tablespoons butter or margarine

Prepare turnover pastry. In a bowl, stir together steak, potato, onion, turnip, salt, and pepper.

Cut pastry dough in half lengthwise, then cut each half into 4 equal pieces. Shape dough pieces into balls; roll each ball out on a floured board to a 7-inch round. Lightly moisten edges of dough with water. Place about ½ cup of the meat filling on half of each round, spreading it to within ½ inch of edges; then fold other half over to enclose filling. With a fork, press edges together to seal; prick top in several places.

Using a wide spatula, transfer turnovers to a greased baking sheet, placing them 1 inch apart. Bake in a 350° oven for 50 to 60 minutes or until lightly browned. Serve warm. Makes 8 turnovers.

...Savory pastry turnovers

Piroshkis

Russia   (Pictured on facing page)

Typically offered alongside tea or cocktails, traditional *piroshkis* are small enough to eat in one or two bites. We've come up with a larger version—a plump, hearty luncheon entrée.

>   Turnover pastry (page 73)
> 1   teaspoon salt
> 1   pound lean ground beef
> 1   medium-size onion, chopped
> 2   cloves garlic, minced or pressed
> ½   pound mushrooms, chopped
> 1   teaspoon dill weed
> ½   cup half-and-half (light cream)
> 2   hard-cooked eggs, chopped
> ¼   cup chopped parsley
>   Pepper

Prepare turnover pastry. Sprinkle salt into a wide frying pan over medium-high heat. Crumble in beef; cook, stirring, for 2 minutes. Add onion and garlic; cook, stirring occasionally, for 5 minutes. Stir in mushrooms and cook until meat is no longer pink and vegetables are soft (about 5 more minutes). Add dill weed and half-and-half; cook, stirring, until all liquid has evaporated. Remove from heat and stir in eggs and parsley. Season to taste with pepper.

Cut pastry dough in half, then cut each half into 4 equal pieces. Shape dough pieces into balls; roll each ball out on a floured board to a 7-inch round. Place about ½ cup of the meat filling on half of each round, spreading it to within ½ inch of edges; then lightly moisten edges of dough with water. Fold other half over to enclose filling. With a fork, press edges together to seal; prick top in several places. With a knife, trim off excess dough to form an even half moon.

Using a wide spatula, transfer turnovers to an ungreased baking sheet, placing them 1 inch apart. Bake in a 425° oven for 20 to 25 minutes or until lightly browned. Serve warm. Makes 8 turnovers.

Chicken Empanadas

Argentina

The South American version of the turnover is the *empanada*, a tasty pie that comes in a variety of sizes and flavors. Our meal-size empanadas hold a chile-spiked chicken filling.

> 3   chicken breast halves (1½ lbs. *total*), skinned
> 1   thin-skinned potato, quartered
> 1   can (14½ oz.) regular-strength chicken broth or 1¾ cups homemade chicken broth (page 33)
> 2   tablespoons salad oil
> 2   medium-size onions, chopped
> 2   cloves garlic, minced or pressed
> ¼   cup finely chopped fresh cilantro (coriander)
> 6   tablespoons canned diced green chiles
> 1½ tablespoons all-purpose flour
> ½   cup sliced pimento-stuffed olives
>   Turnover pastry (page 73)

Place chicken in a 5-quart kettle. Add potato and broth. Bring to a boil over high heat; then cover, reduce heat, and simmer until potato is tender when pierced (20 to 25 minutes). Lift out chicken and potato; reserve broth. When chicken is cool enough to handle, cut meat off bones, then cut into bite-size pieces. Finely dice potato. Set chicken and potato aside.

Heat oil in a wide frying pan over medium heat. Add onions and garlic and cook, stirring occasionally, until onions are soft (about 10 minutes). Stir in cilantro, chiles, flour, and olives; cook for 1 minute. Stir in reserved broth and cook, stirring, until mixture is thick and bubbly. Remove from heat and stir in chicken and potato. Let cool.

Prepare turnover pastry; refrigerate while chicken mixture cools.

Cut pastry dough in half, then cut each half into 4 equal pieces. Shape dough pieces into balls; roll each ball out on a floured board to a 7-inch round. Lightly moisten edges of dough with water. Place about ½ cup of the chicken filling on half of each round, spreading it to within ½ inch of edges; then fold other half over to enclose filling. With a fork, press edges together to seal; prick top in several places.

Using a wide spatula, transfer turnovers to an ungreased baking sheet, placing them 1 inch apart. Bake in a 400° oven for 20 to 25 minutes or until lightly browned. Serve warm. Makes 8 turnovers.

Preparing Piroshkis (Recipe on facing page)·

1 Heat a wide frying pan over medium-high heat. Sprinkle salt into pan to prevent meat from sticking; then quickly crumble beef over salt. Meat will sizzle and start to cook as soon as it hits pan.

2 Spread filling on half of the dough circle; then moisten edges of circle with water.

3 Fold uncovered half of circle over filling; lightly press edges together (don't worry if edges are uneven). The dampened edges will stick firmly together, preventing leakage during cooking.

4 With a knife, trim off excess dough to make an even half moon. Press edges together with back of a fork. Prick top in several places to allow steam to escape.

5 For a hearty lunch or a light supper, serve this winning combination: golden, flaky Russian Piroshkis and Finnish Beet and Cabbage Soup (page 32).

MEATS

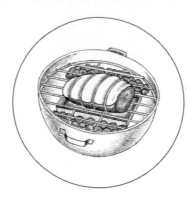

Around the world, the availability of meat—beef, veal, pork, and lamb—varies greatly. Meatless or near-meatless meals are the norm in many countries. In other lands, though, substantial roasts, juicy chops or steaks, or hearty stews are daily dinnertime stars.

No matter how often you serve meat, you'll be a wiser shopper if you know a few basic facts. Those fancy names on many meat counter labels—"London broil," "Texas steak," "veal scaloppine," and the like—often promise nothing more than a higher price. These aren't necessarily the most tender or flavorful cuts you could choose.

All cuts of meat fall into two general categories: naturally tender cuts and those that are fibrous and relatively tough. Tender cuts come from the least exercised parts of an animal—the middle back (loin) and rib, for example. The loin of a steer yields porterhouse and T-bone steaks; lamb, pork, and veal loin chops come from the loin portions of lambs, pigs, and calves. As distance from the loin increases, so does toughness. Hardworking muscles such as the shoulder (chuck) and shank produce fibrous, tough meat.

Cooking techniques

Tender cuts retain their succulence best if cooked by dry heat—oven-roasting, barbecuing, broiling, and pan-frying. Tougher cuts, though, need the moist heat of stewing or braising. Long, slow simmering in liquid breaks down the connective tissue that makes such cuts tough, leaving them tender and flavor-rich.

Thrifty tips

As you explore the cooking styles of other lands, you'll soon discover new ways to save both time and money when cooking meat. For example, many Asian dishes are designed to stretch a little meat a long way—and they require only brief cooking. Asian cooks combine thinly sliced meat with an abundance of fresh vegetables in speedy stir-fries, and skewer small cubes of beef or pork for quick grilling over hot coals.

Cooks in other parts of the world economize by using one large piece of meat—cooked in the oven or on the range—for more than just one meal. Our Harvest Ham & Cabbage is a succulent boiled dinner that could easily make a curtain call as a whole-meal soup. You can use leftover cooked meat in many other ways, too—in hot and cold sandwiches, French omelets, Italian frittatas, and Asian rice or noodle dishes.

You can use leftover cooked meat in many other ways, too: in hot and cold sandwiches, main-dish salads, French omelets, Italian frittatas, Asian rice and noodle dishes, and Indian-style curries. Don't be timid—just stir up your imagination, then blend compatible ingredients for a sparkling new creation.

Oven-roasting

In many of the world's countries, oven-cooking isn't a widely used technique. But in numerous other lands, it's a popular way to prepare naturally tender cuts of beef, pork, lamb, and veal.

To oven-roast meat, place it (usually on a rack) in a shallow roasting pan; do not cover. Insert a meat thermometer in thickest portion of meat (not touching bone). Remove roast from oven when desired interior temperature is reached; let stand for 10 to 20 minutes before carving.

Roast Leg of Lamb

Pakistan

Cool cucumber-yogurt sauce dotted with green peas makes a tangy topping for this roast lamb.

> 1 **leg of lamb (6 to 8 lbs.)**
> 1 **cup soy sauce**
> 1 **tablespoon grated fresh ginger**
> ¼ **cup salad oil**
> 4 **cloves garlic, minced or pressed**
> **Cucumber-Yogurt Sauce (page 143)**

Place lamb in a shallow pan. In a 2-cup glass measure, combine soy, ginger, oil, and garlic; pour over meat. Cover and refrigerate for 24 hours, turning occasionally. Also prepare Cucumber-Yogurt Sauce; cover and refrigerate.

Lift lamb from marinade, drain briefly, and place, fat side up, on a rack in a shallow roasting pan. Insert a meat thermometer in thickest portion of meat (not touching bone). Roast in a 325° oven, uncovered, for about 22 minutes per pound or until thermometer registers 150° for medium-rare.

Lift lamb to a carving board. Let rest for 10 minutes, then cut into thin slices. Pass Cucumber-Yogurt Sauce at the table. Makes 6 to 8 servings.

Quebec Roast Beef with Madeira Sauce

Canada

British fondness for beef and French flair for elegant sauces are both apparent in this roast.

> 1 **beef rib roast (6 to 8 lbs.)**
> **Pepper**
> 1 **can (10½ oz.) condensed consommé**
> ¼ **cup Madeira**
> 4 **tablespoons butter or margarine**

Sprinkle all sides of beef with pepper; place, fat side up, on a rack in a shallow roasting pan. Insert a meat thermometer in thickest portion of meat (not touching bone). Roast in a 325° oven, uncovered, for about 20 minutes per pound or until thermometer registers 135° for rare.

Transfer meat to a carving board; keep warm. Skim and discard fat from drippings, then pour consommé and Madeira into pan. Bring to a boil over high heat; boil until reduced to about 1 cup, scraping up browned particles from pan. Reduce heat to low or remove pan from heat. Then stir in butter with a wire whisk, blending constantly to incorporate butter as it melts. Pass sauce at the table. Makes 8 to 10 servings.

Pork Roast with Black Gravy

Czechoslovakia

When you roast a pork loin in a cast-iron or heavy aluminum roasting pan, the drippings caramelize into black bits that make a dark, rich gravy. (Don't use a pan with a nonstick finish; if you do, the drippings won't caramelize.)

> 1 **pork loin roast (4 to 4½ lbs.)**
> 1 **clove garlic, cut in half**
> 1 **teaspoon caraway seeds**
> ¼ **teaspoon pepper**
> 3 **beef bouillon cubes**
> 2 **cups hot water**
> 3 **tablespoons each cornstarch and water**
> **Salt and pepper**

Place roast, fat side up, in a cast-iron or heavy aluminum roasting pan. Rub flesh with cut sides of garlic, then drop garlic into pan. Sprinkle meat with caraway seeds and the ¼ teaspoon pepper. Then insert a meat thermometer in thickest portion of meat (not touching bone).

Roast on bottom rack in a 350° oven, uncovered, for 2 to 2½ hours or until thermometer registers 170°; baste with drippings several times. Transfer to a platter; keep warm.

Discard garlic and all but about 2 tablespoons fat from drippings. Add bouillon cubes and the 2 cups hot water; bring to a boil over high heat, scraping up all black bits from pan. Stir cornstarch and the 3 tablespoons water together; then stir into drippings and cook, stirring, until bubbly and thickened. Season to taste with salt and pepper. Pass gravy at the table. Makes 6 servings.

Assembling Veal Roast Orloff (Recipe on facing page)

1 Place boneless, tied veal, fat side up, on a rack in a shallow roasting pan. Insert a meat thermometer in thickest portion of meat.

2 While veal roasts, prepare soubise sauce: stir flour into puréed cooked onions, then blend in broth and cream. Cook until very thick; set aside.

3 Let cooked roast stand for 15 to 30 minutes. Then remove string and cut roast into ½-inch-thick slices, cutting to within ½ inch of bottom.

4 Using about half the sauce, spread one side of each veal slice with sauce. Insert a slice of bacon and then a slice of cheese, next to sauce-spread surface of each slice.

5 Retie roast; spread remaining sauce over top and sprinkle with shredded cheese. At this point, you may loosely cover and refrigerate roast; to serve, just bake until heated through.

6 Place cheese-crowned veal on a platter; remove string. Accompany with colorful, lightly cooked vegetables such as Basil Tomatoes (page 167) and green beans.

Oven roasting

Veal Roast Orloff

France   (Pictured on facing page)

European cooks are renowned for sublime veal dishes, among them Italy's Osso Buco (page 92). Here's a festive veal entrée from France: a rolled roast laced with cheese and bacon, topped with a rich onion sauce.

- 1 **boneless leg of veal (4½ to 5 lbs.), tied**
  Pepper
  Soubise sauce (recipe follows)
- ½ **pound fully cooked Canadian bacon, thinly sliced**
- 6 **ounces Gruyère or Swiss cheese, thinly sliced**
- ¼ **cup shredded Gruyère or Swiss cheese**

Sprinkle all sides of veal with pepper and place, fat side up, on a rack in a shallow roasting pan. Insert a meat thermometer in thickest portion of meat. Roast in a 325° oven, uncovered, for about 2½ hours or until thermometer registers 160°. Meanwhile, prepare soubise sauce; set aside.

Remove roast from oven. Let stand for 15 to 30 minutes, then remove strings. Cut roast crosswise into ½-inch-thick slices, cutting to within ½ inch of bottom. Using about half the sauce, evenly spread sauce over one side of each slice. Insert 1 slice bacon, then 1 slice cheese, next to sauce-spread surface of each veal slice. Tie a string around roast to hold it together. Spread remaining sauce over top; sprinkle with shredded cheese. (At this point, you may cover roast loosely and refrigerate until next day.)

Place roast in a 325° oven and bake, uncovered, for about 45 minutes or until heated through and lightly browned on top. Remove string and cut between veal slices. Makes 8 to 10 servings.

Soubise sauce. Melt 3 tablespoons **butter** or margarine in a wide frying pan over medium heat; add 1 large **onion,** chopped, and cook until soft (about 15 minutes). Spoon into a blender or food processor and whirl until puréed; return to pan and stir in ¼ cup **all-purpose flour,** ¼ teaspoon **ground nutmeg,** and a dash of **pepper.** Cook, stirring, for 2 minutes; then gradually add ½ cup each **regular-strength chicken broth** and **whipping cream.** Cook, stirring, until bubbly and very thick.

Strudel Meat Roll

Austria

Time-saving packaged fila stands in for traditional strudel dough in this grand pastry-wrapped meat loaf. You can bake the roll a day in advance, then reheat it at serving time.

- 4 **tablespoons butter or margarine**
- 1 **small onion, finely chopped**
- ¼ **pound mushrooms, chopped**
- 2 **pounds lean ground beef**
- 1 **teaspoon salt**
- ¼ **teaspoon pepper**
- ½ **teaspoon oregano leaves**
- 2 **cloves garlic, minced or pressed**
- 3 **eggs**
- 1½ **cups (6 oz.) shredded Swiss cheese**
- ¼ **cup each finely chopped parsley and fine dry bread crumbs**
- 12 **sheets fila**
  Sour cream

Melt 2 tablespoons of the butter in a wide frying pan over medium heat; add onion and cook until soft. Add mushrooms; then crumble beef into pan and cook until meat is no longer pink. Spoon mixture into a large bowl; add salt, pepper, oregano, and garlic. Let cool. Mix in eggs, cheese, parsley, and crumbs. Cover and refrigerate until cold.

In a small pan, melt remaining 2 tablespoons butter. Overlap 6 sheets of the fila (keep remainder covered with plastic wrap) to make a 15 by 24-inch rectangle, arranging sheets so rectangle has an even thickness and brushing each sheet lightly with butter so layers stick together.

Spread filling over fila rectangle to within 1½ inches of long sides and within 3 inches of ends. Fold side edges over filling. Then fold one end over filling; roll up jelly roll style. Lay out remaining 6 sheets fila to make a 15 by 24-inch rectangle, brushing each sheet with butter. Fold in 1½ inches of each long side. Set meat roll across one end; roll up. Place, seam side down, on a 10 by 15-inch baking pan; brush with butter.

Bake in a 375° oven for 30 to 35 minutes or until golden brown. If made ahead, let cool; then cover and refrigerate until next day. To reheat, bake in a 375° oven, uncovered, for 30 minutes.

Transfer meat roll to a board; cut crosswise into 1-inch-thick slices. Pass sour cream to spoon over each slice. Makes 6 to 8 servings.

Homemade sausage

If you've never thought about making your own sausage, take a moment to consider the advantages. Homemade sausage contains no preservatives. And since you can adjust the amount of fat, salt, and spice to suit your taste, sausage you make yourself always has just the right flavor.

Buying and grinding the meat

Our recipes begin with boneless, untrimmed pork butt. For the juiciest, most flavorful sausage, you'll need equal amounts of lean meat and fat; ask for extra pork fat to be sure you have enough. If you prefer relatively lowfat sausage, use ⅔ lean meat to ⅓ fat; a mix that's much leaner than this will probably yield dry, rather tasteless sausage.

Separate lean meat from fat, cut both into 1-inch cubes, and determine the quantity of each, measuring by weight or volume (1 pound equals a scant 2 cups). Combine meat and fat in the desired proportions, then refrigerate until cold—grinding is easiest if the mix is chilled. Then put through an electric or hand food chopper fitted with the coarsest blade. Or use a food processor; process the mix in 1-pound batches, whirling just until coarsely ground (only a few seconds).

Season the mixture as the following recipes direct, starting with the minimum amount of garlic, chiles (if used), and salt. Fry a small patty and taste it; then add more seasonings, if desired. Refrigerate the mixture for at least 2 hours—or, for best flavor, until next day.

Shaping and storing sausage

Shape meat mixture into ½-inch-thick patties; then stack, placing 2 sheets of wax paper between patties for easy separation. Or, if you plan to use your sausage as bulk sausage, just shape it into 1-pound loaves. Wrap airtight and refrigerate for 2 or 3 days; freeze for longer storage.

HOW TO COOK HOMEMADE SAUSAGES

Place a wide frying pan over medium heat; lightly coat with **butter** or margarine. Add **sausage patties** (thawed if frozen) and cook until well browned on both sides and no longer pink in center when slashed.

Sweet Italian Sausage

Italy

Depending on where it's made—and on each cook's preference—sausage varies from sweet to spicy to hot. Garlic, fennel, and sage give this Italian sausage its sweet gusto.

- 4½ **pounds boneless pork butt**
- 2¼ **teaspoons** *each* **fennel seeds and white pepper**
- 1½ **teaspoons sage leaves**
- 3 **to 5 cloves garlic, minced or pressed**
- 2½ **to 3½ teaspoons salt**
- ¾ **cup dry white wine**

Separate lean meat from fat, then cut both into cubes. Measure or weigh; you should have equal parts (2¼ lbs. *each*) fat and lean meat. Grind fat and meat coarsely; place in a large bowl.

Add fennel seeds, pepper, sage, garlic, salt, and wine to fat and meat. Mix well with your hands. Cover and refrigerate for at least 2 hours or until next day. Shape and store according to directions at left. Makes 4½ pounds.

GREEK LOUKANIKA SAUSAGE

Cut and grind pork butt as directed for **Sweet Italian Sausage.** Place in a large bowl and add 1 tablespoon *each* **thyme leaves** and **marjoram leaves;** 4 to 6 cloves **garlic,** minced or pressed; 1½ teaspoons *each* **ground allspice** and **ground coriander;** ¾ teaspoon **cracked bay leaves;** 1½ tablespoons grated **orange peel;** 2½ to 3½ teaspoons **salt;** and ¾ cup **dry red wine.**

Mix, chill, shape, and store as for **Sweet Italian Sausage.** Makes 4½ pounds.

PORTUGUESE LINGUISA SAUSAGE

Cut and grind pork butt as directed for **Sweet Italian Sausage,** but use only 4 pounds. Place in a large bowl and add 4 to 7 cloves **garlic,** minced or pressed; 4 to 6 **small dried whole hot red chiles,** crushed; 1 tablespoon *each* **ground coriander** and **paprika;** ½ teaspoon *each* **ground cinnamon, cloves,** and **allspice;** 2½ to 3½ teaspoons **salt;** ¼ cup **cider vinegar;** and ½ cup **cold water.**

Mix, chill, shape, and store as for **Sweet Italian Sausage.** Makes 4 pounds.

Covered barbecue: Indirect heat

Whole birds and large, very thick pieces of meat require slow, even cooking—and that's just what the indirect heat of a covered grill gives them. Begin by banking glowing coals on either side of the fire grate; then place a drip pan in the center. Set the meat on the cooking grill, directly above the drip pan, and cover the barbecue. Heat reflected from every angle provides the same even cooking as an oven does. To control the temperature, just regulate the flow of air by adjusting the dampers in the barbecue lid and the firebox.

You can also spit-roast whole poultry and large pieces of meat. Follow manufacturer's directions in the use and care manual for your barbecue.

Barbecued Leg of Lamb

Turkey

Succulent lamb is a favorite throughout the Middle East. Our Turkish-style leg of lamb is especially flavorful; it's studded with slivered garlic before cooking, then basted with a spicy sauce as it grills. Serve cool, tangy Cucumber-Yogurt Sauce (page 143) with the sliced meat, if you wish.

>   1   **leg of lamb (5 to 7 lbs.)**
>   4   **or 5 cloves garlic, slivered**
>   **Pepper**
>   **Lamb basting sauce (recipe follows)**

Using a small pointed knife, slit lamb on all sides; insert garlic in slits. Rub pepper evenly over meat.

About 45 minutes before cooking, start barbecue fire (see "Barbecuing Using Indirect Heat," right). Insert a meat thermometer in thickest portion of lamb (not touching bone). Prepare lamb basting sauce.

Cook meat for 30 minutes, then baste with sauce. Continue to cook, basting occasionally, until thermometer registers 145° for rare, 155° for medium (about 1½ more hours). Lift lamb to a platter; let stand for about 10 minutes before slicing. Makes about 8 servings.

Lamb basting sauce. In a 2-cup glass measure, stir together ½ cup **red or white wine vinegar;** ⅓ cup **olive oil** or salad oil; 2 tablespoons **lemon juice;** 1 small **onion,** finely chopped; ¼ teaspoon each **ground nutmeg, ground ginger,** and **pepper;** and ⅛ teaspoon **ground cloves.**

BARBECUING USING INDIRECT HEAT

Open or remove lid from a covered barbecue, then open bottom dampers. Pile about 40 long-burning briquets on fire grate and ignite. Let briquets burn until they reach the "glowing" stage (30 to 40 minutes). Using long-handled tongs, bank about half the briquets on each side of fire grate; then place a metal drip pan in center.

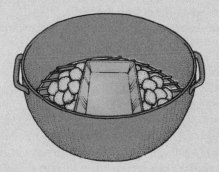

Set cooking grill in place 4 to 6 inches above pan. Lightly grease grill.

Set meat on grill, fat side up, directly above drip pan (drain marinated meat briefly before placing on grill). Insert a meat thermometer in thickest portion (not touching bone). Cover barbecue; adjust dampers as necessary to maintain an even heat. Cook for time specified in recipe or until thermometer registers desired degree of doneness. To keep temperature constant during cooking, add 5 or 6 briquets to each side of fire grate at 45-minute intervals.

Three different terms are commonly used to indicate desired fire temperatures at the start of cooking. Use this guide to help you determine fire temperature:

● *Glowing* describes the hottest fire; coals are just covered with gray ash. You can't hold your hand near the grill over this fire for more than 2 to 3 seconds.

● *Medium-glowing* describes coals that glow through a layer of gray ash. At this stage, you can't hold your hand near the grill for more than 4 to 5 seconds.

● *Low-glowing* describes coals covered with a thick layer of gray ash. You should be able to hold your hand near the grill over low-glowing coals for 6 to 7 seconds.

...Covered barbecue: Indirect heat

Barbecued Leg of Pork

Jamaica   (Pictured on facing page)

A citrus-and-spice marinade gives this Jamaican barbecue its tangy flavor.

>   1 **shank-end leg of pork (7 to 8 lbs.)**
>   ½ **large orange (unpeeled), cut into pieces**
>   ½ **large lime (unpeeled), cut into pieces**
>   1 **clove garlic, quartered**
>   3 **tablespoons salad oil**
>   2 **tablespoons cider vinegar**
>   ¼ **teaspoon** *each* **ground ginger and ground nutmeg**

Using a sharp knife, cut leathery skin from pork. Then score through fat just to meat, making diagonal cuts ½ to ¾ inch apart.

In a blender or food processor, combine orange, lime, garlic, oil, vinegar, ginger, and nutmeg. Whirl until thoroughly combined. Smear mixture over all sides of pork. Place in a deep container, cover, and refrigerate until next day.

About 45 minutes before cooking, start barbecue fire (see "Barbecuing Using Indirect Heat," page 81). Insert a meat thermometer in thickest portion of pork (not touching bone).

Cook pork until thermometer registers 170° (3 to 3½ hours). Lift to a platter; let stand for 10 minutes before slicing. Makes about 8 servings.

Glazed Pork Loin

Philippines

A baste of pineapple, ginger, and soy makes this Filipino roast a winner.

>   1 **pork loin roast (3½ to 4 lbs.)**
>   1 **cup unsweetened pineapple juice**
>   3 **tablespoons soy sauce**
>   1 **clove garlic, minced or pressed**
>   ¼ **teaspoon ground ginger**

About 45 minutes before cooking, start barbecue fire (see "Barbecuing Using Indirect Heat," page 81). Place pork, fat side up, on grill; insert a meat thermometer in thickest portion (not touching bone). Combine pineapple juice, soy, garlic, and ginger.

Cook meat for 1 hour; then baste with soy mixture. Continue to cook, basting often, until thermometer registers 170° (1 to 1½ more hours).

Lift pork to a platter; let stand for 10 minutes, then cut between ribs into individual servings. Meanwhile, if desired, skim and discard fat from drippings in drip pan; pour into a bowl and pass at the table. Makes about 6 servings.

Barbecued Beef

Argentina

On the Argentine pampas, gauchos still roast meat over an open campfire. Here's a modern barbecue adaptation of their open-air feast.

>   **Chimichurri sauce (recipe follows)**
>   1 **boneless beef cross rib or sirloin tip roast (4 to 5 lbs.)**

Prepare chimichurri sauce. Spoon about half into a bowl; cover and refrigerate until serving time. Pour remaining sauce over roast. Cover; let stand for 1 to 2 hours, turning often.

About 45 minutes before cooking, start barbecue fire (see "Barbecuing Using Indirect Heat," page 81). Insert a meat thermometer in thickest portion of roast. Cook, basting occasionally with sauce, until thermometer registers 135° for rare, 155° for medium (1½ to 2 hours). Lift to a platter; let stand for 10 minutes before slicing. Pass reserved sauce at the table. Makes about 8 servings.

Chimichurri sauce. You'll need 2 medium-size **carrots,** 1 large **tomato,** 1 stalk **celery,** 1 clove **garlic,** ½ **green pepper** (seeded), and 1 **lemon** (unpeeled). Cut all into pieces; then whirl in a food processor or blender, a portion at a time, until finely chopped. Add ½ teaspoon *each* **salt, crushed red pepper,** and **black pepper,** then stir in 1½ cups **salad oil** and ¼ cup *each* **dry red wine** and **red wine vinegar.**

EL SALVADORAN BEEF

Follow directions for **Barbecued Beef,** but omit chimichurri sauce. Instead, marinate beef in a mixture of ½ cup **orange juice,** 2 tablespoons minced **onion,** 2 cloves **garlic** (minced or pressed), ¼ teaspoon **pepper,** 3 tablespoons **salad oil,** 2 tablespoons **red wine vinegar,** and ¾ teaspoon **ground cumin.** Baste beef with marinade during cooking. Also prepare **Chirmol** (page 138); pass at the table to top individual portions of meat.

Preparing Barbecued Leg of Pork (Recipe on facing page)

1 Cut leathery skin from pork. With a sharp knife, score rough fat just to meat, making agonal cuts ½ to ¾ inch apart.

2 In a blender, whirl orange, lime, and seasonings until well blended. Smear mixture evenly over pork, then cover and refrigerate until next day.

3 Ignite charcoal. When briquets reach the "glowing" stage—just covered with gray ash—bank about half of them on each side of fire grate. Place drip pan in center.

4 Set cooking grill in place. Position meat on grill directly above drip pan. Cover barbecue, then adjust dampers to maintain an even temperature.

5 Carve pork into thick slices. Fresh tropical fruits in season and sweet potatoes or squash complement the meat's mild, smoky flavor.

Open grill & broiling: Direct heat

For open grilling over a solid bed of coals, you'll need a built-in brick barbecue, brazier, hibachi or other small portable grill (some box-style barbecues are also suitable). You can use a kettle barbecue, too, though most manufacturers advise keeping the kettle covered when it's being used this way.

Choose cuts of meat that lie fairly flat and measure no more than 2 inches thick. Steaks, cubes (for skewering), and chops are all excellent candidates for open grilling; ground meat patties are a good choice, too. You'll find that the direct heat of hot coals cooks these meats very quickly, so be prepared to tend them with care. Turn as needed to ensure even cooking and a richly browned exterior; baste often (if recipe directs) to make the meat extra flavorful and juicy.

Most meats that cook well on an open grill also broil nicely. The barbecue heat comes from below, the broiler from above—but both produce marvelous results (barbecued meats gain added flavor from the smoke of the open fire).

Pounded Pork & Chili Chops

Mexico

Pounding is a time-honored technique for tenderizing meat; here it also works in the seasonings. Flattened meat takes less time to cook.

    1   tablespoon chili powder
    ½   teaspoon ground cumin
    2   cloves garlic, minced or pressed
    1   small onion, minced
    2   tablespoons salad oil
    4   rib or loin pork chops, *each about ½ inch thick
        (about 1¼ lbs. total)*
    2   ripe avocados
        Fresh cilantro (coriander) sprigs
    1   small orange (unpeeled), cut into wedges

Stir together chili powder, cumin, garlic, onion, and oil. Slash fat around edges of chops at 1-inch intervals; spread about 1 tablespoon chili mixture on each side of each chop. Place 1 or 2 chops between 2 sheets of plastic wrap, making sure sheets are large enough to cover meat after pounding (chops will expand to 2 to 3 times original size). With a flat-surfaced mallet, pound meat evenly and firmly around bone until about ¼ inch thick. Repeat with remaining chops.

About 35 minutes before cooking, start barbecue fire (see "Barbecuing Using Direct Heat," below). Place chops on grill 4 to 6 inches above a solid bed of glowing coals. Or place about 2 inches below heat on a rack in a broiler pan (see "How to Broil Meat," facing page). Cook, turning once, until meat near bone is no longer pink when slashed (5 to 6 minutes *total*). Halve and pit avocados; serve each chop with cilantro, an avocado half, and orange wedges to squeeze over meat and avocado. Makes 4 servings.

PORTUGUESE POUNDED LAMB CHOPS

Follow directions for **Pounded Pork & Chili Chops,** but use 4 **rib or loin lamb chops.** Substitute ¾ teaspoon **ground cinnamon** and ¼ teaspoon **ground cloves** for chili powder. Cook for about 4 minutes *total* for medium-rare.

BARBECUING USING DIRECT HEAT

Spread briquets on the fire grate in a solid layer that's 1 to 2 inches bigger than grill area required for meat. Then mound charcoal and ignite.

Fire temperatures are usually described as glowing, medium-glowing, or low-glowing coals (see page 81). When coals have reached fire temperature specified in recipe, spread out into a single layer again.

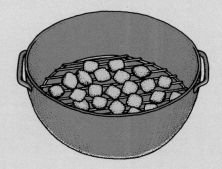

Set grill in place at recommended height above coals; grease lightly.

Skewered Meatballs

Turkey

For an open-air meal Turkish style, try these simple, succulent skewers: mint-seasoned lamb meatballs paired with mellow green peppers.

> 2 **medium-size green peppers**
> 1 **pound** *each* **lean ground lamb and lean ground beef**
> ¼ **cup** *each* **fine dry bread crumbs, chopped onion, and chopped parsley**
> 2 **eggs**
> 1 **tablespoon dry mint**
> 1 **teaspoon salt**
> ¼ **teaspoon pepper**
> **Olive oil**
> **Cucumber-Yogurt Sauce (page 143)**

Cut green peppers into 24 pieces, each 1 to 1½ inches square; remove any seeds. In a 3-quart pan, bring about 4 cups water to a boil over high heat; add peppers and boil for 1 minute. Drain and set aside.

In a large bowl, combine lamb, beef, crumbs, onion, parsley, eggs, mint, salt, and pepper. Mix well, then shape into 30 balls. Alternately thread 5 meatballs and 4 pepper squares on each of 6 long skewers. Lightly brush skewers with oil on all sides. Prepare Cucumber-Yogurt Sauce.

About 35 minutes before cooking, start barbecue fire (see "Barbecuing Using Direct Heat," page 84). Place skewers on grill 4 to 6 inches above a solid bed of glowing coals. Or place about 4 inches below heat on a rack in a broiler pan (see "How to Broil Meat," right). Cook, turning as needed to brown all sides, until meat is done to your liking when slashed (about 8 minutes *total* for medium). Pass sauce at the table. Makes 6 servings.

Teriyaki Beef

Japan

A favorite with barbecue cooks everywhere, Japan's famous *teriyaki* sauce adds magical flavor to beef, chicken, pork—even seafood.

> 1 **to 1½ pounds lean boneless beef steak (sirloin or flank)**
> **Teriyaki sauce (recipe follows)**

HOW TO BROIL MEAT

First check the manufacturer's operational instructions for your broiler. Then choose a large, shallow pan with a rack; place the meat on the rack. Position the pan below the heat source in your broiler, adjusting the pan (or the oven rack on which the pan is resting) until the top of the meat is the recommended distance below the heat source.

Remove the meat from the broiler, leaving the pan and rack inside. Preheat the broiler for 5 to 7 minutes. Meanwhile, if the meat has a border of fat, slash through the fat to the lean meat at 1-inch intervals to prevent curling. Remove the pan from the broiler and lightly grease the hot rack.

Place the meat on the rack and broil, turning as needed, for the time specified in the recipe or until it's done to your liking when slashed in the thickest portion.

Trim and discard excess fat from beef, then cut diagonally across the grain into ¼-inch-thick slices. Place meat in a bowl.

Stir together teriyaki sauce; pour over meat. Let stand at room temperature for about 1 hour.

About 35 minutes before cooking, start barbecue fire (see "Barbecuing Using Direct Heat," page 84). Lift meat slices from marinade and drain briefly, reserving marinade. Place slices on grill 3 to 4 inches above a solid bed of glowing coals. Or place 2 to 3 inches below heat on a rack in a broiler pan (see "How to Broil Meat," above). Cook, turning and basting with marinade, until browned on all sides and done to your liking when slashed (1 to 2 minutes per side for medium-rare). Makes 4 to 6 servings.

Teriyaki sauce. In a 1-cup glass measure, stir together ⅓ cup **soy sauce,** 2 tablespoons *each* **sugar** and **dry sherry,** ¾ teaspoon grated **fresh ginger,** and 2 cloves **garlic,** minced or pressed.

Preparing Ripple-skewered Steak (Recipe on facing page)

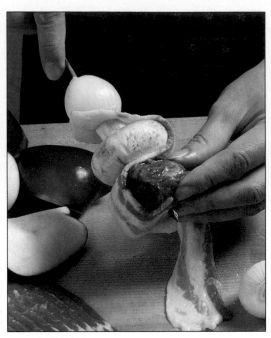

1 Assemble all ingredients, ready for threading on long metal skewers: apple quarters, bacon strips, mushrooms, onions, and marinated beef cubes.

2 Thread 1 onion on skewer; then pierce one end of a bacon strip. Add a mushroom; lap bacon over and pierce it again. Thread on beef, then lap bacon over and pierce it.

3 Add apple, then more beef, weaving bacon in and out. Secure bacon end; slide all up on skewer. Repeat with another bacon strip, 1 mushroom, 1 apple quarter, and 2 beef cubes; end with an onion.

4 Arrange skewers on grill 4 to 6 inches above a solid bed of medium-glowing coals. Cook, basting and turning as needed, until bacon is crisp and beef is done to your liking when slashed.

5 Richly browned, hearty-skewers take the spotlight at a summer barbecue. Sharing the applause: corn on the cob and juicy watermelon.

.Open grill & broiling: Direct heat

Ripple-skewered Steak

United States   (Pictured on facing page)

Shish kebab is a Turkish phrase (from *shish* "sword" plus *kebab* "roasted meat")—but the technique of cooking skewered foods over a fire is practiced worldwide. Here's one irresistible example from the United States.

    1½ to 2 pounds tender boneless beef steak
        (from the rib, loin, or fillet), cut about
        1½ inches thick
        Red wine marinade (recipe follows)
    8   small white boiling onions
    8   strips bacon
    8   large mushrooms
    2   large Red Delicious apples, cored and
        quartered

Cut meat into 16 cubes, each about 1½ inches on each side. Stir together red wine marinade; pour over meat. Cover and refrigerate, stirring several times, for at least 4 hours or until next day.

Lift meat from marinade, reserving marinade. Then assemble 4 skewers. For each one, run tip of a long metal skewer through 1 onion, then through one end of a bacon strip. Pierce 1 mushroom through stem; lap bacon over it and pierce bacon. Thread on 1 beef cube; lap bacon over and pierce it. Add 1 apple quarter and 1 more beef cube, lapping bacon over each; secure bacon end on skewer. Starting with another bacon strip, repeat threading and "rippling" with 1 more mushroom, another beef cube, an apple quarter, and a final beef cube. Secure bacon end; add 1 more onion.

About 35 minutes before cooking, start barbecue fire (see "Barbecuing Using Direct Heat," page 84). Place skewers on grill 4 to 6 inches above a solid bed of medium-glowing coals. Cook, turning and basting with marinade, until bacon is crisp and beef is done to your liking when slashed (about 15 minutes for medium-rare). Makes 4 servings.

Red wine marinade. In a 2-cup glass measure, stir together ¾ cup **dry red wine,** ½ cup **salad oil,** 1 tablespoon each minced **onion** and **Worcestershire,** ⅓ cup **catsup,** 1 teaspoon **dry rosemary,** ¼ teaspoon **pepper,** and 6 drops **liquid hot pepper seasoning.**

Grilled Pork

Indonesia

Sate babi—marinated morsels of pork, skewered and grilled—are a typical part of the sumptuous Indonesian buffet called *rijsttafel* ("rice table").

        Peanut Sauce (page 143)
    1   pound lean boneless pork butt
        Soy marinade (recipe follows)

Prepare Peanut Sauce; cover and set aside.

Cut pork into ¼ by 1 by 2-inch strips; place in a small bowl. Prepare soy marinade and pour over meat; mix well. Cover and refrigerate for about 1 hour, stirring several times.

Lift meat from marinade and drain briefly; reserve marinade. Then thread meat, 2 or 3 strips to a bamboo skewer, weaving skewer in and out "ripple" fashion to make meat strips lie flat.

About 35 minutes before cooking, start barbecue fire (see "Barbecuing Using Direct Heat," page 84). Place skewers on grill 4 to 6 inches above a solid bed of glowing coals. Or place 2 to 3 inches below heat on a rack in a broiler pan (see "How to Broil Meat," page 85). Cook, turning and basting with marinade, until browned on all sides and no longer pink in center when slashed (10 to 12 minutes *total*).

Arrange skewers on a platter with sauce for dipping. Makes about 4 servings.

Soy marinade. In a small bowl, stir together 2 tablespoons each **sugar, salad oil,** and **soy sauce;** 1 tablespoon **lemon juice;** ½ small **onion,** minced; 2 cloves **garlic,** minced or pressed; and ⅛ teaspoon **crushed red pepper.**

HOW TO TOAST ALMONDS

Brief toasting in the oven enhances the rich, nutty flavor of almonds. Spread slivered, sliced, or whole blanched nuts in a shallow baking pan; bake in a 350° oven, uncovered, for 8 to 10 minutes or until golden. Stir nuts (or shake pan) often.

Stir-frying & pan-frying

For dinners in a hurry, choose stir-frying or pan-frying—two classic range-top techniques you can use to turn out hearty meals in just minutes.

To make a stir-fry, you cook several foods in sequence, all in the same pan. Since cooking goes quickly, have everything ready for the pan before you begin. Pan-frying typically uses larger pieces of food than stir-frying—but this method, too, requires close attention. Tend the meat carefully to assure even cooking without overcooking.

Stir-fried and pan-fried meats taste best when served right after cooking, so choose accompaniments that don't require last-minute attention.

Picadillo

Cuba

Cuba's *picadillo* ("minced meat") includes such favorite Latin ingredients as olives, raisins, and green pepper.

> 1 **pound lean ground beef**
> 1½ **tablespoons white (distilled) vinegar**
> 1 **clove garlic, minced or pressed**
> 1 **teaspoon ground cumin**
> 2 **tablespoons salad oil**
> 1 **small onion, chopped**
> 1 **small green pepper, seeded and cut into strips**
> 1 **small can (8 oz.) tomato sauce**
> ½ **cup water**
> ½ **teaspoon cracked bay leaves**
> 6 **pimento-stuffed green olives, sliced**
> 1 **tablespoon raisins**
> **Salt and pepper**
> 1 **can (4 oz.) shoestring potatoes (or use hot cooked rice)**

In a bowl, combine beef, vinegar, garlic, and cumin; mix well and let stand for 15 minutes.

Heat 1 tablespoon of the oil in a wide frying pan over medium-high heat. Add meat mixture; cook, stirring often, until meat is browned and liquid has evaporated. Lift out and set aside.

Heat remaining 1 tablespoon oil in pan over medium heat; add onion and green pepper and cook until onion is soft. Stir in tomato sauce, water, bay leaves, olives, and raisins. Bring to a boil; reduce heat and simmer, uncovered, until slightly reduced (about 5 minutes). Add meat mixture and cook until heated through (about 2 more minutes). Season to taste with salt and pepper. Mound on a rimmed platter; surround with potatoes (or serve over rice). Makes 4 servings.

Ground Steak with Onions

Denmark

A topping of delicate, creamy sauce and mellow golden onions adds a little glamor—and a lot of good flavor—to Danish *hakkebøf*.

> 4 **tablespoons butter or margarine**
> 4 **medium-size onions, thinly sliced**
> **Salt and white pepper**
> 1½ **pounds lean ground beef**
> **All-purpose flour**
> 1 **tablespoon salad oil**
> 1 **tablespoon butter or margarine**
> ½ **cup whipping cream**
> ½ **teaspoon Worcestershire**
> **Chopped parsley**

Melt the 4 tablespoons butter in a wide frying pan over medium heat; add onions and cook, stirring often, until soft and golden (20 to 25 minutes). Season to taste with salt and pepper; keep warm.

Meanwhile, shape beef into 6 patties, each ½ to ¾ inch thick. Sprinkle lightly with salt and pepper, then coat with flour; shake off excess.

Heat oil and the 1 tablespoon butter in a wide frying pan over medium-high heat. When fat is hot, add patties and cook until well browned on both sides and done to your liking when slashed (8 to 10 minutes *total* for medium).

Transfer patties to a platter. Discard excess fat from pan drippings; add cream and Worcestershire and cook, stirring to loosen browned bits, until sauce is bubbly and slightly thickened.

Spoon onions over meat, then pour sauce over all and sprinkle with parsley. Makes 6 servings.

Pork with Pea Pods

China

Hoisin sauce adds spicy flavor to this stir-fry of pork and crisp snow peas (also called Chinese pea pods). Use purchased hoisin (available in Asian markets and well-stocked supermarkets) or try the simple substitute on page 143.

1 pound lean boneless pork
1 tablespoon *each* catsup, dry sherry, cornstarch, and hoisin sauce
1 tablespoon sesame oil, or 1 tablespoon sesame seeds, toasted (page 99) and crushed
1 teaspoon Worcestershire
1 clove garlic, minced or pressed
6 tablespoons salad oil
2 tablespoons soy sauce
¾ pound snow peas, ends and strings removed
1 tablespoon water
1 small onion, cut into thin slivers
1 teaspoon sugar

Trim and discard fat from pork; cut meat into 1-inch chunks. With a flat-surfaced mallet, pound meat to a thickness of ¼ inch. In a bowl, stir together catsup, sherry, cornstarch, hoisin, sesame oil, Worcestershire, garlic, 2 tablespoons of the salad oil, and 1 tablespoon of the soy. Add pork and mix well; cover and refrigerate, stirring several times, for at least 2 hours or until next day.

Heat a wok or wide frying pan over high heat. When pan is hot, add 2 tablespoons of the salad oil, peas, then water; stir-fry until peas are tender-crisp to bite (2 to 3 minutes). Pour into a serving dish.

Add remaining 2 tablespoons salad oil to pan. When oil is hot, add pork mixture and stir-fry until meat is no longer pink when slashed (3 to 4 minutes). Add onion, remaining 1 tablespoon soy, and sugar; stir-fry for 1 more minute. Serve over peas. Makes 4 or 5 servings.

Veal with Peppers

Italy

Here, juicy pepper strips mingle with tender veal; on page 95, you'll find them combined with pork in a colorful Hungarian entrée.

½ pound sliced boneless veal, cut into 3-inch squares
All-purpose flour
About 1 tablespoon salad oil
About 1 tablespoon butter or margarine
3 Italian frying peppers or 1 large green or red bell pepper, seeded and cut into ½-inch strips
½ teaspoon oregano leaves
1 clove garlic, minced or pressed
½ cup dry white wine
Salt and pepper

Veal should be about ³⁄₁₆ inch thick; if necessary, pound between sheets of plastic wrap to achieve the proper thickness. Coat veal with flour, then shake off excess and set meat aside.

Heat 1 tablespoon *each* of the oil and butter in a wide frying pan over medium heat. Add peppers, oregano, and garlic; cook, stirring, until peppers are soft (about 5 minutes). With a slotted spoon, transfer peppers to a serving dish.

Increase heat to medium-high; add veal and more oil and butter, if needed, to prevent sticking. When edges of veal turn white (about 1 minute), turn pieces over and cook until lightly browned.

Place veal in serving dish with peppers. Add wine to pan and boil, scraping to loosen browned bits, until liquid is reduced by about half. Season to taste with salt and pepper, then pour over peppers and veal. Makes 2 servings.

Carpetbagger Steaks

Australia

This hearty dinner combines two Australian favorites—fine beef and juicy local oysters.

4 beef tenderloin fillets, *each* 2 inches thick
7 tablespoons butter or margarine
2 tablespoons lemon juice
1 tablespoon minced parsley
4 shucked oysters, *each* 2 to 3 inches long
Salt and pepper
1 tablespoon salad oil

In one side of each fillet, cut a pocket about 2 inches deep and 2½ to 3 inches long. *Do not cut completely through fillet.*

Melt 5 tablespoons of the butter in a small pan over low heat; stir in lemon juice and parsley. Spoon about 1 teaspoon of the butter mixture into each pocket; keep remaining mixture warm. Sprinkle oysters with salt and pepper, then insert one in each fillet. Fasten pockets with small skewers; make sure oysters are completely enclosed.

Heat oil and remaining 2 tablespoons butter in a wide frying pan over medium-high heat. Sprinkle both sides of each fillet with pepper, then place in pan and cook, turning with tongs as needed, until well browned and done to your liking when slashed (10 to 12 minutes *total* for rare).

Lift fillets to a warm platter; drizzle reserved butter mixture over tops. Makes 4 servings.

Braising: Top of the range

How do you make tough meat tender? Worldwide, one good answer is *braising*. Cooks in many nations use this technique to render sinewy cuts of meat deliciously tender and juicy.

For range-top braising, you begin by browning meat in a small amount of fat. Then you pour in liquid, cover the cooking pan tightly, and simmer the meat slowly and gently. (You can braise meats in the oven, too—see page 93.)

Braised Flank Steak

Colombia

In *sobrebarriga*, a richly seasoned marinade and long, slow braising work tenderizing magic.

    1 large flank steak (1½ to 2 lbs.)
       Salt and pepper
    1 cup coarsely chopped onion
    ¾ cup diced celery
    2 large cloves garlic, minced or pressed
    2 small tomatoes, peeled and chopped
    2 tablespoons chopped parsley
    1 can (12 oz.) beer or 1½ cups water
    2 cups regular-strength beef broth
    1 teaspoon ground cumin
    3 tablespoons salad oil

Trim and discard excess fat from steak, then sprinkle both sides with salt and pepper. Roll up meat with the grain, then tie tightly (see photo 3, facing page) and place in a 9 by 13-inch baking pan. Combine ½ cup of the onion with celery, garlic, tomatoes, parsley, beer, broth, and cumin; pour over meat. Cover and refrigerate for at least 4 hours or until next day, turning occasionally.

Lift meat from marinade and pat dry. Heat 2 tablespoons of the oil in a wide, deep kettle over medium heat; add meat and cook, turning, until well browned on all sides. Pour in marinade. Bring to a boil over medium-high heat; cover, reduce heat, and simmer, turning meat over several times, until tender when pierced (2 to 2½ hours).

About 20 minutes before serving, heat remaining 1 tablespoon oil in a small frying pan over medium heat; add remaining ½ cup onion and cook until soft and golden. Then lift meat to a carving board and spoon onions over top. Keep warm. Skim and discard fat from cooking broth; boil over high heat, uncovered, until slightly reduced. Pass at the table. Makes about 6 servings.

Rolled Flank Steak

Italy   (Pictured on facing page)

Neapolitan cooks take deserved pride in their "gravy"—a robust, garlicky tomato sauce. Here, a rolled flank steak simmers in the rich sauce to make a splendid dish called *braciola*.

    1 large flank steak (1½ to 2 lbs.)
    2 tablespoons grated Parmesan cheese
    5 strips bacon
    4 slices provolone cheese
    6 thin slices salami
    3 hard-cooked eggs
    1 tablespoon olive oil or salad oil
       Italian gravy (recipe follows)
       Hot cooked spaghetti

Trim and discard excess fat from steak. Then butterfly steak: Split it horizontally, leaving one long edge attached. Open steak out and place between sheets of plastic wrap; pound with a flat-surfaced mallet until evenly flattened, especially at center ridge. Discard top piece of plastic. Sprinkle meat evenly with Parmesan.

Render excess fat from bacon by partially cooking it in a wide frying pan over medium heat; it should still be limp. Arrange bacon strips across steak; top with provolone, then with salami. Place eggs, end to end, on salami. Using plastic wrap to help you lift, tightly roll up meat to enclose filling. Tie roll lengthwise, tucking in ends; then tie crosswise at 2-inch intervals.

Heat oil in a wide, deep kettle over medium heat; add meat and cook, turning, until well browned on all sides. Prepare Italian gravy; spoon over meat. Bring to a boil over medium-high heat. Cover, reduce heat, and simmer, turning meat over occasionally, until very tender when pierced (2½ hours).

Lift out meat; skim and discard fat from gravy. Cut meat crosswise into ½-inch slices; arrange around spaghetti on a rimmed platter. Pass gravy at the table. Makes about 6 servings.

Italian gravy. Combine 1 can (28 oz.) **tomato purée;** 1 clove **garlic,** minced or pressed; ¼ cup chopped **parsley;** ¼ pound **mushrooms,** sliced; ⅓ cup **dry red wine;** 1 tablespoon **dry basil;** 1½ teaspoons **oregano leaves;** ½ teaspoon *each* **salt** and **sugar;** ¼ teaspoon **pepper;** and ¾ cup **water.**

Preparing a Rolled Flank Steak (Recipe on facing page)

1 Begin by butterflying steak: Split it horizontally almost all the way through, leaving one long edge attached. Then open up meat, place between sheets of plastic wrap, and pound to an even thickness.

2 Arrange filling of bacon, cheese, salami, and hard-cooked eggs on steak. Using plastic wrap to help you lift, tightly roll up meat to enclose filling completely.

3 Tie string lengthwise around stuffed meat roll, tucking in ends of roll. Then tie roll crosswise at intervals of about 2 inches.

4 Stir together mushroom-laden Italian gravy; spoon over browned beef roll, then cover and simmer until meat is very tender when pierced.

5 Each slice of cooked beef reveals tempting filling of salami, egg, and cheese. Arrange slices on a platter around spaghetti; pass Italian gravy to spoon over all.

...Braising: Top of the range

Sauerbraten

Germany

In the days before refrigeration, meats were often preserved by a soak in a pickling "bath." German *Sauerbraten* is probably the best known of these pickled meats; our herb-fragrant version features a rich sour cream gravy.

> Wine vinegar marinade (recipe follows)
> 1 boneless beef rump roast (about 6 lbs.)
> 1 strip bacon, diced
> 1 large carrot, diced
> 1 medium-size onion, sliced
> 1 can (10½ oz.) condensed beef broth
> Sautéed Apples (page 140)
> 3 tablespoons cornstarch
> 2 tablespoons water
> ½ pint (1 cup) sour cream

In a large bowl or pan, stir together wine vinegar marinade; add beef and turn over once. Cover and refrigerate for 3 to 4 days, turn meat daily.

Remove meat from marinade and pat dry. Pour marinade through a wire strainer; reserve ½ cup of liquid and discard remainder. Cook bacon in a 6-quart kettle over medium heat until drippings form. Add meat and cook, turning, until well browned on all sides. Add carrot, onion, broth, and reserved marinade. Bring to a boil; then cover, reduce heat, and simmer until meat is tender when pierced (2½ to 3 hours). Lift meat to a platter and keep warm. Meanwhile, prepare Sautéed Apples; cover and keep warm.

Pour cooking juices through a wire strainer; discard residue. Return juices to kettle and bring to a boil over high heat. In a small bowl, stir together cornstarch and water; then add sour cream, stirring until smooth. Stir mixture into juices and cook, stirring, until thickened. Pour into a bowl.

Thinly slice meat across the grain and surround with Sautéed Apples. Pass gravy at the table. Makes about 12 servings.

Wine vinegar marinade. Combine 1½ cups **white wine vinegar;** 3 cups **water;** ¼ teaspoon *each* **pepper, dry rosemary, marjoram leaves, dry basil,** and **oregano leaves;** 1 **bay leaf;** 6 **whole cloves;** and 2 teaspoons **salt.** Then add 1 **carrot,** diced; 1 stalk **celery,** cut up; and 1 large **onion,** sliced.

Osso Buco

Italy

Osso buco means "hollow bones"—but the veal shanks used in this classic Italian dish are scarcely hollow. Each meaty piece contains a tasty treasure of marrow to scoop out with a marrow spoon or knife tip.

> 7 to 8 pounds meaty veal shanks, cut through bone into 2-inch-thick slices
> Salt
> All-purpose flour
> ½ cup (¼ lb.) butter or margarine
> 1½ cups dry white wine
> 1 cup regular-strength chicken broth
> ½ cup chopped parsley
> 1½ tablespoons grated lemon peel
> 1 clove garlic, minced or pressed

Sprinkle veal with salt, then roll in flour; shake off excess. Melt butter in a 6 to 8-quart kettle over medium heat. Add some of the veal and cook, turning, until browned on all sides; remove and set aside. Repeat until meat is browned. Add wine and broth to kettle, then return meat; bring to a boil. Cover, reduce heat, and simmer until meat is very tender when pierced and pulls easily from bones (1½ to 2 hours).

Combine parsley, lemon peel, and garlic; set aside. With a slotted spoon, transfer meat to a warm platter; keep warm. Skim and discard fat from sauce; bring to a boil over high heat, stirring to loosen browned bits. Add half the parsley mixture to sauce; simmer just until parsley is wilted. Pour sauce over meat and garnish with remaining parsley mixture. Makes 6 to 8 servings.

CHOPPING & STORING PARSLEY

Having a supply of chopped fresh parsley on hand can be a real timesaver at mealtime. For perfectly chopped parsley, discard the tough stems, then wash and thoroughly dry the feathery sprigs (wet parsley turns to mush). Using a sharp knife or a food processor, chop 1 to 2 cups of parsley at a time. Store chopped parsley in a tightly covered jar in the refrigerator; use within a week.

Braising: In the oven

Oven braising is extremely easy. It's simpler than range-top braising, since you don't need to brown the meat. You just place it in an ovenproof casserole or kettle, add liquid and seasonings, and pop it into the oven. After baking (usually at a high temperature) for a few hours, the meat will be tender and juicy—and every bit as tasty as meat braised by the conventional range-top method.

Baked Lamb Shanks

Greece

Greek cooks serve lamb many ways—*moussaka* (page 172) is one example. Here's another lamb specialty: meaty shanks baked in a pungent tomato-herb sauce, topped off with lemon peel, parsley, and tangy feta cheese. Crusty rolls and hot buttered broccoli or green beans make appropriate accompaniments.

    4   meaty lamb shanks (¾ to 1 lb. *each*)
        Pepper
    1   large onion, thinly sliced
    1   medium-size green pepper, seeded and cut
        into thin strips
    1   small can (8 oz.) tomato sauce
    1   clove garlic, minced or pressed
    ⅓   cup dry white wine
    ¼   teaspoon *each* salt, sugar, ground cinnamon,
        and dry rosemary
    ½   teaspoon oregano leaves
    1   teaspoon grated lemon peel
    1   tablespoon chopped parsley
        Crumbled feta cheese (optional)

Sprinkle lamb with pepper; then place in a 4-quart casserole along with onion and green pepper.

In a small bowl, combine tomato sauce, garlic, wine, salt, sugar, cinnamon, rosemary, and oregano; pour over lamb. Cover and bake in a 400° oven for about 2¼ hours or until meat is very tender when pierced.

Transfer meat to a rimmed platter and keep warm. Skim and discard fat from cooking liquid; pour over meat. Garnish with lemon peel and parsley; sprinkle with cheese, if desired. Makes 4 servings.

Cinnamon-spiced Lamb with Apricots

Morocco

This cinnamon-spiked stew of lamb and apricots illustrates the North African fondness for combinations of meat, fruit, and sweet spices—a blend of flavors that's also characteristic of Middle Eastern and some European cooking.

    3   pounds boneless lamb stew meat, cut into
        1½-inch pieces
    ⅓   cup honey
    1   large onion, chopped
    3   large cloves garlic, minced or pressed
    2   cinnamon sticks (*each* 3 inches long)
    2   tablespoons lemon juice
    2   teaspoons turmeric
    2   tablespoons water
    1   teaspoon cornstarch
    1   package (6 oz.) moist pack dried apricots
        Salt
        Hot cooked rice

Combine lamb, honey, onion, garlic, cinnamon sticks, lemon juice, and turmeric in a 5-quart kettle; cover tightly. Bake in a 350° oven, stirring occasionally, for about 2 hours or until lamb is very tender when pierced.

Remove kettle from oven. Blend water with cornstarch; pour into kettle, then add apricots. Cook over medium-high heat, stirring, until sauce boils (about 3 minutes). Season to taste with salt. Serve with rice. Makes 6 to 8 servings.

STABILIZING SOUR CREAM

Smooth, rich sour cream sauces and gravies are popular from Scandinavia through eastern and central Europe. Traditionally, these sauces have had one drawback: Excessive heat can break down the sour cream, causing the sauce to curdle. But you needn't worry about curdling if you first stabilize the sour cream by stirring cornstarch or all-purpose flour into it—a minimum of 1 teaspoon to each cup of sour cream. With a wire whisk, mix this amended sour cream into the hot cooking liquid; then cook over low heat, stirring, until sauce is bubbly and thickened.

Making Pork with Sautéed Peppers (Recipe on facing page)

1 Cut country-style spareribs (butterflied pork loin end) between ribs into meaty pieces. Then finely chop onions.

2 Place chopped onions in a 3 to 4-quart casserole. Rub seasonings over pork pieces; arrange pork atop onions. Add broth and lemon juice; cover and bake.

3 While pork bakes, prepare pepper sauté. First cook onions until soft; then add green peppers and cook for 1 minute. Add red peppers; cook for 2 more minutes. Stir in tomato and paprika.

4 Add mixture of cornstarch and sour cream to cooking liquid and stir until bubbly and thickened. Cornstarch stabilizes the sour cream, giving you a smooth sauce that won't separate.

5 Arrange a bed of hot, buttered noodles on a serving plate, if desired; place meat and colorful sautéed peppers on top. Pass creamy sauce at the table.

..Braising: In the oven

Pork with Sautéed Peppers

Hungary   (Pictured on facing page)

To serve Hungarian style—and catch every last bit of the sprightly sauce—spoon this stew over hot buttered noodles.

    About 3½ pounds country-style spareribs
2 medium-size onions, finely chopped
2 teaspoons sweet Hungarian paprika or regular paprika
1 teaspoon dry mustard
¼ teaspoon caraway seeds
⅛ teaspoon pepper
1 can (14½ oz.) regular-strength chicken broth or 1¾ cups homemade chicken broth (page 33)
1 tablespoon lemon juice
    Pepper sauté (recipe follows)
1 tablespoon cornstarch
¾ cup sour cream

Trim and discard excess fat from pork, then cut between ribs into meaty pieces (remove blade bone first, if necessary). Place onions in a 3 to 4-quart casserole. Combine paprika, mustard, caraway seeds, and pepper; rub over all sides of meat. Arrange meat on top of onions, then pour in broth and lemon juice. Cover and bake in a 400° oven for 1¼ to 1½ hours or until meat is tender when pierced.

About 30 minutes before pork is done, prepare pepper sauté. Lift out meat; mound on a platter. Surround with peppers; keep warm.

Skim and discard fat from cooking broth. Blend cornstarch and sour cream until smooth, then stir into broth and cook over medium-high heat, stirring, until bubbly and thickened. Pass sauce at the table. Makes 4 to 6 servings.

Pepper sauté. Seed 1 to 1½ pounds **green or red bell peppers** (or a combination); then cut into ¼ to ½-inch strips. Melt 2 tablespoons **butter** or margarine in a wide frying pan over medium heat; add 1 medium-size **onion,** chopped, and cook until soft. Add peppers; cook, stirring, for 3 minutes if using green peppers, 2 minutes if using red peppers. If using both types, cook green peppers for 1 minute, then add red ones and cook for 2 more minutes. Stir in 1 large **tomato,** peeled and chopped, and 2 teaspoons **sweet Hungarian paprika** or regular paprika. Cook, uncovered, stirring often, until almost all juices have evaporated (about 5 minutes). Season to taste with **salt;** keep warm.

SWEDISH-STYLE PORK RIBS

Follow directions for **Pork with Sautéed Peppers,** but omit paprika, dry mustard, and caraway seeds. Instead, use ½ teaspoon **dill weed** and ¼ teaspoon **thyme leaves.** Substitute **cooked whole thin-skinned potatoes** for pepper sauté. Surround meat with potatoes; sprinkle with **dill weed.**

Pickled Pork

Norway

Like *Sauerbraten* (page 92), Norwegian pickled pork must marinate before cooking. Gjetost cheese and currant jelly lend Nordic flavors.

1 lean boneless pork shoulder or butt (about 5 lbs.), rolled and tied
    White wine marinade (recipe follows)
1 can (14½ oz.) regular-strength beef broth or 1¾ cups homemade beef broth (page 33)
1 tablespoon cornstarch
½ cup sour cream
2 tablespoons red currant jelly
¼ cup shredded gjetost cheese
2 tablespoons butter or margarine
1 pound small mushrooms

Place pork in a large bowl. Prepare marinade; pour over meat. Cover and refrigerate for 3 to 4 days, turning daily. Place meat in a 5-quart kettle. Add 1 cup marinade (discard remaining marinade), cover, and bake in a 400° oven for 2½ to 3 hours or until a meat thermometer registers 170°. Lift meat to a platter.

Skim and discard fat from pan juices; strain juices into a small pan. Add broth. Stir together cornstarch and sour cream until smooth; stir into broth mixture and cook over medium heat, stirring, until thickened. Add jelly and cheese and cook, stirring, just until smooth; keep warm.

Melt butter in a wide frying pan over medium heat; add mushrooms and cook until lightly browned, then spoon around meat. Pass gravy at the table. Makes about 10 servings.

White wine marinade. Combine 1 bottle (750 ml) **dry white wine,** ¾ cup **white wine vinegar,** 2 teaspoons **salt,** 1 tablespoon **sugar,** 1 teaspoon **thyme leaves,** 1 **bay leaf,** 6 each **whole cloves** and **whole allspice,** 2 tablespoons **olive oil** or salad oil, and 1 medium-size **onion,** sliced.

One-pot meals

In almost every country, a few classic one-pot recipes have been handed down from one generation of cooks to the next. It's no wonder these dishes have been so popular for so long; they're both simple and delicious.

Worldwide, basic ingredients are the same: meat, vegetables, and broth. Cooking technique varies, though. Japan's Shabu Shabu is prepared at the table; diners cook their own servings in bubbling broth. In other lands, one-pot meals simmer atop the range, then come to the table as stews—as in France's Lamb Ragoût.

Harvest Ham & Cabbage

Switzerland

It may remind you of St. Patrick's Day corned beef and cabbage—but this boiled dinner is Swiss, and it celebrates the autumn harvest season.

  Harvest Mustard Sauce (page 143)
 1 picnic ham (smoked pork shoulder, 6 to 7 lbs.)
 2 large onions, thinly sliced
 1½ pounds kielbasa (Polish sausage), cut into 1½-inch slices
 1 bay leaf
 6 each whole black peppers and whole allspice
 2 cups dry white wine
 10 to 12 small red thin-skinned potatoes
 1 large head cabbage (about 2½ lbs.), cut into 10 to 12 wedges
  Chopped parsley
  Prepared horseradish

Prepare Harvest Mustard Sauce.

Rinse ham; place in a 6 to 8-quart kettle. Cover with water and bring to a boil over high heat, then drain. Add onions, sausage, bay leaf, peppers, allspice, and wine. Bring to a boil; cover, reduce heat, and simmer until ham is very tender when pierced (about 3½ hours). Lift out ham and set aside.

Add potatoes and cabbage to kettle. Cover and simmer until vegetables are tender when pierced (about 25 minutes).

Meanwhile, discard rind, bone, and excess fat from ham. Separate meat into large chunks and keep warm. To serve, lift vegetables and sausage from kettle with a slotted spoon; arrange on a large rimmed platter along with ham. Sprinkle parsley over all. Pass mustard sauce and horseradish at the table. Makes 10 to 12 servings.

Beef Brisket & Sweet Potatoes

Jewish heritage

This hearty combination of beef, sweet potatoes, and prunes belongs to the class of Jewish dishes called *tzimmes*—a name that applies to almost any selection of meats, vegetables, or fruits that cook together until their juices merge into one delicious blend.

 1 fresh beef brisket (3 to 4 lbs.)
 3 medium-size onions, thinly sliced
 1 lemon, thinly sliced
 2 cans (10½ oz. each) condensed beef broth
 2 tablespoons honey
 1 tablespoon white wine vinegar
 ¼ teaspoon ground cloves
 ½ teaspoon ground cinnamon
 6 to 8 large carrots, cut into 2-inch chunks
 3 medium-size sweet potatoes, peeled and quartered
 1 package (12 oz.) pitted prunes
 2 tablespoons each cornstarch and water
  Salt and pepper

Place beef in a large roasting pan. Bake in a 500° oven, uncovered, for 30 minutes (turn after 15 minutes). Remove pan from oven. Decrease oven temperature to 300°.

Lift up meat and arrange onions and half the lemon slices on pan bottom; place meat on top, then pour beef broth into pan. Cover and bake for 1½ to 2 hours or until meat is barely tender when pierced.

Combine honey, vinegar, cloves, and cinnamon; stir into pan juices. Arrange carrots, potatoes, and prunes around meat. Cover and bake for 2 more hours or until meat is very tender when pierced.

With a slotted spoon, lift meat, vegetables, and prunes to a rimmed platter. Skim and discard fat from pan juices. Combine cornstarch and water, stir into juices, and cook, stirring, until bubbly and thickened; season to taste with salt and pepper. Garnish meat with remaining lemon slices; pass gravy at the table to spoon over individual portions. Makes 6 to 8 servings.

Short Ribs with Rice

Korea

Sesame, nippy fresh ginger, and garlic flavor meaty braised short ribs (*kalbi chim*).

- 2 **tablespoons sesame seeds, toasted (page 99)**
- 4 **pounds lean beef short ribs, cut into 2 to 3-inch lengths**
- ⅓ **cup soy sauce**
- 3 **tablespoons sugar**
- 2 **teaspoons minced garlic**
- 3 **thin slices fresh ginger**
- 3 **cups water**
- 2 **large carrots, cut into ¼-inch slices**
- 1 **tablespoon sesame oil (optional)**
  Thinly sliced green onions (including tops)
  Hot cooked rice

Coarsely crush sesame seeds and set aside.

Trim and discard excess fat from ribs, then place them in a 5 to 6-quart kettle. Add sesame seeds, soy, sugar, garlic, ginger, and water. Bring to a boil over high heat; cover, reduce heat, and simmer, turning ribs occasionally, until meat is very tender when pierced (2½ to 3 hours).

Add carrots and simmer until tender when pierced (15 to 20 minutes). Skim and discard fat. Add sesame oil, if desired. Ladle ribs, broth, and carrots into wide soup plates; garnish with onions and accompany with rice. Makes 4 to 6 servings.

Sausage & Sauerkraut Stew

Poland

A centuries-old classic, vigorous *bigos* helps fend off the chill during long, cold Polish winters.

- 4 **tablespoons butter or margarine**
- 1 **large onion, chopped**
- ¼ **pound mushrooms, sliced**
- ¾ **pound kielbasa (Polish sausage), cut into ¼-inch slices**
- 1 **can (1 lb.) sauerkraut, rinsed and drained well**
- 2½ **cups water**
- 1½ **to 2 pounds ham hocks**
- 4 **quarts shredded cabbage**
- 2 **tart apples, peeled, cored, and thickly sliced**
- 10 **to 12 pitted prunes**
- 6 **small red thin-skinned potatoes, each 1½ to 2 inches in diameter**

In a 6 to 8-quart kettle, combine butter, onion, mushrooms, and sausage. Cook over medium-high heat, stirring often, until onion is lightly browned. Remove from kettle; set aside.

Add sauerkraut, water, and ham hocks to kettle. Bring to a boil; then cover, reduce heat, and simmer for 1½ hours. Add sausage mixture and cabbage; cover and simmer until ham pulls easily from bones (about 45 minutes).

Remove from heat; lift out ham and let cool. Discard bones and fat; cut meat into bite-size pieces and return to kettle. Add apples, prunes, and potatoes; bring to a boil. Cover, reduce heat, and simmer until potatoes are tender when pierced (20 to 30 minutes). Makes 6 servings.

Provincial Lamb Ragoût

France

Raisins, almonds, and fragrant nutmeg add an exotic Middle Eastern accent to this simple stew.

- 2 **tablespoons salad oil**
- 2½ **pounds boneless lamb shoulder, cut into 1-inch cubes**
- 2 **tablespoons butter or margarine**
- 2 **onions, chopped**
- 1 **cup long-grain white rice**
- ⅛ **teaspoon pepper**
- ½ **teaspoon ground nutmeg**
- ½ **cup golden raisins**
- 3 **large carrots, sliced**
- 1 **can (14½ oz.) regular-strength chicken broth or 1¾ cups homemade chicken broth (page 33)**
- 3 **tablespoons lemon juice**
  About ½ cup boiling water
  Salt
- ⅔ **cup sliced almonds, toasted (page 87)**

Heat oil in a 5-quart kettle over medium-high heat. Add lamb and cook until browned on all sides; lift out with a slotted spoon and set aside. Melt butter in kettle over medium heat; add onions and rice and cook, stirring often, until rice is opaque. Stir in pepper, nutmeg, raisins, carrots, broth, and lemon juice. Return meat to kettle. Bring to a boil; then cover, reduce heat, and simmer until lamb is tender when pierced (about 45 minutes); stir in boiling water, if needed, to keep rice moist). Season to taste with salt.

Spoon ragoût into a serving dish and heap almonds on top. Serve at once. Makes 6 servings.

...One-pot meals

Hot Pot Supper

Vietnam

Everybody's a chef at this cook-at-the-table meal from Vietnam.

> 1½ **to 2 pounds lean boneless beef steaks (sirloin or flank)**
> **Dipping sauce (recipe follows)**
> 8 **cups water**
> 4 **ounces thin rice noodles (rice sticks)**
> 1 **large cucumber**
> ½ **pound bean sprouts**
> 2 **large heads butter lettuce, separated into leaves**
> 1 **bunch fresh cilantro (coriander)**
> **Lemony broth (recipe follows)**

Freeze beef until firm (30 to 45 minutes). Trim and discard excess fat, then slice meat very thinly across the grain. Arrange on a platter. Prepare dipping sauce; set aside.

Pour water into a large kettle; bring to a boil over high heat. Add noodles and cook, uncovered, just until tender to bite (3 to 4 minutes). Drain, rinse under cold water, and drain again.

Peel cucumber, if desired. Cut in half lengthwise, then cut each half crosswise into thin slices. Arrange cucumber, bean sprouts, lettuce, and cilantro sprigs in bowls or on platters. (At this point, you may cover and refrigerate noodles, meat, and vegetables separately for up to 6 hours.)

Shortly before serving, prepare lemony broth. Pour steaming broth into an electric wok, an electric frying pan, or a fondue pot over an alcohol burner. Set noodles, meat, and vegetables on the table; provide a small bowl of dipping sauce at each place. Cook a few slices of meat at a time in broth, then top a lettuce leaf with noodles, cooked meat, and vegetables. Fold lettuce to form a packet; dip into sauce. Makes 4 to 6 servings.

Dipping sauce. In a bowl, stir together ¾ cup **soy sauce** or fish sauce; ½ cup **cider vinegar;** ⅔ cup **sugar;** 3 tablespoons **water;** ½ to 1 teaspoon **crushed red pepper;** and 2 cloves **garlic,** minced or pressed. Add ¾ cup finely shredded **carrot.**

Lemony broth. In a small pan combine ½ cup **cider vinegar,** ⅓ cup **sugar,** zest from 1 **lemon,** 3 quarter-size slices **fresh ginger,** 3 **chicken bouillon cubes,** and 4 cups **water.** Simmer over medium heat, covered, until hot (about 10 minutes).

Shabu Shabu

Japan   (Pictured on facing page)

Shabu shabu is a favorite Japanese way to warm up in blustery winter weather. It's easiest to lift cooked foods from the steaming broth if you use a slotted spoon or hot-pot strainer.

> 1½ **pounds lean boneless beef steak (sirloin or flank)**
> 4 **large carrots**
> ½ **head napa cabbage**
> 8 **ounces firm tofu (bean curd)**
> ½ **to ¾ pound spinach**
> 10 **to 12 large mushrooms, sliced**
> 6 **to 8 green onions (including tops), cut into 1 to 2-inch lengths**
> 3 **cans (14½ oz. each) regular-strength beef broth or 5½ cups homemade beef broth (page 33)**
> ¼ **cup soy sauce**
> 3 **tablespoons dry sherry**
> **Dipping sauce (recipe follows)**
> **Hot cooked rice**

Freeze beef until firm (30 to 45 minutes). Trim and discard excess fat; slice meat very thinly. Cut carrots diagonally into thin slices. Cut cabbage into shreds and tofu into small cubes. Discard tough spinach stems; rinse leaves well and pat dry. Arrange beef, carrots, cabbage, tofu, spinach, mushrooms, and onions in individual bowls or on a platter in separate rows. (At this point, you may cover and refrigerate for up to 6 hours.)

Combine broth, soy, and sherry in a 3-quart pan. Then prepare dipping sauce; pour into small individual bowls. Heat broth mixture until bubbly; pour into an electric wok, an electric frying pan, or a fondue pot over an alcohol burner. Cook small quantities of meat and vegetables briefly in broth, then lift out and dip into sauce. Serve individual bowls of rice; ladle broth into bowls for sipping after all food is cooked. Makes 4 servings.

Dipping sauce. Place ½ cup **sesame seeds** in a small, heavy, dry frying pan over medium heat. Toast, stirring often, until golden brown (about 2 minutes). Spoon seeds into a blender; add 6 tablespoons of the **cooking broth mixture,** 3 tablespoons **white wine vinegar,** 1 teaspoon **sugar,** and 2 tablespoons *each* **soy sauce** and **dry sherry.** Whirl until well blended. Pour through a wire strainer, pressing to extract liquid.

Cooking Shabu Shabu at the table (Recipe on facing page)

1 To make beef easier to slice, freeze it just until firm (30 to 45 minutes). Trim and discard excess fat, then cut meat across the grain into very thin slices.

2 For an attractive presentation, cut carrots on the diagonal. Slice them very thinly so they'll cook quickly in the bubbling broth.

3 To toast sesame seeds, pour them into a heavy, dry frying pan over medium heat. Toast, stirring seeds or shaking pan often, until seeds are golden (about 2 minutes).

4 It's fun to cook at the table! Add your choice of meat and colorful vegetables to bubbling broth and cook briefly—then season with sauce and enjoy.

POULTRY

"Poultry is for cookery what canvas is for paint... It is served to us boiled, roasted, hot or cold, whole or in portions, with or without sauce, and always with equal success." These words, written over 150 years ago by the French food philosopher Brillat-Savarin, express something that cooks have always known. For culinary artistry and delicious taste, there is no better choice than poultry.

Chicken is still a worldwide favorite, of course, but birds of a different feather are increasing in popularity. Turkey is now sold in parts as well as whole; duck, goose, and game hen, both fresh and frozen, also come to today's market. Squab and quail are appearing more often, too, thanks to stepped-up production by commercial breeders.

This chapter offers a gallery of good-looking, good-tasting poultry recipes, all grouped by cooking method. Whatever your favorite bird, you'll find plenty here to please both eye and palate.

Roast poultry

The magnificent appearance of a whole roasted bird belies its ease of preparation. There are just two simple secrets to a succulent success: cook the bird on a rack in a shallow roasting pan, and baste it during the last half of the cooking time. Elevating the bird on a rack allows the dry oven heat to cook it evenly on all sides; basting keeps the flesh moist as the skin turns crisp and golden.

Let the roasted bird rest for about 10 minutes on platter or carving board; then carve with knife and fork (or cut up with poultry or kitchen shears).

Cantonese Roast Chicken

China

Juicy roast chicken is popular in virtually every cuisine. Seasonings vary from one region to another; here, cilantro (also called coriander and Chinese parsley) lends its zest to a Cantonese treat.

- 1 **frying chicken (3 to 3½ lbs.)**
  Salt and pepper
- 1 **bunch fresh cilantro (coriander)**
- 1 **tablespoon *each* soy sauce, salad oil, and lemon juice**
- 1 **teaspoon Chinese five-spice**

Remove chicken giblets and reserve for other uses; pull off and discard lumps of fat. Sprinkle body cavity lightly with salt and pepper. Remove and discard root ends from cilantro; reserve a few sprigs for garnish, then tuck remainder into cavity. Combine soy, oil, lemon juice, and five-spice; rub into skin all over chicken.

Place chicken, breast up, on a rack in a roasting pan. Roast in a 375° oven, uncovered, for 1 to 1½ hours or until meat near thighbone is no longer pink when slashed. Baste with pan drippings every 15 minutes during last half of cooking time. Transfer chicken to a platter, reserving all juices. Garnish with reserved cilantro. Spoon some of the juices over each serving. Makes 4 servings.

Roast Chicken with Swiss Chard

Italy

Where the northwestern rim of Italy's "boot" meets France, cooking shows many a tasty influence from neighboring Provence. This succulent chicken stuffed with chard and rice is one example.

- ¾ pound Swiss chard
- ¼ cup olive oil or salad oil
- ¼ cup pine nuts
- 1 medium-size onion, chopped
- 1 clove garlic, minced or pressed
- ¾ cup cooked brown or white rice
- ¼ cup grated Parmesan cheese
- 1 teaspoon dry rosemary
  Salt and pepper
- 1 roasting chicken (4 to 5 lbs.)
- 2 tablespoons butter or margarine, softened

Rinse and drain chard. Cut off white stems and slice ¼ inch thick; coarsely chop leaves. Set stems and leaves aside in separate piles.

Heat oil in a wide frying pan over medium heat; add pine nuts and cook, stirring, until golden. Lift out and set aside. Stir in chard stems, onion, and garlic; cover and cook until chard is tender when pierced (4 to 5 minutes). Stir in chard leaves; cover and cook until wilted (3 minutes). Remove from heat and mix in nuts, rice, cheese, and rosemary. Season to taste with salt and pepper.

Remove chicken neck and giblets and reserve for other uses; also pull off and discard lumps of fat. Stuff neck and body cavities with chard mixture and secure skin over openings with metal skewers. Place chicken, breast down, on a rack in a shallow roasting pan. Rub with butter. Roast in a 325° oven, uncovered, for 45 minutes. Turn bird breast up and roast for 1 to 1¼ more hours or until meat near thighbone is no longer pink when slashed. Baste with pan drippings every 15 minutes during last half of cooking time.

Transfer bird to a platter and remove skewers. Makes 5 or 6 servings.

Roast Ducklings & Yams

United States

Traditional staple of the American South, yams combine with a tangy tangerine sauce to enhance tender roast ducklings.

- 2 ducklings (4½ to 5 lbs. each)
  About 3 pounds yams, peeled and cut into 2-inch chunks
  Tangerine sauce (recipe follows)

Remove duck necks and giblets; reserve for sauce. Pull off and discard lumps of fat. Fasten each duck's neck skin to its back with a metal skewer. Prick skin with a fork.

Place ducks, breast down, on a rack in a large roasting pan (at least 12 by 17 inches). Roast in a 375° oven, uncovered, for 1 hour; then, using a bulb baster, siphon off and discard fat from pan. While ducks roast, cook necks and giblets for tangerine sauce.

Turn ducks breast up. Arrange yams around rack in pan; turn to coat with drippings. Roast for 1 more hour or until yams are tender when pierced and duck skin is crisp, browned, and beginning to pull away from leg bone; turn yams several times and baste ducks with drippings every 15 minutes. Transfer ducks and yams to a platter; keep warm. Skim and discard fat from drippings. Finish preparing tangerine sauce.

Cut ducks into quarters; spoon sauce over each serving. Makes 6 to 8 servings.

Tangerine sauce. In a 2-quart pan, combine **duck necks and giblets** (reserve liver for other uses); 2 cups **water;** 1 large **onion,** quartered; and 1 **bay leaf.** Bring to a boil over high heat; cover, reduce heat, and simmer for 1 hour. Pour through a wire strainer. If necessary, boil broth to reduce to ½ cup. Add to drippings in roasting pan.

Pare zest (colored outer layer of peel) from 1 large **tangerine;** cut into thin slivers (you should have 3 tablespoons). Squeeze 4 large **tangerines** to make 1½ cups juice. Add zest, juice, and 3 tablespoons **honey** to roasting pan. Combine 1½ tablespoons each **cornstarch** and **water;** add to pan. Bring to a boil over high heat; boil, stirring, until sauce thickens and turns clear (about 1 minute). Season to taste with **salt** and **pepper.**

Roasting a goose (Recipe on facing page)

1 Pull out lumps of fat from neck and body cavities of goose. Then, with a fork, prick skin at 1-inch intervals to allow excess fat to drain off during roasting.

2 Roast goose, breast down, for 1 hour; siphon off fat every 30 minutes. If you wish, refrigerate rendered fat and use it in cooking— for frying potato pancakes, for example.

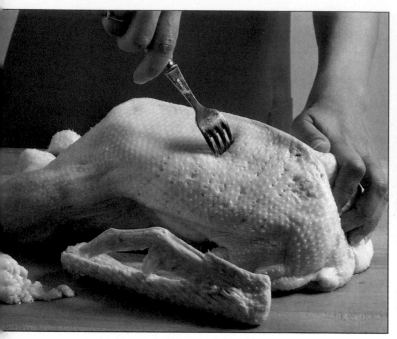

3 To make giblet wine sauce, pour hot giblet mixture into roasting pan; stir to scrape flavorful browned bits free. Strain mixture into a 2-quart pan to complete cooking.

4 French Potato Pancakes (page 165) and a garland of apples and prunes complement the richness of goose. Garnish the bird with thin strips of orange zest, if you like.

.Roast poultry

Roast Goose with Port-Poached Fruit

Czechoslovakia   (Pictured on facing page)

Those accustomed to a turkey's plump girth may be somewhat surprised at the elongated look of a roast goose. Both body and wings are long and slim; the breastbone is quite prominent. But for all its angular appearance, this all-dark-meat bird has richly succulent flesh. Unlike leaner poultry such as chicken and turkey, a goose has a wealth of natural fat. As it renders away during roasting, the fat bastes the bird—leaving it with crisp skin and flesh that's deliciously moist. When cooked with skill, a roast goose is a special treat indeed— especially when accompanied with fruit (as in our recipe).

In American markets, fresh and frozen goose is easiest to find during autumn and winter. To thaw frozen goose, let the bird stand (in its original wrapping) in the refrigerator for 1½ to 2 days. An 8 to 9-pound goose serves 5 or 6 diners; for 8 to 10 people, choose a 10 to 12-pound bird.

> 1 **goose (8 to 12 lbs.)**
> **Giblet wine sauce (recipe follows)**
> **Port-poached fruit (recipe follows)**

Remove giblets from goose; reserve for sauce. Pull out and discard lumps of fat from neck and body cavities. With a fork, prick skin all over at 1-inch intervals. Fasten neck skin to back with a metal skewer. Tie drumsticks together at ends.

Place goose, breast down, on a rack in a large roasting pan. Roast in a 400° oven for 1 hour. Every 30 minutes, siphon off fat in pan (reserve 2 tablespoons fat for sauce).

Reduce oven temperature to 325°. Turn goose breast up; insert a meat thermometer in thickest part of breast (not touching bone). Continue to roast bird, siphoning fat from pan every 30 minutes, until thermometer registers 175°—about 1½ hours for an 8-pound bird, up to 2½ hours for a 12-pounder. While goose roasts, simmer giblets for sauce; also prepare port-poached fruit.

Lift bird from pan and place on a platter; remove skewer and untie drumsticks. Finish preparing giblet wine sauce.

Surround goose with fruit. Carve as directed at right; pass sauce to spoon over meat. Makes 5 to 10 servings.

Giblet wine sauce. Reserve goose liver for other uses; coarsely chop remaining **giblets** and set aside. Pour 2 tablespoons **goose fat** into a 2 to 3-quart pan. Add giblets; cook over medium-high heat, stirring, until well browned. Add 1 small **onion,** chopped; cook until golden. Add 2 cups **water;** 1 **chicken bouillon cube;** 1 stalk **celery,** cut into pieces; 1 **bay leaf;** and ¼ teaspoon **thyme leaves.** Cover and simmer for 1½ hours.

Add hot giblet mixture to browned bits in roasting pan; stir to scrape bits free. Pour mixture through a wire strainer into a 2-quart pan; discard residue in strainer. Boil broth rapidly until reduced to 1¼ cups. Add ½ cup **port;** return to a boil. Season to taste with **salt** and **pepper,** then serve. If desired, thicken sauce by stirring in a mixture of 1½ tablespoons **cornstarch** and 2 tablespoons **water;** cook and stir until sauce boils and thickens slightly (about 1 minute).

Port-poached fruit. In a pan, heat 1½ cups **port** just until hot. Remove from heat, add 2 cups (one 12-oz. package) **pitted prunes,** and let stand for 10 minutes; then drain off port and reserve. Meanwhile, peel, core, and quarter 4 or 5 **Golden Delicious apples.**

In a wide frying pan, melt 2 tablespoons **butter** or margarine. Add apples and 2 tablespoons **lemon juice;** turn fruit to coat. Add port; cover and simmer over medium-low heat until apples begin to soften (about 4 minutes). Uncover; increase heat to high, add prunes, and cook, turning fruit frequently, until apples are translucent and sauce clings to fruit (about 2 minutes).

Carving the bird. Begin by cutting off tips and first joints of wings. To sever each wing from body, hold remaining wing section and force knife through side of breast into joint while twisting wing.

A goose's hip joints are almost at its backbone. To carve legs, turn bird breast down and cut through back skin to expose joints next to center back. Anchor a fork firmly in thigh and press drumstick down to board; then cut between thigh and body at joint. Repeat for other leg. Separate thighs and drumsticks at joints, then slice meat off thighbone.

Remove each side of breast by sliding knife between meat and keel bone. Cut down to breastbone along wishbone and around to wing joint, then cut meat free in one piece. Thinly slice each breast crosswise.

Barbecued & broiled poultry

Barbecuing and broiling are similar cooking methods that both produce moist, tender poultry with flavorful, lightly charred skin. But the barbecue heats from below, the broiler from above; and the burning charcoal of a barbecue produces more intense heat than an oven broiler. Because of these differences, you may need to adjust timing and distance from heat if you substitute one method for the other.

Tandoori Chicken

India   (Pictured on page 163)

This spicy North Indian chicken gets its name from *tandoor*—the bucketlike, charcoal-fired oven in which it's traditionally cooked.

> 1 teaspoon *each* grated fresh ginger and ground allspice
> ¼ to ½ teaspoon crushed red pepper
> 2 cloves garlic, minced or pressed
> 1 tablespoon lemon juice
> 4 large chicken legs with thighs attached
> Plain yogurt

Mash together ginger, allspice, pepper, garlic, and lemon juice to make a paste. Then lift skin of each chicken leg; spread 1 teaspoon paste over flesh of each. Brush any remaining paste evenly over skin.

About 35 minutes before cooking, start barbecue fire (see "Barbecuing Using Direct Heat," page 84). Place chicken on grill 6 inches above a solid bed of medium-glowing coals. Cook, turning frequently, until meat near thighbone is no longer pink when slashed (about 45 minutes). Pass cold yogurt to spoon over chicken. Makes 4 servings.

Bangkok-style Barbecued Birds

Thailand

When you barbecue chickens on an open grill, first cut them into halves, quarters, or other pieces that will lie fairly flat. But if you're using smaller birds such as game hens, squab, or quail, just split them open and spread them out; then thread them side by side on parallel pairs of long skewers. In addition to making the birds lie flat and helping them to cook evenly, this skewering technique allows you to turn them all at once.

> Thai sauce (recipe follows)
> 8 Rock Cornish game hens (1¼ lbs. *each*); or 8 squab (1 lb. *each*); or 16 quail (3 oz. *each*); or 2 or 3 frying chickens (3 to 3½ lbs. *each*)
> ½ cup minced fresh cilantro (coriander)
> ⅓ cup coarsely ground pepper
> 24 cloves garlic, minced or pressed

Prepare Thai sauce and set aside. With poultry or kitchen shears, split game hens, squab, or quail lengthwise through breastbone. Spread birds open; place skin side up and press firmly to crack bones so birds lie reasonably flat. (If using chicken, cut into quarters.)

Thread small birds on long metal skewers (18 inches or longer) as follows: Force one skewer into drumstick and through thigh, then under backbone, through other thigh, and out through other drumstick. Run a second skewer parallel to the first, forcing it through one side of breast and middle section of one wing, then over backbone, through middle section of other wing, and out through other side of breast. On each pair of skewers, thread as many birds as will fit; 18-inch skewers hold 2 or 3 game hens or squab or up to 6 quail. (Don't thread chicken.) Mash together cilantro, pepper, and garlic; rub evenly over poultry.

About 35 minutes before cooking, start barbecue fire (see "Barbecuing Using Direct Heat," page 84). Place poultry on grill 4 to 6 inches above a solid bed of medium-glowing coals. Cook, turning as needed, until meat near thighbone of game hens or chicken is no longer pink when slashed (25 to 30 minutes for game hens, 40 to 45 minutes for chicken) or until squab or quail are cooked rare (12 to 15 minutes for squab, 8 to 10 minutes for quail). Serve with Thai sauce. Makes 8 to 12 servings.

Thai sauce. In a blender or food processor, whirl until blended: 1 small can (8 oz.) **tomato sauce,** 3 tablespoons firmly packed **brown sugar,** 6 cloves **garlic,** ⅛ to ½ teaspoon **ground red pepper** (cayenne), and ¼ cup **cider vinegar.** Add 1¼ cups **golden raisins** and ⅓ cup **water;** whirl until raisins are coarsely chopped. Pour sauce into a 2 to 3-quart pan; bring to a boil over high heat. Boil, stirring, until reduced to 1½ cups. Let cool, then refrigerate until cold.

Chicken Yakitori

Japan

Before heading home at day's end, Tokyo office workers often stop at a street stall for beer, gossip, and the skewered grilled chicken called *yakitori*. (Use chicken breasts in place of thighs, if you wish.)

- ½ **cup soy sauce**
- ½ **cup sweet sherry, sake, or mirin**
- 3 **tablespoons sugar**
- 6 **large chicken thighs, skinned, boned, and cut into bite-size pieces**
- ½ **pound chicken livers**
- 2 **bunches green onions (including tops), cut into 1½-inch lengths**

In a pan, bring soy, sherry, and sugar to a boil over high heat; reduce heat and simmer, uncovered, for 3 minutes. Thread thigh meat and livers on separate 6-inch skewers, including several onion pieces on each skewer; marinate in soy mixture for 15 minutes.

Place skewers 4 inches below heat on a rack in a broiler pan (see "How to Broil Meat," page 85). Cook, turning as needed and basting with soy mixture, for 5 to 7 minutes for livers, 7 to 9 minutes for thigh meat. Makes about 16 skewers.

Lemony Broiled Chicken

Lebanon

Lebanese cooks, like many others, have found that a skillfully herbed and spiced marinade produces exceptionally flavorful chicken.

- 3 **tablespoons olive oil or salad oil**
- ¼ **cup lemon juice**
- ¾ **teaspoon salt**
- 1 **teaspoon oregano leaves**
- ½ **teaspoon pepper**
- ¼ **teaspoon ground cinnamon**
- 1 **frying chicken (3 to 3½ lbs.), cut into quarters**

In a 9 by 13-inch baking pan, combine oil, lemon juice, salt, oregano, pepper, and cinnamon. Place chicken in marinade; turn to coat both sides. Let stand for 30 minutes, turning occasionally.

Lift chicken from marinade and place, skin side down, 6 inches below heat on a rack in a broiler pan (see "How to Broil Meat," page 85). Cook for 15 minutes, basting once or twice with marinade. Turn chicken over; cook, basting several more times with marinade, until meat near thighbone is no longer pink when slashed (15 to 20 more minutes). If chicken skin begins to burn, complete cooking in a 350° oven. Makes 4 servings.

Broil-Bake Chicken with Onions

El Salvador

For the sake of convenience, we've Americanized the cooking technique in this recipe—but the dish retains its zesty Latin temperament.

- 4 **tablespoons butter or margarine**
- 4 **large onions, thinly sliced**
- 1 **small can (8 oz.) tomato sauce**
- 1 **tablespoon Worcestershire**
- 1 **tablespoon chopped fresh cilantro (coriander)**
- 1 **frying chicken (3 to 3½ lbs.), cut up**
  Salt, pepper, and garlic powder
  Boiling water

Melt butter in a wide frying pan over medium heat. Add onions; cook, stirring often, until golden (about 20 minutes). Stir in tomato sauce, Worcestershire, and cilantro; bring to a boil, then set aside.

Sprinkle chicken with salt, pepper, and garlic powder; then place, skin side down, 6 inches below heat on a rack in a broiler pan (see "How to Broil Meat," page 85). Cook until lightly browned (about 10 minutes). Remove pan from broiler; adjust oven rack to center of oven. Set oven at 500°. Turn chicken over and place pan in oven, then pour boiling water into pan (under chicken on rack) to a depth of ½ inch. Bake for 20 to 25 minutes or until meat near thighbone is no longer pink when slashed. Reheat onion-tomato sauce; serve with chicken. Makes 4 servings.

Boned poultry breast entrées

Time spent learning basic cooking techniques is time well spent—once you've mastered a fundamental skill, you can capitalize on it to create dozens of new dishes. Boning a poultry breast is one such basic technique; you follow the same steps to bone a breast of chicken, turkey, or any other bird. Each time you practice, you both sharpen your skills and reward yourself with tender, boneless meat to use in these entrées or in one of the stir-fries on page 114.

Turkey Scaloppine

Italy   (Pictured on facing page)

In Italy, *scaloppine* usually means veal. But when sliced thin and sautéed in the same fashion, economical turkey breast tastes just as exquisite.

To ensure fork-tender texture, you'll need to pound the sliced turkey before cooking it. If you wish, pound the meat up to 2 days ahead of time, then keep the turkey scallops in the refrigerator until you're ready to cook them.

   1½ **pounds boned turkey breast (about half of one boned breast), cut into ¼-inch-thick slices**
       All-purpose flour
   ½ **cup (¼ lb.) butter or margarine**
   ½ **pound large mushrooms, cut into quarters**
   ½ **cup Marsala**

Space turkey slices slightly apart between 2 sheets of wax paper, then pound with a mallet to a thickness of ⅛ inch. Coat turkey lightly with flour.

Melt 2 tablespoons of the butter in a wide frying pan over medium-high heat. When butter is foamy, add as many slices of meat as will fit without crowding. Cook, turning once, until lightly browned on both sides (about 1 minute *total*). Transfer to a platter and keep warm. Repeat with remaining turkey, adding more butter to pan as needed, a tablespoon at a time.

Add mushrooms to pan and stir until they begin to brown; then pour in Marsala and stir to scrape up browned bits. With a slotted spoon, transfer mushrooms to platter.

Bring sauce to a boil over high heat; boil, stirring, until large, shiny bubbles form. Turn off heat. Add remaining butter (you should have about 4 tablespoons) and stir until completely blended. Pour sauce over turkey. Makes 6 servings.

Chicken with a Pocketful of Mushrooms

Japan/France

Of recent fascination to avant-garde chefs have been such cross-cultural marriages as this: Japanese seasonings combined with French technique.

       Sautéed mushrooms (recipe follows)
   3 **large whole chicken breasts, skinned, boned, and split**
   3 **tablespoons butter or margarine**
   6 **large fresh shiitake or regular mushrooms**
   ½ **teaspoon minced fresh ginger**
   ⅓ **cup sake or dry sherry**
   1 **cup regular-strength chicken broth**
   1½ **tablespoons soy sauce**
   ½ **teaspoon *each* sugar and vinegar**
   1 **tablespoon cornstarch**
   2 **tablespoons water**

Prepare sautéed mushrooms. Pull slim fillet off inside of each breast half, then cut a 3½-inch-long, 2-inch-deep pocket in thickest part of each breast. Fill each pocket with 2 tablespoons mushrooms.

Melt butter in a wide frying pan over medium-high heat. Add fillets and as many breasts as will fit; cook until browned on both sides. Remove from pan. Add remaining breasts and whole mushrooms and cook until browned. Add ginger, sake, broth, soy, sugar, vinegar, and all breasts; cover and simmer for 7 minutes. Turn breasts over and add fillets. Cover; simmer until meat in thickest part of breasts is no longer pink when slashed (about 3 minutes). With a slotted spoon, transfer chicken and mushrooms to serving dish; keep warm.

Mix cornstarch and water; stir into pan juices. Increase heat to high; bring to a boil, stirring. Add juices that have drained from chicken. Thin sauce with a few drops of water, if necessary. Spoon sauce over chicken; place mushrooms on top for garnish. Makes 6 servings.

Sautéed mushrooms. Melt 2 tablespoons **butter** or margarine in a wide frying pan over medium-high heat. Add ½ pound **fresh shiitake or regular mushrooms,** finely chopped; 1 medium-size **onion,** finely chopped; ½ teaspoon minced **fresh ginger;** and 1 clove **garlic,** minced or pressed. Cook, stirring, until mushrooms and onions are very soft and all liquid has evaporated. Add 1 teaspoon **soy sauce.**

Making Turkey Scaloppine (Recipe on facing page)

1 Pull off and discard skin from turkey breast. Then cut down side of breastbone and along ribs to free meat. Cut around wishbone; lift out breast and slice crosswise, ¼ inch thick.

2 Space turkey slices slightly apart between 2 sheets of wax paper. Using a flat-surfaced mallet, pound to a thickness of ⅛ inch.

3 Heat butter until foamy. Then add turkey, a portion at a time, placing slices in a single layer (don't crowd). Cook until lightly browned (about 30 seconds per side). Transfer to a platter.

4 Cook and stir mushrooms until lightly browned, then pour in Marsala and scrape pan to loosen browned bits. Spoon mushrooms alongside turkey slices on platter.

5 Boil sauce until large, shiny bubbles form. Turn off heat; add butter and stir constantly until completely blended.

6 Tender turkey breast, juicy mushrooms, and smooth, buttery wine sauce combine for an elegant entrée that you can prepare in minutes. Bright green basil makes a perky garnish.

...Boned poultry breast entrées

Coconut Chicken with Fresh Fruit

Tahiti

Tahitian cooking shows a happy blend of French and native Polynesian traits. Here, local ingredients—coconut and fresh tropical fruits—enhance chicken simmered in ginger-seasoned cream.

⅓ cup sweetened flaked coconut
2 large whole chicken breasts, skinned, boned, and split
   Salt and pepper
1 tablespoon salad oil
1 tablespoon butter or margarine
1 teaspoon minced fresh ginger
1 lime, cut in half
½ cup whipping cream
2 bananas
1 papaya

Spread coconut in a shallow rimmed baking pan; toast in a 350° oven, stirring frequently, for 4 to 5 minutes or until lightly browned. Set aside.

Sprinkle chicken with salt and pepper. Heat oil and butter in a wide frying pan over medium-high heat; add ginger and stir for 30 seconds. Add chicken and cook turning once, until lightly browned on both sides (about 3 minutes per side). Squeeze juice from one lime half into pan and cook for 1 minute. Add ¼ cup of the coconut; then pour cream over all. Cover, reduce heat, and simmer, turning once, until meat in thickest part is no longer pink when slashed (8 to 10 minutes).

Peel and quarter bananas. Peel and halve papaya; scoop out seeds, then slice fruit. Remove chicken from pan and arrange on a platter with fruit. Spoon sauce over chicken; sprinkle with remaining coconut. Cut remaining lime half into quarters; use as garnish. Makes 4 servings.

USING LEFTOVER GIBLETS

When you buy whole poultry rather than parts, you get a bonus in the little bag of giblets that comes with the bird. If you don't need the giblets right away, freeze them—neck in one container, heart and gizzard in another, liver in a third. Keep adding to your store until you have enough to use in a recipe.

Chicken Breasts with Caramelized Apples

France

Normandy's famous Calvados—an aromatic apple brandy distilled from cider—lends distinctive flavor to much of the region's cooking. Combined with cream, it makes a marvelous sauce for chicken.

   Caramelized apples (recipe follows)
4 large whole chicken breasts, skinned, boned, and split
   Salt and pepper
4 tablespoons butter or margarine
½ cup apple juice or apple cider
⅓ cup Calvados or brandy
3 green onions (including tops), thinly sliced
½ cup whipping cream
2 tablespoons lemon juice

Prepare caramelized apples; keep warm in a 200° oven. Sprinkle chicken lightly with salt and pepper. Melt butter in a wide frying pan over medium-high heat; add half the chicken and cook, turning once, until lightly browned on both sides (about 3 minutes per side). Remove from pan. Repeat with remaining chicken.

Return all chicken to pan; add apple juice. Cover, reduce heat, and simmer, turning once, until meat in thickest part is no longer pink when slashed (8 to 10 minutes). Add Calvados, heat mixture until bubbly, and ignite (see page 210). When flames disappear, lift chicken from pan and arrange on a platter.

Add onions to pan, increase heat to high, and cook until sauce is reduced by half. Add cream and lemon juice and cook until large, shiny bubbles form and sauce is slightly thickened. Spoon sauce over chicken; serve apples alongside. Makes 8 servings.

Caramelized apples. Peel and core 4 **Golden Delicious apples,** then cut into ¼-inch slices. Place in a well-greased 2½-quart baking dish. Sprinkle with 3 tablespoons **lemon juice,** 2 tablespoons **sugar,** and ¼ teaspoon **ground cinnamon.** Pour ¼ cup **Calvados** or apple juice over top. Cover; bake in a 400° oven for 10 minutes. Uncover and bake for 20 more minutes or until tender. Sprinkle with ¼ cup **sugar.** Broil 3 to 4 inches below heat until golden brown.

Baked poultry

These no-fuss entrées are just right for days when you can't spend much time cooking. In each one, a hearty accompaniment bakes along with the poultry; to complete the menu, you need only add a salad.

Baked Chicken with Bulgur

Middle East

Nutty-tasting bulgur has been used in Middle Eastern cooking for centuries. Here, a lightly spiced bulgur pilaf dotted with currants pairs up with tender chicken.

- 1 **frying chicken (3 to 3½ lbs.), cut up**
- ½ **teaspoon** *each* **salt, ground cinnamon, and ground allspice**
- ⅛ **teaspoon pepper**
- 2 **tablespoons salad oil**
- 4 **tablespoons butter or margarine**
- 1 **small onion, chopped**
- 1½ **cups bulgur (quick-cooking cracked wheat)**
- ½ **cup currants**
- 1 **can (14½ oz.) regular-strength chicken broth or 1¾ cups homemade chicken broth (page 33)**
- ½ **cup water**
- ¼ **cup chopped parsley mixed with 2 tablespoons chopped fresh mint**

Sprinkle chicken with salt, cinnamon, allspice, and pepper. Heat oil in a wide frying pan over medium-high heat. Add chicken and cook, turning, until browned on all sides. Lift from pan and set aside; discard pan drippings.

Melt butter in pan; add onion and cook, stirring, until soft. Add bulgur and currants and stir to coat with butter.

Spread bulgur mixture in a 9 by 13-inch baking pan; arrange chicken on top. Pour in broth and water. Cover pan tightly with foil. Bake in a 375° oven for 40 to 45 minutes or until meat near thighbone is no longer pink when slashed and bulgur has absorbed all liquid. Sprinkle with parsley and mint. Makes 4 servings.

Dijon-style Chicken & Potatoes

France

Unlike the sophisticated selections of many French restaurants, *poulet à la dijonnaise* reflects the hearty simplicity of country cuisine.

- ½ **cup (¼ lb.) butter or margarine**
- 2 **tablespoons Dijon mustard**
- 1½ **pounds russet potatoes, scrubbed and cut lengthwise into 1-inch-thick wedges**
- 4 **large chicken legs with thighs attached**
- 1½ **to 2 cups seasoned croutons, finely crushed**

Place butter in a broiler pan that's at least 1 inch deep, or in a 9 by 13-inch baking pan. Place pan in a 400° oven to melt butter. Pour 3 tablespoons of the melted butter into a shallow dish and blend in mustard; set aside. Put potatoes in pan and turn to coat all sides with butter.

Set broiler rack in place on broiler pan (or rest a cake rack on baking pan). Coat chicken with mustard mixture, then with crumbs; shake off excess. Arrange on rack, skin side up. Bake, uncovered, until meat near thighbone is no longer pink when slashed and potatoes are tender when pierced (about 45 minutes). Makes 4 servings.

Yorkshire Chicken

England

In England, golden Yorkshire pudding traditionally pairs off with roast beef. But it makes just as savory a sensation with baked chicken.

- 1¼ **cups all-purpose flour**
- ⅛ **teaspoon pepper**
- 1½ **teaspoons salt**
- 4 **large chicken legs with thighs attached**
- 2 **tablespoons salad oil**
- 2 **tablespoons butter or margarine**
- 1 **teaspoon** *each* **baking powder and rubbed sage**
- 3 **eggs**
- 1½ **cups milk**

Stir together ¼ cup of the flour, pepper, and ½ teaspoon of the salt. Dredge chicken in flour mixture.

Heat oil and butter in a wide frying pan over medium heat; add chicken and cook, turning, until browned on all sides. Transfer chicken and drippings to a 9 by 13-inch baking pan. Tilt pan to distribute drippings; place in a 350° oven.

Stir together remaining 1 cup flour, remaining 1 teaspoon salt, baking powder, and sage. In a blender, whirl eggs, milk, and dry ingredients until smooth. Pour evenly over chicken. Bake, uncovered, for 1 hour or until puffy and browned. Serve at once. Makes 4 servings.

Composing an Indian curry (Recipe on facing page)

1 *Garam masala*, a condiment that's sprinkled atop curry, includes (clockwise from top) cinnamon stick, cumin seeds, whole black peppers, whole cloves, coriander seeds, and bay leaves.

2 To start the flavorful sauce, purée onions, garlic, jalapeño pepper, and a few pieces of fresh ginger with a little water.

3 Cook onion-garlic purée until thick and dry. Then reduce heat and stir in salad oil, tomato paste, salt, turmeric, ground red pepper, and yogurt.

4 Turn chicken pieces in sauce to coat on all sides. Then cover pan and simmer until chicken is tender. (If you wish, cook up to a day ahead; reheat at serving time.)

5 Exotic-looking Indian curry has mild, mellow flavor. Mango chutney and garam masala are traditional condiments; Rice with Green Peas (page 154) and raw vegetables complete the meal.

Curried poultry

Most of us are familiar with Western-style curries: meat, fish, or poultry in a flour-thickened sauce flavored with preblended curry powder. But these dishes are a far cry from the authentic curries served in India and neighboring countries and in Southeast Asia. In these lands, cooks don't use a standard spice mixture for every curry; they prepare a different blend for each dish, pounding together intricate combinations of spices, herbs, and roots. Long, slow cooking removes every trace of harshness from this curry paste, as well as reducing and thickening the sauce.

Our two chicken curries are both relatively mild. The Nepalese dish is fragrant with sweet spices; the Indian one has a more savory flavor.

Fragrant Chicken Curry

Nepal

- ¼ cup salad oil
- 1 large onion, thinly sliced
- 12 cloves garlic (leave whole)
- 2 tablespoons minced fresh ginger
- 1 cinnamon stick (about 2 inches long)
- 2 whole cardamom pods, shells removed
- 1 large tomato, peeled and cut into 8 wedges
- 1 tablespoon *each* ground coriander and unsweetened shredded coconut
- 1½ teaspoons ground cumin
- 1 frying chicken (3 to 3½ lbs.), cut up
- ½ cup regular-strength chicken broth
- 1 tablespoon *each* cashews and raisins
  Salt
- 2 hard-cooked eggs, sliced
  Fresh cilantro (coriander) leaves

Heat oil in a wide frying pan over medium heat. Add onion, garlic, ginger, cinnamon stick, and cardamom; cook until onion is browned (5 to 7 minutes). Add tomato and cook until liquid has evaporated.

Stir in ground coriander, coconut, cumin, chicken, and broth. Bring to a boil; then cover, reduce heat, and simmer, turning chicken once, until meat near thighbone is no longer pink when slashed (40 to 45 minutes). Lift out chicken.

Stir cashews and raisins into sauce. Increase heat to high; bring sauce to a boil, then boil until reduced to 1 cup. Skim and discard fat; season to taste with salt. Pour sauce over chicken. Garnish with eggs and cilantro. Makes 4 servings.

Spicy Chicken Curry

India   (Pictured on facing page)

Pleasantly spicy but not too hot, *murg masalam* features a thick sauce of onion-nippy yogurt. Offer *garam masala*, a mixture of pulverized spices, to sprinkle atop each serving.

- Garam masala (recipe follows)
- 2 medium-size onions, cut into chunks
- 2 cloves garlic
- 1 to 2 teaspoons minced fresh or canned jalapeño pepper (remove seeds for a milder curry)
- 3 tablespoons coarsely chopped fresh ginger
  About ¼ cup water
- ⅓ cup salad oil
- 2 tablespoons tomato paste
- 1½ teaspoons salt
- 1 teaspoon turmeric
- ¼ teaspoon ground red pepper (cayenne)
- ½ cup plain yogurt
- 6 *each* chicken legs and thighs
  Fresh cilantro (coriander) leaves

Prepare garam masala; set aside. In a blender, whirl onions, garlic, jalapeño pepper, ginger, and ¼ cup of the water until puréed. Pour into a wide frying pan and cook over medium heat, stirring occasionally, until dry and thick (15 to 20 minutes). Reduce heat to medium-low; stir in oil, tomato paste, salt, turmeric, red pepper, and yogurt. Cook, uncovered, for 8 more minutes.

Add chicken to sauce and turn to coat. Cover and simmer, turning chicken once, until meat near thighbone is no longer pink when slashed (40 to 45 minutes); add about 1 tablespoon more water if sauce begins to stick to pan. Transfer chicken to a serving dish. Skim and discard fat from sauce, then spoon over chicken. Garnish with fresh cilantro. Pass garam masala at the table. Makes 6 servings.

Garam masala. In a small frying pan over medium-low heat, cook 3 tablespoons **coriander seeds** and 2 teaspoons **cumin seeds,** shaking pan often, until lightly browned (about 4 minutes). Place in a blender. Add 8 **whole cloves,** 1 **cinnamon stick** (about 2 inches long), ½ teaspoon **whole black peppers,** and 4 **bay leaves.** Whirl until finely ground. Store in an airtight jar. Makes ⅓ cup.

Braised poultry

What makes a particular dish a favorite? For most of us, it's marvelous flavor. From the cook's point of view, convenience is important, too. Braised poultry appeals on both counts, offering great taste plus the ease of make-ahead preparation.

Each of our entrées features tender chicken in a sweet, savory, or spicy sauce. The sauce keeps the chicken moist, so you can make these dishes in advance without worrying that reheating will dry out the meat.

Chicken Peanut Stew

Ghana

In Africa, this popular dish is flavored with peanuts pulverized to a paste; we've substituted peanut butter. Traditional accompaniments include rice and spinach—prepare them while the stew simmers.

    2   tablespoons salad oil
    4   *each* chicken legs and thighs
    2   medium-size onions, chopped
    2   medium-size tomatoes, peeled, seeded, and
        chopped
    1   can (14½ oz.) regular-strength chicken broth or
        1¾ cups homemade chicken broth (page 33)
    ½   teaspoon liquid hot pepper seasoning
    1   tablespoon lime juice
    ¼   teaspoon ground nutmeg
    ⅛   teaspoon ground cloves
    1   cinnamon stick (about 2 inches long)
    5   carrots, cut diagonally into 3-inch pieces
    2   green peppers, seeded and chopped
    ½   cup creamy peanut butter
    2   tablespoons cornstarch
        Accompaniments (suggestions follow)

Heat oil in a 5 to 6-quart kettle over medium-high heat. Add chicken and cook, turning, until browned on all sides; remove from kettle and set aside. Discard all but 2 tablespoons drippings.

Add onions to kettle; reduce heat to medium and cook, stirring, until soft. Add tomatoes, 1½ cups of the broth, hot pepper seasoning, lime juice, nutmeg, cloves, cinnamon stick, and carrots. Return chicken to kettle. Bring to a boil; cover, reduce heat, and simmer for 20 minutes. Add green peppers and continue to simmer until meat near thighbone is no longer pink when slashed (20 to 25 more minutes). Push chicken to one side and skim fat from sauce.

In a bowl, blend peanut butter with cornstarch; then smoothly stir in remaining broth. Pour into stew. Cook, stirring, until sauce thickens (about 5 minutes). Serve with accompaniments as directed below. Makes 4 servings.

Accompaniments. You will need 4 cups hot **cooked rice,** 2 or 3 cups hot **cooked spinach,** ½ cups chopped **green onions** (including tops), and 1 cup *each* **roasted salted peanuts** and **shredded coconut.** Spoon rice into wide soup bowls or rimmed plates; top with spinach, stew, onions, peanuts, and coconut.

Chicken & Pork Adobo

Philippines

Popular *adobo* exists in countless versions in the Philippines. Usually made with pork or chicken (or both), it may feature liver as well.

    2   pounds mixed chicken legs and thighs
    1   pound lean boneless pork, cut into 1-inch
        cubes
    ½   cup *each* wine vinegar and water
    ¼   cup soy sauce
    8   whole black peppers
    1   bay leaf
    4   cloves garlic, minced or pressed
    2   tablespoons salad oil
        Chopped parsley
        Hot cooked rice

In a bowl, combine chicken, pork, vinegar, water, soy, peppers, bay leaf, and garlic. Cover and refrigerate for 1 hour, turning meats occasionally.

Remove meats from marinade and pat dry; reserve marinade. Heat oil in a 5-quart kettle (not a cast-iron kettle) over medium-high heat. Add chicken and cook, turning, until browned on all sides; remove from kettle and set aside. Add pork to kettle and cook, stirring occasionally, until browned. Pour in marinade. Bring to a boil; cover, reduce heat, and simmer for 15 minutes. Return chicken to kettle; simmer, covered, until meat near thighbone is no longer pink when slashed (40 to 45 minutes). Transfer both meats to a platter.

Skim and discard fat from sauce; also discard peppers and bay leaf. Increase heat to high. Bring sauce to a boil, then boil until reduced to about ¾ cup. Pour over meats. Sprinkle with parsley; serve with rice. Makes 6 servings.

Caribbean Chicken

Cuba

Raisins and ripe olives dot a spicy tomato sauce in this exuberant Cuban creation.

>   2 **tablespoons olive oil or salad oil**
>   1 **frying chicken (3 to 3½ lbs.), cut up**
>   2 **cloves garlic, minced or pressed**
>   1 **large onion, chopped**
>   1 **large green pepper, seeded and chopped**
>   4 **small thin-skinned potatoes, scrubbed**
>   ¾ **teaspoon** *each* **oregano leaves and ground cumin**
>   1 **large can (15 oz.) tomato sauce**
>   ⅓ **cup dry white wine or water**
>   ½ **cup** *each* **raisins and pitted ripe olives**
>   1 **cup frozen peas, thawed**

Heat oil in a 5-quart kettle over medium-high heat. Add chicken and cook, turning, until browned on all sides. Remove from kettle and set aside. Discard all but 2 tablespoons drippings.

Add garlic, onion, and green pepper to kettle; reduce heat to medium and cook, stirring, until onion is soft. Cut potatoes into 1-inch cubes; add to kettle along with chicken, oregano, cumin, tomato sauce, wine, raisins, and olives. Bring to a boil; then cover, reduce heat, and simmer, turning chicken once, until meat near thighbone is no longer pink when slashed (40 to 45 minutes). Stir in peas; cook just until heated through. Makes 4 servings.

Chicken Paprika

Hungary

In *paprikás csirke*, sweet Hungarian paprika adds a flaming glory of flavor and color to a creamy sauce for chicken.

>   1 **frying chicken (3 to 3½ lbs.), cut up**
>   **Salt and pepper**
>   1 **tablespoon salad oil**
>   1 **tablespoon butter or margarine**
>   1 **large onion, chopped**
>   1½ **tablespoons sweet Hungarian paprika or regular paprika**
>   ¾ **cup regular-strength chicken broth**
>   ½ **cup sour cream**

Sprinkle chicken lightly with salt and pepper. Heat oil and butter in a wide frying pan over medium-high heat. Add chicken and cook, turning, until golden on all sides; remove from pan.

Add onion to pan; reduce heat to medium and cook, stirring, until soft. Stir in paprika and broth and return chicken to pan. Bring to a boil; then cover, reduce heat, and simmer, turning once, until meat near thighbone is no longer pink when slashed (40 to 45 minutes). Lift out chicken.

Skim and discard fat from sauce. Reduce heat to very low; whisk in sour cream until smoothly blended. Add chicken and turn to coat. Makes 4 servings.

Chicken with Oranges

Mexico

For a fiesta of flavor, serve *pollo con naranjas:* chicken with aromatic oranges, spices, and raisins.

>   1 **frying chicken (3 to 3½ lbs.), cut up**
>   **Salt and pepper**
>   ⅛ **teaspoon** *each* **ground cinnamon and ground cloves**
>   2 **tablespoons salad oil**
>   1 **medium-size onion, chopped**
>   2 **cloves garlic, minced or pressed**
>   1 **cup orange juice**
>   2 **tablespoons raisins**
>   1 **tablespoon capers, drained well**
>   ½ **cup coarsely chopped blanched almonds**
>   3 **oranges, peeled and sliced**

Sprinkle chicken lightly with salt, pepper, cinnamon, and cloves. Heat oil in a wide frying pan over medium-high heat. Add chicken and cook, turning, until browned on all sides; remove from pan and set aside. Pour off and discard all but 2 tablespoons drippings.

Add onion and garlic to pan; reduce heat to medium and cook, stirring, until onion is soft. Return chicken to pan. Add orange juice, raisins, and capers. Bring to a boil; then cover, reduce heat, and simmer, turning once, until meat near thighbone is no longer pink when slashed (40 to 45 minutes). Transfer chicken to a platter.

Skim and discard fat from sauce; stir in almonds. Pour sauce over chicken and garnish with oranges. Makes 4 servings.

Stir-fried poultry

Since stir-frying is so rapid, it demands your full attention—so have everything ready beside pan or wok before you start to cook. Our stir-fries call for boned chicken breast, but turkey breast also gives good results. (It's coarser grained than chicken, so don't expect the same velvety texture after cooking.) If you're a dark-meat fan, you can substitute boned chicken legs or thighs (or turkey thighs) for breasts; just be sure to increase the cooking time by 1 to 2 minutes.

Once you've begun to cook, how often should you stir? That depends on the intensity of the heat and on how much food you've added to the pan. When you add poultry or meat, oil temperature drops; spread the pieces evenly over the pan's surface to let heat rise again and to seal in juices (10 to 15 seconds), then give a stir.

Give each morsel a chance to cook on one side before stirring to expose another side; stir more frequently near the end of cooking time, scraping pan bottom to prevent sticking. To test for doneness, cut into a piece. Breast meat should be opaque; dark meat should no longer look pink.

After you add vegetables, stir them constantly to prevent browning. Stir until done—or until recipe instructs you to add a bit of water and cover the pan (liquid keeps vegetables from browning).

Chicken & Snow Peas

China

This stir-fried chicken—briefly marinated first, sauced at the last minute—is one tantalizing example of a favorite Cantonese cooking style.

>   5   medium-size Oriental dried mushrooms
>   2   teaspoons *each* soy sauce, cornstarch, dry sherry, and water
>   Dash of white pepper
>   1½ pounds chicken breasts, skinned and boned
>   3½ tablespoons salad oil
>   Cooking sauce (recipe follows)
>   1   clove garlic, minced
>   ½   teaspoon minced fresh ginger
>   ½   cup sliced bamboo shoots or 1 whole bamboo shoot, cut into small pieces
>   ¼   pound snow peas, ends and strings removed

Soak mushrooms in warm water to cover for 30 minutes, then drain. Cut off and discard stems; squeeze caps dry, cut into ¼-inch slices, and set aside. In a bowl, combine soy, cornstarch, sherry, water, and pepper. Cut chicken into bite-size pieces; add to marinade and stir to coat, then stir in 1½ teaspoons of the oil. Let marinate for 15 minutes. Prepare cooking sauce and set aside.

Place a wok or wide frying pan over high heat. When pan is hot, add 2 tablespoons of the oil. When oil begins to heat, add garlic and ginger and stir once. Add chicken and stir-fry until opaque (about 3 minutes), then remove from pan.

Add remaining 1 tablespoon oil to pan. When oil is hot, add mushrooms and bamboo shoots. Stir-fry for 1 minute, adding a few drops of water if pan appears dry. Add snow peas and stir-fry for 1½ minutes, adding a few drops more water if necessary. Return chicken to pan. Stir the cooking sauce, add to pan, and cook, stirring, until sauce bubbles and thickens. Makes 3 or 4 servings.

Cooking sauce. Mix together ½ cup **water,** 1 tablespoon **dry sherry,** 2 tablespoons **soy sauce** or oyster sauce, ¼ teaspoon **sugar,** 1 teaspoon **sesame oil,** and 1 tablespoon **cornstarch.**

CHINESE CHICKEN & ZUCCHINI

(Pictured on facing page)

Follow directions for **Chicken & Snow Peas,** but add garlic and ginger to marinade; also add 2 teaspoons **fermented black beans,** rinsed, drained, and finely chopped. Substitute ½ pound **zucchini** and 1 **red or green bell pepper** for snow peas.

Roll-cut zucchini by making a diagonal slice straight down through squash, then rolling squash a quarter turn and slicing again. Seed pepper and cut into 1-inch squares. Stir-fry zucchini and pepper with mushrooms and bamboo shoots for 1 minute; then add 2 tablespoons water, cover, and cook until vegetables are tender-crisp to bite (about 3 minutes). Return chicken to pan, then proceed as directed above.

CANTONESE JADE CHICKEN

Follow directions for **Chicken & Snow Peas,** but add ½ teaspoon **crushed red pepper** to marinade. Substitute 1½ cups **seedless green grapes** for mushrooms and bamboo shoots; omit snow peas. In place of cooking sauce, use a mixture of ½ cup **regular-strength chicken broth,** 2 teaspoons **cornstarch,** and ½ teaspoon **sugar.**

Stir-frying Chicken & Zucchini (Recipe on facing page)

1 Soak dried mushrooms in warm water for 30 minutes. Cut off and discard hard stems; cut caps to ¼-inch-thick slices.

2 Cut boned chicken breasts into bite-size pieces. Then add chicken to soy marinade flavored with garlic, ginger, and fermented black beans; stir to coat and let marinate for 15 minutes.

3 Roll-cut zucchini by making a diagonal slice straight down through squash, giving it a quarter turn, and slicing again. Cut pepper into 1-inch squares; cut bamboo shoot into small pieces.

4 When vegetables are tender-crisp, return cooked chicken to pan and toss to heat through.

5 Add cooking sauce, pouring it in around edges of pan so it will heat quickly. Cook, stirring constantly, until sauce thickens (about 30 seconds).

6 Stir-fried vegetables have bright color, crisp texture; chicken morsels are tender and juicy. To serve the meal Chinese style, provide each diner with an individual bowl of rice.

Cooked & boned poultry

For sheer convenience, nothing beats having a cache of cooked, boned poultry on hand. When you roast an extra chicken or prepare a bird that's sure to provide more servings than you need, you gain a supply of leftover meat to use in another night's entrée. If you're starting from scratch, you can poach chicken breasts in a seasoned broth that gives the meat a marvelous flavor.

Turkey Tetrazzini

United States

A San Francisco chef of the early 1900s created this creamy casserole especially in honor of the opera singer Luisa Tetrazzini.

> 6　tablespoons butter or margarine
> 5　tablespoons all-purpose flour
> 2½　cups regular-strength chicken broth
> 1¼　cups half-and-half (light cream)
> ½　cup dry white wine
> ¾　cup grated Parmesan cheese
> ¾　pound mushrooms, sliced
> 12　ounces spaghetti
> 　Boiling salted water
> 3　to 4 cups bite-size pieces cooked turkey
> 　Salt and white pepper

In a 2-quart pan, melt 3 tablespoons of the butter over medium heat. Mix in flour; cook, stirring, until bubbly. Remove from heat and stir in broth, half-and-half, and wine. Return to heat; cook, stirring, until sauce boils and thickens. Stir in cheese and set sauce aside.

Melt remaining 3 tablespoons butter in a wide frying pan over medium-high heat. Add mushrooms and cook, stirring, until liquid has evaporated and mushrooms are lightly browned.

Following package directions, cook spaghetti in a large kettle of boiling salted water until *al dente;* drain. Reserve 1 cup of the sauce; combine remainder with spaghetti, mushrooms (save a few slices for garnish), and turkey. Mix lightly. Season to taste with salt and pepper. Turn into a greased shallow 2-quart casserole. Spoon reserved sauce evenly over surface; top with reserved mushroom slices.

Cover and bake in a 375° oven for about 45 minutes or until hot and bubbly. Uncover; broil 4 inches below heat until top is lightly browned. Makes 6 to 8 servings.

Pastel de Montezuma

Mexico

Pastel means "pie"—and in Mexican cuisine, the word promises tortillas or pastry in a pie or casserole.

> 　Green sauce (recipe follows)
> 6　cups bite-size pieces cooked turkey or chicken
> 1　pint (2 cups) sour cream
> 1　dozen 6-inch corn tortillas, cut into 2-inch squares
> 6　cups (1½ lbs.) shredded jack cheese

Prepare green sauce. Arrange half the turkey in a lightly greased 9 by 13-inch baking pan or shallow 3-quart casserole. Spread with half the green sauce, then with half the sour cream; top with half the tortilla pieces and half the cheese. Repeat layers, ending with cheese. Cover pan with foil.

Bake in a 375° oven for 40 minutes (55 minutes if refrigerated); uncover and bake for 8 more minutes or until cheese is bubbly and casserole is heated through. Cut into squares to serve. Makes 8 to 10 servings.

Green sauce. In a food processor or blender, combine 1 can (13 oz.) **tomatillos,** drained; 1 small **onion,** cut into pieces; 2 cloves **garlic;** 1 can (4 oz.) **diced green chiles,** drained; 1 bunch fresh **cilantro** (coriander), chopped (about ½ cup); 1 teaspoon **salt;** and ½ teaspoon **sugar.** Whirl until puréed.

ADD ZEST WITH FRESH GINGER

Fresh ginger tastes quite unlike the powdered spice—it's zestier and more aromatic. You'll find it for sale in most supermarkets. Choose firm roots with unwrinkled skin (see photo 2, page 110); peel before slicing, mincing, or grating. To store, wrap in a paper towel, then enclose in a plastic bag and refrigerate for up to 2 weeks. Or place peeled chunks in a jar, pour in sherry to cover, and refrigerate. When you need ginger for cooking, just pull out a piece and cut off the desired amount. Ginger stored this way keeps indefinitely (the sherry's good for flavoring, too).

Fila Chicken & Artichoke Casserole

Greece

Overlapping layers of delicate fila pastry enclose a creamy mixture of chicken, rice, and artichokes in this company casserole from Greece.

 ¾ cup (¼ lb. plus 4 tablespoons) butter or margarine
 ¼ cup all-purpose flour
 ½ cup half-and-half (light cream)
 3½ cups regular-strength chicken broth
  Salt and white pepper
 2 cloves garlic, minced or pressed
 1 large onion, chopped
 ½ pound mushrooms, sliced
 ¾ cup long-grain white rice
 ¾ teaspoon each summer savory and thyme leaves
 1 package (10 oz.) frozen artichoke hearts, thawed
 3 to 4 cups bite-size pieces cooked chicken
 16 sheets fila

In a 3-quart pan over medium heat, melt 4 tablespoons of the butter. Blend in flour and cook, stirring, until bubbly. Remove from heat; stir in half-and-half and 2 cups of the broth. Return to heat and cook, stirring, until sauce boils and thickens. Season to taste with salt and pepper. Set aside.

In a 2-quart pan over medium heat, melt 3 tablespoons of the butter. Add garlic, onion, and mushrooms and cook until vegetables are soft. Add rice and stir to coat. Add remaining 1½ cups broth, savory, and thyme; bring to a boil. Cover, reduce heat, and simmer until all liquid is absorbed (about 20 minutes). Stir in artichokes; cover and simmer for 5 more minutes. Stir in 1 cup of the cream sauce; remove from heat and let cool. Stir chicken into remaining cream sauce.

Stack fila; keep sheets covered with plastic wrap while you work. In a small pan, melt remaining 5 tablespoons butter; brush some on bottom and sides of a 9 by 13-inch baking pan. Place 1 sheet fila in bottom of pan, folding it to fit; brush lightly with butter. Repeat with 7 more sheets, brushing each with butter.

Spread half the rice mixture over fila in pan; top with all the chicken mixture. Then spoon on remaining rice mixture. Cover with 7 sheets fila, folding edges under to fit pan and lightly brushing each sheet with butter. Add remaining sheet of fila, tucking edges down inside pan; brush lightly with butter.

With a sharp knife, score the top 3 or 4 layers into 8 to 12 sections. (At this point, you may cover and refrigerate until next day.) Bake in a 350° oven, uncovered, for about 45 minutes (1 hour if refrigerated) or until golden brown and heated through. Makes 8 to 12 servings.

Szechwan Chicken with Spicy Peanut Sauce

China

Depending on the amount of lettuce you use, you can serve this salad as a main course or an appetizer. Be sure to shred the chicken rather than cutting it, so each piece has rough edges that absorb plenty of the flavorful dressing.

 1½ pounds chicken breasts
 1 green onion (including top), cut in half
 1 quarter-size slice fresh ginger, crushed
 1 tablespoon dry sherry
 ½ teaspoon each salt and sugar
 2 cups water
  Spicy peanut sauce (recipe follows)
 1 to 3 cups shredded iceberg lettuce

Place chicken in a 2-quart pan with onion, ginger, sherry, salt, sugar, and water. Bring to a boil over high heat; then cover, reduce heat, and simmer until meat in thickest part is no longer pink when slashed (15 to 20 minutes). Remove from heat, uncover, and let stand until cool enough to handle. Lift out chicken; strain broth and reserve for other uses. Discard chicken skin and bones; tear meat into long shreds. (At this point, you may cover and refrigerate for up to 2 days.)

Prepare peanut sauce. Mound lettuce on a platter or on individual plates. Arrange chicken over lettuce; drizzle peanut sauce over all. Makes 3 main-dish or 6 appetizer servings.

Spicy peanut sauce. In a bowl, stir together 1½ tablespoons **creamy peanut butter** and 2½ tablespoons **salad oil** until blended. Stir in 2 tablespoons each **soy sauce** and **sugar,** 2 teaspoons **white (distilled) vinegar,** ½ teaspoon **sesame oil,** ¼ to ½ teaspoon **ground red pepper** (cayenne), and 1 tablespoon each minced **green onion** (including top) and **fresh cilantro** (coriander) leaves.

Making Moroccan Bastilla (Recipe on facing page)

1 Saffron threads, cinnamon stick, and other fragrant spices season chicken as it simmers. Cook and shred chicken a day ahead, if you wish.

2 Eggs will cook into curds when stirred into hot chicken broth. Pour through a wire strainer; let drain very well to prevent bastilla from becoming soggy.

3 Arrange sheets of butter-streaked fila, cartwheel fashion, in pan. Sprinkle with sugar and cinnamon, then build layers of shredded chicken, drained eggs, and chopped almonds.

4 Cover pie with sheets of fila, tucking edges down inside pan. Brush with melted butter. (At this point, you may cover with plastic wrap and refrigerate for up to 4 hours.)

5 Sift powdered sugar over warm bastilla. Sprinkle ground cinnamon over sugar in a crisscross design, holding pinches of spice between thumb and forefinger.

6 Bastilla is traditionally served as a first course, but it's good enough to make a meal. Serve with forks—or, to eat Moroccan style, plunge fingers into pastry and lift out a piece.

Poultry in a pie

Poultry baked in a pie—what a dainty dish to set before your guests! And what an elegant way to stretch a small amount of meat a long way. Chicken pot pie, long a favorite in the United States, has cousins in many other lands; we give recipes for just two of these. Sumptuous Moroccan *bastilla* is wrapped in fila pastry; Chilean *pastel de choclo* has a flavorful creamed-corn "crust."

Bastilla

Morocco   (Pictured on facing page)

- 1 **frying chicken (3 to 3½ lbs.)**
- 2 **medium-size onions, chopped**
- 1 **large can (49½ oz.) regular-strength chicken broth or 6 cups homemade chicken broth (page 33)**
- 1 **cup chopped parsley**
- 1 **cinnamon stick (about 3 inches long)**
- 1 **teaspoon ground ginger**
- ¼ **teaspoon pepper**
- ½ **teaspoon saffron threads**
- 6 **eggs**
- 8 **sheets fila**
- 4 **tablespoons butter or margarine, melted**
- 1 **tablespoon granulated sugar**
- 1 **teaspoon ground cinnamon**
- ⅔ **cup finely chopped blanched almonds**
  Powdered sugar and ground cinnamon

Chop chicken giblets and place in a 5 to 6-quart kettle; then add chicken neck, chicken, onions, broth, parsley, cinnamon stick, ginger, pepper, and saffron. Bring to a boil over high heat; then cover, reduce heat, and simmer until chicken pulls easily from bones (1 to 1¼ hours).

Lift chicken and neck from broth and let stand until cool enough to handle. Discard skin and bones, then shred meat into bite-size pieces.

Bring broth to a boil over medium heat. Lightly beat eggs; pour slowly into broth, stirring until curds form (1 to 2 minutes). Pour through a wire strainer placed over a bowl. Let stand until well drained (reserve broth for soup, if desired). Discard cinnamon stick.

Stack fila; keep it covered with plastic wrap while you work. Brush some of the butter over bottom and sides of a deep 10-inch pie pan. Arrange 6 sheets fila in pan, overlapping them to cover pan bottom and extend 8 to 10 inches beyond edges. Brush fila with butter. Sprinkle granulated sugar and the 1 teaspoon cinnamon over fila; top

evenly with chicken. Spread egg mixture over chicken, then sprinkle with almonds. Fold edges of fila over filling; brush with butter. Fold remaining 2 sheets fila in half crosswise and place on pie. Tuck edges inside pan. Brush with butter.

Bake in a 425° oven, uncovered, for 20 minutes or until golden brown. Shake pan to loosen pie; then hold an unrimmed baking sheet loosely over top of pie and invert pan. Lift off pan, place baking sheet in oven, and bake pie for 10 more minutes or until golden. Invert pie onto a platter; let stand for 5 minutes. Sift powdered sugar generously over top, then decorate with crisscrossing lines of cinnamon. Makes 8 servings.

Chicken-Corn Pie

Chile

- 3 **tablespoons butter or margarine**
- 1 **medium-size onion, chopped**
- 1 **clove garlic, minced or pressed**
- 2 **tablespoons all-purpose flour**
- 1 **cup regular-strength chicken broth**
- ½ **teaspoon each paprika and ground cumin**
- ¼ **teaspoon crushed red pepper**
- 3 **cups bite-size pieces cooked chicken**
- 2 **hard-cooked eggs, chopped**
- ⅓ **cup pitted ripe olives, drained well**
- ¼ **cup raisins**
- 1 **can (about 1 lb.) cream-style corn**
- 1 **egg, lightly beaten**
- 4 **teaspoons sugar**

Melt 2 tablespoons of the butter in a wide frying pan over medium heat. Add onion and garlic and cook until onion is soft. Stir in 1 tablespoon of the flour and cook for 1 minute, then stir in broth. Add paprika, cumin, and pepper and cook, stirring, until sauce boils and thickens. Remove from heat and stir in chicken, hard-cooked eggs, olives, and raisins. Spoon mixture into a greased shallow 1½-quart casserole.

Wipe frying pan clean, then add remaining 1 tablespoon butter and melt over medium heat. Stir in remaining 1 tablespoon flour and corn; cook, stirring, until bubbly. Remove from heat. Pour egg into corn mixture and stir until well combined. Spoon evenly over chicken; sprinkle with sugar. Bake in a 350° oven for 35 minutes or until heated through, then broil 2 inches below heat until top is golden brown. Makes 4 servings.

FISH & SHELLFISH

From oceans, rivers, and lakes, fishermen around the world reap a daily harvest unsurpassed in variety and abundance: halibut and delicate sole, trout and rosy-fleshed salmon, clams, crabs, and scallops, and countless others. For many of the world's people, fish and shellfish are the major source of protein. And for all of us, they provide magnificent eating.

Today, as interest in lean, protein-rich foods increases, the popularity of fish and shellfish is definitely on the rise. New local fish markets are opening to enthusiastic customers; supermarkets offer a selection that's wider than ever.

When you shop for fish, don't be surprised if you run across an unfamiliar variety or two. And if you'd like to taste a new type, feel free to try it in our recipes. Though this chapter focuses on generally available kinds of fish, the cooking methods we present apply to many varieties.

To estimate cooking time for any fish, follow this rule: *For pan-frying, poaching, steaming, barbecuing, and broiling,* allow 8 to 10 minutes per inch of thickness. For example, a ½-inch-thick fillet will cook in 4 to 5 minutes; a 1½-inch-thick piece will cook in 12 to 15 minutes. This rule doesn't always apply to *baked* fish, since a sauce or topping affects cooking time.

For shellfish cooking times, see individual recipes.

TESTING FISH FOR DONENESS

For years, recipes have recommended cooking fish until it flakes easily when prodded in the thickest portion with a fork. ("Flaking" means that the flesh slides apart along natural divisions.)

Our testing indicates that cooking to this stage is usually a touch too much, since fish continues to cook from its own internal heat during the interval between cooking and serving. A better method is to cook the fish until the flesh inside is just opaque. If you do this, the fish will flake by the time it arrives at the table.

As fish cooks, its translucent flesh changes to opaque white (or pink, in the case of salmon). *Near the end of the estimated cooking time, make this test for doneness: Cut a slit in the center of the thickest portion of the fish. When the flesh inside has lost its wet look, take the fish off the heat.*

Fish from the oven

Great-tasting fish without a fuss—that's what you get when you oven-cook. Oil or butter added to the pan gives you fish with a pan-fried flavor; if you add a little liquid, the fish poaches, releasing juices you can use in a flavorful sauce.

Roman Sole

Italy

The Roman way with sole calls for a one-step oven-frying technique that eliminates turning the fragile fish during cooking.

> 1½ **pounds sole fillets**
> **Salt and pepper**
> **All-purpose flour**
> 4 **tablespoons butter or margarine, or**
> **2 tablespoons butter or margarine**
> **and 2 tablespoons olive oil**

Choose an ovenproof dish in which sole will just fit without overlapping. Place dish in a 500° oven. Sprinkle fish with salt and pepper; coat with flour.

Remove dish from oven and add butter; swirl dish until butter is melted. Turn fish in butter to coat. Return to oven; bake for 4 to 8 minutes or until fish is browned and tests done (see facing page). Makes 4 servings.

Coconut Oven-fried Fish

Caribbean

The tang of lime and the sweetness of coconut give whole fish or fillets a Caribbean flavor.

> 5 **tablespoons butter or margarine, melted**
> 2 **tablespoons lime juice**
> ⅛ **teaspoon *each* salt and pepper**
> 1 **cup sweetened flaked coconut**
> ½ **cup fine dry bread crumbs**
> 4 **whole cleaned trout (about 8 oz. *each*); or**
> **2 pounds white fish fillets or steaks such**
> **as halibut, rockfish, or turbot, *each* about**
> **1 inch thick**
> 1 **tablespoon salad oil**
> 1 **tablespoon butter or margarine**

In a shallow dish, combine the 5 tablespoons butter, lime juice, salt, and pepper. In another dish, combine coconut and crumbs.

Brush cavity of each trout with butter mixture, then turn in butter mixture to coat. (Or simply coat fillets or steaks with butter mixture.) Then roll in coconut mixture to coat all sides; reserve any unused coconut mixture.

Place oil and the 1 tablespoon butter in a 12 by 17-inch shallow rimmed baking pan and set in a 400° oven. When butter is melted (2 to 3 minutes; don't let it burn), swirl pan to coat bottom. Place fish in pan and sprinkle with half the reserved coconut mixture. Bake for 4 minutes. Carefully turn fish with a wide spatula; sprinkle with remaining coconut mixture. Bake for 4 to 6 more minutes or until done (see facing page). Makes 4 servings.

Baked Salmon Steaks with Fish Mousse

France

Golden puffs of sole mousse top succulent salmon steaks in this elegant company dish.

> ½ **pound sole or lingcod fillets**
> 1 **egg**
> ½ **cup whipping cream**
> 4 **salmon steaks, *each* about 1 inch thick**
> 1 **cup dry white wine**
> ½ **teaspoon thyme leaves**
> 1 **tablespoon minced green onion (including top)**
> **or shallot**
> 4 **tablespoons butter or margarine**
> **Salt and pepper**

Pull any bones from sole with pliers or tweezers, then cut fish into chunks. Place in a food processor and whirl until puréed (or put through a food chopper fitted with a fine blade). Add egg and ¼ cup of the cream; mix well.

Arrange salmon steaks side by side in a 9 by 13-inch baking dish. Spoon sole mixture evenly over salmon. (At this point, you may cover and refrigerate for up to 6 hours.)

Just before baking, pour wine around fish. Bake in a 450° oven, uncovered, for 15 to 20 minutes or until mousse topping is lightly browned and fish tests done (see facing page).

With a slotted spatula, transfer fish to a platter; keep warm. Pour cooking liquid through a wire strainer into a wide frying pan. Add remaining ¼ cup cream, thyme, and onion; boil rapidly over high heat until reduced to ½ cup.

Reduce heat to low. Add butter all at once, stirring constantly to incorporate butter as it melts. Season to taste with salt and pepper. Spoon sauce over and around fish. Makes 4 servings.

Fish & shellfish wrapped & baked

Securely packaged in a leakproof packet during cooking, fish and shellfish stay wonderfully moist and succulent. Europeans know this method as cooking en *papillote*—in an envelope of parchment. In other parts of the world, though, a folded leaf is the wrapper of choice: taro in Polynesia (see Shrimp Palusami, page 129), banana in India and Southeast Asia. Bamboo leaves are traditional in Japan, though today's cooks use foil.

Because foil and cooking parchment are more readily available (and easier to use), our recipes call for these materials. Parchment is sold alongside the wax paper in many supermarkets.

Dilled Fish Fillets in Parchment

Sweden   (Pictured on facing page)

Salmon and fresh dill are a favorite Swedish combination—and when you sample this entrée, you'll see why. (For tips on boning fillets, see page 134.)

>   4   **equal-size pieces salmon or sea bass fillet (1½ lbs. *total*), each ¾ to 1 inch thick**
>   3   **tablespoons *each* olive oil, white wine vinegar, and chopped green onions (including tops)**
>   1   **teaspoon chopped fresh dill or ½ teaspoon dry dill weed**
>   1   **teaspoon grated orange peel**
>   3   **tablespoons butter or margarine, melted**
>   **Salad oil**
>   **Fresh dill sprigs (optional)**

Skin fish; pull out any bones with pliers or tweezers. In a 1-cup glass measure, combine olive oil, vinegar, onions, dill, and orange peel; set aside.

Cut 4 sheets of cooking parchment, each about 4 times wider and 6 inches longer than each fish portion. Brush each parchment sheet with about 2 teaspoons of the butter, starting 1 to 2 inches from the long side and covering an area the size of fish to be wrapped. Place one fish portion on buttered area of each sheet; spoon ¼ of the olive oil mixture over each.

To make each packet, fold parchment over fish, then roll over twice to enclose. Double-fold ends; tuck them under packet to seal. Place packets, folded ends down, slightly apart in a shallow rimmed baking pan; brush with salad oil.

Bake in a 500° oven for 6 to 10 minutes or until fish tests done (see page 120; to test, cut a tiny slit through parchment into fish). Garnish each serving with dill, if desired. Makes 4 servings.

ITALIAN SHRIMP OR SCALLOPS WITH PESTO

Make pesto: In a food processor or blender, place ¾ cup lightly packed **fresh basil leaves,** ⅓ cup grated **Parmesan cheese,** and 3 tablespoons *each* **olive oil** and **lemon juice.** Whirl until basil is finely chopped. Shell and devein 1½ pounds large **raw shrimp** or rinse 1½ pounds scallops; pat dry.

Divide shellfish into 4 portions. Wrap and bake as directed for **Dilled Fish Fillets in Parchment.** Omit olive oil mixture; instead, top each portion with ¼ of the pesto, 1 thin **lemon slice,** 1 **pitted ripe olive,** and a sprinkling of **salt** and **pepper.** (Shrimp are done when they turn pink, scallops when they're opaque throughout—takes 8 to 10 minutes.)

Fish Baked in Foil

Japan

Snug in a shiny foil wrapper, fish bakes to juicy, gingery perfection in just minutes.

>   4   **equal-size pieces salmon, sea bass, or halibut fillet (1½ lbs. *total*), each ¾ to 1 inch thick; or 4 whole cleaned trout (about 8 oz. *each*)**
>   ½   **teaspoon salt**
>   **Salad oil**
>   ½   **small onion, thinly sliced**
>   1   **teaspoon grated fresh ginger**
>   4   **large shiitake or regular mushrooms**
>   4   **thin lemon slices**
>   2   **tablespoons sake or dry sherry**

Skin fillets; pull out any bones with pliers or tweezers. Sprinkle fish with salt and let stand for 10 minutes.

Cut 4 pieces of foil, each 3 times as wide and 1½ times as long as fish. For each packet, brush center of a foil sheet with oil, then center ¼ of the onion on oiled area. Top with a portion of fish, ¼ teaspoon ginger, 1 mushroom, and 1 lemon slice. Sprinkle with ½ tablespoon sake. Bring long sides of foil together; fold to seal. Double-fold ends.

Place packets, sealed sides up, slightly apart in a shallow rimmed baking pan. Bake in a 425° oven for 6 to 10 minutes for fillets, 12 to 15 minutes for trout, or until fish tests done (see page 120; to test, cut a slit through foil into fish). Serve in packets. Makes 4 servings.

Preparing paper-wrapped fish, Swedish style (Recipe on facing page)

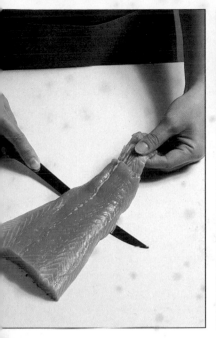

1 To skin fish most easily, use a knife with a flexible blade. Make a cut ½ inch from end of fillet down to skin, then turn blade flat. Holding end, cut between skin and flesh.

2 Brush parchment with melted butter 1 to 2 inches from one long edge. Place fish on buttered area; spoon on dill-flavored seasoning mixture.

3 Fold parchment forward to enclose fish; then roll over 2 times to seal packet completely.

4 Double-fold ends of parchment; tuck under packet to hold in place. Brush sealed packets with oil and set in a rimmed baking pan. If you wish, refrigerate until next day before baking.

5 Slash open the packet and enjoy dill-seasoned salmon, moist and delicious in its own juices. For a Swedish-style meal, top fish with dill sprigs and offer small boiled potatoes and asparagus alongside.

Broiled & barbecued seafood

Steaks, fillets, skewered chunks of fish, even delicate shellfish—all cook beautifully in the direct heat of barbecue or oven broiler. Both methods produce tasty results (the barbecue adds a wonderful smoky flavor), and actual cooking time is about the same for each. But if you're in a hurry, choose broiling; there's no waiting for coals to burn to the right stage.

Fish on Skewers

Greece

Fresh bay leaves alternate with marinated chunks of fish for a simple, aromatic entrée. Firm fish such as halibut and swordfish are best for skewering; more delicate types will fall apart.

> 2 **pounds halibut or swordfish steaks,** *each* **about 1 inch thick**
> ½ **cup lemon juice**
> ½ **cup olive oil or salad oil**
> 2 **tablespoons chopped parsley**
> 1 **teaspoon oregano leaves**
> 1 **clove garlic, minced or pressed**
> ½ **teaspoon salt**
> ¼ **teaspoon pepper**
> 20 **fresh or dry bay leaves**

Skin fish and pull out any bones with pliers or tweezers; then cut fish into 1-inch cubes and place in a bowl.

In another bowl, combine lemon juice, oil, parsley, oregano, garlic, salt, and pepper; stir until blended. Pour ⅔ of marinade over fish and stir to coat; reserve remaining marinade to pass at the table. Cover and refrigerate fish for 2 hours. If using dry bay leaves, place in a bowl, cover with boiling water, and let stand for 5 minutes; then drain.

Lift fish from marinade and drain briefly, reserving marinade for basting. Alternately thread fish cubes and bay leaves on 6 skewers, each at least 12 inches long.

Place fish 4 inches below heat on a greased rack in a broiler pan (see "How to Broil Meat," page 85); or barbecue 4 inches above a solid bed of medium-glowing coals (see "Barbecuing Using Direct Heat," page 84). Cook, turning several times and basting occasionally with marinade, until fish is browned and tests done (8 to 10 minutes; see page 120). Pass reserved marinade at the table. Makes 4 to 6 servings.

Broiled Fish Sinaloa

Mexico

On the beaches of Sinaloa, you can buy this lemony, anchovy-anointed fish hot from a vendor's stall. It makes good eating at home, too, especially when paired with cold beer.

> 2 **tablespoons butter or margarine**
> 2 **tablespoons lemon juice**
> 1 **clove garlic, minced or pressed**
> 1 **to 1½ pounds firm-textured white fish fillets or steaks such as halibut, rockfish, sea bass, or swordfish,** *each* **¾ to 1 inch thick**
> 1 **teaspoon dry mustard**
> 6 **anchovy fillets, drained and chopped**

In a small pan, heat butter, lemon juice, and garlic until butter is melted. Place fish on a greased rack in a broiler pan (see "How to Broil Meat," page 85); brush with half the butter mixture. Broil 4 inches below heat until just slightly translucent inside (about 3 minutes; to test, cut into center of thickest part).

Stir mustard and anchovies into remaining butter mixture. Turn fish over, baste, and continue to cook until done (3 to 7 more minutes; see page 120). Remove pan from oven. Makes 3 servings.

Grilled White Fish

Japan

A delicate soy-lemon sauce flavors these quick-to-fix skewered fillets. Japanese cooks like to use the parallel-skewer technique for whole fish, too, rippling the skewers in and out to make the fish look as though it's actively swimming.

> 1 **to 1½ pounds firm-textured white fish fillets such as red snapper or sea bass,** *each* **¾ to 1 inch thick**
> 3 **tablespoons soy sauce**
> 2 **tablespoons mirin or 2 teaspoons sugar**
> 1 **tablespoon lemon juice**
> 1½ **teaspoons salad oil**

Cut fish into serving-size pieces. For easy handling, run 2 bamboo skewers lengthwise through each piece, spacing them about 1 inch apart. In a small bowl, mix soy, mirin, lemon juice, and oil. Brush some of soy mixture over fish; let stand for about 10 minutes.

Place fish 4 inches below heat on a greased rack in a broiler pan (see "How to Broil Meat," page 85), or barbecue 4 inches above a solid bed of medium-glowing coals (see "Barbecuing Using Direct Heat," page 84). Cook until just slightly translucent inside (about 3 minutes; to test, cut into center of thickest part). Turn fish over and continue to cook, basting several times with soy mixture, until fish tests done (3 to 7 more minutes; see page 120). Makes 3 or 4 servings.

Spicy Marinated Shrimp

United States

Zesty with Creole seasonings, these skewered shrimp are perfect for a summertime barbecue.

- ¼ cup salad oil
- 1 teaspoon salt
- ½ teaspoon pepper
- 1 clove garlic, minced or pressed
- ⅓ cup each vinegar and tomato-based chili sauce
- 2 tablespoons Worcestershire
- ⅛ teaspoon liquid hot pepper seasoning
- ½ cup minced parsley
- 2 pounds medium-size raw shrimp, shelled and deveined

In a bowl, combine oil, salt, pepper, garlic, vinegar, chili sauce, Worcestershire, hot pepper seasoning, and parsley. Stir in shrimp; cover and refrigerate for 1 to 2 hours.

About 35 minutes before cooking, start barbecue fire (see "Barbecuing Using Direct Heat," page 84). Lift shrimp from marinade and drain briefly, reserving marinade. Thread on metal skewers and place on a well-greased grill 4 to 6 inches above a solid bed of low-glowing coals. Cook, basting with marinade and turning once, until shrimp turn pink (about 4 minutes per side). Makes 6 servings.

MEXICAN GARLIC SHRIMP

Skewer and grill shrimp as directed for **Spicy Marinated Shrimp,** but omit marinade. Instead, baste shrimp with a mixture of ½ cup **olive oil,** ½ cup melted **butter** or margarine, 2 tablespoons **lemon juice,** 3 cloves **garlic** (minced or pressed), and 3 tablespoons minced **parsley.**

QUICK SAUCES FOR FISH & SHELLFISH

These flavorful cold sauces pair well with hot or chilled fish and shellfish.

Aïoli (Garlic Mayonnaise)/French Provence. In a blender or food processor, whirl until blended: 1 large **egg,** 1½ tablespoons each **white wine vinegar** and **lemon juice,** ½ teaspoon **salt,** and 4 to 6 cloves **garlic.** With motor running, gradually add a mixture of ½ cup each **olive oil** and **salad oil**— a few drops at a time at first, then increasing to a slow, steady stream. Season to taste with **liquid hot pepper seasoning.** Cover and refrigerate. Makes 1¼ cups.

Skordalia (Garlic Almond Mayonnaise)/ Greece. Prepare **Aïoli,** but reduce garlic to 2 cloves and omit hot pepper seasoning. After blending in oil, add ⅓ cup finely chopped **blanched almonds, toasted** (page 87); blend for 3 seconds. Cover and refrigerate. Makes 1⅓ cups.

Cucumber Sauce/Scandinavia. Peel and finely chop 1 **cucumber.** Place in a bowl and stir in ½ teaspoon **salt;** let stand for 15 minutes, then drain well. Add ½ cup **sour cream** or plain yogurt, ½ cup **mayonnaise,** and 1½ teaspoons **dill weed;** mix well. Cover and refrigerate. Makes about 2 cups.

Tahini Sauce/Middle East. In a bowl, stir ½ cup **water** into ½ cup **tahini** (sesame-seed paste). Add ½ cup **lemon juice** and blend well. Stir in 1 clove **garlic** (minced or pressed), ½ teaspoon **salt,** ¼ teaspoon **ground cumin,** and ½ cup chopped **parsley.** Cover and refrigerate. Makes 1½ cups.

Tomato Chile Salsa/Mexico. Seed and chop 1 medium-size **tomato.** Mix with ¼ cup chopped **green pepper,** 2 tablespoons each chopped **green onion** (including top) and chopped **radishes,** and 1 tablespoon each **canned diced green chiles** and chopped **fresh cilantro** (coriander). Cover and refrigerate. Makes ¾ cup.

Deep-frying Fish & Chips (Recipe on facing page)

1 To slice a potato quickly, cut a thin strip off one side; then place on cutting board, cut side down. Cut lengthwise into ⅜-inch slices. Stack slices, a few at a time; cut into ⅜-inch-wide strips.

2 As you cut potatoes, drop them into cold water for a quick rinse to prevent discoloration and sticking during cooking. Dry thoroughly before frying—wet food and hot oil create spatters.

3 Lower limp prefried potatoes into hot oil for second cooking to turn them crisp and brown. Keep cooked potatoes warm in a 200° oven while you fry fish. Salt potatoes just before serving.

4 Use tongs to lower batter-coated fish into hot oil. Don't crowd—allow each piece enough room to develop a crisp coating on all sides.

5 Offer golden, crunchy Fish & Chips with malt vinegar and salt for an authentic English meal. Or serve American style—with catsup and tartar sauce.

Deep-fried fish

There's no denying it. Batter-fried fish can be sublime—or it can be a disappointment. If you want delectably crunchy results every time, fry fast, at the proper temperature, and serve hot. This is the kind of production that goes smoothly when two cooks team up—one to fry, the other to assemble the rest of the meal.

The larger the pan, the faster you can fry, so don't be tempted to skimp on oil by frying in a small pan. We strongly recommend using a large pan: a 5-quart kettle, a wide, heavy frying pan at least 3 inches deep, or a wok set in a ring stand for stability. An electric deep-fryer, frying pan, or wok is fine, too, and has the advantage of a built-in heat control. (If you don't use electric equipment, you'll need to attach a clip-on deep-frying thermometer to the side of the pan.)

Colorless, odorless salad oil such as corn, peanut, or cottonseed oil is best for deep-frying. Heat oil to the temperature specified in the recipe, then add food (be careful; there's sure to be some spattering). Fry only small amounts at a time—if you crowd too much into the pan, the oil temperature will drop and the food will turn out greasy and sodden.

As you fry, remove the browned bits of batter floating on the oil before they burn. This helps keep oil fresh enough to re-use for another batch of fish. After you're done cooking, let oil cool completely; then pour it through a strainer lined with several layers of cheesecloth into a wide-mouthed jar. Refrigerate oil until needed; discard it when it darkens or begins to smell rancid.

Fish & Chips

England   (Pictured on facing page)

The English call them chips. We call them French fries. By either name, they taste marvelous, especially with batter-fried fish. If you want to make your own fries, allow enough time for double frying, a technique that gives you wonderfully crisp potatoes. (If you're short on time, just deep-fry frozen French fries, following package directions.)

It's not essential to make the batter ahead, but for best results, prepare it 1 to 2 hours in advance.

Our batter fries up into a light, crisp coating that holds up quite well, so you can keep cooked fish warm in a 200° oven until you've finished frying the entire batch. For a thicker batter (and a thicker coating), decrease beer by 2 tablespoons.

1 **cup all-purpose flour**
½ **teaspoon baking powder**
¾ **teaspoon salt**
⅛ **teaspoon pepper**
1 **cup beer, at room temperature**
4 **to 6 large russet potatoes (2 to 3 lbs. *total*), scrubbed**
  About 3 cups salad oil
2 **pounds firm-textured white fish fillets such as red snapper, rockfish, or sea bass, *each* ½ to ¾ inch thick**
1 **egg white**
  Salt
  Malt vinegar

In a large bowl, combine flour, baking powder, the ¾ teaspoon salt, and pepper. Slowly add beer, blending with a wire whisk until smooth. Let batter stand at room temperature for 1 to 2 hours.

Meanwhile, peel potatoes, if desired; then cut lengthwise into ⅜-inch-thick strips, dropping strips into a bowl of cold water as you cut them.

Into a heavy pan, pour oil to a depth of 1½ to 2 inches and heat to 325° on a deep-frying thermometer. (If you're using a basket liner, heat in oil for last 3 minutes before cooking potatoes.) Lift potatoes from water; *dry thoroughly* in a clean towel. Using tongs or a large spoon, lower about 1½ cups potatoes into oil; cook until limp but not golden (4 to 5 minutes). Lift out with a slotted spoon or an Oriental wire skimmer and drain on paper towels. Repeat until all are cooked; turn off heat under oil. Let potatoes cool for at least 30 minutes or up to 2 hours.

Pull any bones from fish with pliers or tweezers, then cut fish crosswise into 1½-inch-wide strips. Beat egg white until frothy; fold into batter. Place fish in batter and turn to coat.

Reheat oil to 375° (also reheat basket liner, if you're using one). Cook potatoes, about 1½ cups at a time, until nicely browned (2 to 3 minutes). Drain in a single layer on paper towels; keep warm in a 200° oven.

Reheat oil to 375°, if necessary. Using tongs, lower 4 to 6 pieces of fish into oil, one piece at a time. Cook, turning, until coating is golden brown and fish tests done (3 to 5 minutes; see page 120). Remove with a slotted spoon, drain on paper towels, and keep warm. Repeat until all fish is cooked.

Sprinkle salt over potatoes (or pass salt at the table). Serve fish and potatoes with malt vinegar. Makes 4 to 6 servings.

Steamed fish

Steaming is a technique that's common throughout the Orient, where it's especially popular for cooking fish. Moist, gentle steam heat preserves natural juices, fresh flavor, and bright color.

A variety of steaming equipment is readily available, from Chinese stacked bamboo baskets to stacked metal steamers. But you can improvise, too. Just set a plate (Illustration 1) or wire rack (Illustration 2) on supports—such as large tuna cans with both ends removed—inside a deep kettle or frying pan with a tight-fitting lid.

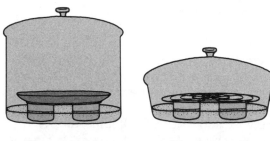

Illustration 1   *Illustration 2*

Start with a container full of steam and keep it that way. Begin with enough water to last the full cooking time; if you need to add more, make sure it's boiling when you pour it in. During steaming, water droplets gather on the steamer lid, then drip down from it—so shield food contained in a dish with a piece of wax paper.

Though steam looks harmless, it can burn you. Always lift the steamer lid away from you, then give steam a few seconds to disperse.

Gingered Steamed Fish

China

  1 or 2 whole fish (1½ to 2½ lbs. *total*) such as red snapper, rockfish, or kingfish, cleaned and scaled; or 1½ pounds white fish fillets, *each* ¾ to 1 inch thick
  1 teaspoon salt
  3 quarter-size slices fresh ginger
  4 green onions (including tops), cut into 1½-inch pieces
  2 to 3 tablespoons salad oil
  5 sprigs fresh cilantro (coriander)
  2 tablespoons matchstick pieces fresh ginger
  2 tablespoons soy sauce

Make 3 diagonal slashes across whole fish on each side of body; then rub with salt, inside cavity and outside. (Or rub salt over all sides of fillets.)

Place fish on a heatproof dish or plate that will fit inside a steamer. Top fish with ginger slices and half the onion; shred remaining onion.

Place dish on rack in steamer. Cover and steam over 1 to 2 inches of boiling water until fish tests done (see page 120; allow 6 to 10 minutes for fillets or small fish, 10 to 12 minutes for a 1½-pound fish, and 16 to 18 minutes for a 2½-pound fish).

Heat oil in a small pan until hot but not smoking. Remove dish with fish from steamer, discard ginger slices and onion pieces, and tip dish slightly to drain off liquid. Sprinkle fish with onion shreds, cilantro, matchstick pieces ginger, and soy; pour oil over fish. Makes 3 to 6 servings.

Chilled Salmon with Lomi Lomi Relish

United States—Hawaii

Classic *lomi lomi* is a combination of chopped salted salmon, tomatoes, and onions. In this variation, the salmon is steamed and chilled separately, then served with a zippy lomi lomi relish.

      Lomi lomi relish (recipe follows)
      About 2 pounds salmon or turbot fillets, *each* ¾ to 1 inch thick
   1 or 2 bay leaves
      Whole black peppers
   4 lemon slices
      Butter lettuce leaves
      Lemon wedges

Prepare lomi lomi relish; cover and refrigerate.

Place fish on a double layer of cheesecloth that's slightly bigger all around than fish. Then place fish on rack in steamer, folding cheesecloth up around edges. Place bay leaves, peppers, and lemon slices on fish. Cover and steam over 1 to 2 inches of boiling water until fish tests done (6 to 10 minutes; see page 120). Grasp cheesecloth and lift out fish; let cool, then cover and refrigerate.

Arrange lettuce on 4 individual plates and top with serving-size pieces of fish. Serve with relish and lemon wedges. Makes 4 to 6 servings.

Lomi lomi relish. In a bowl, combine 2 medium-size **tomatoes,** chopped; 1 large **green pepper,** seeded and chopped; ½ cup thinly sliced **green onions** (including tops); 1 small **onion,** chopped; 2 to 3 tablespoons **canned diced green chiles;** 2 tablespoons **lemon juice;** and 1 teaspoon **salt.** Makes about 2 cups.

Shellfish sampler

If you're looking for especially tempting ways to serve shellfish, these recipes are for you. Here and on the next three pages, we present a mouth-watering collection employing a variety of cooking techniques. Try shrimp baked with feta cheese, saucy stir-fried crab, or simmered mussels—or make a very special dish of cheese-stuffed squid baked in rich tomato sauce. (Though squid isn't really a shellfish—or a fish either, for that matter—we've included it in this section.)

Baked Shrimp with Feta

Greece

Plump shrimp and chunks of feta cheese bake in a garlicky tomato sauce for *garithes yiouvetsi*, a waterfront specialty of Piraeus.

    2 tablespoons olive oil or salad oil
    1 small onion, chopped
    1 clove garlic, minced or pressed
    2 green onions (including tops), finely chopped
    1 can (about 1 lb.) Italian-style tomatoes
    ¼ cup dry white wine
    2 tablespoons chopped parsley
    ½ teaspoon oregano leaves
    1 pound medium-size raw shrimp, shelled and deveined
    3 ounces feta cheese, cut into ½-inch cubes

Heat oil in a wide frying pan over medium heat. Add onion; cook, stirring occasionally, until soft. Add garlic and green onions; cook for 1 minute. Chop tomatoes; add tomatoes and their liquid, wine, parsley, and oregano. Simmer, uncovered, until sauce is slightly thickened (about 10 minutes).

Remove pan from heat and stir in shrimp. Spoon into a 1½-quart casserole. Scatter cheese over top, pushing it in slightly. Bake in a 375° oven, uncovered, for 15 to 20 minutes or until shrimp turn pink and cheese is slightly softened. Makes 4 servings.

Shrimp Palusami

Samoan Islands

This Samoan favorite features a luscious combination of shrimp, coconut, and ripe banana. We've substituted spinach and cooking parchment for the traditional (and edible) taro-leaf wrapper.

    1 pound spinach, rinsed well, tough stems removed
    1 medium-size onion, chopped
    2 cups cooked rice mixed with ¾ teaspoon salt
    1 pound medium-size raw shrimp, shelled and deveined
    1⅓ cups canned or thawed frozen coconut milk, or 1⅓ cups whipping cream mixed with ¾ teaspoon *each* coconut extract and sugar
    1 firm ripe banana, thinly sliced
    4 lime wedges

Tear or cut four 15-inch-square pieces of cooking parchment or foil. Mound ¼ of the spinach in center of each piece; scatter onion and rice evenly over spinach. Top each mound with ¼ of the shrimp, then spoon on ⅓ cup of the coconut milk.

Bring opposite sides of parchment together and fold down to food; double-fold ends and tuck under packet. Place packets, folded ends down, in a shallow rimmed baking pan. Bake in a 350° oven for 30 minutes or until onion is tender and shrimp turn pink (to test, cut a slit through parchment). Slash open each packet and add ¼ of the banana; squeeze lime wedges over food. Makes 4 servings.

Scallops with Saffron Cream

United States

Delicate white scallops are briefly broiled, then served with a golden cream-and-wine sauce.

    1 pound sea scallops, rinsed and drained
       Melted butter or margarine
    ½ cup *each* dry white wine and regular-strength chicken broth
    2 tablespoons minced shallots or onion
       Pinch of ground saffron
    ½ cup whipping cream

Thread scallops on 4 skewers, then brush generously with butter. Place about 3 inches below heat on a greased rack in a broiler pan (see "How to Broil Meat," page 85); cook, turning occasionally and basting with butter, just until opaque throughout (3 to 5 minutes). Keep warm.

In a wide frying pan, combine wine, broth, shallots, and saffron. Bring to a boil over high heat; boil, uncovered, until reduced by half. Add cream; continue to boil until reduced to ¾ cup. Pour sauce into a rimmed platter; arrange scallops in sauce. Makes 4 servings.

...Shellfish sampler

Ricotta-stuffed Squid

Italy   (Pictured on facing page)

In recent years, Americans have learned what Mediterranean and Asian cooks have long known—squid (*calamari* in Italian) makes marvelous eating. The white flesh has a mild, sweet flavor and an abalone-like texture. Squid does take time to clean, but the job goes faster with a little practice.

> 1 **pound squid**
> 1 **cup (8 oz.) ricotta cheese**
> ½ **cup *each* grated Parmesan cheese and chopped parsley**
> 2 **cloves garlic, minced or pressed**
> ⅓ **cup fine dry bread crumbs**
> 1 **tablespoon butter or margarine**
> ⅓ **cup chopped green onions (white part only)**
> 2 **cans (about 1 lb. *each*) Italian-style tomatoes**
> 1 **teaspoon granulated beef stock base**
> ⅛ **teaspoon pepper**
>   **Chopped parsley**
>   **Lemon slices**

Clean squid as shown in photographs 1, 2, and 3 on facing page. Set mantles aside. Chop tentacles; place in a bowl and add ricotta, Parmesan, the ½ cup parsley, garlic, and crumbs. Mix well.

Melt butter in a wide frying pan over medium heat; add onions and cook until soft. Add tomatoes (break up with a spoon) and their liquid, stock base, and pepper. Simmer, uncovered, until sauce is thickened (about 20 minutes).

Using a small spoon or your fingers, stuff squid mantles with ricotta mixture; then place squid in a shallow 1½-quart baking dish and pour tomato sauce over them. Bake in a 300° oven, uncovered, for about 30 minutes or until squid is tender when pierced. Garnish with parsley and lemon slices. Makes 4 servings.

Spiced Clams & Rice

Turkey

Turkish, Greek, and Armenian cooks all serve versions of this sensational shellfish supper. For the sake of convenience, we've substituted canned clams for the mussels more typically used in Turkey. The spicy seafood-rice mixture is traditionally served in small clam or mussel shells.

> ⅓ **cup olive oil**
> 1 **large onion, finely chopped**
> 1 **cup short-grain (pearl) rice**
> ¼ **cup pine nuts**
> 2 **cans (6½ oz. *each*) chopped or minced clams**
> ⅓ **cup tomato sauce**
> ½ **teaspoon dill weed**
> ¼ **teaspoon ground allspice**
> ¼ **cup currants**
>   **Lemon wedges**

Heat oil in a wide frying pan over medium heat; add onion and cook until soft. Stir in rice and pine nuts and cook, stirring, until nuts are golden.

Drain clams and measure liquid; add water, if necessary, to make 1 cup. Pour liquid over rice mixture. Stir in tomato sauce, dill weed, allspice, and currants. Cover and bring to a boil; then reduce heat and simmer for 15 minutes. Remove from heat and let stand, covered, for 10 minutes. With a fork, lightly stir in clams.

Serve hot as an entrée. Or let cool, then spoon into small shells and serve as an appetizer. Offer lemon wedges to squeeze over top. Makes 4 main-dish servings or about 2 dozen appetizers.

Crab in Black Bean Sauce

China

For the juiciest results, Chinese chefs cook shellfish in the shell—as in this crab stir-fry.

> 3 **tablespoons salad oil**
> 1½ **tablespoons fermented black beans, rinsed, drained, and finely chopped**
> 1 **large clove garlic, minced or pressed**
> ¾ **teaspoon minced fresh ginger**
> 1 **green pepper, cut into 1-inch squares**
> 1 **cooked crab in shell (about 2 lbs.), cleaned and cracked**
> 1 **tablespoon *each* soy sauce and dry sherry**
> 2 **green onions (including tops), cut into 1-inch lengths**
> ⅓ **cup regular-strength chicken broth**

Place a wok or wide frying pan over high heat. When pan is hot, add oil. When oil begins to heat, add black beans, garlic, and ginger and stir once. Add green pepper and stir-fry for 1 minute. Add crab, soy, sherry, onions, and broth; cook, stirring, until crab is heated through (about 3 minutes). Makes 2 servings.

Preparing Ricotta-stuffed Squid (Recipe on facing page)

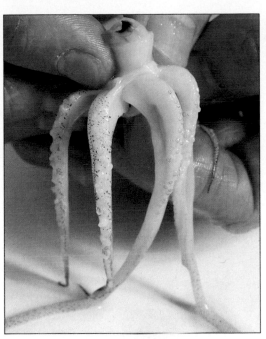

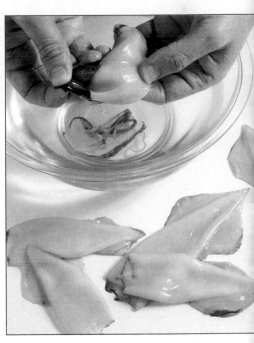

1 To clean squid: Gently pull body to separate from mantle. Then pull long, clear quill from mantle and discard. With fingers or spoon, scoop out and discard interior of mantle. Rinse out mantle.

2 With a sharp knife, sever body between eyes and tentacles; discard eyes and material attached. Pop out and discard hard black beak in center of tentacles.

3 With your fingers, pull off and discard thin speckled membrane to expose white meat of mantle. Rinse and drain mantle.

4 With fingers, fill mantles with cheese mixture. Stuff loosely— filling expands during baking. Pour tomato sauce over and around squid.

5 Plump stuffed squid mantles bake to tenderness in savory tomato sauce. Garnish with thin lemon slices and parsley; offer Parmesan cheese for sprinkling and parsley-flecked rice alongside.

...Shellfish sampler

Cracked Crab with Ginger Sauce

Japan

Here's a simple dish from the *sunomono* ("vine-gar-dressed") category of Japanese cooking.

>   4 **to 6 pounds cooked crab in shell, cleaned and cracked**
>   ½ **cup rice vinegar**
>   1 **tablespoon water**
>   1 **teaspoon grated fresh ginger**
>   ¼ **teaspoon salt**
>   2 **to 3 tablespoons mirin or cream sherry**
>   **Pickled ginger (optional)**

Mound crab on a tray; cover and refrigerate until serving time. In a cup, stir together vinegar, water, fresh ginger, and salt; then add mirin. Pour into small individual bowls; garnish each with pickled ginger, if you wish. To eat, dunk crab pieces into sauce. Makes 4 to 6 servings.

HOW TO HANDLE MUSSELS

Though mussels have been familiar favorites in many countries for years, they've only recently begun to appear regularly in American markets. Now grown and harvested commercially, these shellfish are available all year. (If you gather them yourself, be sure to check for local seasonal quarantines.) The oval blue-black shell conceals buttery-textured flesh that's white in males, coral colored in females; the flavor is delicate but distinctive.

You'll get about 2 dozen mussels to the pound. Like other shellfish, they should be used within a day after purchase. Store them in the refrigerator, wrapped loosely in damp newspaper or paper towels (never plastic, in which they suffocate). Sort through mussels before cleaning, discarding any with open shells that don't close when submerged in water. Then scrub shells under running water, using a stiff brush. Pull out and discard the tough, brown, hairlike "beard" (the *byssus*).

After cooking mussels, check to make sure all the shells have popped open; discard any that are still closed.

Mussels from Brussels

Belgium

After simmering in an herb-seasoned wine broth, mussels are lavished with a last-minute addition of cream and butter.

>   ¾ **cup coarsely chopped shallots or green onions (white part only)**
>   ½ **teaspoon pepper**
>   ¾ **cup lightly packed parsley sprigs**
>   1 **tablespoon *each* cracked bay leaves and coarsely chopped garlic**
>   ¼ **cup salad oil**
>   1 **cup dry white wine**
>   3 **pounds mussels, scrubbed, beards removed**
>   ½ **pint (1 cup) whipping cream**
>   2 **tablespoons butter or margarine**
>   **Hot cooked rice or crusty French bread**
>   **Lemon wedges**

In a food processor or blender, combine shallots, pepper, parsley, bay leaves, garlic, and oil; whirl until blended. Pour mixture into a 5-quart kettle; add wine. Place mussels in kettle and stir to coat. Cover and cook over medium heat until shells open (7 to 10 minutes). Stir in cream and butter; cook until liquid is heated through.

Place a large spoonful of rice in each of 4 wide soup bowls; ladle on mussels, discarding any unopened ones. (Or just pass bread to dunk into sauce.) Garnish with lemon wedges. Makes 4 servings.

INDIAN CURRY-SPICED MUSSELS

Heat 3 tablespoons **salad oil** in a 5-quart kettle over medium heat. Add 1 large **onion,** chopped, and 3 large cloves **garlic,** minced or pressed; cook until onion is golden. Stir in ½ teaspoon *each* **turmeric, ground cumin,** and **crushed red pepper,** and ¼ teaspoon *each* **ground cloves** and **black pepper;** cook for 2 minutes. Add 2 large **tomatoes,** peeled, seeded, and chopped, and cook for 2 more minutes. Add 1⅓ cups **water** and 3 pounds **mussels** (scrubbed, beards removed); stir to coat mussels.

Cook as directed for **Mussels from Brussels,** but omit cream and butter. Serve mussels over **hot cooked rice;** sprinkle evenly with 3 tablespoons **lemon juice.** Garnish with ½ cup **fresh cilantro** (coriander) leaves.

Seafood stews & soups

Originally a catchall for each day's unsold fish and shellfish, seafood soups and stews have become classics in fishing countries around the world. Since local ingredients and favorite seasonings differ from one land to another, these dishes exist in impressive variety—a marvelous state of affairs for seafood lovers.

When you prepare our recipes, follow the example of seaport cooks of old—experiment with amounts and types of seafood to find the combination you like best. And keep tasting as you cook; that's the way to produce a really splendid dish.

San Francisco-style Cioppino

United States

Probably invented by Italian fishermen in San Francisco, *cioppino* combines Dungeness crab and other shellfish in a bold, tomato-bright broth. It's wonderfully messy to eat, so provide big bibs and plenty of napkins.

    ¼ cup olive oil or salad oil
    1 large onion, chopped
    2 cloves garlic, minced or pressed
    1 large green pepper, seeded and chopped
    ⅓ cup chopped parsley
    1 large can (15 oz.) tomato sauce
    1 large can (28 oz.) tomatoes
    1 cup dry red or white wine, or ¾ cup water and
       ¼ cup lemon juice
    1 bay leaf
    1 teaspoon dry basil
    ½ teaspoon oregano leaves
    1 dozen small hard-shell clams, scrubbed
    1 pound medium-size raw shrimp, shelled and
       deveined
    2 cooked Dungeness or other hard-shelled crabs
       in shell (about 2 lbs. *each*), cleaned and
       cracked

Heat oil in a 6 to 8-quart kettle over medium heat. Add onion, garlic, green pepper, and parsley; cook, stirring often, until onion is soft. Stir in tomato sauce, tomatoes (break up with a spoon) and their liquid, wine, bay leaf, basil, and oregano. Bring to a boil; then cover, reduce heat, and simmer until slightly thickened (about 20 minutes).

Add clams, shrimp, and crabs. Cover and simmer until clams open and shrimp turn pink (10 to 15 minutes). Ladle into large soup bowls, discarding any unopened clams. Makes 6 servings.

Seafood Firepot

Thailand

Shellfish simmer in a clear broth infused with citrus and chiles to make a hot-tart, enticingly aromatic soup.

    2 large cans (49½ oz. *each*) regular-strength
       chicken broth or 3 quarts homemade chicken
       broth (page 33)
    3 cups water
    1 each lemon and lime
    1 or 2 fresh or pickled hot chiles (*each* about 2½
       inches long), thinly sliced and seeded
    1½ dozen small hard-shell clams, scrubbed
    1¼ pounds medium-size raw shrimp, shelled and
       deveined
    1 cooked crab in shell (1½ to 2 lbs.), cleaned
       and cracked
    ⅔ cup lime juice
    ½ cup fresh cilantro (coriander) sprigs
    3 green onions (including tops), cut into 1-inch
       lengths
       Lime wedges

Combine broth and water in an 8 to 10-quart kettle. Using a vegetable peeler, pare zest (colored outer layer of peel) from lemon and lime (reserve pulp for other uses, if desired). Loosely tie lemon and lime zest and chile (reserve 4 to 6 slices for garnish) in a piece of cheesecloth; place in broth. Bring broth to a boil over high heat. Cover, reduce heat, and simmer for 45 minutes. Discard seasonings.

Add clams, shrimp, and crab to kettle. Cover and simmer until clams open and shrimp turn pink (about 10 minutes). Stir in lime juice. Garnish with reserved chile slices, cilantro, and onions. Serve with lime wedges. As you serve soup, discard any unopened clams. Makes 6 to 8 servings.

HOW TO CLEAN & CRACK A CRAB

If your market sells only whole cooked crab, you'll need to clean and crack it before further use. First, twist off legs and claws where they join body. Holding each leg and claw on its narrow edge, crack shell with a mallet. Then pull off heavy back shell from body; discard shell, gills, and spongy parts. Using a heavy knife, cut body into quarters.

Making a Spanish seafood stew (Recipe on facing page)

1 The fried bread called *migas* starts with leftover bread. Shave bread into thin slices; then combine it with onion, bacon, and garlic and moisten the mixture with water.

2 Clam juice intensifies the flavor of the sea in this quick stock. You can prepare stock ahead, then add fish and shellfish at the last minute.

3 To bone a fillet, rub fingers along it to feel any bones; then pull out bones with pliers or tweezers. Live hard-shell clams have tightly closed shells; if shells are open, discard.

4 To complete migas, drizzle olive oil around edges and in crevices of bread mixture. Cook until browned on bottom, then turn and brown other side (migas will break into irregular pieces).

5 Ladle Spanish seafood stew into wide soup bowls; accompany with Marinated Vegetable Medley (page 137) and crusty, garlicky migas.

Seafood stews & soups

Seafood Soup with Migas

Spain   (Pictured on facing page)

Like the fishermen's soup-stews of other countries, this satisfying Spanish dish combines a superbly seasoned broth with a wealth of succulent seafood. The crusty, crumbly Iberian garlic bread called *migas* is perfect for nibbling alongside.

  Spanish fried bread (recipe follows)
3 **tablespoons olive oil or salad oil**
2 **medium-size onions, finely chopped**
2 **cloves garlic, minced or pressed**
1 **green pepper, seeded and chopped**
1 **can (15 oz.) tomato purée**
2 **bottles (8 oz. *each*) clam juice**
¾ **cup dry white wine**
2 **cans (14½ oz. *each*) regular-strength chicken broth or 3½ cups homemade chicken broth (page 33)**
2 **bay leaves**
1 **small dried whole hot red chile**
½ **teaspoon *each* ground coriander, dry basil, and thyme leaves**
1 **lemon, thinly sliced**
2 **medium-size carrots, sliced**
1½ **pounds firm-textured white fish fillets such as halibut, rockfish, or sea bass**
1½ **dozen small hard-shell clams, scrubbed**
½ **pound medium-size raw shrimp, shelled and deveined**
  Chopped parsley

Prepare bread for frying and set aside.

Heat oil in a 5-quart kettle over medium heat. Add onions, garlic, and green pepper and cook, stirring occasionally, until soft. Stir in tomato purée, clam juice, wine, broth, bay leaves, chile, coriander, basil, thyme, half the lemon slices, and carrots. Bring to a boil; then cover, reduce heat, and simmer until carrots are tender to bite (about 20 minutes).

Meanwhile, pull any bones from fish with pliers or tweezers; cut fish into 1-inch chunks. Add fish, clams, and shrimp to broth; cover and simmer until clams open and shrimp turn pink (7 to 10 minutes). Meanwhile, fry bread. Garnish soup with parsley and remaining lemon slices; serve bread alongside. (As you serve soup, discard any unopened clams.) Makes 6 to 8 servings.

Spanish fried bread. You'll need half of 1 large round loaf (about 1½ lbs.) day-old **French bread.**

Shave bread into very thin slices; you'll have about 8 cups. Place in a bowl and mix in 1 medium-size **onion,** finely chopped; 1 to 2 cloves **garlic,** minced or pressed; ¼ cup crumbled crisply cooked **bacon;** and ¼ teaspoon *each* **salt** and **pepper.** Gradually sprinkle in ½ cup **water,** tossing until bread is evenly dampened. Cover and set aside for at least 30 minutes. Stir together ½ cup **olive oil** and 2 cloves **garlic,** crushed.

To fry bread, heat a wide frying pan over medium-high heat; generously brush with garlic-oil mixture. Scoop 2 to 3 cups of the bread mixture into pan, then flatten into a ¼-inch-thick round. Cook until bottom is well browned (about 3 minutes), drizzling oil around edges and through crevices once or twice. Turn in sections and cook until browned on other side, drizzling with oil as needed. Repeat with remaining bread mixture.

Tomatillo Fish Stew

Mexico

Mild white fish and mellow corn balance the tartness of tomatillos in this chile-seasoned stew. Tomatillos are like small green tomatoes with papery husks, typically used fresh in Mexican cooking; we've substituted the canned variety for the sake of convenience.

2 **tablespoons salad oil**
1 **medium-size onion, chopped**
1 **fresh hot chile (2½ inches long), seeded and minced**
2 **cans (13 oz. *each*) tomatillos, drained**
1 **can (12 oz.) whole kernel corn, drained**
2 **cans (14½ oz. *each*) regular-strength chicken broth or 3½ cups homemade chicken broth (page 33)**
⅓ **cup dry white wine**
1½ **pounds firm-textured white fish fillets or steaks such as halibut, lingcod, or sea bass**
½ **cup chopped parsley**

Heat oil in a 5-quart kettle over medium heat. Add onion and cook, stirring, until soft. Add chile and cook for 3 minutes. Chop tomatillos; add to kettle with corn, broth, and wine. Bring to a boil; then cover, reduce heat, and simmer for 10 minutes.

Pull any bones from fish with pliers or tweezers; cut fish into bite-size pieces. Add fish to kettle and simmer until done (6 to 8 minutes; see page 120). Stir in parsley. Makes 4 to 6 servings.

RELISHES & SAUCES

A special accompaniment is the magic touch that makes a simple meal memorable, the "something extra" that can turn an everyday dinner into a celebration. And when you want to add authenticity to an ethnic menu, just include an appropriate accompaniment or two.

Our accompaniments offer you an easy way to bring international flair to your meals—and a good opportunity to explore a whole world of taste combinations. You'll find marinated vegetables, fresh fruit treats, chutneys, sauces, homemade mustards, and more. And with our easy-to-make fruit and vegetable garnishes, you can add a lively decorative touch to any night's dinner.

Most of these recipes store well—some for a week or so, others for much longer—so you can make them well in advance, and sample them with a number of different entrées.

Vegetable accompaniments

Use this potpourri of vegetable go-alongs to give your menus a change of pace. Just a small serving of pickled vegetables or a dollop of tangy relish can do a lot to perk up a meal, adding delightful contrast in color, texture, and flavor.

Cold Spiced Cabbage

China

This slightly sweet, mildly hot cabbage is a natural for Oriental meals, but it's just as tasty alongside grilled Polish or German sausages.

> **About ½ large head cabbage**
> 2 **tablespoons salad oil**
> 2 **cloves garlic, minced or pressed**
> ⅓ **cup water**
> 3 **tablespoons** *each* **sugar and white wine vinegar**
> ½ **teaspoon salt**
> 1½ **teaspoons sesame oil (optional)**
> ¼ **to ½ teaspoon crushed red pepper**

Cut cabbage in half lengthwise. Cut out core; then cut cabbage into 2-inch squares (you should have 8 cups).

Heat salad oil in a wok or wide frying pan over high heat; add cabbage, garlic, and water. Cover and cook, stirring occasionally, until cabbage is just barely wilted (about 1½ minutes). Pour off and discard any liquid, then spoon cabbage into a bowl and stir in sugar, vinegar, salt, sesame oil (if used), and pepper. Let cool; cover and refrigerate, stirring occasionally, for up to 1 week. Serve cold. Makes 4 to 6 servings.

Marinated Beets & Onions

Sweden

Vegetable salads are popular throughout Scandinavia, where leafy greens are expensive much of the year. Here's one favorite combination: bright beets and thin-sliced onions.

    2   cans (1 lb. *each*) sliced beets
    2   medium-size mild red onions, thinly sliced
    ½   cup red wine vinegar
    1   teaspoon dill weed
    1½ tablespoons sugar
    ½   teaspoon salt
    ¼   teaspoon pepper

Drain beets, reserving 1 cup of the liquid. In a deep bowl, combine beets, reserved liquid, onions, vinegar, dill weed, sugar, salt, and pepper. Cover and refrigerate for several hours or until next day. Makes about 8 servings.

Tomato-Lemon Chutney

Sri Lanka

In India and neighboring countries, you'll find spicy chutneys in countless variety. Try this one with curry, or tuck a small spoonful into a chicken sandwich or a hamburger.

    1   lemon, peeled, white membrane removed
    1   can (about 1 lb.) tomatoes
        Spice mix (recipe follows)
    1   tablespoon salad oil or olive oil
    ½   cup *each* raisins and sugar

In a blender or food processor, whirl lemon with tomatoes and their liquid just until blended.

In a 2-quart pan, stir together spice mix; add oil. Cook over medium-high heat, stirring, until seeds begin to pop. Add tomato mixture, raisins, and sugar. Boil gently, stirring often, until mixture has a jamlike consistency (about 20 minutes). If made ahead, let cool; then cover and refrigerate for up to 3 days. Serve at room temperature. Makes 1¾ cups.

Spice mix. Combine 1 **small dried whole hot red chile,** 2 teaspoons grated **lemon peel,** 1 teaspoon **mustard seeds,** ½ teaspoon **cumin seeds,** and ¼ teaspoon **ground nutmeg.**

Marinated Vegetable Medley

Spain   (Pictured on page 134)

Lightly cooked, marinated vegetables add a cool and refreshing crunch alongside spicy entrées. This colorful Spanish medley has a close relative in Italy's *giardiniera*.

    1   small head cauliflower, separated into
        flowerets (cut any large flowerets in half
        lengthwise)
    4   medium-size carrots, cut into ½ by 4-inch sticks
    1   large red or green bell pepper, seeded and cut
        into ½-inch-wide strips
    6   tablespoons olive oil or salad oil
    3   tablespoons *each* white wine vinegar and
        minced parsley
        Salt and pepper

Bring a large quantity of water to a boil in a 5-quart kettle over high heat. Add cauliflower and cook just until tender-crisp when pierced (3 to 5 minutes). Lift out with a slotted spoon; plunge into cold water to cool quickly. Drain well.

Return water to a boil; add carrots and bell pepper and cook just until tender-crisp to bite (1 to 2 minutes). Drain, then plunge into cold water to cool quickly; drain well.

In a plastic bag, combine oil, vinegar, and parsley; season to taste with salt and pepper. Add vegetables and mix well to coat evenly; close bag. Refrigerate for at least 2 hours or until next day, turning occasionally. Makes 6 to 8 servings.

ITALIAN MARINATED MUSHROOMS

Follow directions for **Marinated Vegetable Medley,** but omit cauliflower, carrots, and bell pepper. Instead, use 1 pound small whole **mushrooms** (uncooked). Add ½ teaspoon **dry basil** to marinade. Makes about 6 servings.

SPANISH ROASTED PEPPERS

Follow directions for **Marinated Vegetable Medley,** but substitute **4 *each* large green and red bell peppers, roasted** (page 45) for cauliflower, carrots, and bell pepper. Cut peppers into ½-inch-wide strips; discard seeds. Add to marinade along with 1 clove **garlic,** minced or pressed. Serve at room temperature. Makes about 8 servings.

...Vegetable accompaniments

Pub Onions

England   (Pictured on facing page)

A popular relish in English pubs, these sweet-tart onions are a piquant reminder of India's influence on English cooking.

    1½ **cups Madeira or port**
    ¾ **cup white (distilled) vinegar**
    ½ **cup firmly packed brown sugar**
    ½ **cup currants or raisins**
    ⅛ **teaspoon ground red pepper (cayenne)**
    2 **pounds small white boiling onions, *each* ¾ to 1½ inches in diameter**
    3 **tablespoons salad oil**
      Salt

In a 3 to 4-quart pan, combine Madeira, vinegar, sugar, currants, and pepper. Bring to a boil over high heat; then boil rapidly, uncovered, until reduced to 1¼ cups. Set aside.

    Prepare onions as shown in photos 1, 2, and 3 on facing page. Arrange a single layer of onions in a wide frying pan; pour oil over them. Cook over medium heat until lightly browned (5 to 7 minutes), shaking pan to turn onions. Transfer to Madeira sauce. Repeat with remaining onions.

    Bring onion mixture to a boil over high heat; cover, reduce heat, and simmer until onions are tender-crisp when pierced (about 10 minutes). Let cool, then season to taste with salt. If made ahead, cover and refrigerate for up to 2 weeks; serve at room temperature. Makes 6 to 8 servings.

Tomato Salsa

Mexico   (Pictured on page 67)

All over Mexico, fresh *salsa* appears on the table just as routinely as salt and pepper.

    2 **medium-size tomatoes, quartered**
    ½ **small onion**
    3 **tablespoons canned diced green chiles**
    4 **teaspoons white (distilled) vinegar**
    1 **tablespoon chopped fresh cilantro (coriander)**
      Salt

In a blender or food processor, combine tomatoes, onion, chiles, vinegar, and cilantro. Whirl until puréed; season to taste with salt. If made ahead, cover and refrigerate until next day. Makes 1½ cups.

Tomato-Pepper Relish

Yugoslavia

Zesty *pindzur* adds a bold flourish to cheese sandwiches, barbecued meats, or pan-fried liver. You'll find the dried chiles used in this relish in markets offering Mexican products.

    1 **large can (28 oz.) Italian-style tomatoes**
    1 **ounce (3 or 4) dried red California or New Mexico chiles**
    2 **tablespoons *each* olive oil and salad oil**
    3 **or 4 cloves garlic, minced or pressed**
    ½ **teaspoon sugar**
      Salt and ground red pepper (cayenne)

Drain tomatoes, pouring off liquid into a 2-quart pan. Bring liquid to a boil over high heat; then add chiles, remove from heat, and let stand for 2 hours. Lift out chiles. Scrape pulp and seeds from skins and reserve; discard skins and stems.

    In a wide frying pan, combine chile pulp and seeds, tomato liquid, tomatoes (break up with a spoon), olive oil, salad oil, garlic, and sugar. Cook over medium-high heat, uncovered, until juices have evaporated (about 20 minutes); stir frequently. Let cool, then season to taste with salt and pepper. Serve at once; or, if made ahead, cover and refrigerate for up to 1 week. Serve at room temperature. Makes 1¾ cups.

Chirmol

El Salvador

Chunky *chirmol* is typically served with grilled meats such as Barbecued Beef (page 82).

    4 **medium-size tomatoes**
    1 **medium-size onion, finely chopped**
    ⅓ **cup finely chopped green pepper**
    1 **tablespoon finely chopped fresh cilantro (coriander)**
    2 **teaspoons finely chopped fresh mint or 2 teaspoons dry mint**
    ½ **teaspoon garlic salt**
    ¼ **to ½ teaspoon liquid hot pepper seasoning**

Peel, seed, and chop tomatoes (you should have about 2 cups). Combine tomatoes, onion, green pepper, cilantro, and mint. Stir in garlic salt and hot pepper seasoning. Cover and refrigerate for up to 3 days; serve cold. Makes about 2½ cups.

Preparing piquant Pub Onions (Recipe on facing page)

1 To peel boiling onions easily, place unpeeled onions in a bowl; cover with boiling water and let stand for 3 to 5 minutes. Drain well.

2 With your fingers, peel back each onion's tissuelike skin to root end. Cut off root ends with a sharp knife; discard.

3 To help onions hold their shape during cooking, use a sharp knife to cut a shallow "x" in the trimmed root end of each one.

4 In a wide frying pan, cook onions in oil until lightly browned. Then transfer to Madeira sauce with a slotted spoon; cook just until tender-crisp. Serve at room temperature.

5 Plump onions in a spicy, currant-laden sauce are much like relishes offered in English pubs. Sweet-tart in flavor, they pair well with grilled meats.

Fruit accompaniments

Whether served almost "as is" or transformed into flavorful relishes or chutneys, fruits are a universally popular partner for entrées. These six accompaniments are equally good with spicy fare and simple broiled and roasted meats.

Fried Plantains

Nicaragua

Popular in Central and South American cooking, plantains taste much like starchy bananas. When ripe, they're almost entirely black. If you can't find them, substitute large green bananas.

   2 **ripe plantains or 3 large green bananas**
   3 **to 5 tablespoons salad oil**
      Salt

Peel plantains; cut in half crosswise, then thinly slice lengthwise. Heat 3 tablespoons of the oil in a wide frying pan over medium heat. Add about half the plantains (or bananas) and cook, turning, until golden on both sides (10 to 12 minutes *total*; 5 to 6 minutes *total* for bananas). Drain on paper towels; keep warm. Repeat with remaining plantains, adding more oil as needed. Sprinkle with salt and serve at once. Makes about 4 servings.

Glazed Papaya Quarters

United States–Hawaii

With its enticing blend of seasonings reflecting Hawaii's rich ethnic diversity, this luscious glazed fruit enhances roast pork, chicken, and ham.

   2 **large papayas, unpeeled**
   4 **tablespoons butter or margarine**
   1 **teaspoon *each* ground ginger and ground coriander**
   ¼ **teaspoon curry powder**
   2 **tablespoons *each* honey and lime juice**

Cut papayas lengthwise into quarters; discard seeds. Place in a baking dish, cut side up.

   In a small pan, combine butter, ginger, coriander, and curry powder. Cook over low heat until bubbly, then stir in honey and lime juice. Brush mixture over fruit. Bake in a 325° oven, uncovered, for about 25 minutes or until heated through; baste occasionally. Pour any remaining honey mixture into papaya cavities. Makes 8 servings.

Sautéed Apples

Germany

Simply sliced and sautéed, apples add a sweet-tart accent to roasted or braised meats.

   3 **to 4 tablespoons butter or margarine**
   ¼ **teaspoon grated lemon peel**
   3 **large Golden Delicious apples, cored and cut into ½-inch-thick slices**
      Ground nutmeg

Melt 2 tablespoons of the butter in a wide frying pan over medium heat; add lemon peel and a single layer of apples. Cook, uncovered, until translucent (about 10 minutes); turn slices with a wide spatula to ensure even cooking. Transfer apples to a platter; sprinkle lightly with nutmeg and keep warm. Repeat with remaining apples, adding more butter as needed. Makes 4 to 6 servings.

Plum & Pear Chutney

England

When summer fruits are at their peak, English cooks preserve part of the plenty in chutneys.

         About 2 pounds firm red plums
         About 2 pounds firm ripe pears
   1½ **cups sugar**
    1 **cup cider vinegar**
    2 **tablespoons minced fresh ginger**
    2 **teaspoons curry powder**
   ½ **teaspoon crushed red pepper**
    1 **teaspoon salt**
    1 **clove garlic, minced or pressed**
    1 **large onion, chopped**
    1 **small orange (unpeeled), finely chopped**
    1 **cup raisins**

Quarter and pit plums; peel, core, and coarsely chop pears. You should have 5 cups plums and 4 cups pears.

   In a 6 to 8-quart kettle, combine sugar, vinegar, ginger, curry powder, pepper, salt, garlic, onion, orange, and raisins. Bring to a boil over medium-high heat; then add plums and pears. Reduce heat and boil gently, uncovered, until thickened (30 to 40 minutes); stir frequently. Let cool, then cover and refrigerate for up to 2 months. Makes about 3½ pints.

Orange-Date Chutney

India

To those who think that "chutney" just means Major Grey's (made with mangoes), the diversity of these spicy condiments will come as a surprise. This sweet chutney is based on oranges and dates; serve it with curry, roast pork, and chicken.

> About 6 large oranges
> 1 large red bell pepper, seeded and chopped
> 2½ tablespoons minced fresh ginger
> 1 large onion, coarsely chopped
> 8 ounces pitted dates, chopped
> 1½ cups white (distilled) vinegar
> 2¼ cups firmly packed brown sugar
> 1 teaspoon ground cinnamon
> ½ teaspoon *each* ground allspice and crushed red pepper
> ¼ teaspoon ground cloves

Cut peel and white membrane from oranges. Dice and measure flesh; you should have 4 cups.

In a 5 to 6-quart kettle, combine diced oranges, bell pepper, ginger, onion, dates, vinegar, sugar, cinnamon, allspice, red pepper, and cloves. Simmer over medium heat, uncovered, until reduced to 4 cups (about 1½ hours); stir often.

Fill hot sterilized canning jars to within ¼ inch of rims. Wipe rims; put hot sterilized lids and rings in place. Set jars on a rack in a kettle; cover with boiling water. Bring water to a simmer; cook for 10 minutes. Lift out jars; let cool. Makes 2 pints.

Cranberry-Orange Relish

United States

Tart-sweet cranberry relish traditionally accompanies Thanksgiving turkey, but it's just as good with other roast poultry or roast pork.

> 1 pound (4 cups) cranberries
> 1 large orange (unpeeled), cut into chunks
> 1 cup sugar

Using a food processor or a food chopper fitted with a fine blade, grind together cranberries and orange. Spoon into a small pan and add sugar; bring to a boil over medium heat, stirring constantly. Remove from heat and let cool; cover and refrigerate for up to 4 days. Makes about 3 cups.

CREATING YOUR OWN MUSTARDS

Making good mustard is easy—just combine a seasoned vinegar mixture with a paste of dry mustard and water, then cook the blend to thicken it.

The concentration of the vinegar mixture determines the mustard's pungency; if you reduce it by half (as we suggest here), you'll get a medium-hot mustard. For a hotter product, reduce the mixture further.

Dijon-style mustard. Smoothly stir ½ cup **cold water** into 1 cup (4 to 5 oz.) **dry mustard;** let stand for at least 10 minutes.

Meanwhile, in a 3-quart noncorrosive pan, combine 1⅓ cups *each* **dry white wine** and **white wine vinegar;** 1 small **onion,** chopped; 3 large cloves **garlic,** minced or pressed; 2 **bay leaves;** 8 **whole allspice;** 2 teaspoons *each* **salt** and **sugar;** and 1 teaspoon **dry tarragon.** Bring to a boil over high heat; boil, uncovered, until reduced by half (15 to 20 minutes). Press through a wire strainer into top of a double boiler. Stir in mustard paste; cook over simmering water, stirring often, until as thick as very heavy cream (10 to 15 minutes). Let cool (mixture will thicken slightly). Cover and refrigerate for up to 2 years. Makes 2 cups.

Spiced German mustard. Combine ⅓ cup **white mustard seeds,** ¼ cup **dry mustard,** and ½ cup **cold water;** let stand for 3 hours.

In a 2-quart noncorrosive pan, combine 1 cup **cider vinegar;** 1 small **onion,** chopped; 2 tablespoons firmly packed **brown sugar;** 1 teaspoon **salt;** 2 cloves **garlic,** minced or pressed; ½ teaspoon **ground cinnamon;** ¼ teaspoon *each* **ground allspice, dill seeds,** and **dry tarragon;** and ⅛ teaspoon **turmeric.** Simmer over medium heat, uncovered, until reduced by about half (10 to 15 minutes). Pour liquid through a wire strainer into mustard mixture; whirl in a blender or food processor until as smooth as you like. Pour into top of a double boiler and cook as for **Dijon-style mustard.** Stir in 1 to 2 tablespoons **honey.** Store as for **Dijon-style mustard.** Makes about 1 cup.

Colorful vegetable & fruit garnishes

Carrot twists. With a vegetable peeler, pare thin 3-inch-long strips from carrot. Cut a 1-inch slit in center of each, then soak in cold salted water for 10 minutes. Slip one end of strip through slit; pull back.

Green onion brushes. Cut root end from onion, then cut a 2 to 3-inch section from white part. Hold one end; make many cuts through remaining portion to form a "brush." Soak in ice water until curled.

Lemon stars. Insert knife on the diagonal into middle of lemon, piercing to center. Make a second cut angled the other way; continue to alternate cuts around lemon. Separate halves; garnish with parsley.

Orange curls. Slice orange in half lengthwise. Turn so cut side is down and slice ¼ inch thick. Cut each slice between peel and flesh, leaving about 1 inch of peel attached; curl loose peel under.

Turnip flowers. Peel turnip; set between 2 chopsticks. Make parallel cuts, ⅛ inch apart, through turnip to sticks. Make a second set of cuts at right angles. Soak in cold salted water until "petals" open.

Cucumber twigs. Cut sides from a 2-inch length of cucumber in five ¼-inch-thick pieces. Trim long edges of pieces. In each remaining piece, cut 2 lengthwise slits, one from each end. Cross cut ends over.

Sauces

When you keep a sauce or two on hand in the refrigerator, it's easy to give a unique touch to your meals. The quick-to-make sauces we feature here are versatile—tasty with their traditional partners, and just as appealing with companions from other lands.

Cucumber-Yogurt Sauce

Pakistan

Through much of the Middle East, soothing yogurt-based sauces help temper the heat of spicy entrées. Pair up this refreshing example with Pakistani Roast Leg of Lamb (page 77).

- 1 pint (2 cups) plain yogurt
- 1 small cucumber, peeled, shredded, and drained well
- ½ cup chopped green onions (including tops)
- ½ teaspoon *each* salt and sugar
- 1 teaspoon ground cumin
- ¼ teaspoon chili powder
- 1 package (10 oz.) frozen peas, thawed and drained well

In a bowl, stir together yogurt, cucumber, onions, salt, sugar, cumin, chili powder, and peas. Cover and refrigerate for at least 8 hours or up to 2 days. Stir before serving. Makes about 4 cups.

Hoisin-style Sauce

China

Often used to flavor cooking sauces (as in Pork with Pea Pods, page 88), spicy hoisin also joins many Chinese meals as a table condiment. Our easy-to-make alternative to canned or bottled sauce gets its sweet spiciness from apple butter.

- ½ cup apple butter
- 3 tablespoons soy sauce
- 1 teaspoon white (distilled) vinegar
- ¼ teaspoon *each* ground red pepper (cayenne), ground ginger, and garlic powder

In a small pan, combine apple butter, soy, vinegar, pepper, ginger, and garlic powder. Cook over medium heat, uncovered, until very thick (about 15 minutes); stir frequently. Let cool. If made ahead, cover and refrigerate for up to 2 weeks. Serve at room temperature. Makes ½ cup.

Harvest Mustard Sauce

Switzerland

Offer this pungent sauce with Harvest Ham & Cabbage (page 96), frankfurters, or corned beef.

- 2 tablespoons dry mustard
- 5 tablespoons port or apple juice
- 1 cup water
- ½ cup firmly packed brown sugar
- 2 cinnamon sticks (*each* about 3 inches long)
- 1½ teaspoons anise seeds
- 1 tablespoon *each* cornstarch and water
- ¼ teaspoon salt

Stir together dry mustard and 2 tablespoons of the port; set aside. In a 1-quart pan, combine the 1 cup water, sugar, cinnamon sticks, and anise seeds. Bring to a boil over high heat; then cover, reduce heat, and simmer for 1 hour. Pour through a fine wire strainer, then return hot syrup to pan.

Combine cornstarch and the 1 tablespoon water; stir into hot syrup and cook, stirring, until thickened. Add salt, remaining 3 tablespoons port, and mustard mixture. Remove from heat and beat with a wire whisk until smooth. Let cool, then cover and refrigerate for up to 2 weeks. Serve cold; stir before serving. Makes 1 cup.

Peanut Sauce

Indonesia   (Pictured on page 147)

Traditional accompaniment to Grilled Pork (page 87), this sauce also makes a tempting dip for raw vegetables and crisp baked chicken wings.

- 1 cup unsweetened pineapple juice
- ⅔ cup crunchy peanut butter
- 2 cloves garlic, minced or pressed
- 2 tablespoons firmly packed brown sugar
- 1½ tablespoons lemon juice
- 1 tablespoon soy sauce
- ¼ to ½ teaspoon crushed red pepper

In a small pan, combine pineapple juice, peanut butter, and garlic. Cook over medium heat, stirring, until mixture boils and thickens. Remove from heat and stir in sugar, lemon juice, soy, and pepper. Let cool to room temperature. If made ahead, cover and refrigerate for up to 3 days; serve at room temperature. Makes about 2 cups.

PASTA, GRAINS & BEANS

Down through the ages, grains and beans have provided nourishment for mankind; almost every inhabited area in the world will support some kind of grain or bean. And wherever the land favors it, each variety tends to grow in abundance —corn in the Americas, lentils in the Middle East, and rice in Asia, for example.

As a group, these field-grown products— including pasta, made mostly from wheat flour— can be stored for long periods of time without refrigeration. As a result, beans, grains, and the products made from them have traditionally cost little; yet they provide a wealth of vitamins, minerals, and protein. As a special advantage to cooks everywhere, these staples also provide a quiet background for more assertive seasonings, condiments, sauces, fillings, or stews. By the same token, they naturally enhance leftovers and extend limited portions of meat.

In this chapter, we present a sampling of the world's creativity with grains and beans—simple dishes that have evolved, with time and imagination into gourmet feasts. On our tour, you'll taste such well loved classics as Italian tortellini, Jewish kreplach, Moroccan couscous, Spanish paella, Chinese fried rice, and French cassoulet—as well as other tempting recipes based on the world's field-grown sustenance.

Pasta entrées

Though the word is Italian, our pasta recipes span the globe. Cook all noodles just until *al dente*, or tender but firm to bite.

Linguine with Clam Sauce

Italy

Elegant yet effortless, *linguine con vongole* has become a pasta classic.

> ½ cup (¼ lb.) butter
> ¼ cup olive oil
> 4 cloves garlic, minced or pressed
> 3 cans (6½ oz. each) chopped clams
> 1 teaspoon *each* oregano leaves and dry basil
> ¼ teaspoon crushed red pepper
> 1½ cups chopped parsley
> 1 pound linguine or spaghetti
> Boiling salted water

Heat butter and oil in a 2-quart pan over low heat. Add garlic and cook until golden (about 10 minutes); don't let garlic scorch. Drain juice from 2 cans clams into butter mixture; drain third can and reserve juice for other uses, if desired. Increase heat to medium; add oregano, basil, pepper, and parsley to pan and simmer, uncovered, for 5 minutes. Add drained clams and heat through.

Meanwhile, following package directions, cook linguine in a large kettle of boiling salted water until *al dente;* then drain. Toss linguine with clam sauce. Makes 5 or 6 servings.

Pansit

Philippines

Chinese in origin, this quick, savory noodle entrée is so popular with Filipinos that local Chinese restaurants are often called *pansiterias.*

    2 tablespoons salad oil
    1 medium-size onion, cut in half, then thinly
      sliced
    3 cloves garlic, minced or pressed
    1 cup *each* bite-size pieces cooked chicken and
      boiled ham
    1 cup small cooked shrimp
    2 tablespoons soy sauce
    1 cup coarsely shredded, firmly packed napa
      cabbage
    1 cup regular-strength chicken broth
    1 pound fresh Chinese egg noodles or dried
      spaghetti
      Boiling salted water
      Salt and pepper
    2 lemons, cut into wedges

Heat oil in a wide frying pan over medium-high heat; add onion and garlic and cook until onion is tender-crisp to bite (about 4 minutes). Remove from pan and set aside. Add chicken, ham, and shrimp to pan and cook until lightly browned. Remove part of each from pan; set aside to use for garnish.

Return onion and garlic to pan. Add soy, mix well, and cook for 2 minutes. Add cabbage and broth; bring to a boil, then reduce heat and simmer for 2 minutes. Remove pan from heat and keep warm.

Meanwhile, following package directions, cook noodles in a large kettle of boiling salted water until *al dente.* Drain well; then add to cabbage mixture and mix lightly. Season to taste with salt and pepper. Serve in shallow bowls; garnish with lemon wedges and reserved chicken, ham, and shrimp. Makes 6 servings.

Spring Green Noodles & Shrimp

United States

Green spinach noodles and fresh vegetables combine in a pretty entrée that's just right for a springtime luncheon.

    ¾ pound asparagus, rinsed well, tough stalk
      ends trimmed
    ¼ pound snow peas, ends and strings removed
    8 ounces spinach noodles
      Boiling salted water
    4 tablespoons butter or margarine
    1 cup dry white wine
    ½ pint (1 cup) sour cream
    2 teaspoons all-purpose flour
    ½ pound small cooked shrimp

Cut asparagus into bite-size pieces. In a wide frying pan, bring 1 inch water to a boil; add asparagus and boil, uncovered, for 3 minutes. Add peas, pushing them under water; boil, uncovered, until both vegetables are tender-crisp to bite (about 1 more minute). Drain; keep warm.

Meanwhile, following package directions, cook noodles in a large kettle of boiling salted water until *al dente;* then drain. Mix in 1 tablespoon of the butter. Keep warm.

In a 2 to 3-quart pan, bring wine to a boil over medium-low heat. Add remaining 3 tablespoons butter; whisk constantly until butter is completely melted. Combine sour cream and flour; stir into wine mixture and cook until bubbly. Gently toss together pasta, shrimp, vegetables, and sauce. Makes 4 servings.

HOW TO COOK PASTA

For each 8 ounces (½ pound) **pasta,** bring 3 quarts **water** to a rapid boil in a large kettle. Add 2 teaspoons **salt.** For a pound of pasta, double the water only.

Add pasta to boiling water. When water returns to a boil, stir pasta once to separate. Boil, uncovered, for the time suggested on the package or just until pasta is *al dente*—tender, but still firm to bite. Drain cooked pasta at once, then mix with **sauce.** (Rinse with cold water only if specified in recipe.)

...Pasta entrées

Noodles & Beef with Black Bean Sauce

China

Fermented black beans combined with beef and vegetables dress up noodles in this Cantonese favorite. Look for black beans in Asian markets. After opening, store them at room temperature in a tightly covered jar.

  4 **ounces medium-wide noodles**
    Boiling salted water
  4 **tablespoons salad oil**
  ½ **pound lean boneless beef (flank or top round)**
  1 **teaspoon** *each* **cornstarch, dry sherry, and soy sauce**
  1 **tablespoon water**
    Cooking sauce (recipe follows)
  2 **tablespoons fermented black beans, rinsed, drained well, and finely chopped**
  2 **large cloves garlic, minced or pressed**
  1 **teaspoon minced fresh ginger**
  ¼ **teaspoon crushed red pepper**
  1 **green pepper, seeded and cut into 1-inch squares**
  2 **green onions (including tops), cut into 1-inch lengths**

Following package directions, cook noodles in a large kettle of boiling salted water until *al dente*. Drain, rinse with cold water, and drain again. Toss noodles with 1 tablespoon of the oil.

Cut beef with the grain into 1½-inch-wide strips; then cut each strip diagonally across the grain into ⅛-inch-thick slices. In a bowl, combine cornstarch, sherry, soy, and the 1 tablespoon water. Add beef and 1½ teaspoons of the oil, and stir to coat. Let stand for 15 minutes. Prepare cooking sauce.

Heat a wok or wide frying pan over high heat. When pan is hot, add 1 tablespoon of the oil. When oil begins to heat, add noodles and stir-fry until heated through. Remove from pan; then add remaining 1½ tablespoons oil to pan. When oil begins to heat, add black beans, garlic, ginger, and pepper; stir once. Add beef and stir-fry for 2 minutes. Add green pepper and onions and stir-fry for 1 more minute, adding a few drops of water if vegetables stick to pan. Stir cooking sauce, pour into pan, and cook, stirring, until sauce boils and thickens. Return noodles to pan and toss lightly to mix. Makes 2 servings.

Cooking sauce. In a bowl, combine ½ cup **water** and 1 tablespoon *each* **cornstarch** and **soy sauce.**

Bahmi Goreng

Indonesia   (Pictured on facing page)

Almost every Southeast Asian cuisine shows some Chinese characteristics, whether in ingredients, cooking methods, or both. *Bahmi goreng* ("fried noodles") is one hearty example of China's influence on Indonesian cooking. It's traditionally served with peanut sauce as a quick family supper—but this presentation, crowned with a lattice of golden egg shreds, is easily elegant enough for a party entrée.

     Egg Shreds (page 57)
     Peanut Sauce (page 143)
  2 **tablespoons soy sauce**
  1¼ **teaspoons salt**
  ¼ **teaspoon anchovy paste (optional)**
  4 **cups shredded cooked chicken, pork, or beef**
  1 **pound medium-wide noodles**
    Boiling salted water
  2 **tablespoons salad oil**
  4 **cloves garlic, minced or pressed**
  ½ **to 1 teaspoon crushed red pepper**
  2 **medium-size onions, cut in half, then thinly sliced**
  3 **cups thinly sliced celery**
  1 **small head cabbage (about 1¼ lbs.), coarsely chopped**
  2 **cups snow peas, ends and strings removed**
  2 **large tomatoes, coarsely chopped**
    Red bell pepper strips and celery leaves

Prepare Egg Shreds, but use a 10-inch frying pan and make only 2 sheets of egg. Cut sheets into ¼-inch-wide strips, then cover and refrigerate. Prepare Peanut Sauce.

In a bowl, combine soy, salt, anchovy paste (if used), and chicken; set aside. Following package directions, cook noodles in a large kettle of boiling salted water until *al dente*; drain and keep warm.

Heat oil in a heavy 5 to 6-quart kettle over medium-high heat; add garlic, pepper, onions, and celery. Stir-fry until vegetables are tender-crisp to bite (about 3 minutes). Add chicken mixture; reduce heat to medium and stir-fry for 3 more minutes. Add cabbage and peas and cook for 2 minutes. Add noodles and tomatoes and cook, stirring, until heated through. Turn onto a large platter and arrange Egg Shreds on top in a lattice-work design. Garnish with bell pepper strips and celery leaves, if desired. At the table, pass Peanut Sauce. Makes 6 to 8 servings.

Preparing fried noodles, Indonesian style (Recipe on facing page)

1 Make egg shreds: Let sheets of cooked egg cool, then roll loosely, jelly roll style. Cut roll crosswise into ¼-inch-wide slices. Cover and refrigerate for up to a day, if desired.

2 Prepare all vegetables before you begin to stir-fry. To slice celery quickly, stack stalks, then cut across whole bundle.

3 *Bahmi goreng* is fast to cook. You stir-fry firmer vegetables with soy-seasoned cooked chicken, then stir in drained noodles and quick-cooking vegetables near end of cooking time.

4 Topped with a lattice of egg shreds and garnished with red bell pepper and celery leaves, Indonesian fried noodles make a festive party dish. Spoon Peanut Sauce (page 143) over noodles at the table.

...Pasta entrées

Chicken Soba

Japan

In Japan, noodles in broth are sold from little stands as a quick snack. You can find *soba*—thin buckwheat noodles—in Asian markets and in some supermarkets.

> 4 ounces soba (buckwheat noodles)
> Boiling water
> ½ cup cold water
> 1 large can (49½ oz.) regular-strength chicken broth or 6 cups homemade chicken broth (page 33)
> 2 tablespoons *each* dry sherry and soy sauce
> ¼ pound snow peas, ends and strings removed
> 1½ to 2 cups shredded cooked chicken
> 2 green onions (including tops), thinly sliced

Drop soba into a large kettle of boiling water; stir to separate. When water returns to a boil, add cold water. Bring to a boil again, then cook, uncovered, until noodles are *al dente* (6 to 7 minutes). Drain well.

Meanwhile, bring broth, sherry, and soy to a simmer in a 3-quart pan. Add peas and chicken and cook for 1 minute. Divide hot noodles among 3 or 4 large soup bowls. Ladle hot broth over noodles, distributing peas and chicken evenly. Sprinkle some of the onions over each serving. Makes 3 or 4 servings.

Green Chile Pasta

Mexico

This moist, flavorsome pasta is a spirited example of Mexican *sopa seca*, or "dry soup." As the name implies, the pasta is cooked in only the amount of liquid it can absorb.

> 6 strips bacon, diced
> 1 large onion, chopped
> 8 ounces vermicelli or thin spaghetti
> 1 can (about 1 lb.) Italian-style tomatoes
> 1 can (14½ oz.) regular-strength beef broth or 1¾ cups homemade beef broth (page 33)
> 1 can (4 oz.) diced green chiles, drained well
> 2 tablespoons red wine vinegar
> Salt and pepper
> Grated Parmesan cheese

In a 3 to 4-quart pan over medium heat, cook bacon until crisp. Lift out, drain on paper towels, and set aside. Measure drippings; you should have ¼ cup (discard any excess).

Add onion to drippings in pan and cook, stirring, until soft. Break vermicelli into 2-inch pieces (you should have about 2 cups); stir into onion and continue cooking until onion is golden brown. Add tomatoes (break up with a spoon) and their liquid, broth, chiles, and vinegar; stir well. Cover and simmer until vermicelli is tender and almost all liquid has been absorbed (about 15 minutes). Season to taste with salt and pepper.

Spoon into a serving dish; top with bacon. At the table, pass cheese to sprinkle on pasta. Makes 4 servings.

Bean Threads with Szechwan Sauce

China

Translucent bean threads (see page 12) soak up the flavor of a spicy pork and mushroom sauce in this Szechwan specialty. In China, the dish is called "ants climbing a tree."

> 2 ounces bean threads
> 2 medium-size Oriental dried mushrooms
> 3 tablespoons salad oil
> 1 teaspoon minced fresh ginger
> 2 cloves garlic, minced
> 2 ounces lean boneless pork, finely chopped
> ¼ to ½ teaspoon crushed red pepper
> 1 green onion (including top), thinly sliced
> ½ cup regular-strength chicken broth
> 1 tablespoon *each* dry sherry and soy sauce
> 1 teaspoon sesame oil

Place bean threads and mushrooms in separate bowls; cover both with warm water and let stand for 30 minutes. Drain bean threads and cut into 4-inch lengths. Drain mushrooms; cut off and discard stems, then thinly slice caps.

Heat a wok or wide frying pan over high heat. When pan is hot, add salad oil. When oil begins to heat, add ginger and garlic and stir once. Add pork and pepper; stir-fry until pork loses its pinkness (about 4 minutes). Reduce heat to medium. Add mushrooms, bean threads, onion, broth, sherry, and soy. Simmer, uncovered, until all liquid has been absorbed (about 5 minutes), stirring occasionally. Stir in sesame oil just before serving. Makes 2 servings.

Stuffed pasta from purchased wrappers

There's no getting around it—making filled pastas the classic way is time-consuming. But you can produce delicious and impressive results in half the time by starting with purchased egg roll skins, won ton skins, or pot sticker wrappers. You might even prefer the commercial wrappers, since they're often thinner than those you'd make at home.

Chicken Liver Kreplach

Jewish heritage

Cousin to Italy's ravioli and China's won ton, *kreplach* are savory dumplings stuffed with chopped chicken liver or chopped beef.

- 2 **tablespoons rendered chicken or goose fat, or salad oil**
- ½ **small onion, finely chopped**
- ¼ **pound mushrooms, sliced**
- 2 **tablespoons chopped parsley**
- ¼ **teaspoon thyme leaves**
- ½ **teaspoon salt**
  Dash of white pepper
- ½ **pound chicken livers, cut in half**
- 4 **dozen won ton skins**
- 1 **egg white, lightly beaten**
  Boiling salted water
  Hot regular-strength chicken broth (1 cup per serving)

Heat chicken fat in a wide frying pan over medium-high heat. Add onion and mushrooms; cook for 5 minutes. Add livers, parsley, thyme, salt, and pepper; reduce heat to medium and cook just until livers are firm but still slightly pink in center (about 7 minutes). In a food processor or blender, whirl mixture until smooth. Let cool.

Place about 1 teaspoon filling in center of each won ton skin. Moisten edges with egg white, then fold skin in half to make a triangle and press edges to seal. Cook immediately; or transfer to floured baking sheets and freeze until firm, then transfer to plastic bags and store in freezer for up to 3 months.

Figure on 6 kreplach per serving. Drop freshly made or frozen kreplach into a large kettle of boiling salted water. Reduce heat to medium and boil gently, uncovered, until tender (4 minutes; 6 minutes if frozen). Drain. Place 6 kreplach in each individual bowl; ladle 1 cup hot broth over each serving. Makes 4 dozen kreplach.

Pot Stickers

China

The Chinese call these dim sum delicacies *guotie*; we know them as pot stickers. They're plump, filled dumplings, delectable as an appetizer, a light lunch, or even as an entrée along with stir-fried vegetables. Pot sticker wrappers are sold in Asian markets and some supermarkets; they're labeled as *gyoza*, their Japanese name.

- ½ **pound lean ground pork**
- ½ **pound small cooked shrimp, chopped**
- 1 **can (8 oz.) water chestnuts, drained well and chopped**
- ½ **cup chopped green onions (including tops)**
- 3 **tablespoons soy sauce**
- 3 **tablespoons dry sherry or regular-strength chicken broth**
- 1 **tablespoon cornstarch**
- 1 **teaspoon minced fresh ginger**
- ½ **teaspoon sugar**
- 4 **dozen pot sticker wrappers (gyoza)**
- 4 **tablespoons salad oil**
  White (distilled) vinegar, soy sauce, and chili oil

Combine pork, shrimp, water chestnuts, onions, the 3 tablespoons soy, sherry, cornstarch, ginger, and sugar; mix well.

To make each pot sticker, place 2 teaspoons filling in center of a wrapper. Moisten edges with water, then fold in half and press edges together to seal. (For an authentic-looking pot sticker, make 3 tucks along edge facing you as you seal wrapper.) Set pot sticker down firmly, seam side up, so it will sit flat on a flour-dusted baking sheet. Cover while you shape remaining pot stickers. (At this point, you may freeze pot stickers in a single layer until firm, then transfer to plastic bags and store in freezer for up to 3 months.)

Cook pot stickers 12 at a time. For each batch, heat 1 tablespoon of the oil in a wide, heavy frying pan over medium heat. Set pot stickers (don't thaw if frozen), seam side up, in pan. Cook, uncovered, until bottoms are deep golden brown (5 to 7 minutes). Pour in ¼ cup water; immediately cover, reduce heat to low, and cook for 10 more minutes (15 minutes if frozen). Uncover and continue to cook until all liquid has been absorbed.

Using a wide spatula, transfer pot stickers, browned side up, to a platter. Serve hot, with vinegar, soy, and chili oil. Makes 4 dozen pot stickers.

Preparing two Italian classics with one filling (Recipes on facing page)

1 For a two-way pasta filling, combine Italy's favorite cured ham—prosciutto—with chicken, onion, ricotta and Parmesan cheeses, and nutmeg.

2 *To make cannelloni,* mound ⅓ cup filling along one long edge of egg roll skin; roll to enclose. Place filled pasta in tomato-mint sauce. Top with more sauce and cheese slices.

3 Swathed in creamy teleme cheese and bubbly sauce, cannelloni make a rich and special entrée. To complete the meal, you need only a simple green salad and a loaf of good crusty bread.

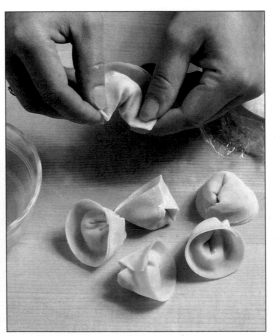

4 *To make each tortellini,* place 1 teaspoon filling in middle of a pot sticker wrapper. Moisten edges with egg white, then fold wrapper in half and press firmly to seal.

5 To form traditional belly button shape, draw ends of filled wrapper together and overlap. Moisten ends and press to seal. You can store tortellini in the freezer, ready to cook at a moment's notice.

6 Plump tortellini cloaked in silky cheese sauce and accented with freshly grated nutmeg illustrate Italian dining at its most satisfying. Small portions make an extra-elegant first course.

.Stuffed pasta from purchased wrappers

Chicken & Prosciutto Cannelloni

Italy   (Pictured on facing page)

Cannelloni made with egg roll skins are a bit larger and more generously filled than their classic counterparts, since the purchased wrappers are bigger than typical homemade ones.

>   **Chicken & prosciutto filling (recipe follows)**
>   **Creamy tomato-mint sauce (recipe follows)**
> 1 **dozen egg roll skins**
> 1 **pound teleme or jack cheese**

Prepare filling and sauce. Mound about ⅓ cup filling along one long edge of each egg roll skin; roll to enclose. Divide half the sauce evenly among 6 individual baking dishes, each about 4 by 6 inches. Place 2 cannelloni in each dish, seam side down and slightly apart. Spread with remaining sauce. Cut cheese into 12 slices, each just slightly larger than top of each cannelloni; place one slice on each cannelloni. Bake in a 400° oven, uncovered, for 30 to 40 minutes or until heated through. Makes 6 servings.

Chicken & prosciutto filling. Skin and bone 1 pound **chicken breasts;** cut meat into ½-inch pieces. Coarsely chop 6 ounces thinly sliced **prosciutto** or ham. Melt 2 tablespoons **butter** or margarine in a wide frying pan over medium heat. Add 1 large **onion,** chopped, and cook until soft. Add chicken; cook until opaque (about 3 minutes). Remove from heat; add prosciutto.

Whirl mixture in a food processor until coarsely ground (or mince with a knife). Place in a bowl; mix in 2 **egg yolks,** ⅔ cup grated **Parmesan cheese,** 1 cup (8 oz.) **ricotta cheese,** and ⅛ to ¼ teaspoon **ground nutmeg.** Season to taste with **salt** and **white pepper.**

Creamy tomato-mint sauce. Heat 3 tablespoons **salad oil** in a wide frying pan over medium heat. Add 2 medium-size **onions,** finely chopped, and 2 cloves **garlic,** minced or pressed; cook until soft. Add 1 large can (28 oz.) and 1 can (about 1 lb.) **Italian-style tomatoes** and their liquid, 1½ tablespoons **dry mint,** 1½ teaspoons **dry basil,** and 1 cup **regular-strength chicken broth.** Break tomatoes up with a spoon. Simmer, uncovered, until sauce is slightly thickened and reduced to 6 cups (about 20 minutes). Stir in ½ cup **whipping cream.** Season to taste with **salt** and **pepper.**

Tortellini

Italy   (Pictured on facing page)

Bellybutton-shaped tortellini (literally "little twists") are a specialty of Bologna.

>   **Chicken & prosciutto filling (recipe at left)**
> 6 **to 7 dozen pot sticker wrappers (gyoza) or**
>   **won ton skins (about 1 lb.)**
> 1 **egg white, lightly beaten**
>   **Supreme sauce (recipe follows)**
>   **Freshly grated nutmeg**

Prepare filling. Assemble tortellini a few at a time, keeping wrappers you're not working with covered to prevent drying. (If using won ton skins, cut skins, a few at a time, into rounds with a 3 to 3¼-inch cooky cutter; discard trimmings.) Place about 1 teaspoon filling on each wrapper; moisten edges with egg white, fold wrapper in half, and press to seal. Overlap ends of folded wrapper; moisten with egg white and press to seal. As you prepare tortellini, place them in a single layer on flour-dusted baking sheets; cover with plastic wrap. (At this point, you may cover and refrigerate for up to 4 hours. Or freeze until solid, then transfer to plastic bags and store in freezer for up to 3 months.) Prepare sauce.

Pour about 4 quarts water into a 5 to 6-quart kettle and bring to a boil over high heat. Drop in about half the tortellini, freshly made or frozen. Reduce heat to medium and boil gently, uncovered, just until tender to bite (about 4 minutes; 6 minutes if frozen). Drain. Repeat with remaining tortellini. Place all tortellini in a wide bowl, then pour in supreme sauce and gently turn tortellini in sauce to coat. Sprinkle with nutmeg. Makes 6 servings.

Supreme sauce. Melt ½ cup (¼ lb.) **butter** in a 2-quart pan over medium heat. Add 2 tablespoons **all-purpose flour** and ¼ teaspoon **ground nutmeg** and cook, stirring, until bubbly. Remove pan from heat and stir in 1 pint (2 cups) **whipping cream.** Return to heat and cook, stirring, until sauce is smooth and thickened. Stir in 1 cup (4 to 5 oz.) grated **Asiago, Romano, or Parmesan cheese** and cook until cheese is melted. If made ahead, let cool; then cover and refrigerate until next day. To reheat, place over hot water; stir constantly until smooth and heated through.

Grains

Grains provide an astonishing 80 percent of the calories people eat worldwide. Here are a few choice examples of how such nourishment comes to tables around the world.

Sesame-Wheat Pilaf

Armenian heritage

Wish your guests *pari akhorjhag*, Armenian for "bon appetit," as you present this crunchy pilaf.

> 2 **tablespoons butter or margarine**
> 1 **small onion, chopped**
> ¼ **pound mushrooms, sliced**
> 1 **cup bulgur (quick-cooking cracked wheat)**
> ¼ **cup sesame seeds, toasted (page 99)**
> 1 **can (14½ oz.) regular-strength chicken broth or 1¾ cups homemade chicken broth (page 33)**
> 1 **tablespoon chopped parsley**
> 1 **clove garlic, cut in half**

Melt butter in a 2-quart pan over medium heat. Add onion and mushrooms and cook until vegetables are soft and liquid has evaporated. Stir in bulgur and sesame seeds and cook for 1 minute. Add broth, parsley, and garlic. Bring to a boil; then cover, reduce heat, and simmer until bulgur is *al dente* and all liquid has been absorbed (about 20 minutes). Remove garlic. Makes 4 servings.

Lentil-Wheat Pilaf

Lebanon

This savory marriage of lentils and wheat is high in protein—a fact that's of special significance to Lebanese Christians, who observe many days of meatless fasting throughout the year.

> ½ **cup lentils, rinsed well**
> 2 **cups water**
> 1 **teaspoon salt**
> 3 **tablespoons olive oil**
> 1 **small onion, chopped**
> ¼ **pound mushrooms, sliced**
> ½ **cup bulgur (quick-cooking cracked wheat)**
>   **Plain yogurt**
>   **Sliced green onions (including tops)**

Combine lentils, water, and salt in a 2-quart pan. Bring to a boil over high heat; then cover, reduce heat, and simmer for 20 minutes. Set aside.

Heat oil in a wide frying pan over medium heat. Add onion and mushrooms; cook, stirring occasionally, until onion is soft. Add bulgur and cook for 2 minutes. Pour lentil mixture into pan and bring to a boil; then cover and simmer just until bulgur is *al dente* and all liquid has been absorbed (about 20 minutes). Serve with yogurt and onions. Makes 4 servings.

Kasha

Russia

Kasha—deliciously crunchy buckwheat groats— has long been a staple of Russian cuisine.

> 1 **can (14½ oz.) regular-strength chicken broth or 1¾ cups homemade chicken broth (page 33)**
> ¼ **teaspoon salt**
> ⅛ **teaspoon pepper**
> 2 **tablespoons butter or margarine**
> 1 **egg**
> 1 **cup kasha (toasted buckwheat groats)**
> 2 **green onions (including tops), sliced**

Place broth, salt, pepper, and butter in a pan; bring to a boil. Meanwhile, in an ungreased wide frying pan, stir together egg and kasha. Cook over medium-high heat, stirring constantly, until egg is set and dry (about 2 minutes). Slowly pour hot broth over kasha. Cover, reduce heat, and simmer until kasha is dry and fluffy (15 to 20 minutes). Turn off heat and stir in onions; cover and let stand for 5 minutes. Makes 4 servings.

Rice with Mushrooms & Peas

Hungary

Festive with mushrooms and peas, *gombás rizs* makes a tasty partner for ham or roast turkey.

> 4 **tablespoons butter or margarine**
> 1 **cup long-grain white rice**
> 1 **can (14½ oz.) regular-strength chicken broth or 1¾ cups homemade chicken broth (page 33)**
> ½ **pound mushrooms, sliced**
> 1 **cup frozen peas, thawed**
>   **Salt and pepper**
>   **Grated Parmesan cheese**

Melt 2 tablespoons of the butter in a 2-quart pan over medium heat. Add rice and cook, stirring occasionally, until golden (about 5 minutes). Add broth. Bring to a boil; then cover, reduce heat, and simmer until rice is *al dente* and all liquid has been absorbed (20 to 25 minutes).

While rice is cooking, melt remaining 2 tablespoons butter in a wide frying pan over medium-high heat. Add mushrooms and cook until mushrooms are soft and all liquid has evaporated. Add mushrooms and peas to rice and mix lightly with a fork. Season to taste with salt and pepper. Cover and let stand for 5 minutes before serving. Pass cheese to sprinkle over each serving. Makes 4 servings.

Yellow Rice with Raisins

South Africa   (Pictured on page 174)

Fragrant, golden, and studded with raisins, this South African pilaf makes a tempting presentation. And it tastes just as good as it looks, especially alongside Spicy Cabbage Rolls (page 175).

- 1 **tablespoon salad oil**
- 1 **tablespoon curry powder**
- 1 **teaspoon salt**
- ¾ **teaspoon ground cumin**
- ½ **teaspoon turmeric**
- 1½ **cups long-grain white rice**
- 3 **cups water**
- ¾ **cup raisins**
- 2 **bay leaves**

Heat oil in a 3-quart pan over medium-low heat. Add curry powder and cook, stirring, for 2 minutes. Stir in salt, cumin, turmeric, and rice. Add water and bring to a boil over high heat; then cover, reduce heat to low, and cook until rice is *al dente* and liquid has been absorbed (20 to 25 minutes). Remove from heat and stir in raisins and bay leaves. Cover and let stand for 5 minutes before serving. Makes 6 servings.

Shrimp Fried Rice

China

Fried rice is a popular family dish in central and southern China, where it's used to convert leftovers into a quick meal. You can add just about any meat or vegetable you wish, but always start with cold, cooked rice so the grains stay separate during stir-frying.

- 4 **cups cold cooked long-grain white rice**
- 2 **eggs**
- ¼ **teaspoon salt**
- 4 **tablespoons salad oil**
- 2 **green onions (including tops), thinly sliced**
- 1 **cup small cooked shrimp, diced cooked ham, or diced cooked chicken**
- ½ **cup *each* thawed frozen peas and roasted, salted cashews**
- 2 **tablespoons soy sauce**

Rub rice with wet hands so all grains are separated; set aside. In a bowl, beat eggs with salt. Heat 1 tablespoon of the oil in a wide frying pan over medium heat; add onions and stir-fry for 30 seconds. Add eggs and cook, stirring, until soft curds form; remove from pan and set aside.

Heat 1 more tablespoon oil in pan. Add shrimp, peas, and cashews. Stir-fry for 2 minutes to heat through; remove from pan and set aside. Heat remaining 2 tablespoons oil in pan. Add rice and stir-fry for 2 minutes to heat through. Stir in soy and shrimp mixture. Add eggs; stir mixture gently until eggs are in small pieces. Makes 4 servings.

WHEN IS GRAIN DONE?

The doneness test for grains is like that for pasta: *al dente*, or tender but firm to bite. At this stage, each grain has a slightly resilient core, and all the cooking liquid has been absorbed.

For basic grain cooking instructions, check the package label. Some grains cook more quickly than others; some require more liquid than others. Bulgur takes only about 20 minutes, while short-grain rice needs up to half an hour. And short-grain rice (favored by Japanese and Korean cooks) takes less water than the long-grain varieties used in Chinese, Middle Eastern, and much American cooking.

When you're deciding how much grain to cook, plan on about 1 cup uncooked grain for each 3 cups cooked.

...Grains

Paella

Spain (Pictured on front cover and facing page)

Today, *paella* is a sumptuous feast of poultry, shellfish, and saffron rice—but this celebrated classic started out as a poor man's supper in the Spanish province of Valencia. The dish gets its name from *paellera*, the shallow iron pan in which it is traditionally cooked.

> 1 **dozen mussels, scrubbed, beards removed; or 1 dozen small hard-shell clams, scrubbed**
> ½ **cup water**
> 6 **chicken legs**
> **Salt and pepper**
> 2 **tablespoons olive oil or salad oil**
> ¾ **pound chorizo or linguisa sausage, casings removed, cut into ½-inch-thick slices**
> 1 **large onion, chopped**
> 1 **red or green bell pepper, seeded and chopped**
> 2 **large cloves garlic, minced or pressed**
> 2 **cups long-grain white rice**
> ⅛ **teaspoon ground saffron**
> ½ **teaspoon** *each* **dry basil and oregano leaves**
> 1 **package (10 oz.) frozen artichoke hearts, thawed**
> **About 3½ cups regular-strength chicken broth**
> 1 **dozen large raw shrimp, shelled (leave tails attached) and deveined**
> ¼ **cup frozen peas, thawed**

Place mussels (or clams) and water in a 2-quart pan. Bring to a boil; then cover, reduce heat to low, and cook until shells open (5 to 8 minutes). Remove from heat and let cool.

Sprinkle chicken with salt and pepper. Heat oil in a wide frying pan over medium-high heat. Add chicken and cook, turning as needed, until well browned on all sides. Remove from pan and set aside. Add sausage and cook until browned; remove and set aside.

Discard all but 3 tablespoons of pan drippings. Add onion, bell pepper, and garlic to drippings; cook, stirring occasionally, until onion is soft. Add rice, saffron, basil, and oregano; stir to coat rice with drippings.

Transfer rice mixture to a wide, shallow 4-quart casserole. Arrange chicken, sausage, and artichoke hearts over rice.

Measure mussel liquid; add enough broth to make 4 cups. Pour into a pan and bring to a boil over high heat, then pour over rice mixture.

Tightly cover casserole with foil. Bake in a 350° oven for 30 minutes. Uncover and stir lightly to mix ingredients. Push shrimp into top of rice. Cover and bake for 10 more minutes or until shrimp turn pink. Uncover; push mussels into rice and scatter peas over top. Cover and bake for about 5 more minutes or until mussels are heated through and all liquid is absorbed. Makes 6 servings.

Rice with Green Peas

India (Pictured on page 110)

Sweet spices and turmeric flavor golden *mattar pilau*. Try it as an accompaniment to Spicy Chicken Curry (page 111).

> 2 **tablespoons salad oil**
> 4 **whole cloves**
> 2 **cardamom pods, cracked open**
> 1 **cinnamon stick (about 2 inches long)**
> 1½ **cups long-grain white rice**
> ½ **teaspoon turmeric**
> 2½ **cups water**
> 1 **cup frozen peas, thawed**
> **Salt**

Heat oil in a 2 to 3-quart pan over low heat; add cloves, cardamom pods, and cinnamon stick. Cook, stirring, for 2 minutes. Stir in rice and turmeric and cook for 2 more minutes. Add water. Bring to a boil over high heat; then cover, reduce heat to low, and cook for 15 minutes. Scatter peas over rice and continue to cook until rice is *al dente*, peas are tender to bite, and all liquid has been absorbed (about 5 more minutes). Remove whole spices; fluff rice with a fork and season to taste with salt. Makes 6 servings.

SRI LANKAN SAVORY RICE

Prepare **Rice with Green Peas.** While rice is cooking, cut 2 **leeks** (white and tender green sections only) crosswise in ¼-inch thick slices; separate white part into rings. Shred 2 small **carrots.** Melt 2 tablespoons **butter** or margarine in a wide frying pan over medium heat. Add leeks and carrots and cook, stirring occasionally, until soft. Stir in ¼ cup *each* roasted salted **cashews** and **raisins** and heat through, then stir into cooked rice. Makes 6 servings.

Making Spanish Paella (Recipe on facing page)

1 Scrub mussels; pull off beards. Shells should be closed before cooking; they'll open with application of heat. (Discard any mussels that are open before cooking or still closed after cooking.)

2 Cook chicken legs until browned on all sides; remove from pan. Add sliced chorizos and cook until browned on edges; sausages turn bright brick red as they cook.

3 Onion, red bell pepper, and garlic absorb spicy flavor as they cook in chorizo drippings. Cook vegetables until soft but not browned.

4 Arrange chorizos, chicken, and artichokes atop rice mixture. At this point, you may cover and refrigerate up to 4 hours; add hot liquid and bake about 45 minutes before serving.

5 Shells clatter when you serve Paella—the Spanish dish of shellfish, chicken, sausages, and vegetables in saffron-flavored rice.

...Grains

Lamb & Chicken Couscous

Morocco

Couscous has two meanings. It's a nutty-tasting grain product made from durum wheat; it also names a famous one-dish Moroccan banquet of various meats and vegetables, all served with a platter of fluffy steamed couscous.

- 2 tablespoons olive oil or salad oil
- 3 each chicken legs and thighs
- 2 pounds lamb stew meat (with bones), cut into 2-inch pieces
- 1 medium-size onion, chopped
- 5 medium-size carrots, cut into 1-inch pieces
- ¼ teaspoon black pepper
- 4 cups regular-strength chicken broth
- 3 stalks celery, cut into 1-inch pieces
- 1 green pepper, seeded and cut into strips
- 1 can (15 oz.) garbanzo beans, drained well
- 1 can (14 oz.) artichoke hearts in water, drained well
  Hot sauce (recipe follows)
  Steamed couscous with raisins (recipe follows)

Heat oil in a 5 to 6-quart kettle over medium-high heat. Add chicken and cook, turning, until browned on all sides. Remove chicken and set aside. Add lamb and cook, turning, until browned on all sides. Remove lamb and set aside. Add onion to kettle; reduce heat to medium and cook, stirring, until soft. Return chicken and lamb to kettle and add carrots, black pepper, and broth. Bring to a boil; then cover, reduce heat, and simmer until chicken and lamb are tender when pierced (about 50 minutes).

When meats are tender, add celery, green pepper, and garbanzos and simmer for 5 more minutes. Add artichokes and heat through. Prepare hot sauce and couscous. Just before serving, pour broth from meat mixture into a bowl; skim and discard fat, then pour broth into a teapot or pitcher for serving.

Mound couscous in center of a large platter. Arrange meats and vegetables around sides. To eat, take a portion of couscous and add some meat and vegetables; pour over broth to moisten, then sprinkle with hot sauce. Makes 6 servings.

Hot sauce. In a bowl, stir together 2 tablespoons **catsup** and 1 tablespoon **olive oil**. Stir in ½ teaspoon each **ground red pepper** (cayenne),

ground cumin, and **white pepper;** then add ¼ teaspoon each **ground nutmeg** and **ground cloves.** Before serving, stir in ⅓ cup **cooking broth** from chicken and lamb mixture.

Steamed couscous with raisins. Pour 3 cups **regular-strength chicken broth** into a 4 to 5-quart kettle; bring to a boil over high heat. Add 6 tablespoons **butter** or margarine, ⅓ cup **raisins,** and ¼ teaspoon **ground cinnamon.** Stir until butter is melted. Quickly stir in 3 cups (one 1-lb. package) **quick-cooking couscous;** cover, remove from heat, and let stand until liquid has been absorbed (about 5 minutes). With a fork, toss couscous until light, fluffy, and free of lumps. Makes 6 servings.

Festive Yellow Rice

Indonesia

Once reserved for religious ceremonies, nasi kuning is still served on special occasions. This sweet, aromatic rice dish pairs well with Grilled Pork (page 87). For a traditional presentation, as part of an Indonesian buffet called rijsttafel ("rice table"), shape the rice into a cone on a serving plate and surround with the tomato and cucumber garnish and skewered grilled pork.

- 1½ cups long-grain white rice
- ¾ cup canned or thawed frozen coconut milk, or ¾ cup whipping cream mixed with ¼ teaspoon each coconut extract and sugar
- 1½ cups water
- 1½ teaspoons turmeric
- 1 strip lemon zest (colored outer part of peel), 1 inch wide and 2 inches long
- 1 thin slice fresh ginger
- ½ bay leaf
  Salt
  Tomato and cucumber slices

In a 2-quart pan, combine rice, coconut milk, water, turmeric, lemon zest, ginger, and bay leaf. Bring to a boil over medium heat. Reduce heat to medium-low; cook, uncovered, until liquid has been absorbed (about 10 minutes). Cover, reduce heat to low, and cook until rice is al dente (15 to 20 minutes). Halfway through cooking, gently fluff rice with 2 forks to cook evenly. Season to taste with salt. Remove lemon zest, ginger, and bay leaf. Fluff rice with a fork, then shape into a cone on a serving plate. Garnish with tomato and cucumber. Makes 4 to 6 servings.

Beans

Plump, meaty seeds of the legume family, beans pack in a wealth of good-tasting nourishment that's appreciated by cuisines throughout the world. Moreover, beans lend themselves to rich culinary diversity and a variety of seasonings.

For most beans, cooking until they're tender can take a long time. To shorten the cooking time, soak all dried beans except lentils before you use them—unless the recipe calls for simmering the beans slowly, as in Corned Beef Simmered with White Beans (at right) and Cassoulet (page 159).

The standard soaking method is to combine 1 pound dried beans, 2 quarts cold water, and 2 teaspoons salt and soak overnight. Drain the beans before cooking. Or combine beans, water, and salt in a large pan; bring to a boil for 2 minutes, then turn off heat, cover, and let stand for 1 hour. Drain before cooking.

Lemon Pinto Beans

Turkey

Called *fasulye pilaki*, this hearty vegetarian mélange of beans and vegetables tastes best at room temperature.

- 1 **pound dried pinto or pink beans**
- 12 **cups water**
- ½ **cup olive oil**
  Salt
- 2 **medium-size onions, chopped**
- 3 **medium-size carrots, diced**
- ⅓ **cup tomato paste**
- 1 **teaspoon sugar**
- ½ **teaspoon black pepper**
- ¼ **teaspoon ground red pepper (cayenne)**
- 1 **large thin-skinned potato**
- ⅔ **cup lemon juice**
  Garnishes: Lemon slices, parsley sprigs, and sliced green onions (including tops)

Sort beans to remove debris; rinse well, then drain. Combine beans, 8 cups of the water, and 2 teaspoons salt in a 4 to 5-quart kettle; bring to a boil over high heat, cover, and cook for 2 minutes. Remove from heat and let stand for 1 hour. Drain well.

Heat oil in a wide frying pan over medium heat; add onions and cook, stirring occasionally, until soft but not browned. Add onion mixture to beans, along with remaining 4 cups water, carrots, tomato paste, sugar, black pepper, and red

pepper; bring to a boil over high heat. Cover, reduce heat to low, and simmer for 30 minutes. Peel and dice potato; add to beans and cook until potato and beans can be mashed easily (about 30 more minutes). Let cool; stir in lemon juice and season to taste with salt. Serve at room temperature, topped with garnishes. Makes 8 servings.

Corned Beef Simmered with White Beans

United States

The beans for this savory dish don't need to be soaked ahead of time. Instead, they cook slowly with the meat and vegetables until very tender.

- 1 **pound dried small white beans**
- 1 **corned beef brisket (5 to 6 lbs.)**
- 2 **large leeks**
- 2 **tablespoons salad oil**
- 2 **tablespoons butter or margarine**
- 1 **large onion, chopped**
- 2 **large carrots, chopped**
- 2 **cloves garlic, minced or pressed**
- ¼ **cup chopped parsley**
- 2 **small cans (6 oz. *each*) tomato paste**
- 1 **teaspoon *each* dry rosemary, thyme leaves, and dry mustard**
- 1 **bay leaf**
- ½ **teaspoon pepper**

Sort beans to remove debris; rinse well, drain, and set aside. Trim and discard excess fat from beef. Place meat in a 10 to 12-quart kettle; cover with water and bring to a boil over high heat. Boil for 2 minutes; drain. Repeat with fresh water.

Meanwhile, trim and discard tough outer leaves from leeks. Split lengthwise, rinse well, and chop. Heat oil and butter in a wide frying pan over medium heat. Add leeks, onion, carrots, garlic, and parsley. Cook, stirring often, for 10 minutes; then add to drained meat in kettle. Add 10 cups water, tomato paste, rosemary, thyme, mustard, bay leaf, and pepper. Stir in beans. Bring to a boil over high heat; then cover, reduce heat, and simmer until meat is tender when pierced and beans mash easily (3½ to 4 hours).

Lift out meat and cut into chunks. Skim and discard fat from sauce. Spoon out 1½ cups beans and some sauce; purée or mash well, then stir back into kettle. Return meat to kettle. Serve in wide soup bowls. Makes 10 to 12 servings.

Assembling a French Cassoulet (Recipe on facing page)

1 Cut roast duck apart with poultry shears. Meat from lamb shanks, cooked with beans, will be stripped from bones in bite-size pieces. Kielbasa and garlic sausages only need slicing.

2 Cut roasted onions in half lengthwise; slip off and discard skins. Then press onion halves into bean mixture, distributing them evenly among sausage slices.

3 Last touch before serving: Spoon on sliced garlic, mellowed and lightly browned in duck fat.

4 A splendid dish for entertaining, Cassoulet bakes untended as guests gather. For a satisfying country-style French meal, add a simple green salad, crusty bread, and a good jug wine.

Cassoulet

France   (Pictured on facing page)

Though the meats used in *cassoulet* vary by locality, the French all agree on the white beans that soak up the rich flavors in the broth.

> **Cooked beans (recipe follows)**
> **Roast duck & onions (recipe follows)**
> 1 **large can (28 oz.) tomatoes**
> 1 **small can (6 oz.) tomato paste**
> 10 **cloves garlic, minced or pressed**
> 4 **kielbasa (Polish sausage) or garlic sausages (or 2 of each kind), cut into 1 to 1½-inch slices**
> **Fried garlic (recipe follows)**

Prepare beans; also prepare roast duck and onions.

In a shallow 9 to 10-quart casserole, combine tomatoes (cut in half) and their liquid, tomato paste, and minced garlic. Add beans; mix well.

Poke sausages down into beans. Arrange roast onion halves, cut side up, on beans; press into beans to cover almost completely. Place duck pieces, skin side up, on beans. (At this point, you may cover and refrigerate for up to 2 days.) Bake in a 300° oven, uncovered, for about 2 hours (3 hours if refrigerated) or until heated through in center. Prepare fried garlic; sprinkle over cassoulet just before serving. Makes 10 servings.

Cooked beans. Place ¼ pound **salt pork,** diced, and 2 **lamb shanks** in an 8 to 10-quart kettle. Cook over medium heat, stirring, until pork is browned. Add 1 large **onion,** chopped; 2 teaspoons **thyme leaves;** 2 **bay leaves;** and ½ teaspoon *each* **ground red pepper** (cayenne) and **ground cloves.** Cook, stirring, until onion is soft.

Sort 1½ pounds **dried Great Northern beans** to remove debris. Rinse beans and add to kettle along with 10 cups **water.** Bring to a boil over high heat; then cover, reduce heat, and simmer, stirring occasionally, until beans mash easily (about 2½ hours). Lift out lamb shanks; let cool. Pull meat from bones in bite-size pieces; return meat to beans. Discard bay leaves. Season to taste with **salt.**

Roast duck & onions. Remove giblets from 1 **duckling** (4 to 5 lbs.); reserve for other uses. Pull off lumps of fat; discard. Rinse duck and pat dry.

Place duck, breast down, on a rack in a 12 by 15-inch roasting pan. Arrange 4 large **onions** (unpeeled) around duck. Roast at 375° for 1 hour; remove fat as necessary and reserve for fried garlic. Turn duck over and roast for 1 more hour, removing onions after 30 minutes. Let duck and onions cool. Using poultry shears or a heavy knife, cut duck into 10 to 12 pieces of about equal size. Cut onions in half lengthwise; slip off skins.

Fried garlic. Peel and slice 15 cloves **garlic.** In a wide frying pan, combine garlic and ½ cup **duck fat.** Place over medium heat and stir until garlic is very light brown; don't let garlic scorch. Lift out slices with a slotted spoon and drain.

Hot & Spicy Lentils

Ethiopia

Berberé, a popular Ethiopian seasoning mixture, gives extra bite to savory *misser wat.*

> **Berberé (recipe follows)**
> ¼ **cup salad oil**
> 2 **large onions, chopped**
> ⅓ **cup tomato paste**
> 5½ **cups water**
> 2 **cups lentils (one 12-oz. package)**
> 1 **small hot fresh chile (such as jalapeño)**
> **Salt**
> 2 **limes, cut into wedges**

Prepare Berberé. Heat oil in a 5-quart kettle over medium heat; add onions and cook until soft. Stir in berberé, tomato paste, and ½ cup of the water; reduce heat to medium-low and cook, stirring, for 5 minutes.

Add remaining 5 cups water. Sort lentils to remove debris, rinse well, and drain; then add lentils and chile to onion mixture. Bring to a boil; cover, reduce heat, and simmer, stirring occasionally, until lentils are soft (about 45 minutes). Discard chile; season stew to taste with salt. Serve hot, with lime wedges to squeeze over each serving. Makes 8 servings.

Berberé (Ethiopian spices). In a bowl, stir together 1 to 2 teaspoons **ground red pepper** (cayenne), 1 teaspoon **paprika,** ½ teaspoon *each* **ground ginger** and **ground cardamom,** ¼ teaspoon *each* **garlic powder** and **salt,** and ⅛ teaspoon *each* **ground coriander** and **ground cinnamon.** Mix in 2 teaspoons **white wine vinegar** and 2 tablespoons **water** to form a smooth paste.

VEGETABLES

Buttery yellow corn, deep green spinach, glossy purple eggplant—you can't beat fresh vegetables for naturally gorgeous color. They offer unbeatable flavor, too, from mellow to robust to incredibly sweet. At one time, many fresh vegetables could be purchased only during a limited season. But today, thanks to advances in agriculture, storage, and transportation, availability has been extended dramatically—letting you enjoy most vegetables fresh almost all year round.

In this chapter, we focus first on side dishes, then close with a small, select group of entrées. The spotlight's on widely available vegetables, so you'll have no trouble trying out all the recipes in this international sampler.

Side dishes

Dressed up with a simple sauce or a sprinkle of seasonings, any vegetable can put on an impressive solo performance—a point amply proved by Ginger-Garlic Broccoli, Roasted Potatoes, and the other recipes on pages 160 to 167. Our medleys (pages 168 to 170) show that vegetables perform beautifully in concert, too; hearty Stamppot and succulent Tourlu are just two examples.

Select a dish that suits the main course. Sauced vegetables or combinations go best with plain meats, poultry, or fish; simpler choices provide good contrast to saucy or highly spiced entrées.

Artichokes with Tomatoes

Italy

In *carciofi in umido* ("stewed artichokes"), a sauce of fresh tomatoes, garlic, and basil enhances small, tender artichokes.

> Acid water (2 tablespoons lemon juice to each 4 cups water)
> 16 small artichokes, *each* about 3 inches long (not including stem); or 2 packages (9 to 10 oz. *each*) frozen artichoke hearts, thawed
> 2 tablespoons olive oil
> 1 large onion, chopped
> 2 medium-size tomatoes, peeled and chopped
> 1 clove garlic, minced or pressed
> ½ teaspoon dry basil
> ¼ cup water
> Salt and pepper
> Grated Parmesan cheese

Have ready a large quantity of acid water. Using a stainless steel knife, cut off stem and top third of each fresh artichoke; peel off outer leaves until you reach pale green inner ones. Drop artichokes into acid water.

Heat oil in a wide frying pan over medium heat. Add onion and cook for 10 minutes; then add tomatoes, garlic, basil, and water. Drain fresh or frozen artichokes well; stir into sauce. Bring to a boil over high heat; cover, reduce heat, and simmer until artichokes are tender when pierced (15 to 20 minutes). Season to taste with salt and pepper; sprinkle with cheese. Makes 4 servings.

Lemon Green Beans

Mexico

Like every cuisine, Mexican cooking has its quiet, simple dishes—such as these Guadalajara-style beans, lightly seasoned with lemon butter.

- 1½ **pounds green beans, ends removed, cut into 1½-inch lengths**
- 3 **tablespoons butter or margarine, melted**
- ½ **teaspoon salt**
- ¼ **teaspoon pepper**
- 1 **tablespoon minced parsley**
- 2 to 3 **tablespoons lemon juice**

In a 3-quart pan, bring 1 inch water to a boil over high heat; add beans. When water returns to a boil, cover pan, reduce heat, and simmer until beans are tender when pierced (5 to 10 minutes). Meanwhile, combine butter, salt, pepper, parsley, and lemon juice. Drain beans well; add butter mixture and stir to coat. Makes 6 servings.

Ginger-Garlic Broccoli

China

Stir-frying is a Chinese technique that's ideal for vegetable cookery. Just a quick tumble in hot oil enhances flavor, intensifies color, and produces a wonderful tender-crisp texture.

- 1 **pound broccoli**
- 2 **tablespoons salad oil**
- 1 **large clove garlic, minced or pressed**
- ½ to 1 **teaspoon grated fresh ginger**
- 2 **tablespoons water**

Cut off broccoli flowerets and slash their stems; peel and thinly slice stalks. Heat a wok or wide frying pan over high heat. When pan is hot, add oil. When oil begins to heat, add garlic and ginger and stir once; then add broccoli and stir-fry for 1 minute. Add water; cover and cook until broccoli is tender-crisp (3 to 4 minutes). Makes 4 servings.

CHINESE GINGER-GARLIC ASPARAGUS

Follow directions for **Ginger-Garlic Broccoli,** but substitute 1 pound **asparagus,** cut diagonally into ¼-inch slices, for broccoli. Cook for only 2 to 3 minutes after adding water.

Sweet-Sour Cabbage

Germany

This popular German side dish gets its sweet-sour flavor from shredded apple, currant jelly, and a healthy splash of red wine vinegar.

- 3 **tablespoons butter or margarine**
- 1 **tablespoon salad oil**
- 1 **small onion, thinly sliced**
- 1 **small tart apple, cored and shredded**
- ½ **cup water**
- ¼ **cup each dry red wine, red wine vinegar, and red currant jelly**
- 1 **large head red cabbage (about 2½ lbs.), cored and finely shredded**
- 1 **teaspoon caraway seeds**

Heat butter and oil in a 5 to 6-quart kettle over medium heat. Add onion; cook, stirring occasionally, until soft but not browned (15 to 20 minutes). Stir in apple, water, wine, vinegar, and jelly; then add cabbage. Cover; cook, stirring occasionally, for 30 minutes. Stir in caraway seeds and cook until cabbage is soft and juices have evaporated (about 30 more minutes). Makes 6 to 8 servings.

Toasted Cabbage

Hungary

There's a lot more to cabbage than great coleslaw (page 41)! Chopped and "toasted" in the frying pan, this versatile vegetable makes a sensational partner for roast pork or chicken.

- 1 **large head cabbage (about 2½ lbs.), cored and finely chopped**
- 1 **tablespoon salt**
- ½ **cup (¼ lb.) butter or margarine**
- 3 **tablespoons sugar**
- ¼ **teaspoon freshly ground pepper**

In a bowl, mix cabbage and salt; let stand for 30 minutes. Pour into a colander and rinse under cold running water, then squeeze out as much liquid as possible. Melt butter in a wide frying pan over medium heat. Add cabbage; cook, uncovered, stirring occasionally, until bright green and limp (about 20 minutes). Add sugar and pepper. Cook, stirring frequently, until cabbage is soft and tinged with gold (about 30 more minutes). Makes 6 to 8 servings.

...Side dishes

Mustard-glazed Carrots

France

If you think you don't like cooked carrots, try this French recipe—and think again. Cloaked with a sweet mustard glaze, the tender-crisp slices taste marvelous, especially with barbecued meats.

> 2 **pounds carrots, cut diagonally into ¼-inch-thick slices**
> 3 **tablespoons Dijon mustard**
> 3 **tablespoons butter or margarine**
> 2 **tablespoons firmly packed brown sugar**
>   **Chopped parsley**

In a wide frying pan, bring ½ inch water to a boil over high heat; add carrots. When water returns to a boil, cover pan, reduce heat, and simmer until carrots are tender-crisp to bite (5 to 10 minutes). Drain thoroughly.

Add mustard, butter, and sugar to carrots in pan; cook over medium heat, stirring, until carrots are glazed (1 to 2 minutes). Sprinkle with parsley. Makes 6 to 8 servings.

Spicy Tomato-topped Eggplant

India   (Pictured on facing page)

Eggplant's mellowness makes it a perfect foil for livelier flavors. In this showy Indian side dish, the tender slices are topped twice: first with cool and tangy yogurt, then with a gingery-hot tomato sauce.

> ⅓ **cup olive oil or salad oil**
> 1 **large eggplant (1¼ to 1½ lbs.), cut crosswise into ¾-inch-thick slices**
> 2 **tablespoons butter or margarine**
> 1 **tablespoon olive oil**
> 1 **medium-size onion, chopped**
> 1 **large clove garlic, minced or pressed**
> 1 **teaspoon *each* grated fresh ginger, ground cumin, and ground coriander**
> ¼ **teaspoon ground ginger**
> 1 **can (about 1 lb.) Italian-style tomatoes**
> 1 **tablespoon sugar**
> 2 **tablespoons chopped parsley**
>   **Salt and pepper**
> ¾ **to 1 cup plain yogurt**
>   **Fresh cilantro (coriander) leaves (optional)**

Brush the ⅓ cup oil over cut sides of eggplant slices. Arrange in a single layer on a baking sheet; bake in a 450° oven for 20 minutes or until tender in center when pierced.

Meanwhile, heat butter and the 1 tablespoon oil in a wide frying pan over medium heat. Add onion and garlic and cook, stirring occasionally, until soft (about 10 minutes). Add fresh ginger, cumin, coriander, ground ginger, tomatoes (break up with a spoon) and their liquid, and sugar. Cook, uncovered, stirring occasionally, until mixture is thickened and almost all liquid has evaporated (about 10 minutes). Remove from heat and stir in parsley. Season to taste with salt and pepper.

Place baked eggplant slices on a platter; spoon yogurt over each slice, then top with a generous spoonful of tomato sauce. Garnish with cilantro, if desired. Makes 6 servings.

Mushrooms in Sour Cream

Russia

Sour cream gives a special richness to many Russian soups and sauces. Here, the addition of sour cream transforms simple sautéed mushrooms into a sumptuous side dish. Serve alongside broiled or barbecued fish, poultry, or meat; or, for a brunch treat, pair the mushrooms with poached or scrambled eggs.

> 4 **tablespoons butter or margarine**
> 1 **medium-size onion, chopped**
> 1 **pound mushrooms, sliced**
> 1 **teaspoon all-purpose flour**
> ½ **cup sour cream**
>   **Salt and pepper**
> 2 **tablespoons chopped parsley**

Melt butter in a wide frying pan over medium heat. Add onion and cook for 10 minutes, stirring occasionally. Add mushrooms and cook, stirring occasionally, until soft (about 10 more minutes). Combine flour and sour cream; stir into mushrooms.

Cook, stirring occasionally, until sauce boils. Season to taste with salt and pepper. Stir in parsley. Makes 4 to 6 servings.

Preparing Spicy Tomato-topped Eggplant (Recipe on facing page)

1 Brush eggplant slices with olive oil to prevent them from sticking to baking sheet and to give baked eggplant a rich brown hue. (Slices will absorb oil as soon as you brush it on.)

2 Cook onion and garlic until soft; then stir in grated fresh ginger and spices. (For tips on purchasing and storing fresh ginger, see page 116.)

3 Parsley retains its bright green color best when you stir it in at the very last—after sauce has thickened and you've removed pan from heat.

4 Mild-tasting eggplant, cool yogurt, and spicy tomato sauce stack up to take center stage in this Indian meal. Supporting cast includes Tandoori Chicken (page 104) and chewy Chapaties (page 177).

...Side dishes

Crisp-fried Onions

Denmark

Stegte løg are a popular snack in Denmark. Try them as a crunchy garnish on soups or salads, too.

> ½   **cup all-purpose flour**
> 2   **large onions (about 1 lb.** *total*)**, thinly sliced and separated into rings**
>   **Salad oil**
>   **Salt**

Place flour in a bag; then add onions, close bag, and shake to coat onions evenly.

Into a deep 2½ to 3-quart pan, pour oil to a depth of 1½ inches and heat to 300° on a deep-frying thermometer. Add about ¼ of the onions and cook, stirring often, until golden (about 5 minutes). Oil temperature will drop at first, then rise again; regulate heat to keep temperature at 300°. With a slotted spoon, lift out onions and drain on paper towels (discard scorched bits); keep warm. Repeat with remaining onions.

Pile onions in a napkin-lined basket or a warmed bowl; sprinkle with salt and serve at once. If made ahead, let cool; then wrap airtight and refrigerate for up to 3 days. To reheat, spread out in a shallow rimmed baking pan. Heat in a 350° oven for 2 to 3 minutes. Makes about 6 servings.

Peas with Pimentos

Italy

Colorful, zesty, and quick—that describes this bright combination of peas, pimentos, and onions.

> 3   **tablespoons olive oil**
> 1   **large onion, finely chopped**
> 1   **clove garlic, minced or pressed**
> 1   **jar (2 oz.) diced pimentos, drained well**
> 4   **cups shelled fresh peas (about 4 lbs. unshelled); or 1 large package (1 lb.) frozen peas, thawed**
> 3   **tablespoons water**

Heat oil in a wide frying pan over medium heat. Add onion and garlic and cook, stirring occasionally, until onion is golden (about 15 minutes). Stir in pimentos, peas, and water. Cover and cook until peas are tender to bite (8 to 12 minutes; 5 minutes for frozen peas). Makes 6 to 8 servings.

CHOPPING BULB ONIONS

To chop an onion without shedding a tear, follow this simple technique. By minimizing exposure to the onion's cut surfaces to air, you minimize release of the volatile oils that cause tearing. First, cut off stem end, leaving root end intact. Peel off papery outer skin under cold running water; then cut onion in half through root end. Place halves on a cutting board, cut side down. Thinly slice each half parallel to board, stopping short of root end; then cut thin lengthwise slices down through to board, again stopping short of root end. Finally, slice onion crosswise, starting at stem end; onion will fall into pieces.

Fried Bell Peppers

Italy

In the bright Mediterranean sun, bell peppers grow plump and sweet. Sautéing makes them taste even sweeter.

> 2   **tablespoons butter or margarine**
> 2   **tablespoons olive oil**
> 4   **large green or red bell peppers, seeded and cut into 1½-inch-wide strips**
> 1   **clove garlic, minced or pressed**
> ⅛   **teaspoon pepper**
> 1   **teaspoon oregano leaves**
>   **Salt**

Heat butter and oil in a wide frying pan over medium heat. Add bell peppers and garlic; cook, stirring occasionally, until peppers are lightly browned. Sprinkle with pepper and oregano. Cover, reduce heat, and cook until tender (about 15 minutes). Season to taste with salt; serve hot or at room temperature. Makes 4 servings.

Potatoes with Cheese

Colombia

Boiled potatoes are dressed up with a tomato-flecked cheese sauce for *papas chorreadas*, a festive companion to Braised Flank Steak (page 90).

8 to 12 small red thin-skinned potatoes (*each 1½ to 2 inches in diameter*)
2 tablespoons butter or margarine
1 medium-size onion, finely chopped
4 large green onions (including tops), cut into 1-inch lengths
2 large tomatoes, peeled, seeded, and chopped
½ cup whipping cream
1 tablespoon finely chopped fresh cilantro (coriander)
½ teaspoon oregano leaves
¼ teaspoon ground cumin
Salt and pepper
1 cup (4 oz.) shredded mozzarella cheese

Place potatoes in a 3-quart pan, then pour in water to a depth of 2 inches. Bring to a boil over high heat; cover, reduce heat, and simmer until potatoes are tender when pierced (about 20 minutes).

While potatoes are cooking, melt butter in a wide frying pan over medium heat. Add chopped onion and green onions; cook until soft. Add tomatoes and cook, stirring occasionally, for 5 minutes. Stir in cream, cilantro, oregano, and cumin; then season to taste with salt and pepper. Stirring constantly, slowly add cheese; cook, stirring, until cheese is completely melted. Drain potatoes and place in a serving dish; immediately spoon sauce over top. Makes 4 to 6 servings.

Roasted Potatoes

Italy

Cooks everywhere know the convenient and fuel-saving secret of baking potatoes and other vegetables alongside a roast. In *patate arroste*, a mixture of diced potatoes and onions bakes up crusty on top, tender inside.

4 large russet potatoes (about 2 lbs. *total*)
3 large onions, coarsely chopped
½ cup olive oil or salad oil
1 teaspoon salt
¼ teaspoon pepper

Peel potatoes, if desired; then cut into ½-inch cubes. Place potatoes and onions in a shallow 3-quart casserole. Add oil, salt, and pepper; stir to mix. Bake in a 325° oven, uncovered, for 2 to 2½ hours or until mixture is crisp and golden on top and potatoes are very soft; stir every 20 minutes after the first hour. Makes 6 to 8 servings.

Crisp Potato Pancakes

Germany   (Pictured on page 166)

Like many other tasty creations, the potato pancake comes in a stack of regional variations. These German cakes are light, fragile, and flavored with a touch of caraway.

2 tablespoons lemon juice
4 cups water
1 large or 2 small russet potatoes (about ½ lb. *total*)
¼ cup minced onion
1 teaspoon caraway seeds
2 tablespoons chopped parsley
2 tablespoons all-purpose flour
1 egg
1 tablespoon milk
Salt and pepper
4 to 6 tablespoons butter or margarine

In a large bowl, combine lemon juice and water. Peel potato and coarsely shred it into acid water; stir well, then pour mixture through a colander. Squeeze as much liquid out of potato as possible and spread out on paper towels to drain further. In dry bowl, combine onion, caraway seeds, parsley, flour, egg, and milk; then stir in potato. Season to taste with salt and pepper.

Melt 2 to 3 tablespoons of the butter in a wide frying pan over medium heat. When butter is foamy, add about 2 tablespoons of the potato mixture and spread into a 4-inch pancake (don't worry if small holes appear). Repeat to make 2 or 3 more cakes. Cook, turning once, until golden brown on both sides (4 to 5 minutes per side); add butter as needed. With a wide spatula, lift pancakes from pan and place slightly apart in a rimmed baking pan; keep warm in a 200° oven. Repeat with remaining potato mixture, adding more butter to pan as needed.

Serve at once; or let cool completely, then cover and let stand for up to 6 hours. To reheat, place in a single layer in a rimmed baking pan; bake in a 400° oven, uncovered, for 8 to 10 minutes or until crisp. Makes 4 servings.

FRENCH POTATO PANCAKES

(Pictured on page 102)

Follow directions for **Crisp Potato Pancakes,** but omit caraway seeds and parsley.

Making German potato pancakes (Recipe on page 165)

1 Shred peeled potato directly into a bowl of water mixed with lemon juice. This acid water prevents shreds from discoloring, and rinses off potato starch so pancakes fry up crisp.

2 Drain potato shreds and squeeze dry; then spread out on paper towels to drain thoroughly. For brown, lacy cakes, potatoes must be dry; excess water leads to mushy pancakes.

3 Heat butter until foamy. Then drop in about 2 tablespoons potato mixture and spread out to a 4-inch pancake with back of spoon. You can cook 3 or 4 pancakes at a time.

4 When pancakes are golden brown on the bottom and edges on top surface are dry, turn cakes over and cook until browned on other side.

5 Top crisp, golden pancakes with chunky applesauce and a dollop of sour cream for a satisfying breakfast or brunch. For heartier appetites, accompany pancakes with sausages and fruit.

.Side dishes

Hot Fried Potato Chips

Brazil

These oniony pan-fried potato "chips" are a bit different from the packaged chips enjoyed by American snackers—but they're just as delectable alongside hamburgers or steak.

> **About 5 tablespoons butter or margarine**
> 4 **medium-size russet potatoes (about 2 lbs.** *total*)**, unpeeled, very thinly sliced**
> 1 **large onion, thinly sliced and separated into rings**
> **Salt and pepper**

Melt 3 tablespoons of the butter in a 12-inch frying pan over medium heat. Add some of the potato slices and turn to coat well with butter; push to sides of pan. Repeat with remaining potatoes, adding more butter as needed to prevent sticking.

Add onion, then spread mixture evenly in pan and season to taste with salt and pepper. Cook, turning over often, until vegetables are golden brown. Cover pan and cook until potatoes are tender when pierced (about 5 minutes). Makes 4 servings.

Spinach with Sesame Seeds

Japan

Sesame seeds, soy, and mirin make a nutty-sweet dressing for lightly cooked spinach in this room-temperature vegetable dish.

> 1 **pound spinach, rinsed well, tough stems removed**
> 3 **tablespoons sesame seeds, toasted (page 99)**
> 2 **tablespoons mirin, or 2 tablespoons sake mixed with ½ teaspoon sugar**
> 1 **tablespoon soy sauce**
> 1 **or 2 thin slices red onion**

Place spinach (with water that clings to leaves) in a 5 to 6-quart kettle. Cover and cook over medium heat, stirring occasionally, just until spinach is wilted (6 to 7 minutes). Drain. When spinach is cool enough to handle, squeeze out excess water with your hands; set aside.

Whirl sesame seeds in a blender until coarsely ground. Add mirin and soy; whirl to blend. Add sesame mixture to spinach and toss lightly to coat. Mound spinach on a serving plate,

then cut through with a sharp knife in several places for easier serving. Top with onion. Makes 4 servings.

Basil Tomatoes

France   (Pictured on page 78)

Producing superb flavor from simple ingredients—such finesse has made French cooking famous. Here's one colorful, simple-to-make example.

> 4 **large tomatoes, cut in half crosswise**
> 4 **tablespoons butter or margarine**
> 1 **teaspoon dry basil**
> ¼ **teaspoon *each* oregano leaves and garlic salt**

Arrange tomatoes, cut side up, in a 9-inch square baking dish. Melt butter in a small pan; stir in basil, oregano, and garlic salt. Brush mixture evenly over tomatoes. Broil about 6 inches below heat until topping is bubbly and lightly browned. Makes 8 servings.

Pan-fried Zucchini

Middle East

Abundant crops of the sun-soaked Middle East, zucchini and other summer squash cook to tempting tenderness in just a splash of olive oil.

> 3 **tablespoons olive oil**
> 1 **clove garlic, minced or pressed**
> 6 **medium-size zucchini, cut into ¼-inch slices**
> 1 **teaspoon oregano leaves**
> 1 **tablespoon finely chopped parsley**
> 1 **teaspoon lemon juice**
> **Salt and pepper**

Heat oil in a wide frying pan over medium-high heat. Add garlic and cook for 1 minute. Add zucchini and oregano; cook, uncovered, stirring occasionally, until zucchini is tender when pierced (4 to 8 minutes). Stir in parsley and lemon juice, then season to taste with salt and pepper. Makes 4 to 6 servings.

...Side dishes

Vegetable Mélange

Ethiopia

Ethiopia's *atikelt wat* gets its bright color and pungent aroma from turmeric, a spice that's also a common ingredient in Indian cooking.

        5 tablespoons salad oil
        2 medium-size onions, thickly sliced
        5 cloves garlic, minced or pressed
        4 medium-size carrots, cut in half crosswise, then quartered lengthwise
        4 medium-size thin-skinned potatoes (about 1½ lbs. *total*), cut into 1-inch cubes
        ½ teaspoon turmeric
        ¼ teaspoon *each* pepper and ground coriander
        ½ cup water
        1 small head cabbage (about 1¼ lbs.), cored and cut into 2-inch chunks
        1 medium-size green pepper, seeded and cut into 1-inch-wide strips
           Salt

Heat oil in a 4 to 5-quart pan over medium-high heat. Add onions and garlic; cook, stirring often, until onions are soft (7 to 10 minutes). Add carrots, potatoes, turmeric, pepper, coriander, and water; stir to mix. Cover and cook, stirring occasionally, just until potatoes are tender when pierced (10 to 15 minutes). Stir in cabbage and green pepper, cover, and cook until cabbage is barely wilted (about 5 more minutes). Season to taste with salt. Makes 10 servings.

Acapulco Corn Medley

Mexico

Hot, peppery seasonings give this colorful vegetable tumble its south-of-the-border zest.

        2 tablespoons butter or margarine
        1 medium-size onion, chopped
        1 red or green bell pepper, seeded and chopped
        1 pound zucchini, cut into ½-inch cubes
        1 canned whole green chile, seeded and chopped
      1½ cups fresh corn cut from cob (about 3 large ears); or 1 can (1 lb.) whole kernel corn, drained well
        1 can (about 1 lb.) Italian-style tomatoes
        ¼ teaspoon liquid hot pepper seasoning
        1 teaspoon paprika
        ½ teaspoon chili powder

Melt butter in a wide frying pan over medium heat. Add onion and bell pepper; cook, stirring occasionally, until vegetables are soft (about 10 minutes).

Stir in zucchini, chile, corn, tomatoes (break up with a spoon) and their liquid, hot pepper seasoning, paprika, and chili powder. Increase heat to high; cook, stirring often, until almost all liquid has evaporated and zucchini is tender to bite (about 5 minutes). Makes 4 to 6 servings.

Sesame-topped Vegetables

Malaysia

Called *achar*, this sweet-and-sour medley of tender-crisp vegetables offers cooling contrast to any spicy entrée. English and European cucumbers are much longer than standard salad cucumbers, and have a more delicate flavor.

        ½ English or European cucumber
        3 large carrots
        3 cups cauliflowerets
        ⅓ cup salad oil
        2 cloves garlic, minced or pressed
        ½ cup minced shallots
        ½ cup white (distilled) vinegar
        ¼ cup sugar
           Soy sauce
        ½ cup sesame seeds, toasted (page 99)

Cut cucumber and carrots into thin slivers, 3 to 4 inches long; break cauliflowerets into smaller flowerets. Set vegetables aside.

Heat oil in a wide frying pan over medium heat. Add garlic and shallots; cook, stirring, until shallots are soft. Increase heat to high and add vinegar, sugar, carrots, and cauliflowerets. Cook, stirring, until vegetables are tender-crisp to bite; then add cucumber and cook, stirring, until heated through.

Season to taste with soy. Transfer to a rimmed serving plate; sprinkle with sesame seeds. Serve warm or at room temperature. Makes 6 to 8 servings.

YAMS OR SWEET POTATOES?

What's a yam? It's the root of a tropical vine native to South and Central America, Africa, and Asia—and it's not grown or sold in the United States. The "yams" sold in North American markets (and called for in our recipes) aren't true yams; they're a type of sweet potato, and don't even belong to the same plant family as true yams.

The sweet potatoes marketed as "yams" taper distinctly at both ends. Their skin color ranges from light copper to dark red to purple, and their brilliant orange flesh is sweet and moist when cooked. Another variety of sweet potato, sold simply as "sweet potato," is also widely available; this root has yellowish gray or brown skin and cream to yellow flesh. After cooking, it has a dry, mealy texture. Both "yams" and "sweet potatoes" became established as staple crops in the southern United States many years ago. They're interchangeable in recipes, and taste especially delicious in combination with fruit or fruit juices.

When you purchase these vegetables, choose firm roots of uniform shape and small to medium size, free of cracks and decay. Stored in a cool, dark place, they'll keep for about 2 weeks.

Yam & Orange Casserole

United States

Sliced yams, oranges, and just a kiss of honey add up to a thoroughly delicious casserole—just right alongside a holiday ham or turkey.

    3½ to 4 pounds yams
    1 large onion, thinly sliced
    3 oranges
    ½ cup (¼ lb.) butter or margarine, melted
    2 tablespoons honey
       Salt and pepper
    ¼ cup sliced almonds, toasted (page 87)

In a 3-quart pan, bring 2 inches water to a boil over high heat; then add yams. When water returns to a boil, cover pan, reduce heat, and sim-

mer until yams are tender when pierced (20 to 30 minutes). Drain and let cool; then peel. Cut diagonally into ¼-inch-thick slices.

Arrange ⅓ of the yams in an even layer in a greased shallow 3-quart baking dish. Top with half the onion; arrange half the remaining yams atop onion. Top with remaining onion, then remaining yams.

Remove and discard peel and white membrane from 2 of the oranges; slice oranges and arrange on top of yams. Squeeze juice from remaining orange and combine with butter and honey; pour evenly over yam mixture. Sprinkle lightly with salt and pepper. (At this point, you may cover and refrigerate until next day.)

Bake in a 325° oven, covered, for 45 to 50 minutes (about 1 hour if refrigerated) or until heated through. Sprinkle with almonds. Makes 8 to 10 servings.

Stamppot

Netherlands

Its no-nonsense name tells what happens to the potatoes and other vegetables in this hearty Dutch dish—they're mashed or "stamped" together in the pot.

    1 to 1½ pounds broccoli
    3 medium-size russet potatoes (about 1½ lbs. *total*), peeled and cut into quarters
    2 large carrots, cut into 2-inch lengths
    1 medium-size onion, chopped
    ½ cup water
    4 tablespoons butter or margarine
    2 to 4 tablespoons whipping cream
       Salt and pepper

Cut flowerets from broccoli (cut any large ones in half); then peel stalks and cut into 2-inch lengths. In a 4 to 5-quart kettle, combine broccoli, potatoes, carrots, onion, and water; bring to a boil over high heat. Cover, reduce heat, and simmer until vegetables are tender when pierced (15 to 20 minutes). Remove kettle from heat; drain off any liquid. Stir in butter. Beat mixture with an electric mixer until vegetables are mashed together but still lumpy.

Place kettle over low heat and stir in enough cream to make vegetable mixture moist, but not runny. Cook until heated through; season to taste with salt and pepper. Makes about 4 servings.

...Side dishes

Ratatouille

France

Ratatouille is the classic vegetable stew of southern France. It tastes best a day or two after cooking, when the flavors have had a chance to mingle.

- ¼ **cup olive oil or salad oil**
- 2 **large onions, sliced**
- 2 **large cloves garlic, minced or pressed**
- 1 **medium-size eggplant (about 1 lb.), cut into ½-inch cubes**
- 6 **medium-size zucchini, thickly sliced**
- 2 **green or red bell peppers, seeded and cut into ¼-inch-wide strips**
- 2 **teaspoons dry basil**
- ½ **cup minced parsley**
- 5 **large tomatoes, cut into wedges**
   Salt

Heat oil in a wide frying pan over medium-high heat. Add onions and garlic and cook, stirring often, until onions are soft (7 to 10 minutes). Stir in eggplant, zucchini, bell peppers, basil, and parsley. Reduce heat to medium; cook, uncovered, stirring occasionally, for 30 minutes. Add 4 of the tomatoes and stir to blend. Cook, uncovered, stirring occasionally, until eggplant is tender when pierced (about 15 more minutes). Season to taste with salt.

Serve hot or at room temperature; garnish with remaining tomato just before serving. If made ahead, let cool; then cover and refrigerate for up to 1 week. Serve at room temperature or reheat. Makes 8 to 10 servings.

HOW TO SELECT EGGPLANTS

The eggplant probably gets its name from a white variety that's common in Asia. But in most American markets, you'll find only purple-skinned eggplant—both the larger oval type (used in our recipes) and the smaller, thinner "Japanese" kind. Select firm eggplants that feel heavy for their size, with smooth, shiny, unwrinkled skins and green stems. Stored in plastic bags in the refrigerator, eggplants keep for up to a week. The flesh darkens when exposed to air, so don't cut until just before cooking.

Tourlu

Armenian heritage   (Pictured on facing page)

Armenian *tourlu* is sweeter and saucier than *ratatouille* (left)—but like its French cousin, it's a wonderfully flavored vegetable medley that can be served either hot or at room temperature.

- 1 **can (about 1 lb.) Italian-style tomatoes**
- ¼ **cup olive oil or salad oil**
- ½ **cup catsup**
- 1½ **teaspoons each salt, sugar, and dry basil**
- ¼ **teaspoon freshly ground pepper**
- ½ **pound green beans, ends removed, cut into 1½-inch lengths**
- 2 **large thin-skinned potatoes, peeled and cut into 1-inch cubes**
- 3 **medium-size carrots, cut diagonally into ¾-inch slices**
- 2 **large onions, cut into 1-inch squares**
- 2 **large stalks celery, cut into ½-inch slices**
- 2 **large red or green bell peppers, seeded and cut into 1-inch squares (see photo 2 on facing page)**
- 1 **medium-size eggplant (about 1 lb.), cut into 1-inch cubes (see photo 3 on facing page)**
- 3 **small zucchini**
   Plain yogurt (optional)

Place tomatoes (break up with a spoon) and their liquid in a bowl. Add oil, catsup, salt, sugar, basil, and pepper; set aside.

In a 5 to 6-quart casserole, combine beans, potatoes, carrots, onions, celery, bell peppers, and eggplant. Stir tomato mixture, then pour over vegetables, coating as many vegetables as possible. (Don't stir through vegetables.) Cover and bake in a 350° oven for 1½ hours; baste vegetables with juices every 30 minutes, using a bulb baster.

Cut zucchini into 1½-inch slices. Remove casserole from oven and gently mix in zucchini. Return to oven; bake, uncovered, for 20 to 30 more minutes or until potatoes are tender when pierced.

Serve hot or at room temperature. Stir gently before serving; top each portion with a generous spoonful of yogurt, if desired. If made ahead, let cool; then cover, and refrigerate for up to 1 week. To serve, bring to room temperature or reheat. Makes 8 servings.

Preparing an Armenian vegetable stew (Recipe on facing page)

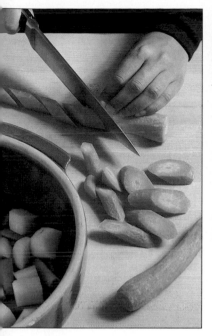

1 To ensure even cooking, all vegetables are cut into equal-size pieces. Here, carrot is cut into ¼-inch-thick slices before joining potatoes in 1-inch cubes, beans in 1½-inch lengths.

2 To seed a bell pepper, first cut a ¼-inch slice off stem end. Hold slice in both hands, thumbs beneath stem; push on stem to snap it out. Tear through seed membranes inside pepper; pull out seeds.

3 Cut eggplant into 1-inch length-wise slices; cut slices length-wise, then crosswise, to make 1-inch cubes. Stir through tomato mixture. Pour over vegetables, coating as many pieces as possible (don't stir).

4 Every 30 minutes, baste vegetables several times to keep them moist, using a bulb baster. Basting vegetables instead of stir-ring them helps each piece keep its shape.

5 Vegetables grown in the Middle East join up in colorful Armenian Tourlu. A topping of cool, tangy yogurt offers a delicious contrast to the casserole's slight sweetness.

Hearty entrées

Around the globe, thrifty and plentiful vegetables often play a prominent role in family dinners. Rich, satisfying Moussaka combines layers of sliced eggplant, cinnamon-spiced meat sauce, and smooth Parmesan custard; in our other savory entrées, vegetables serve as containers or wrappers for flavorful fillings.

Moussaka

Greece

Though *moussaka* is served throughout the eastern Mediterranean world, the Greek version of this layered eggplant casserole is perhaps the most famous. Just one spicy, cheesy bite explains its popularity.

      2 **tablespoons butter or margarine**
      2 **tablespoons olive oil or salad oil**
      2 **large eggplants (2½ to 3 lbs.** *total***), cut crosswise into ½-inch-thick slices**
      2 **pounds lean ground lamb or lean ground beef**
      2 **large onions, chopped**
      2 **cloves garlic, minced or pressed**
      2 **tablespoons all-purpose flour**
      1 **teaspoon** *each* **ground cinnamon, oregano leaves, and salt**
      ½ **teaspoon** *each* **ground nutmeg and pepper**
      ½ **cup** *each* **catsup and water**
      ¾ **cup dry red wine**
      1 **can (about 1 lb.) Italian-style tomatoes**
      ½ **cup minced parsley**
         Custard topping (recipe follows)

Divide butter and oil evenly between 2 large rimmed baking pans. Place pans in a 400° oven until butter is melted; tilt to distribute mixture evenly. Arrange eggplant slices in a single layer in baking pans and turn to coat with butter mixture. Bake, uncovered, for 15 minutes, turning slices over once. Switch positions of pans; bake, turning slices over once, for 15 more minutes or until eggplant is soft. Drain on paper towels.

Crumble lamb into a wide frying pan over medium-high heat. Add onions and garlic and cook, stirring often, until onions are soft. Spoon off and discard excess fat.

Stir in flour, cinnamon, oregano, salt, nutmeg, and pepper. Slowly stir in catsup, water, wine, tomatoes (coarsely chopped) and their liquid, and parsley. Cook, stirring often, until thick (about 15 minutes); set aside.

Prepare custard topping. Arrange half the cooked eggplant in a greased 9 by 13-inch baking dish; evenly spread with meat sauce, then top with remaining eggplant. Spread custard topping evenly over all. (At this point, you may let cool, then cover and refrigerate until next day.)

Bake in a 350° oven, uncovered, for 50 minutes (1 hour if refrigerated) or until custard is bubbly at edges and center appears firm. Let stand for 15 minutes, then cut into squares. Makes 8 to 10 servings.

Custard topping. Melt ½ cup (¼ lb.) **butter** or margarine in a 3-quart pan over medium heat; stir in ½ cup **all-purpose flour** and cook, stirring, until bubbly. Gradually stir in 4 cups **milk**; cook, stirring, until bubbly and thickened.

Beat 6 **eggs** with ¼ teaspoon *each* **ground nutmeg** and **white pepper**; gradually stir in 1 cup of the hot white sauce, then pour egg mixture into remaining white sauce. Cook, stirring constantly, for 1 minute. Remove from heat and stir in 2½ cups (10 to 12½ oz.) grated **Parmesan cheese.**

Chiles Rellenos

Mexico

Chiles rellenos ("stuffed peppers") are one of the best known of all Mexican dishes. Traditionally, the cheese-stuffed chiles are coated with egg batter, then deep-fried. But by using the simplified technique we present here, you can produce authentically tasty results with far less trouble—just arrange the peppers in a pan, pour an eggy batter over them, and bake until the topping is golden and puffy.

      2 **cans (4 oz.** *each***) whole green chiles**
      8 **ounces jack cheese, cut into wide strips**
      4 **eggs**
      1 **cup milk**
      ¼ **cup all-purpose flour**
      1 **teaspoon salt**
      1 **cup (4 oz.) shredded Cheddar cheese**
         Tomato-herb sauce (recipe follows)

Lightly grease a 9-inch square baking pan and set aside. Preheat oven to 375°.

Drain and rinse chiles. Then cut a slit down one side of each and gently remove seeds and pith, trying to preserve shape of chiles. Stuff an equal amount of jack cheese inside each chile. Arrange chiles, side by side, in pan.

In a bowl, beat eggs until frothy; then beat in milk, flour, and salt. Pour batter over chiles. Sprinkle with Cheddar cheese and bake, uncovered, for 30 minutes or until topping is puffy and jiggles only slightly when pan is gently shaken. Meanwhile, prepare tomato-herb sauce and keep warm.

Serve chiles immediately after baking; pass sauce at the table to spoon over individual servings. Makes 4 servings.

Tomato-herb sauce. Melt 2 tablespoons **butter** or margarine over medium heat. Add 3 tablespoons **chopped onion** and 1 clove **garlic,** minced or pressed; cook, stirring occasionally, until golden (about 15 minutes). Stir in 1 large can (15 oz.) **tomato sauce** and ½ teaspoon *each* **ground cumin** and **oregano leaves.** Cover, reduce heat, and simmer for 10 minutes. Makes about 2 cups.

Stuffed Artichokes Omar

Middle East

Chef George Mardikian of Omar Khayyam's Restaurant in San Francisco created this flavorful marriage of Old World lamb stuffing and California artichokes.

>   4 quarts water
>   ½ cup lemon juice
>   8 whole black peppers
>   2 tablespoons olive oil
>   6 large artichokes
>   3 tablespoons salad oil
>   2 medium-size onions, finely chopped
>   2 cloves garlic, minced or pressed
>   1 pound lean ground lamb
>   2 tablespoons chopped parsley
>   3 tablespoons chopped pine nuts
>   ½ teaspoon ground allspice
>   1 egg, lightly beaten
>   Salt and pepper
>   6 slices tomato

Place water, lemon juice, peppers, and olive oil in a 6-quart kettle. Using a stainless steel knife, cut off stem and top third of each artichoke; then remove small, coarse outer leaves. Snip off thorny tips of remaining leaves. As each artichoke is pre-

pared, drop it into lemon water. Bring to a boil over high heat; cover, reduce heat, and simmer for 20 minutes. Lift out artichokes and drain; reserve cooking liquid. Spread leaves apart and pull out inner core of yellow leaves. Using a spoon, scrape out choke (thistle portion), leaving a hollow center (see illustration below).

While artichokes simmer, heat salad oil in a wide frying pan over medium heat. Add onions and garlic. Cook, stirring occasionally, until golden (about 15 minutes); spoon into a bowl. Blend in lamb, parsley, pine nuts, allspice, and egg; season to taste with salt and pepper. Spoon mixture evenly into artichokes, packing it in lightly. Place a slice of tomato atop each stuffed artichoke.

Place artichokes upright in a 9 by 13-inch baking dish and pour in reserved cooking liquid to a depth of 1 inch. Cover and bake in a 350° oven for 30 to 40 minutes or until a leaf can easily be pulled from artichoke. Drain briefly on paper towels before serving. Makes 6 servings.

SELECTING ARTICHOKES

First cultivated in Italy around the 15th century, artichokes were later brought to the United States by French settlers. Today, most of our commercial supply comes from Castroville, California, the self-proclaimed "artichoke capital of the world."

Choose firm, compact, medium-green artichokes that feel heavy for their size. Don't worry about brown frost spots on the leaves—these don't affect flavor. After purchase, place unwashed artichokes in a plastic bag and store in the refrigerator for up to 5 days. Cut them only with a stainless steel knife, and cook only in stainless steel, aluminum, enamel, or heatproof glass; carbon steel and cast iron cause discoloration.

Making spicy stuffed cabbage (Recipe on facing page)

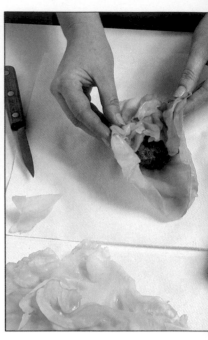

1 To blanch cabbage leaves, drop them into simmering water and cook just until they turn bright green and limp (lift out to test). Lift blanched leaves from water with tongs; drain on paper towels.

2 Cut tough white rib from stem end of each leaf, then mound filling at base of leaf. (If leaf is torn, patch hole with a piece from extra blanched leaves.) Fold bottom edges of leaf in over filling.

3 Fold in both sides, then roll to enclose filling, making sure all meat is covered. Place rolls, seam side down. in baking dish. Pour in broth, add cinnamon sticks; cover, and bake for 1 hour.

4 Skim fat from pan juices; pour into frying pan. Pour in flour-water mixture all at once, stirring with a wire whisk. Cook over medium-high heat, stirring constantly, until sauce boils and thickens.

5 Spicy African cabbage rolls surround cone of Yellow Rice with Raisins (page 153). Pass thickened juices to spoon over rolls, and condiments to sprinkle atop.

.Hearty entrées

Spicy Cabbage Rolls

South Africa   (Pictured on facing page)

Cooks in many lands use pliable blanched cabbage leaves as neat, edible wrappers for savory fillings. Embellish these spicy lamb bundles with condiments such as chutney, sliced green onions, toasted coconut, peanuts, and chopped bananas.

    3 tablespoons salad oil
    1 medium-size onion, chopped
    3 tablespoons curry powder
    3 tablespoons coarsely chopped Major Grey's
      chutney
    1 tablespoon white (distilled) vinegar
    1 teaspoon *each* salt and ground coriander
    ½ teaspoon pepper
    2 pounds lean ground lamb or lean ground beef
      (or a combination)
    ⅓ cup fine dry bread crumbs
    1 egg, lightly beaten
    1 large head cabbage (about 2½ lbs.), cored
    1 can (14½ oz.) regular-strength beef broth or
      1¾ cups homemade beef broth (page 33)
    2 cinnamon sticks (*each* about 2 inches long)
      Yellow Rice with Raisins (page 153)
    3 tablespoons all-purpose flour
    ¼ cup cold water
      Condiments (see recipe introduction)

Heat oil in a wide frying pan over medium heat; add onion and cook for 5 minutes. Stir in curry powder and cook, stirring occasionally, until onion is soft; transfer to a bowl. Mix in chutney, vinegar, salt, coriander, pepper, lamb, crumbs, and egg; set aside.

Hold cabbage head, core side up, under running water and gently peel off leaves, one at a time. (You'll need 12 to 14 large leaves.) Drop leaves into a large pot of simmering water; cook just until bright green and limp. Lift blanched leaves out with tongs; drain on paper towels, then trim off thick white rib at stem end of each to make leaves easier to roll.

Use about ½ cup of the meat filling for larger leaves, a little less for smaller leaves. To stuff each leaf, mound filling at base of leaf; fold in lower edges, then sides, and roll to enclose. Place cabbage rolls, seam side down, in a greased 9 by 13-inch baking dish. (At this point, you may cover and refrigerate for up to 8 hours.)

Pour broth over rolls; add cinnamon sticks, then cover and bake in a 350° oven for 1 hour

(1 hour and 15 minutes if refrigerated). Twenty minutes before rolls are done, prepare Yellow Rice with Raisins; mound rice on a large platter.

With a slotted spoon, lift cabbage rolls from dish; arrange on platter around rice. Skim and discard fat from pan juices; also discard cinnamon sticks. Pour juices into a frying pan. Combine flour and water; stir in. Cook over medium-high heat, stirring constantly, until sauce boils and thickens. Pour into a bowl. Pass sauce and condiments at the table. Makes 6 to 8 servings.

Kasha-stuffed Cabbage Rolls

Russia

      Sweet-sour sauce (recipe follows)
    2 tablespoons butter or margarine
    1 large onion, finely chopped
    ½ pound mushrooms, chopped
    ½ teaspoon marjoram leaves
    ¼ teaspoon ground nutmeg
    ⅛ teaspoon pepper
    1 cup cooked kasha (page 152)
    1 pound lean ground beef
    1 egg, lightly beaten
      Salt
    1 large head cabbage (about 2½ lbs.), cored
      Sour cream

Prepare sweet-sour sauce and set aside. Melt butter in a wide frying pan over medium heat. Add onion, mushrooms, and marjoram; cook, stirring often, until onion is soft and liquid has evaporated. Remove from heat; transfer to a bowl. Blend in nutmeg, pepper, kasha, beef, and egg. Season to taste with salt.

Blanch and stuff cabbage leaves as directed for Spicy Cabbage Rolls (at left). Pour about ⅔ of the sweet-sour sauce into a lightly greased 9 by 13-inch baking dish. Place cabbage rolls, seam side down, in sauce; drizzle with remaining sauce. Cover and bake in a 350° oven for 1 hour. Pass sour cream at the table to spoon over individual servings. Makes 6 to 8 servings.

Sweet-sour sauce. In a pan, combine 2 small cans (8 oz. *each*) **tomato sauce,** 1 cup **water,** ½ cup fine **gingersnap crumbs,** ½ cup **raisins,** 3 tablespoons firmly packed **brown sugar,** and ¼ cup **lemon juice.** Bring to a boil over medium-high heat; then reduce heat and simmer, uncovered, stirring occasionally, for 5 minutes.

BREADS

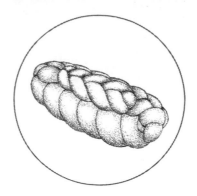

All over the world, the aroma of freshly baked bread fills kitchens with an alluring promise of good eating to come. The simple joys of baking and tasting make homemade bread a supremely satisfying food. Perhaps that's why it's so highly valued, even in countries where good-quality loaves are readily available from bakery or supermarket.

Bread has historical value, too, especially in the Western world. It has nourished people as a daily "staff of life" since ancient times. Today, serving freshly baked rolls or loaves with every meal remains a custom in most of Europe.

Variations on a theme

All breads have essentially the same beginning: flour and liquid. From this basic origin, bakers around the world have created sweet and savory breads in a limitless variety of shapes, textures, and flavors.

A relatively high proportion of flour to liquid yields a dough that's stiff enough to hold its shape. You can mold it into round, sturdy loaves, twine it into braids, or form it into fancifully shaped buns such as Mexico's Pan Dulce. As the amount of liquid increases, the dough becomes more like a batter—thin enough to pour, and almost cakelike after baking (as in Sally Lunn, for example).

What's your flavor preference? What texture do you like best? In the following pages, you'll find hearty, chewy loaves like Dark Rye and Limpa, as well as finer-textured breads such as golden-crusted Challah. Our recipes offer plenty of flavor variety, too. Aromatic fennel seasons crisp bread sticks; lemon, anise, vanilla, and brandy help give Panettone its special flavor. Cheese lovers will want to try France's Gougère, a crusty loaf liberally laced with shredded Swiss cheese. There's even a bread for garlic fans: Hungarian Langos.

Quick versus yeast breads

The breads we call "quick" usually contain some kind of chemical leavening: baking powder, baking soda, or a combination of the two. These agents act quickly, so the bread needn't rise before baking; as soon as you've mixed it, it's ready for the oven.

Yeast breads are leavened by carbon dioxide gas from activated yeast. These breads have a reputation for being difficult—but in fact, the basic techniques of mixing, kneading, and shaping are easy to master. Yeast dough does require plenty of time to rise, but it doesn't demand a lot of attention during that time. As long as you provide a warm place, the dough will do the rest by itself.

Most of the recipes in this chapter adhere as closely as possible to traditional methods. But for breads typically baked in brick or clay ovens or over an open fire, we let custom bow to practicality. In these cases, recipes and baking methods have been adapted to suit the American kitchen.

Flatbreads

Flatbreads offer a delightful range of textures: some are crackling-crisp, others thin and pliable. But whatever the texture, they're easy to mix up and quick to cook.

Potato Lefse

Norway

Chewy and slightly sour, these tortilla-like flatbreads make ideal wrappers for sausages or fingers of cheese.

    2 pounds russet potatoes, peeled and quartered
    2 tablespoons butter or margarine
    ¼ cup milk
    1 teaspoon salt
    3 to 3½ cups all-purpose flour
      Salad oil

Place potatoes in a 3-quart pan and pour in water to cover. Bring to a boil over high heat; then cover, reduce heat, and simmer until tender when pierced (about 20 minutes). Drain. Mash until smooth, then measure; you should have 4 cups. (*Do not use more than 4 cups of potatoes in dough;* if you do, dough will be too sticky to roll out.) Place potatoes in a large bowl and stir in butter, milk, and salt. Let cool to room temperature.

Gradually stir in about 2 cups of the flour, or enough to make a nonsticky dough. Turn out onto a floured board and knead gently to shape into a smooth log. Divide into 24 equal pieces, then shape each into a smooth ball; leave uncovered. On a floured board, roll each ball out to an 8 to 10-inch round. As you roll, turn dough over frequently to keep both sides very lightly coated with flour (this prevents sticking).

Heat a wide frying pan over medium-high heat (or heat an electric griddle to 375°); lightly grease with oil. To cook each lefse, first shake off excess flour; then place in pan. Cook, turning frequently, until bubbles form on surface and lefse is dry and lightly speckled with brown, but still soft to the touch (1½ to 2 minutes). Lefse will puff up briefly, then deflate.

Serve warm. Or let cool completely on wire racks, then wrap airtight and refrigerate for up to 4 days (freeze for longer storage). To reheat, thaw if frozen; then stack, wrap in foil, and heat in a 325° oven for 10 to 15 minutes. Makes 2 dozen.

Chapaties

India

One whole wheat dough, cooked two different ways, yields two different Indian breads. Rounds of dough are cooked in a heavy frying pan for flat, chewy *chapaties*; deep-fried, they puff up into the crisp, balloonlike breads called *puris*.

    1 teaspoon salt
      About 2 cups whole wheat flour
      About ⅔ cup warm water

In a bowl, stir together salt and 2 cups of the flour. Slowly add ⅔ cup of the water, stirring flour mixture with a fork until a crumbly dough forms. Then mix dough with your hands until it holds together (add a few drops of water, if needed). Knead dough on a floured board until smooth but still sticky (about 3 minutes). Wrap tightly in plastic wrap and let rest for 30 minutes.

Shape dough into 16 smooth balls. On a floured board, flatten each ball, then roll each out to a round about 5 inches in diameter. Stack rounds, separating them with wax paper.

Heat an ungreased heavy frying pan over medium-low heat. Place rounds of dough in pan, a few at a time. When top surface of dough has darkened slightly (about 1 minute), press directly on rounds with a wide spatula; blisters will appear as you press. When bottoms are lightly browned (about 2 minutes), turn rounds over and cook until lightly browned on other side (about 2 more minutes). Serve hot. Makes 16.

INDIAN PURIS

Prepare and shape dough as directed for **Chapaties,** but roll out on a board lightly rubbed with **salad oil** rather than flour. Into a deep pan at least 6 inches in diameter, pour **salad oil** to a depth of 1½ inches and heat to 350° on a deep-frying thermometer. Slip one round into hot oil. In a few seconds, it will rise to the surface and start to inflate unevenly. With a slotted spoon, very gently press puri against side or bottom of pan; it will inflate completely. Turn over and continue to cook until golden brown (about 1 minute). Remove and drain on paper towels. Repeat with remaining rounds. Serve hot.

...Flatbreads

Rieska

Finland   (Pictured on facing page)

Rieska tastes best on the day you make it—freshly baked, still warm from the oven.

>   All-purpose flour
> 2 cups rye flour
> ¾ teaspoon salt
> 2 teaspoons *each* sugar and baking powder
> 1 cup half-and-half (light cream)
> 2 tablespoons butter or margarine, melted

Preheat oven to 450°. Generously grease a baking sheet, then dust it with all-purpose flour. Invert a 12-inch plate on center of sheet. Trace around plate with a wooden skewer; lift off plate.

In a bowl, combine rye flour, salt, sugar, and baking powder. Add half-and-half and butter and stir with a fork just until all flour is moistened. Gather dough up into a ball; place in center of circle on baking sheet. Dust hands with all-purpose flour, then press dough out to edge of circle, forming an even layer. Prick top surface all over with a fork. Bake for 10 to 12 minutes or until lightly browned. Makes about 8 servings.

Flour Tortillas

Mexico

The daily bread of northern Mexico, flour tortillas pair well with both mild and spicy foods.

> 2 teaspoons baking powder
> ¾ teaspoon salt
>   About 3 cups all-purpose flour
> ¼ cup solid shortening
>   About 1 cup warm water

In a bowl, stir together baking powder, salt, and 3 cups of the flour. Using a pastry blender or 2 knives, cut in shortening until fine crumbs form. Slowly add 1 cup of the water. Then mix dough with your hands until it holds together (add a few drops more water, if needed). Knead on a floured board until smooth and elastic (about 5 minutes). Shape into 12 balls; cover for 15 minutes.

Shape and cook tortillas one at a time (to prevent drying, cover dough you're not working with). To make each tortilla, flatten a ball of dough on a floured board to a 4 to 5-inch round; using center-to-edge strokes, roll out dough to about 9 inches. Turn dough often as you roll, stretching it slightly as you lift it off board.

Preheat an ungreased wide frying pan over medium-high heat. Place tortilla in pan; blisters will appear almost at once. With a wide spatula, press tortilla gently but firmly all over top; blisters will rise over surface. Turn and cook on other side until blisters are golden brown (tortilla should remain soft). If tortilla sticks or browns too quickly, reduce heat. Stack hot cooked tortillas in a folded cloth towel enclosed in a plastic bag; keep bag closed to let tortillas soften. Makes 1 dozen.

Green Onion Cakes

China

Thin, chewy onion cakes crusted with sesame seeds make a tasty appetizer for a Chinese meal.

> ½ teaspoon salt
>   About 1 cup all-purpose flour
> ⅓ cup boiling water
> 4 strips bacon
> 2 green onions (including tops), thinly sliced
>   About 3 tablespoons sesame seeds
> 1 tablespoon salad oil

In a bowl, combine salt and 1 cup of the flour. Add water, stirring with a fork just until dough begins to hold together. Knead on a lightly floured board until smooth and satiny (about 3 minutes); then cover and let rest for 30 minutes. Meanwhile, in a wide frying pan over medium heat, cook bacon until crisp. Drain, reserving drippings; crumble.

On a lightly floured board, roll out dough to an 8 by 16-inch rectangle; cut crosswise into eight 2-inch-wide strips. Brush each with ½ teaspoon bacon drippings; sprinkle with bacon and onions.

Roll up each strip jelly roll style, starting with the short end; pinch seam to seal. Stand each roll on board and flatten it, then roll out to a 4-inch round. (If filling falls out, press it back into dough.) Sprinkle each side of round with about ½ teaspoon sesame seeds, pressing them in lightly. Stack rounds, separating them with wax paper. (At this point, you may place rounds in a plastic bag and refrigerate for up to 8 hours.)

Heat oil in a wide frying pan over medium-high heat. Cook rounds, a few at a time, until golden brown on both sides (2 to 3 minutes per side). Serve hot. Makes 8.

Making Rieska (Recipe on facing page)

1 Grease and flour-dust a baking sheet. Then make a guide for shaping bread into a round: invert a -inch plate on sheet and trace around it with a wooden skewer.

2 Add half-and-half and melted butter to flour mixture; stir just until dry ingredients are moistened and mixture starts to cling to fork.

3 Gather dough up into a ball and place it in center of circle traced on baking sheet. With your fingertips, gently and evenly press dough out to edge of circle.

4 To prevent bubbles from forming in dough as it bakes, prick top of and all over with a fork. Prick htly; don't pierce all the way rough dough.

5 Let baked bread cool slightly, then break into pieces. Spread lavishly with butter and offer as a hearty snack; or pair with cold beer and assorted cheeses for a satisfying lunch.

Quick breads

Busy cooks the world around add flair to meals with quick breads such as these. No rising time is required—the bread is ready to bake as soon as you've mixed it.

Gougère

France

Add shredded Swiss cheese to cream puff dough, and *voilà!* it's airy French gougère. This golden, crusty, puffy bread is delectable any time of day. Team it with sausages and fruit for breakfast, or offer it at lunchtime (as the French do) with a green salad and red wine. At dinner, it's a welcome accompaniment to barbecued meat or a hearty soup.

Whatever time of day you serve gougère, serve it hot—it tastes best just out of the oven.

> 1 **cup milk**
> 4 **tablespoons butter or margarine**
> ½ **teaspoon salt**
> **Dash of white pepper**
> 1 **cup all-purpose flour**
> 4 **eggs**
> 1 **cup (4 oz.) shredded Swiss cheese**

Preheat oven to 375°. Grease a baking sheet and set aside.

Heat milk and butter in a 3-quart pan over medium-high heat; then add salt and pepper and bring to a rolling boil. Add flour all at once and beat with a wooden spoon until mixture leaves sides of pan and forms a ball (about 2 minutes). Remove from heat. Add eggs, one at a time, beating mixture until smooth after each addition. (Mixture will break apart into slippery clumps after each egg is added, but will become a smooth paste again after vigorous beating.) Beat in ½ cup of the cheese.

Scoop out 7 mounds of dough with an ice cream scoop or a large spoon, using about ¾ of the dough. Arrange mounds, sides barely touching, in a circle on baking sheet. Scoop remaining dough into 7 smaller mounds, placing one atop each larger mound. Sprinkle remaining ½ cup cheese over all.

Bake on center rack of oven for 50 minutes or until puffs are browned and crisp. Serve immediately. Makes 7 servings.

Cornbread

United States

Our version of cornbread might better be called corn*cake*—it's moist, light, and quite sweet, with an exceptionally fine-grained texture.

> ½ **teaspoon baking soda**
> 1 **cup *each* yellow cornmeal and all-purpose flour**
> ½ **teaspoon salt**
> ½ **cup (¼ lb.) butter or margarine**
> ⅔ **cup sugar**
> 2 **eggs**
> 1 **cup buttermilk**

Preheat oven to 375°. Lightly grease an 8-inch square baking pan; set aside. Stir together baking soda, cornmeal, flour, and salt.

Melt butter in a 3-quart pan over medium heat. Remove from heat and stir in sugar; then add eggs and beat until well blended. Stir in buttermilk. Add flour mixture; stir just to moisten.

Pour batter into prepared pan. Bake for 30 minutes or until bread begins to pull away from sides of pan. Serve warm. Makes 6 to 8 servings.

Soda Bread

Ireland

Round, crusty loaves of soda bread are served in Irish country cottages and Dublin hotels alike. If you wish, vary our recipe by adding a handful of currants to the dough.

> **About 4¼ cups all-purpose flour**
> 1 **teaspoon *each* salt and baking soda**
> 1 **tablespoon baking powder**
> ¼ **cup sugar**
> ⅛ **teaspoon ground cardamom or coriander**
> 4 **tablespoons firm butter or margarine, cut into small pieces**
> 1¾ **cups buttermilk**
> 1 **egg**

Preheat oven to 375°. Lightly grease two 8-inch round baking pans; set aside.

Place 4 cups of the flour in a large bowl; then add salt, baking soda, baking powder, sugar, and cardamom. Stir until thoroughly blended. Cut in butter with a pastry blender or 2 knives to make a crumbly mixture. In a 2-cup glass measure, beat together buttermilk and egg; pour all at once into flour mixture and stir just until dry ingredients are moistened. Turn out onto a floured board and knead until smooth (2 to 3 minutes).

Divide dough in half. Shape each half into a smooth, round loaf; place loaves in prepared pans. Evenly press down each loaf until dough comes to edges of pan. With a floured sharp knife, cut a large cross, about ½ inch deep, in center of each loaf. Bake for 35 to 40 minutes or until a wooden skewer inserted in center of bread comes out clean. Makes 2 loaves.

Panettone

Italy

Panettone is a Milanese specialty, a moderately sweet, cakelike bread studded with nuts and candied fruit. Though it's usually made with yeast, a few versions are leavened with baking powder.

Panettone is traditionally baked in a tall, round pan that gives the loaf an impressive domed top. For many years, these pans weren't widely available outside Italy, so Italian-American cooks devised a simple substitute: they baked panettone in a small paper bag, producing a loaf just as lofty as one made in the traditional mold.

- 3 **cups all-purpose flour**
- 1 **tablespoon baking powder**
- ½ **teaspoon salt**
- 1 **cup (½ lb.) butter, softened**
- 1 **cup sugar**
- 3 **eggs**
- 1 **teaspoon** *each* **grated lemon peel and anise extract**
- 2 **teaspoons** *each* **brandy extract and vanilla**
- 1 **cup milk**
- ½ **cup** *each* **chopped nuts, raisins, and coarsely chopped mixed candied fruit**

Preheat oven to 325°.

Fold down top of a paper bag (lunchbag size, measuring 3½ by 6 inches on bottom) to form a cuff, so bag stands about 4 inches high. Butter inside generously, then place bag on a baking sheet. (Or grease and flour-dust a 9 by 5-inch loaf pan.)

In a bowl, stir together flour, baking powder, and salt; set aside. In another bowl, cream butter and sugar until fluffy. Beat in eggs, one at a time, beating well after each addition. Stir in lemon peel, anise extract, brandy extract, and vanilla. Stir in half the flour mixture, then ½ cup of the milk, blending well after each addition. Stir in remaining flour mixture and remaining ½ cup milk; then add nuts, raisins, and candied fruit. Pour batter into bag or pan.

Bake for 1¼ hours (1 hour if using a loaf pan) or until a wooden skewer inserted in center of loaf comes out clean. Place on a wire rack and let cool for 10 minutes. Wrap bag-baked bread in a clean cloth, then in foil, and let cool completely; turn pan-baked bread out onto rack and let cool completely, then wrap in foil. To serve, tear off bag and cut bread into slim wedges (or cut loaf into thin slices). Makes 1 loaf.

Brown Bread

United States

In New England, this moist, sweet bread is a favorite companion for baked beans. It's traditionally steamed, but we've devised a baked version that's easier on the cook—and just as good.

- 2 **cups whole wheat flour**
- 1 **cup all-purpose flour**
- 2 **teaspoons baking soda**
- 1 **teaspoon salt**
- 3 **tablespoons butter or margarine**
- ¾ **cup firmly packed brown sugar**
- 2 **cups buttermilk**
- 3 **tablespoons light molasses**
- 1 **cup** *each* **raisins and chopped walnuts**

Preheat oven to 350°. Rinse out and dry 3 empty 1-pound fruit or vegetable cans (not coffee cans); then grease well. In a large bowl, stir together whole wheat flour, all-purpose flour, baking soda, and salt. In another bowl, cream butter and sugar; stir in buttermilk and molasses. Add flour mixture, raisins, and walnuts; stir just until dry ingredients are moistened. Spoon batter evenly into cans.

Place cans upright on oven rack; bake for about 1 hour or until a wooden skewer inserted in center of bread comes out clean. Transfer cans to a wire rack and let cool for 10 minutes. Then slide loaves from cans, place upright on rack, and let cool completely. Makes 3 small loaves.

Making Dark Rye Bread (Recipe on facing page)

1 Melt sugar in a heavy pan, stirring constantly with a wooden spoon and scraping down undissolved crystals on pan sides. Cook until caramelized sugar turns dark amber, thickens, and smokes.

2 Stirring constantly, pour in boiling water (protect hands from spatters with potholders). Stir to dissolve any sugar lumps on pan bottom. Continue cooking until liquid is reduced to ½ cup.

3 On floured board, knead dough: fold it toward you with fingers, then push away with heel of hand. Rotate dough a quarter turn; repeat folding and pushing. Knead until elastic and just slightly tacky.

4 Push 2 fingers into dough—if indentations remain, it's ready to shape. Punch down dough with your fist; then turn it out onto floured board and knead briefly to release air bubbles. Divide in half.

5 Form each piece of dough into a ball, gently pulling dough from top toward underside to make top smooth. Pinch underside together. Place loaves 4 inches apart on baking sheet, pinched side down.

6 Loaf on baking sheet is ready for the oven; other loaves are ready to enjoy. Fully baked loaf looks nicely browned, sounds hollow when tapped. Let cool completely on wire rack before slicing.

Yeast breads

Crisp bread sticks, egg-rich sweet rolls, sturdy sandwich loaves—the variety of yeast breads is endless. But all begin with the same basic ingredients: yeast, liquid, salt, and flour (and usually sugar and fat). Basic techniques are also much the same; to bake successful bread, you'll need to dissolve yeast properly and measure flour accurately.

Dissolving yeast. Dissolve active dry yeast in liquid that's warm (about 110°). For compressed yeast, use lukewarm liquid (about 95°). If the liquid is too cool, the yeast action will be sluggish; if it's too hot, the yeast will be killed and your dough won't rise. You can make sure the temperature is right by testing the liquid (before adding the yeast) with a candy thermometer.

Measuring flour. There's no need to sift flour before measuring. Just stir it once or twice in the container, then spoon lightly into a cup measure—never pack it into the cup or shake it down. Level off the filled cup with a straight-edged knife or spatula. *NOTE:* The amount of flour any recipe requires will vary slightly from one baking day to the next, depending on the moisture content of the flour and on the temperature and humidity of the air. To accommodate this variation, our recipes state the required amount of flour as an approximate measure rather than a specific amount.

Dark Rye Bread

Russia   (Pictured on facing page)

Scorched sugar gives this deli-style rye its distinctive flavor and rich mahogany color; the sturdy texture comes from stone-ground dark rye flour.

You begin by melting sugar as you would for making caramel (page 206)—but you keep cooking it until it foams into an ebony syrup, then dissolve it with boiling water. *CAUTION:* Sugar smokes as it scorches, and scorched sugar spatters when boiling water is added to it. Make sure your kitchen is well ventilated (use the exhaust fan), and protect yourself with an apron and potholders. After pouring out the sugar mixture, cool pan completely; then add tap water, soak briefly, and wash. The blackened sugar won't mar the pan.

Stone-ground dark rye flour is available in health food stores and some supermarkets. If you can't find it, just use medium rye flour.

½ cup sugar
¾ cup boiling water
2 tablespoons solid shortening, butter, or margarine
3 packages active dry yeast
2 cups warm water (about 110°)
¼ cup unsweetened cocoa
2 teaspoons salt
2 tablespoons caraway seeds
   About 4¾ cups all-purpose flour
2 cups stone-ground dark rye flour
2 tablespoons yellow cornmeal

Pour sugar into a wide, heavy frying pan. Place pan over medium-high heat; with a wooden spoon, stir sugar constantly until it's melted. Continue to cook and stir until sugar smokes and is very dark (about 2½ minutes). When sugar is entirely black, add boiling water and continue to cook, stirring constantly, until all sugar is dissolved and liquid is reduced to ½ cup. Remove pan from heat and pour syrup into a small dish; stir in shortening, then let mixture cool to 110°.

In large bowl of an electric mixer, dissolve yeast in warm water. Stir in sugar syrup, cocoa, salt, caraway seeds, and 2 cups of the all-purpose flour. Beat until smooth. Add rye flour and beat for at least 5 minutes on medium speed. With a wooden spoon or a heavy-duty mixer on low to medium speed, beat in 2 cups more all-purpose flour to make a stiff, very moist dough; then turn dough out onto a floured board. At this stage, it's too moist to knead, so cover it with plastic wrap and let it rest for 10 minutes. As it rests, flour will absorb more of liquid in dough, making it firmer.

Knead dough until elastic and just slightly tacky (5 to 10 minutes), adding all-purpose flour as needed to prevent sticking. Place in a greased bowl and turn to grease top. Cover and let rise in a warm place until doubled (about 1 hour).

Sprinkle cornmeal over a lightly greased baking sheet; set aside. Punch down dough, knead briefly on a lightly floured board to release air, and divide in half. Shape each half into a ball, gently pulling dough toward underside of ball to make top surface smooth; pinch underside together. Place loaves, pinched side down, 4 inches apart on baking sheet. Cover and let rise until almost doubled (about 1 hour and 15 minutes). Meanwhile, preheat oven to 375°.

Bake loaves for 35 minutes or until they sound hollow when tapped. Transfer to a wire rack; let cool completely. Makes 2 loaves.

...Yeast breads

Bolillos

Mexico

Tortillas aren't the only bread served in Mexico—the plain yeast roll called *bolillo* is just as popular. Like hard French and Italian rolls, bolillos have a crisp, chewy crust.

> 2 **cups water**
> 1½ **teaspoons sugar**
> 2 **teaspoons salt**
> 2 **tablespoons butter or margarine**
> 1 **package active dry yeast**
> 5½ **to 6 cups all-purpose flour**
> 1 **teaspoon cornstarch dissolved in ½ cup water**

In a small pan, combine water, sugar, salt, and butter; warm over low heat, stirring constantly, until mixture reaches 110°. Pour into a large bowl; sprinkle on yeast and stir until dissolved. Gradually beat in about 5 cups of the flour to make a stiff dough. Turn dough out onto a floured board; knead until smooth and satiny (5 to 15 minutes), adding flour as needed to prevent sticking. Place dough in a greased bowl; turn to grease top. Cover and let rise in a warm place until doubled (about 1½ hours).

Lightly grease 3 baking sheets; set aside. Punch down dough and knead briefly on a floured board to release air. Divide into 16 pieces; shape each into a smooth ball, then gently pull each ball from center toward ends to make a 4-inch-long oblong (center should be thicker than ends).

Place rolls 3 inches apart on baking sheets. Cover and let rise until almost doubled (about 35 minutes). Meanwhile, adjust oven racks so they're evenly spaced in oven; preheat oven to 375°. (*NOTE: If you have only one oven*, you can bake only 2 sheets of rolls at a time. Cover third sheet with plastic wrap after shaping; refrigerate for up to 30 minutes. Then remove from refrigerator and let rise until almost doubled—about 45 minutes.)

Pour cornstarch-water mixture into a pan; bring to a boil over high heat, then let cool slightly. Brush mixture over raised rolls. With a razor blade or a floured sharp knife, cut a 2-inch-long, ¾-inch-deep slash in top of each roll.

Bake rolls for 35 to 40 minutes or until they're golden brown and sound hollow when tapped; switch position of sheets halfway through baking. Let cool on wire racks. Makes 16.

YEAST DOUGH RISING TIPS

To prepare most yeast breads from mixing to baking, you'll need 3 to 4 hours. If you can't stay near the kitchen for that long, just cover dough with plastic wrap after you've kneaded it; then place in the refrigerator for several hours (or until next day). Dough will rise in the cold—but very slowly. When you're ready to continue, move dough to a warm place and let it finish rising; then shape, let rise again, and bake.

What if you let dough rise too long? You'll find it has ballooned past double its original size; its "skin" is thin and transparent, with bubbles just beneath. Such "over-proofed" dough still makes excellent bread —just punch down and let rise again. Dough can overrise two or three times without harm to the finished loaf (each rising takes a bit less time).

Slavic Farmer's Bread

Yugoslavia

All over Europe, you'll find peasant breads like this one: a big, crusty, freeform loaf made from an unsweetened dough.

> 2 **packages active dry yeast**
> 2 **cups warm water (about 110°)**
> 1 **teaspoon salt**
> **About 6¼ cups all-purpose flour**
> ⅓ **cup firm butter or margarine, cut into small pieces**

In a small bowl, dissolve yeast in water. In a large bowl, combine salt and 4 cups of the flour. Cut in butter with a pastry blender or 2 knives to make a crumbly mixture. Add yeast mixture; stir with a wooden spoon or a heavy-duty mixer until all flour is moistened. Work in 1 more cup of flour to make a stiff dough.

Turn dough out onto a floured board. Knead until smooth and satiny (about 10 minutes); add flour as needed to prevent sticking. Place in a greased bowl and turn to grease top. Cover; let rise in a warm place until doubled (1 to 1½ hours).

Lightly grease a large baking sheet. Punch down dough; knead briefly on a lightly floured board to release air. Shape into an oval loaf (about 7 by 9 inches); place on baking sheet, cover, and let rise in a warm place until almost doubled (about 45 minutes). Preheat oven to 400°.

With a floured sharp knife, cut a ½-inch-deep cross in top of loaf; brush loaf lightly with water. Bake for 25 minutes. Reduce heat to 350° and bake for about 15 more minutes or until loaf sounds hollow when tapped. Let cool on a wire rack before slicing. Makes 1 large loaf.

Pocket Bread

Middle East

For these popular breads to form their characteristic hollow centers, it's crucial that the oven temperature remain constant. After broiling breads to brown tops, *return oven to 475°* before baking the next batch.

- 1 **package active dry yeast**
- 1 **tablespoon sugar**
- 3 **cups warm water (about 110°)**
- 1 **tablespoon *each* salt and salad oil**
   About 9 cups all-purpose flour

In a bowl, dissolve yeast and sugar in water and let stand until bubbly (5 to 12 minutes). Stir in salt and oil. Place 9 cups of the flour in a large bowl and make a well in center. Pour in about half the yeast mixture and mix with your hands until well combined. Add remaining yeast mixture, mixing and kneading until dough holds together.

Turn dough out onto a floured board, shape into a log, and divide into 20 pieces; keep covered. Flour your hands lightly. To shape each bread round, place a piece of dough in your palm. Use your other hand to pull dough out away from sides, then fold it back toward center and press in middle; work around edge, gently pressing and pulling dough until it's smooth. Place round breads, smooth side up, on a cloth-lined tray; cover with a dry cloth, then a damp cloth. Let rise in a warm place until puffy (1 to 1½ hours).

Place each bread on a floured board. Flatten with a rolling pin; then roll out to form a circle 6 inches in diameter, using 4 strokes in each direction around the circle. Shake off excess flour and place breads at least ½ inch apart on a dry cloth. Cover with another dry cloth; top with a damp cloth. Cover all with plastic wrap. Let stand at room temperature until slightly puffy (about 1

hour). Meanwhile, adjust oven rack so it's 2 inches from oven bottom. Then preheat oven to 475°.

Carefully transfer 3 to 5 breads to an ungreased 12 by 15-inch baking sheet, placing them about ½ inch apart. Bake for about 5 minutes or until pockets form and bottoms are lightly browned. Immediately increase heat to broil and move baking sheet to 4 inches below heat. Broil until tops are lightly browned (about 1 minute). Slide breads off baking sheet onto a towel. *Return oven to 475° before baking next batch.*

Let baked breads cool completely. If made ahead, gently flatten; then wrap airtight and refrigerate for up to 5 days. Makes 20.

Fennel Bread Sticks

Italy

Crisp "sticks" of bread are a uniquely Italian creation—sometimes plain, sometimes flavored.

- 1 **package active dry yeast**
- ¾ **cup warm water (about 110°)**
- ¾ **cup *each* beer (at room temperature) and salad oil**
- 1 **teaspoon salt**
- 1 **tablespoon fennel seeds**
   About 4½ cups all-purpose flour
- 1 **egg beaten with 1 tablespoon water**

In a large bowl, dissolve yeast in water. Stir in beer, oil, salt, and fennel seeds. Gradually add 3½ cups of the flour, beating with a wooden spoon or a heavy-duty mixer until dough is elastic (about 5 minutes). Turn dough out onto a board or pastry cloth spread with 1 cup more flour.

To knead dough, lift edge and fold toward center, then push away, keeping fingers on flour-coated part of dough. Knead dough until smooth and elastic, turning it as you work. Place in a greased bowl and turn to grease top; then cover and let rise in a warm place until doubled (1 to 1¼ hours). Preheat oven to 325°.

Punch down dough; knead briefly on a lightly floured board. Pinch off 1½-inch lumps of dough; roll each into an 18-inch rope. Cut each rope in half. Place wire racks on baking sheets; lay ropes across racks, ½ inch apart. Brush on egg-water mixture. Bake for about 35 minutes or until evenly browned and crisp. Serve hot. Or let cool completely on racks, then package airtight and store at room temperature. Makes about 5 dozen.

...Yeast breads

Challah

Jewish heritage   (Pictured on facing page)

Richly glazed and topped with sesame or poppy seeds, *challah* (sometimes spelled hallah) occupies a place of honor on Sabbath and holiday tables in many Jewish homes. To give this loaf its typical deep yellow hue, you can add a few crushed saffron threads to the egg-yeast mixture.

> 1 **package active dry yeast**
> 1¼ **cups warm water (about 110°)**
> 1 **teaspoon salt**
> ¼ **cup each sugar and salad oil**
> 2 **eggs, lightly beaten**
> **Pinch of saffron threads (optional)**
> 5 **to 5½ cups all-purpose flour**
> 1 **egg yolk**
> 1 **tablespoon water**
> 1 **tablespoon sesame seeds or poppy seeds**

In a large bowl, dissolve yeast in warm water. Stir in salt, sugar, oil, eggs, and saffron (if used). Gradually beat in 4½ cups of the flour to make a stiff dough.

Turn dough out onto a floured board and knead until smooth and satiny (5 to 20 minutes), adding flour as needed to prevent sticking. Place in a greased bowl and turn to grease top; then cover and let rise in a warm place until doubled (about 1½ hours). Punch down dough; knead briefly on a lightly floured board to release air. Cut off about ¾ cup of the dough; set aside and cover.

Divide remaining dough into 4 equal portions. On a lightly floured board, roll each portion into 16-inch rope. Place ropes side by side on a greased baking sheet, pinch tops together, and braid as follows: Pick up rope on right and bring it over adjacent rope; then bring it under third rope and over fourth. Repeat until braid is complete, always starting with rope farthest to right. Pinch ends together.

Roll reserved dough into a strip about 15 inches long; cut into 3 shorter ropes. Pinch tops together, then plait into a 3-strand braid and pinch ends to seal. Place atop large braid. Cover loaf and let rise in a warm place until almost doubled (about 1 hour). Meanwhile, preheat oven to 350°.

Beat together egg yolk and the 1 tablespoon water; spread evenly over loaf, using a soft brush or your fingers. Sprinkle with sesame seeds. Bake for 30 to 35 minutes or until loaf is golden brown and sounds hollow when tapped. Serve warm, pulled into chunks; or let cool on a wire rack, then slice. Makes 1 large loaf.

Bohemian Braid

Czechoslovakia

Like braided breads of neighboring countries, this decorative loaf traditionally joins the festivities at weddings and other special occasions.

> 1 **package active dry yeast**
> ¼ **cup warm water (about 110°)**
> 1 **cup warm milk (about 110°)**
> ⅓ **cup sugar**
> 1½ **teaspoons each salt and grated lemon peel**
> 1 **teaspoon ground mace**
> 2 **tablespoons butter or margarine, softened**
> 1 **egg**
> **About 4 cups all-purpose flour**
> ½ **cup each raisins and chopped unblanched almonds**
> **Almond icing (recipe follows)**
> **Pecan halves**
> **Candied red cherries, halved**

In large bowl of an electric mixer, dissolve yeast in water. Stir in milk, sugar, salt, lemon peel, mace, butter, egg, and 1½ cups of the flour; beat for at least 5 minutes on medium speed. With a wooden spoon or a heavy-duty mixer on low to medium speed, beat in about 2½ cups or more flour to form an elastic dough. Place dough in a greased bowl; turn to grease top. Cover and let rise in a warm place until doubled (about 1 hour).

Stir down dough, blending in raisins and almonds. Turn out onto a floured board; knead lightly until satiny. Following directions for Challah (at left), shape dough into a 4-strand braid topped with a smaller 3-strand braid. Cover and let rise in a warm place until almost doubled (30 to 45 minutes). Meanwhile, preheat oven to 350°.

Bake loaf for 25 to 30 minutes or until golden brown. Let cool on a wire rack for 10 minutes; then prepare icing and drizzle over loaf. Decorate with pecans and cherries. Makes 1 large loaf.

Almond icing. In a small bowl, combine ¾ cup sifted **powdered sugar,** 2 to 3 teaspoons **milk,** and ⅛ teaspoon **almond extract;** stir until smooth.

Making Challah (Recipe on facing page)

1 After punching down dough, cut off about ¾ cup; set aside nd cover. Divide remaining dough nto 4 portions. On a floured board, ll each portion into a 16-inch rope.

2 Place ropes on a baking sheet; pinch tops together. Bring right strand over second strand, then under third and over fourth. Repeat until braid is complete, always starting with right rope.

3 Roll reserved dough into a 15-inch rope; divide into 3 equal portions. Pinch tops together and plait into a 3-strand braid; place atop large braid. Cover and let rise.

4 Gently brush risen loaf with egg wash; be careful not to puncture ough, and don't let egg drip onto aking sheet. Sprinkle loaf with esame seeds.

5 Baked loaf is crisp and golden outside, tender within. To make the neatest slices, let cool completely before cutting—but if you can't wait to taste, just break warm loaf into chunks.

...Yeast breads

Portuguese Sweet Bread

Portugal

Portuguese settlers brought this tender bread with them to Hawaii—and today, the same delicious, springy loaf often goes by the name "Hawaiian sweet bread."

   ⅔ **cup boiling water**
   ¼ **cup instant mashed potato granules or flakes**
   ⅔ **cup sugar**
   ¼ **cup instant nonfat dry milk**
   ½ **cup (¼ lb.) firm butter or margarine, cut into small pieces**
   ⅓ **cup warm water (about 110°)**
   2 **packages active dry yeast**
     About 5 cups all-purpose flour
   1 **teaspoon salt**
   ½ **teaspoon vanilla**
   ¼ **teaspoon lemon extract**
   4 **eggs**
     Sugar (optional)

Pour boiling water into a bowl. Beat in potato granules; then stir in the ⅔ cup sugar. Stir in dry milk and butter; let cool to 110°.

Meanwhile, pour warm water into a large bowl; sprinkle on yeast and let stand until bubbly (5 to 12 minutes). Stir in potato mixture, then 2 cups of the flour; beat until blended. Add salt, vanilla, lemon extract, and 3 of the eggs; stir to blend well. Beat in about 2½ cups more flour to make a stiff dough. Turn dough out onto a floured board; knead until smooth and satiny (5 to 20 minutes), adding flour as needed to prevent sticking. Place dough in a greased bowl; turn to grease top. Cover and let rise in a warm place until doubled (about 1 hour).

Punch down dough; knead briefly on a lightly floured board to release air. Cover and let rest for 10 minutes, then shape.

For coiled loaves, divide dough in half. Roll each portion into a 30-inch-long rope. Coil each rope in a greased 9-inch pie pan, starting at outside edge of pan and ending in center; twist rope slightly as you coil it.

For coiled buns, divide dough into 12 equal portions. Roll each into a 12-inch-long rope. On greased baking sheets, coil and twist each rope as described for coiled loaves (above), making buns 2½ to 3 inches in diameter and spacing them at least 2 inches apart.

For round loaves, divide dough in half. Shape each half into a flattened round about 8 inches in diameter, then place each in a greased 9-inch pie pan.

Cover shaped dough and let rise in a warm place until almost doubled (35 to 45 minutes for loaves, 20 to 30 minutes for buns). Preheat oven to 350°. Lightly beat remaining egg, then brush over bread; sprinkle with sugar, if desired.

Bake until lightly browned—25 to 30 minutes for loaves, 20 to 25 minutes for buns. Transfer to wire racks. Let cool slightly and serve warm; or let cool completely and serve at room temperature. Makes 2 loaves or 1 dozen buns.

Sally Lunn

England

This light, eggy yeast cake is named for the pastry cook who created it—Sally Lunn, proprietress of a refreshment house in Bath around 1680.

   ½ **cup warm water (about 110°)**
   1 **package active dry yeast**
   1 **cup milk**
   ½ **cup (¼ lb.) firm butter or margarine, cut into small pieces**
   ⅓ **cup sugar**
   1 **teaspoon salt**
   3 **eggs**
   5½ **to 6 cups all-purpose flour**

Pour water into a large bowl; sprinkle on yeast and let stand until bubbly (5 to 12 minutes). In a small pan, combine milk, butter, sugar, and salt; heat to about 110° (butter need not melt completely). Add to dissolved yeast, then stir in eggs and 3 cups of the flour. Beat until smooth.

With a wooden spoon or a heavy-duty mixer on low to medium speed, beat in 2½ to 3 cups more flour, or enough to make a stiff dough that's too sticky to knead. Cover and let rise in a warm place until doubled (about 1½ hours).

Generously grease a 10-inch tube pan (sides, center tube and bottom) with a removable bottom. Stir down dough, then turn into prepared pan, pushing and punching dough to cover pan bottom evenly. Cover and let rise in a warm place until level with pan top (about 1 hour). Meanwhile, preheat oven to 375°.

Bake for about 35 minutes or until well browned. Run a long spatula around pan sides;

lift out tube and bread. Loosen bottom of bread with spatula; invert bread and gently twist out tube. Place bread upright on a wire rack; let cool completely. Cut into thin wedges to serve. Makes 1 large loaf.

Streuselkuchen

Germany

Streusel is a buttery sprinkle-on topping; *Kuchen* means "cake." Our big coffee cake adds something else: a sweet filling of cheese or apples between tender yeast-dough base and spicy topping.

- ¼ cup milk
- 2 tablespoons granulated sugar
- ¾ teaspoon salt
- 4 tablespoons firm butter or margarine, cut into small pieces
- ¼ cup warm water (about 110°)
- 1 package active dry yeast
- 2 eggs
  About 3¼ cups all-purpose flour
  Apple filling or cheese filling (recipes follow)
  Streusel topping (recipe follows)
  Powdered sugar

Place milk, granulated sugar, salt, and butter in a small pan; heat over medium heat just until butter melts. Let cool to 110°.

Meanwhile, pour water into large bowl of an electric mixer; sprinkle on yeast and let stand until bubbly (5 to 12 minutes). Stir in milk mixture and eggs; then add 2 cups of the flour. Beat mixture on medium speed until batter pulls away from sides of bowl (about 3 minutes). Using a wooden spoon, stir in 1 cup more flour to make a soft dough. Turn dough out onto a floured board; knead until smooth and elastic (5 to 10 minutes). Place in a greased bowl and turn to grease top; then cover and let rise in a warm place until doubled (1 to 1½ hours). While dough is rising, prepare filling of your choice and streusel topping.

Punch down dough and turn out onto a greased 14-inch pizza pan or 10 by 15-inch jelly roll pan; cover with inverted bowl and let rest for 5 to 10 minutes. Then pat dough out to fit pan; cover evenly with filling. Sprinkle an even layer of streusel atop filling. Let rise until puffy (about 20 minutes). Meanwhile, preheat oven to 375°.

Bake for 25 minutes or until crust and streusel are golden brown. Let cool for 20 minutes, then dust with powdered sugar and serve warm.

If made ahead, let cool completely, cover, and store at room temperature until next day. To reheat, cover loosely with foil and bake in a 350° oven for 10 minutes; top with powdered sugar just before serving. Makes 12 to 16 servings.

Apple filling. In a 2-quart pan, combine 5 cups cored, peeled, and chopped **tart cooking apples;** 2 tablespoons **lemon juice;** and 1 tablespoon **water.** Bring to a boil over medium heat; cover, reduce heat, and simmer, stirring occasionally, until apples are just tender when pierced (8 to 10 minutes). In a bowl, combine ¾ cup **sugar,** 2 tablespoons **all-purpose flour,** ½ teaspoon **ground cinnamon,** and ¼ teaspoon **ground nutmeg;** stir into apples and cook, stirring, until thickened. Remove from heat and let cool.

Cheese filling. In a bowl, beat 1 large package (8 oz.) **cream cheese** (softened) until fluffy. Then beat in ½ cup **sugar,** 1 **egg,** and 1 teaspoon *each* grated **lemon peel** and **vanilla.** Stir in ½ cup **golden raisins.**

Streusel topping. In a bowl, stir together 1¼ cups **all-purpose flour,** ½ cup **powdered sugar,** 1 teaspoon **baking powder,** and ½ teaspoon **ground cinnamon.** Add ½ cup (¼ lb.) firm **butter** or margarine, cut into pieces; cut into flour mixture with a pastry blender or 2 knives to form coarse, moist crumbs that just begin to clump together. Mix in ½ teaspoon **vanilla.**

GREASING BAKING PANS

Use only solid shortening to grease baking pans. Butter and margarine tend to burn; vegetable oil may collect at the bottom of the pan, resulting in a damp bottom crust.

Always grease pans *before* you start to prepare the recipe; if batter is allowed to stand after being stirred, the baked product will have a lower volume and a denser texture. For the highest, lightest breads and cakes, grease only the pan bottom unless otherwise noted. By leaving the sides ungreased, you'll give batter a non-slippery surface to use for a "handhold" as it rises.

Shaping Pan Dulce (Recipe on facing page)

1 *To shape as a shell* (concha). Pat dough to a 3-inch round. Squeeze ¼ cup streusel to a firm ball; then press into a patty, score top, and place atop dough. Or just sprinkle streusel atop dough.

2 *To shape as a horn* (cuerno). Roll dough to a 4 by 8-inch oval; top with 3 tablespoons streusel. Roll up halfway; stop and fold in sides. Finish rolling; curl in ends.

3 *To shape as a corn ear* (elote). Roll dough to a 4 by 8-inch oval; top with 3 tablespoons streusel. Roll from one end to the other. Slash top with a knife, cutting halfway through dough each time.

4 A bountiful array of Mexican sweet breads makes a special breakfast treat. To reheat baked buns, just wrap in foil and place in a 350° oven for 10 minutes.

.Yeast breads

Pan Dulce

Mexico   (Pictured on facing page)

You start with an egg-rich yeast dough and some sweet crumb topping—and end up with curved horns, seashells, or whatever your fancy dictates. All of these imaginatively shaped buns are called *pan dulce*, which simply means "sweet bread."

> 6 **tablespoons firm butter or margarine, cut into small pieces**
> 1 **cup milk**
> 1 **package active dry yeast**
> 1 **teaspoon salt**
> ⅓ **cup sugar**
> 5 **to 5½ cups all-purpose flour**
> 3 **eggs**
> **Plain and chocolate egg streusels (recipes follow)**
> 2 **tablespoons milk**

In a small pan, combine butter and the 1 cup milk. Heat over medium heat until very warm (120° to 130°; butter need not melt completely). In large bowl of an electric mixer, combine yeast, salt, sugar, and 2 cups of the flour. Pour in milk mixture and beat on medium speed for 2 minutes, scraping bowl often. Blend in 2 of the eggs, then 1 cup more flour; beat on high speed for 2 minutes. Using a wooden spoon or a heavy-duty mixer on low to medium speed, gradually beat in about 1½ cups more flour, or enough to make a stiff dough.

Turn dough out onto a floured board; knead until smooth and satiny (5 to 10 minutes), adding flour as needed to prevent sticking. Place in a greased bowl and turn to grease top; then cover and let rise in warm place until doubled (about 1½ hours). Meanwhile, prepare both plain and chocolate egg streusels and set aside.

Punch down dough and turn out onto a floured board. Divide into 14 equal pieces; shape each into a smooth ball. Then shape buns as shown on facing page, making 7 oblong buns (horns or corn ears) and 7 round ones (shells). To measure streusel, lightly pack it into cup or spoon. For shells, squeeze measured streusel into a ball; then press it into a smooth patty, score top, and place atop dough. (Or simply break ball of streusel into chunks and sprinkle atop dough.)

Place buns about 2 inches apart on greased baking sheets, placing streusel-topped (round) buns on one sheet and filled (oblong) buns on an-

other. Lightly cover filled buns. Let rise in a warm place until almost doubled (about 45 minutes). Meanwhile, preheat oven to 375°.

Beat together remaining egg and the 2 tablespoons milk; brush over filled buns. Bake buns for 15 to 17 minutes or until tops are lightly browned. Makes 14 buns.

Plain egg streusel. In a bowl, stir together ½ cup **sugar** and ⅔ cup **all-purpose flour.** Cut in 3½ tablespoons firm **butter** or margarine with a pastry blender (or rub mixture between your fingers) until fine crumbs form. Add 2 **egg yolks** and stir with a fork until well blended.

Chocolate egg streusel. Prepare **plain egg streusel,** but stir 2 tablespoons **unsweetened cocoa** into sugar-flour mixture. (If you prefer a sweeter filling, use 2 tablespoons ground chocolate in place of cocoa.)

TYPES OF YEAST

The yeast that leavens bread is a "living leavening," not a chemical agent like baking soda or baking powder. When activated by the warm liquid used to make bread dough, yeast releases carbon dioxide gas. The gas bubbles cause the dough to rise into an airy sponge.

Yeast is available in two forms: granular (active dry yeast) and compressed. Our recipes call for active dry yeast—it's more widely sold, as well as more convenient to use. You'll find it in vacuum-sealed packages (containing about 2¼ teaspoons each) and in small glass jars. Unopened yeast keeps for about a year if stored in a cool, dry place; check the expiration date stamped on package or jar. Dry yeast in jars should be refrigerated after opening.

Compressed yeast, sold in small cakes, is more perishable than the dry form. Always store it in the refrigerator (it will keep for about 2 weeks). Crumble it before using; if it crumbles readily, it's still active. You may substitute 1 cake compressed yeast for each package of active dry yeast—just be sure to dissolve it in water that's lukewarm (95°) rather than warm (110°).

...Yeast breads

Limpa

Sweden

Rye withstands cold Scandinavian winters more easily than wheat, so it's no surprise that the region's breads are typically made with rye flour. Swedish *limpa* is one well-known Scandinavian loaf. It's traditionally flavored with fennel and orange peel; our version also includes chewy nuggets of cracked wheat. Spread thin slices of limpa with butter, top them with a mild cheese, or use for Danish open-faced sandwiches (page 69).

    ½ **cup cracked wheat**
    2 **teaspoons crushed fennel seeds**
    1 **tablespoon grated orange peel**
    2 **teaspoons salt**
    ⅓ **cup dark molasses**
    3 **tablespoons butter or margarine**
    1 **cup boiling water**
    1 **package active dry yeast**
    ¼ **cup warm water (about 110°)**
    1 **cup milk, at room temperature**
    2 **cups rye flour**
    4 **to 4½ cups all-purpose flour**
      Butter or margarine, melted

Place cracked wheat, fennel seeds, orange peel, salt, molasses, and the 3 tablespoons butter in a large bowl. Pour in boiling water; stir, then let mixture cool to 110°. Sprinkle yeast over the ¼ cup warm water; let stand until bubbly (5 to 12 minutes), then stir into wheat mixture. Beat in milk and rye flour; gradually stir in about 3½ cups of the all-purpose flour to make a moderately stiff dough.

    Turn dough out onto a floured board; knead until smooth and elastic (10 to 20 minutes), adding all-purpose flour as needed to prevent sticking. Place dough in a greased bowl and turn to grease top. Cover and let rise in a warm place until doubled (about 2 hours). Punch down dough; knead briefly on a lightly floured board to release air. Divide dough in half, then shape each half into a round loaf about 9 inches across. Place each loaf on a greased baking sheet. Cover and let rise in a warm place until almost doubled (about 1 hour).

    Meanwhile, adjust oven racks so they're evenly spaced in oven; preheat oven to 350°. Bake loaves for about 35 minutes or until they sound hollow when tapped (switch position of baking sheets halfway through baking). Brush tops with melted butter. Transfer to wire racks and let cool. Makes 2 loaves.

Dresden-style Stollen

Germany

Stollen is Germany's traditional Christmas bread, richly laden with fruits and nuts and topped with a snowdrift of powdered sugar. Dresden-style stollen is one of the most popular examples of this holiday treat. Our version has a rich, buttery dough studded with candied orange peel, raisins, currants, and almonds.

    ½ **cup milk**
    1 **cup (½ lb.) firm butter or margarine, cut into small pieces**
    ½ **cup granulated sugar**
    ½ **cup warm water (about 110°)**
    2 **packages active dry yeast**
    ½ **teaspoon salt**
    1 **teaspoon *each* almond extract and grated lemon peel**
      About 5¼ cups all-purpose flour
    2 **eggs**
    ⅓ **cup finely chopped candied orange peel**
    ½ **cup *each* dark raisins, golden raisins, currants, and slivered almonds**
    1 **egg white**
    1 **teaspoon water**
    4 **tablespoons butter or margarine**
    ⅓ **cup powdered sugar**

In a small pan, combine milk, the 1 cup butter, and granulated sugar. Heat to very warm (120° to 130°) over medium heat, stirring to dissolve sugar and melt butter. Set aside; let cool to 110°.

    Pour warm water into a large bowl; sprinkle on yeast and let stand until bubbly (5 to 12 minutes). Add milk mixture, salt, almond extract, lemon peel, and 3 cups of the flour; beat until well blended. Add eggs, one at a time, beating well after each addition. Gradually blend in orange peel, raisins, currants, and almonds; then stir in 2 cups more flour.

Turn dough out onto a floured board; knead until smooth and elastic (about 10 minutes), adding flour as needed to prevent sticking. Place dough in a greased bowl and turn to grease top; then cover and let rise in a warm place until doubled (about 1½ hours).

Punch down dough, turn out onto a floured board, and knead briefly to release air. Divide in half. Place each portion on a lightly greased baking sheet and shape into an oval about 7 inches wide, 9 inches long, and ¾ inch thick.

In a small bowl, beat together egg white and the 1 teaspoon water; brush some of mixture over each oval. Using the back of a knife, mark a lengthwise crease, slightly off center, in each oval. Fold along crease; bottom edge should extend about an inch beyond top edge (see illustrations below).

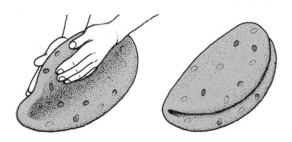

Brush loaves evenly with remaining egg white mixture. Cover and let rise in a warm place until almost doubled (35 to 45 minutes). Meanwhile, adjust oven racks so they're evenly spaced in oven; preheat oven to 375°.

Bake loaves for 25 minutes or until golden brown. Melt the 4 tablespoon butter in a small pan over low heat. Brush baked loaves evenly with melted butter, then sift powdered sugar over tops. Return to oven and bake for 3 more minutes. Transfer to wire racks and let cool slightly, then slice and serve warm.

If made ahead, don't top with butter and sugar after baking. Instead, let cool completely; then wrap airtight and freeze. To reheat, cover thawed loaves loosely with foil and heat in a 350° oven for 20 minutes. Then top with butter and sugar; bake for 3 more minutes. Makes 2 loaves.

Alsatian Kugelhopf

France

France's Alsace region borders on Germany— and both countries claim *kugelhopf* as their own (the name is German). It's traditionally baked in a special mold, but you can use any decorative tube pan.

> ¾ cup raisins
> 1½ tablespoons kirsch
> 1 package active dry yeast
> ¼ cup warm water (about 110°)
> ½ cup (¼ lb.) butter or margarine, softened
> ½ cup granulated sugar
> 1 teaspoon *each* grated lemon peel, vanilla, and salt
> 3 eggs
> 3 cups all-purpose flour
> ½ cup milk
> ⅓ cup coarsely chopped blanched almonds
> ¼ cup sliced almonds
> Powdered sugar

In a small bowl, mix raisins and kirsch; set aside. In another small bowl, sprinkle yeast over water; let stand until bubbly (5 to 12 minutes).

Place butter, granulated sugar, lemon peel, vanilla, and salt in large bowl of an electric mixer; beat on medium speed until well blended. Add eggs, one at a time, beating thoroughly after each addition; then stir in yeast mixture. Add flour alternately with milk, mixing after each addition. Beat on medium speed of electric mixer for 2 minutes. With a wooden spoon, stir in raisin mixture and chopped almonds. Cover and let rise in a warm place until doubled (about 2 hours).

Generously grease a 10-cup decorative tube pan; arrange sliced almonds in bottom. Stir down dough and pour into prepared pan. Cover and let rise in a warm place until dough almost reaches top of pan (about 1 hour). Meanwhile, preheat oven to 350°.

Bake bread on lowest oven rack for about 40 minutes or until top is well browned and a wooden skewer inserted into center comes out clean. Let cool in pan for 15 minutes.

Invert onto a serving plate and serve warm; or invert onto a wire rack, let cool completely, and serve at room temperature. Dust with powdered sugar before serving. Makes 10 to 12 servings.

Deep-fried breads

Golden, chewy-crisp deep-fried breads are enjoyed all over the world. On this page, we offer fried breads from Hungary and the United States; you'll find a third type (Indian *puris*) on page 177.

All fried breads taste best fresh out of the pan. If you must make them a day ahead, let them cool completely; then wrap airtight and store at room temperature. To reheat, place in a single layer on a baking sheet; heat in a 350° oven, uncovered, for about 10 minutes or until heated through.

Langos

Hungary   (Pictured on facing page)

Langos began as a use for leftovers. On baking days in Hungary, these puffy breads were fried up from the scraps of dough left after bread making. Our version of langos starts with a potato-enriched yeast dough; you press it into rounds, then slash each in a few places to give the finished breads an extra-chewy interior and an appealing sand-dollar shape.

    1   large russet potato (about ½ lb.)
    2   cups water
    1   package active dry yeast
    1   teaspoon salt
    ½   teaspoon *each* ground ginger and baking soda
    3   tablespoons cornstarch
        About 3 cups all-purpose flour
        Salad oil
        Salt
        Garlic cloves, peeled and halved

Peel potato, if desired; cut into ¼-inch slices and place in a 1½-quart pan. Add water and bring to a boil over high heat; then cover, reduce heat, and simmer until tender when pierced (about 20 minutes). Drain, reserving ¾ cup of the liquid. Mash potato until smooth and set aside.

Pour reserved potato liquid into a large bowl and let cool to 110°; add yeast and stir to dissolve. Stir in potato, the 1 teaspoon salt, ginger, and baking soda.

Stir cornstarch into 2½ cups of the flour, then gradually beat into yeast mixture with a wooden spoon (dough will be crumbly). Turn dough out onto a floured board; knead until smooth (5 to 10 minutes), adding flour as needed to prevent sticking. Place dough in a greased bowl and turn to grease top; then cover and let rise in a warm place until doubled (about 1½ hours).

Punch down dough and knead briefly on a floured board to release air. Divide dough into 16 pieces, then shape each into a smooth ball; place balls about 1½ inches apart on a greased baking sheet. Cover and let rise until almost doubled (about 45 minutes).

On a floured board, flatten each ball into an evenly thick 4-inch round. Cut 4 or 5 slits in each with a knife. Place rounds 1½ inches apart on greased baking sheets; gently pull slits slightly open. Cover and let rise until puffy (30 minutes).

Into a deep, heavy 10 to 12-inch frying pan, pour oil to a depth of 1 inch and heat to 350° on a deep-frying thermometer. Have 2 spatulas on hand so you'll have a cool one ready for cooking each bread.

To fry each bread, place it on a cool spatula, then lower into oil. Cook, turning often, until golden brown on both sides (1½ to 2 minutes *total*). Lift from oil, let drain briefly, and place on paper towels. Sprinkle lightly with salt.

Serve warm or at room temperature; rub with cut garlic just before eating. Makes 16.

Navajo Fry Bread

United States

These chewy breads—also called Papago popovers—are great for tostada bases. Try them as a snack, too, sprinkled with sugar or drizzled with honey.

        About 2 cups all-purpose flour
    ½   cup instant nonfat dry milk
    1   tablespoon baking powder
    ½   teaspoon salt
    2   tablespoons lard or solid shortening
    ¾   cup water
        Salad oil

In a bowl, stir together 2 cups of the flour, dry milk, baking powder, and salt. With your fingers, crumble in lard until mixture is like cornmeal. Add water; stir with a fork just until dough clings together. Turn out onto a floured board and knead until smooth and satiny (about 5 minutes).

Divide dough into 6 portions; shape each into a ball. On a floured board, press out one ball to a 6 to 7-inch round; cover loosely. Repeat with remaining dough. Deep-fry rounds in hot oil as directed for Langos (left); drain on paper towels and serve hot. Makes 6.

Making Langos (Recipe on facing page)

1 On a floured board, pat each ball of dough into an evenly thick 4-inch round. If round is patted out thinner in center than on edges, center of bread will burn.

2 With a small knife, cut 4 or 5 slits in each round. Make slits about ¾ inch long; if they're much longer, dough will stretch apart when placed in hot oil.

3 Place round on a cold spatula, then lower spatula into oil. Round will immediately puff up and rise off spatula. Cook bread, turning often, until golden on both sides. Drain briefly; place on paper towels.

4 Cooked breads are golden, puffy, chewy. Rub them with cut cloves of garlic, then enjoy as partners to a spicy soup or stew.

DESSERTS

If there's one thing most of the world's people have in common, it's a sweet tooth. Ever since the first samplings of sugar cane and honey, sweets have tempted our palates—and around the globe, recipes for pastries, cakes, puddings, confections, and fresh fruits showcase this favorite taste.

In this chapter, you'll find a gorgeous array of sweet indulgences: simple conclusions and grand finales, homey treats and extravagant show-stoppers. For dessert or any special sweet occasion, these delights are sure to please.

Always choose a dessert that complements the earlier part of the meal. After a substantial main course, it only makes sense to offer something delicate—perhaps a refreshing French Fruit Ice paired with thin, crisp Swedish butter cookies. A light repast, on the other hand, calls for a more lavish and filling close—Black Forest Cherry Cake, Blazing Bananas, or richly glazed Chocolate Almond Torte. And when you make your dessert selection, don't pass up our tempting assortment of cookies and confections. A trayful of these, offered with liqueurs or cups of good hot coffee or tea, ends a meal on a delightful note.

Sometimes, you'll want to serve a dessert that helps satisfy nutritional needs. For example, a cool and protein-rich Mexican Flan provides an especially satisfying finish to a meal that's low in protein.

The recipes in this chapter were selected with convenience in mind. All use the standard baking pans found in grocery and department stores, so there's no need for last-minute trips to a specialty store to purchase an unusual pan or mold. And most of these sweet conclusions can be prepared a day or two in advance—a real plus for the busy cook.

Cookies

The English word "cooky" comes from Dutch *koekje*—literally, "little cake." And the first cookies were just that: small spoonfuls of cake batter, baked separately to let the cook judge flavor, texture, and appropriate oven temperature. Today, of course, cookies aren't just dropped from a spoon. As our international cooky sampler shows, cooky dough can be shaped—and flavored—in all sorts of ways.

Twice-baked Cookies

Italy

In Italy, these hard, crunchy cookies are sometimes called "wine dunkers"—they're typically served with wine, and often dipped into it before being eaten.

2 **cups coarsely chopped almonds or walnuts**
5½ **cups all-purpose flour**
1 **tablespoon baking powder**
2 **cups sugar**
1 **cup (½ lb.) butter or margarine, melted**
¼ **cup** *each* **anise seeds and anisette (or other anise-flavored liqueur)**
3 **tablespoons whiskey, or 2 teaspoons vanilla mixed with 2 tablespoons water**
6 **eggs**

In a bowl, stir together almonds, flour, and baking powder; set aside. In another bowl, combine sugar and butter; blend in anise seeds, anisette, and whiskey. Add eggs, one at a time, beating well after each addition. Stir in flour mixture; blend well. Cover and refrigerate for 2 to 3 hours.

Preheat oven to 375°. Grease 2 baking sheets. With your hands, shape dough directly on sheets into flat loaves about ½ inch thick, 2 inches wide, and as long as sheet. Space loaves, 2 to a baking sheet, 4 inches apart (they spread upon baking). Bake for 20 minutes or until lightly browned.

Let loaves cool on baking sheets until you can touch them (about 5 minutes), then cut into ½ to ¾-inch-thick slanting slices. Place slices close together on baking sheets, cut sides down; return to oven and bake for 15 more minutes or until lightly toasted. Transfer to wire racks and let cool completely. Store in airtight containers for up to 1 month. Makes about 9 dozen.

Teacakes

Mexico (Pictured on page 206)

It's a small world, indeed: Mexico's round, rich nut cookies are virtually identical to teacakes baked in Russia and Sweden.

½ **cup (¼ lb.) butter or margarine (softened) or lard**
2 **tablespoons powdered sugar**
1 **teaspoon vanilla**
1 **cup all-purpose flour**
½ **cup finely chopped nuts**
Sifted powdered sugar

Preheat oven to 325°. Lightly grease a baking sheet; set aside. Cream butter, the 2 tablespoons powdered sugar, and vanilla. Mix in flour and nuts. Pinch off 1-inch lumps of dough, roll into balls, and place 1 inch apart on baking sheet.

Bake for 30 minutes or until lightly browned. Let cool on baking sheet for 5 minutes, then gently roll in sifted powdered sugar until coated. Place on a wire rack and let cool completely; roll in powdered sugar again. Makes 3 dozen.

Filbert Chocolate Bars

Germany

Haselnussecken—"hazelnut corners"—are rich, chocolate-topped bars from the city of Trier, in Germany's Mosel Valley.

1 **cup whole unblanched filberts (hazelnuts) or almonds (to toast almonds, see page 87)**
Press-in pastry (recipe follows)
½ **cup (¼ lb.) butter or margarine, softened**
¾ **cup sugar**
1 **teaspoon vanilla**
3 **eggs**
2 **tablespoons all-purpose flour**
½ **teaspoon ground cinnamon**
¼ **teaspoon ground nutmeg**
2 **ounces semisweet chocolate, grated**

Spread filberts in a shallow baking pan and toast in a 350° oven for 10 to 12 minutes or until golden beneath skins. Let cool, then rub briskly with a dishtowel to remove skins. Whirl in a food processor until finely ground, then set aside.

Grease an 8-inch square baking pan. Prepare pastry; press evenly over bottom of pan. Bake in a 350° oven for 12 minutes or until lightly browned.

Meanwhile, in a bowl, beat butter and sugar until blended; stir in vanilla. Add eggs, one at a time, beating well after each addition. Stir in flour, cinnamon, nutmeg, and filberts.

Spread nut mixture evenly over pastry. Return to oven and bake for 30 to 35 minutes or until a wooden pick inserted in center comes out clean. Remove from oven; immediately sprinkle with chocolate. Let stand for 30 minutes, then spread chocolate evenly over surface and let cool completely. Cut into 1 by 3-inch bars. Makes 24.

Press-in pastry. In a bowl, stir together ¾ cup **all-purpose flour** and ⅓ cup **powdered sugar.** With a pastry blender or 2 knives, cut in 4 tablespoons firm **butter** or margarine until mixture resembles coarse crumbs. Add ¼ teaspoon **almond extract** and 1 **egg yolk;** stir until blended.

Shaping Swedish butter cookies (Recipe on facing page)

1 *For Butter Cut-outs:* After cutting dough into shapes, lift out excess dough with a wooden skewer. Use a wide spatula to lift cookies to baking sheets. Reroll scraps; cut more cookies.

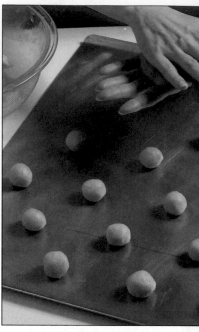

2 *For Almond Refrigerator Cookies:* Chill almond-crusted rolls of dough until firm, then cut into even slices with a thin, sharp knife. Sprinkle more almond mixture over each slice.

3 *For Sandkakor:* Use about 1½ teaspoons dough for each cooky; roll between your palms to form a round ball. Space balls 2 inches apart on baking sheets—they spread out flat upon baking.

4 *For Spritz:* Fill cooky press with slightly chilled dough (if too cold, it crumbles). Use press plate of your choice—we used a star plate, swirling dough into a circle, then pinching it off with fingers.

5 *For Raspberry Strips:* With little finger, make a ½-inch-deep groove down center of each rope. With index fingers, gently push up sides of each rope to make groove deeper. Fill with preserves.

6 Which one to choose? A bountiful array of traditional Swedish butter cookies awaits coffeetime guests. For a festive mood, decorate cut-out cookies with tinted buttercream frosting (page 202).

..Cookies

Butter Cut-outs

Sweden   (Pictured on facing page)

Buttery flavor and crisp texture characterize these melt-in-your-mouth morsels. Easy variations on one rich, simple dough turn out an impressive array of traditional treats. All bake in a 350° oven, but baking time and yield vary slightly for each type.

Stored airtight, these cookies will stay crisp and fresh for 2 to 3 days after baking. If you want to keep them longer, it's best to freeze them (be sure to package each kind separately).

- 1 **cup (½ lb.) butter, softened**
- ½ **cup sugar**
- 1 **egg**
- 1 **teaspoon vanilla**
- ¼ **teaspoon salt**
- 3 **cups all-purpose flour**

In a bowl, cream butter and sugar until light and fluffy. Add egg and vanilla; beat to blend well. Stir in salt and flour until well blended. Cover dough and refrigerate for at least 1 hour or until next day.

Preheat oven to 350°. Lightly grease baking sheets; set aside. On a lightly floured board or pastry cloth, roll dough to a thickness of ⅛ inch; cut into desired shapes with floured 2-inch cooky cutters. Remove excess dough, then transfer cookies to baking sheets with a metal spatula, spacing them about 1 inch apart. Reroll dough scraps and cut additional cookies.

Bake for 12 to 15 minutes or until very lightly browned around edges. Transfer to wire racks; let cool completely. Makes about 5½ dozen.

ALMOND REFRIGERATOR COOKIES

Follow directions for **Butter Cut-outs,** but separate egg. Stir **egg yolk** into butter mixture; reserve **egg white.** Shape dough into 2 rolls, each 1 to 1¼ inches in diameter. Place each roll on a sheet of wax paper that's 2 inches longer than roll. Combine ⅓ cup minced **unblanched almonds** and ¼ cup **sugar.** Lightly beat egg white and brush over rolls; then sprinkle all sides of rolls with almond mixture, pressing it in gently. Reserve any loose almond mixture. Wrap wax paper around rolls; refrigerate for 2 hours. Cut rolls into ¼-inch-thick slices and place on ungreased baking sheets, cut

side down and 1½ inches apart. Sprinkle reserved almond mixture over slices. Bake as for **Cut-out Butter Cookies.** Makes about 7 dozen.

SANDKAKOR

Follow directions for **Butter Cut-outs,** but increase sugar to ⅔ cup and omit egg. Decrease flour to 2 cups and sift it with salt, 1 teaspoon **ground cardamom,** and ¼ teaspoon each **baking soda** and **ground cinnamon.** Don't refrigerate dough; instead, shape it immediately into 1-inch balls. Place balls about 2 inches apart on lightly greased baking sheets. Bake for 13 to 18 minutes or until golden brown. Makes about 4 dozen.

SPRITZ

Follow directions for **Butter Cut-outs,** but increase sugar to ¾ cup and substitute 2 **egg yolks** for whole egg. Decrease flour to 2½ cups. Cover dough and refrigerate for 1 hour, then spoon into a cooky press with a design plate. Force dough onto ungreased baking sheets, spacing cookies about 1 inch apart. Top with halved **candied cherries,** if desired. Bake for 10 to 12 minutes or until very light golden around edges. Makes about 4 dozen.

RASPBERRY STRIPS

Follow directions for **Butter Cut-outs,** but decrease flour to 2½ cups. Cover dough and refrigerate for 1 hour. Divide dough into 4 equal portions; shape each into a rope about ½ inch in diameter. Place ropes lengthwise on an ungreased baking sheet, spacing them about 2 inches apart. With the side of your little finger, press a groove down center of each rope. Push up sides of rope to make a deeper trench.

Fill each groove with **raspberry preserves** (or apricot, peach, or strawberry preserves). You'll need one 10-ounce jar (about 1 cup) *total.*

Bake for 20 minutes or until very lightly browned around edges. Remove from oven; let cool on baking sheet for 10 minutes. Cut each rope at about a 45° angle into 1-inch slices. Let cool on baking sheet for 10 more minutes, then sprinkle with sifted **powdered sugar.** Transfer cookies to a wire rack and let cool completely. Makes about 4 dozen.

...Cookies

Pennsylvania Dutch Spice Cakes

United States

    2 **cups all-purpose flour**
    1 **teaspoon *each* baking soda, ground cinnamon, ground cloves, and ground ginger**
    ½ **cup (¼ lb.) butter or margarine, softened**
    ¼ **cup solid shortening**
  1¼ **cups sugar**
    1 **egg**
    ¼ **cup dark molasses**

Combine flour, baking soda, cinnamon, cloves, and ginger; set aside. In a bowl, beat butter and shortening until creamy. Beat in 1 cup of the sugar, then beat in egg and molasses. Gradually mix in flour mixture. Cover dough and refrigerate until firm (about 2 hours).

    Preheat oven to 350°. Lightly grease baking sheets; set aside. Place remaining ¼ cup sugar in a small dish. Shape dough into 1-inch balls, then roll in sugar to coat. Arrange on baking sheets, 2 inches apart (cookies spread upon baking). Bake for 10 minutes. Let cool on baking sheets for 1 minute. Then transfer to wire racks and let cool completely. Makes about 5 dozen.

Pineapple-Coconut Bars

Tahiti

    ¾ **cup all-purpose flour**
    ¾ **teaspoon baking powder**
    ½ **teaspoon salt**
    ½ **cup (¼ lb.) butter or margarine, softened**
    1 **cup firmly packed brown sugar**
    2 **eggs**
    ¼ **teaspoon almond extract**
    ¾ **cup sweetened flaked coconut**
    1 **can (8 oz.) crushed pineapple packed in its own juice, drained well**

Preheat oven to 350°. Lightly grease and flour-dust a 9-inch square baking pan; set aside. Stir together flour, baking powder, and salt.

    In a bowl, beat together butter and sugar. Add eggs and almond extract; beat until fluffy. Gradually beat in flour mixture, then add coconut and pineapple and mix well. Pour into pan.

    Bake for 25 to 30 minutes or until top springs back when lightly pressed. Transfer to a wire rack. Loosen edges with a spatula, then let cool. Cut into 1 by 2-inch bars. Makes 3 dozen.

Almond Cookies

China

These tender almond-topped cookies are one of the very few traditional Chinese baked desserts.

  2¼ **cups all-purpose flour**
    ⅛ **teaspoon salt**
  1½ **teaspoons baking powder**
    1 **cup (½ lb.) lard or solid shortening**
    ½ **cup granulated sugar**
    ¼ **cup firmly packed brown sugar**
    1 **egg**
    1 **teaspoon almond extract**
    About 5 dozen whole blanched almonds
    1 **egg yolk**
    2 **tablespoons water**

Preheat oven to 350°. Stir together flour, salt, and baking powder. In a bowl, cream lard, granulated sugar, and brown sugar until fluffy. Add egg and almond extract; beat until well blended. Add flour mixture and blend well.

    Pinch off dough, about 1 tablespoon at a time, and roll into balls. Place balls on ungreased baking sheets, 2 inches apart; flatten each to make a 2-inch round. Press an almond into center of each round. Beat together egg yolk and water; brush over each cooky.

    Bake for 10 to 12 minutes or until lightly browned around edges. Transfer to wire racks and let cool completely. Store in airtight containers. Makes about 5 dozen.

BAKING SHEET KNOW-HOW

For evenly baked and browned cookies, use shiny, unrimmed baking sheets. Dark metal sheets retain heat, giving cookies dark (even burned) bottoms; rimmed sheets make it harder for oven heat to reach cookies on all sides.

    Always start out with cool baking sheets. If they're warm, the fat in the dough will begin to melt before dough starts to bake, resulting in flat cookies. And don't grease sheets unless the recipe tells you to do so. Some cookies can't keep their "footing" on a greased sheet—they spread out and lose their shape as the grease melts.

Cakes

The light and lovely cakes we enjoy today have a humble common ancestor: a flat patty of crushed grain and water, baked on a heated stone. Over time, the coarse grain was replaced by finely milled flour; beaten eggs were added to lighten the mixture, and honey or sugar to sweeten it. These four pages offer some of the most delicious results of the world's long history of cake baking.

Sour Cream Coffee Cake

United States

Pecans are widely grown in the southern United States, where they're put to good use in baking—as in this moist coffee cake. (You can use walnuts, almonds, or filberts in place of pecans.)

- ¾ **cup coarsely chopped pecans**
- 1½ **teaspoons ground cinnamon**
- ¾ **cup firmly packed brown sugar**
- 3 **cups all-purpose flour**
- 1½ **teaspoons** *each* **baking powder and baking soda**
- ¼ **teaspoon salt**
- 1 **cup (½ lb.) butter or margarine, softened**
- 1½ **cups granulated sugar**
- 3 **eggs**
- 1½ **teaspoons vanilla**
- 1½ **cups sour cream**
- 2 **tablespoons** *each* **vanilla and water**

Preheat oven to 325°. Lightly grease and flour-dust a 10-inch tube pan; set aside. Combine pecans, cinnamon, and brown sugar; set aside.

Stir together flour, baking powder, baking soda, and salt. In a bowl, beat together butter and granulated sugar until fluffy, using an electric mixer on medium speed. Add eggs, one at a time, beating well after each addition; then beat in the 1½ teaspoons vanilla and sour cream. With mixer on lowest speed, gradually add flour mixture; beat just until blended.

Spoon ⅓ of the batter into pan; sprinkle with ⅓ of the pecan mixture. Repeat with remaining batter and pecan mixture, making 2 more layers of each. Combine the 2 tablespoons vanilla with water; drizzle over top.

Bake for 1 hour and 10 minutes or until a wooden pick inserted in center comes out clean. Transfer to a wire rack and let cool for 20 minutes, then remove from pan. Serve warm or at room temperature. Makes 12 to 16 servings.

Caramel-Walnut Oatmeal Cake

Scotland

Throughout the British Isles, tea brings family and friends together to enjoy a good deal more than late afternoon cups of tea. At a Scottish tea banquet, this spicy oatmeal cake might share the spotlight with cookies, scones, cream cakes, and other delectable fare. It also improves a morning cup of coffee—and makes a satisfying, homey dessert.

- 1 **cup regular or quick-cooking rolled oats**
- 1½ **cups boiling water**
- 1½ **cups all-purpose flour**
- 1 **teaspoon** *each* **baking soda and ground cinnamon**
- ½ **teaspoon salt**
- ¼ **teaspoon ground nutmeg**
- ½ **cup (¼ lb.) butter or margarine, softened**
- 1 **cup** *each* **granulated sugar and firmly packed brown sugar**
- 2 **tablespoons light molasses**
- 2 **eggs**
  Caramel topping (recipe follows)

Preheat oven to 350°. Lightly grease and flour-dust a 9-inch square baking pan; set aside. Place oats in a bowl and pour in boiling water; let cool to lukewarm. Stir together flour, baking soda, cinnamon, salt, and nutmeg. In another bowl, cream butter, then gradually beat in granulated sugar and brown sugar. Mix in molasses, eggs, and oats; then stir in flour mixture just until dry ingredients are moistened. Pour into prepared pan and spread out evenly. Bake for 50 minutes or until center springs back when lightly pressed.

Meanwhile, prepare caramel topping. As soon as cake is done, spread topping over it; then broil about 6 inches below heat until topping is browned and bubbly. Transfer pan to a wire rack and let cake cool for 30 minutes before cutting. Makes 12 servings.

Caramel topping. In a 2 to 3-quart pan, combine 6 tablespoons **butter** or margarine, ¾ cup firmly packed **brown sugar,** and 3 tablespoons **half-and-half** (light cream). Place over medium heat and stir until butter is melted. Stir in 1 cup *each* **sweetened flaked coconut** and chopped **walnuts.** Bring to a boil, stirring; boil and stir for 1 minute.

...Cakes

Black Forest Cherry Cake

Germany   (Pictured on facing page)

Germany's Black Forest region is justly famous for *Schwarzwälder Kirschtorte*, a luscious chocolate cherry cake flavored with the clear cherry brandy called *kirsch*. Use sour cherries, not sweet ones, and soak them overnight in kirsch for the richest taste. It's best to assemble this cake a day ahead to give the flavors time to blend.

        Kirsch cherries (recipe at right)
    2   **cups all-purpose flour**
    1   **teaspoon baking soda**
    ½   **teaspoon salt**
    ½   **cup (¼ lb.) butter or margarine, softened**
    2   **cups sugar**
    4   **eggs, at room temperature**
    4   **ounces unsweetened chocolate, melted and cooled**
    1   **cup milk**
        Two ¾ to 1-inch-thick bars solid milk chocolate (8 oz. *each*), at room temperature
        Whipped cream frosting (recipe at right)
        Buttercream frosting (recipe at right)
        Red maraschino cherries with stems (optional)

Prepare kirsch cherries; cover and refrigerate for at least 4 hours or until next day.

Preheat oven to 350°. Lightly grease and flour-dust two 9-inch round baking pans; set aside.

Stir together flour, baking soda, and salt; set aside. In a bowl, beat together butter and sugar until fluffy. Add eggs, one at a time, beating well after each addition. Stir in unsweetened chocolate. Add flour mixture alternately with milk, starting and ending with flour. Spoon batter into pans.

Bake for 30 to 35 minutes or until tops spring back when lightly pressed and cakes begin to pull away from sides of pans. Transfer pans to wire racks and let cool for 10 minutes; then turn layers out onto racks and let cool completely.

Make chocolate curls from both chocolate bars (see photo 1 on facing page) and refrigerate. Prepare whipped cream frosting; cover and refrigerate for up to 30 minutes (no longer, or gelatin will begin to set, making frosting too stiff to spread). Prepare buttercream frosting; cover and leave at room temperature.

To assemble cake: If desired, place a doily on plate. Then place 4 strips of foil around edge of plate (see photo 4 on facing page) to form a square. Don't use wax paper—it will become soggy and tear apart when you try to pull it away after frosting cake.

Slice each cake layer in half horizontally (see photo 3 on facing page), forming 4 thin layers. Place one layer on plate. Strain juices from kirsch cherries into a small bowl; reserve cherries. Drizzle 2 tablespoons cherry juice over cake layer on plate; spread with 1 cup whipped cream frosting and top with ⅓ of the cherries. Add another cake layer; gently press down. Drizzle with 2 tablespoons cherry juice; spread with all the buttercream frosting and half the remaining cherries. Place a third layer atop cherries; press down. Sprinkle with 2 tablespoons cherry juice, then top with 1 cup whipped cream frosting and remaining cherries.

Add remaining cake layer and press down. Spread a thin layer of whipped cream frosting over sides and top of cake; refrigerate for 30 minutes. (Leave remaining cream at room temperature.) Reserve 1 cup of whipped cream frosting for rosettes, if desired; then smoothly spread on remaining cream.

Reserve the largest, prettiest chocolate curls for top of cake; sprinkle remaining curls over sides, pressing them in gently. If desired, decorate top of cake with cream rosettes and place a maraschino cherry on each. Lift reserved chocolate curls onto cake with a wooden skewer. Refrigerate for at least 8 hours or until next day. Pull out foil before slicing. Makes 12 servings.

Kirsch cherries. Thaw and drain one bag (16 oz.) **frozen pitted red cherries** (or use one 16-ounce can pitted sour cherries, drained). Cut cherries in half; place in a bowl and stir in ¼ cup **kirsch.**

Whipped cream frosting. Soften 1 envelope **unflavored gelatin** in 2 tablespoons **cold water;** heat over hot water just until gelatin dissolves. Using an electric mixer, beat 1 pint (2 cups) **whipping cream** with 1 tablespoon **kirsch** and ¼ cup sifted **powdered sugar** until softly set; drizzle with gelatin mixture and continue beating until soft peaks form.

Buttercream frosting. Place 2 cups sifted **powdered sugar** in a bowl. Add 4 tablespoons **butter** or margarine, melted; 3 tablespoons **milk;** and 1 teaspoon **kirsch** or vanilla; beat with an electric mixer on high speed until light and fluffy (about 4 minutes).

Frosting a Black Forest Cherry Cake (Recipe on facing page)

1 Chocolate must be at room temperature to make chocolate curls. Press blade of a vegetable peeler down into chocolate bar and draw it down surface, forming curls.

2 After letting cake layers cool completely, brush loose crumbs away from sides and bottom of each. This gives cake a smoother surface, making it easier for frosting to adhere.

3 To split cake layers, place wooden picks at 2-inch intervals all around sides of cake, just below the middle. Using picks as your guide, cut cake in half (just above picks) with a sharp knife.

4 Spread frosting just to edges of cake. Scatter kirsch-flavored cherries evenly over frosting, starting with a circle of cherries around outside edge, then moving in toward center.

5 Holding spatula vertically, spread a thin layer of whipped cream frosting over sides and top of assembled cake to seal in crumbs. Refrigerate for 30 minutes. Apply more frosting to sides and top of cake.

6 Black Forest Cherry Cake takes time to make—but the result is worth it. When you want a dessert that looks and tastes spectacular, you can't do better than this irresistible chocolate layer cake.

...Cakes

Apple Cake

Denmark

Apple cake is a dessert that's enjoyed all over Scandinavia; some versions are more like puddings than cakes. Our Danish variation is a tender layer cake topped with thinly sliced apples.

    ½ **cup (¼ lb.) butter or margarine, softened**
    1 **cup sugar**
    2 **eggs**
    1 **cup all-purpose flour**
    ½ **teaspoon vanilla**
    ¼ **teaspoon** *each* **salt and lemon extract**
    3 **large Golden Delicious apples, peeled, cored, and cut into ¼-inch-thick slices**
    ¼ **teaspoon ground nutmeg**

Preheat oven to 350°. Lightly grease an 8-inch spring-form pan; set aside. In a bowl, beat together butter and ¾ cup of the sugar until light and fluffy. Add eggs, one at a time, beating well after each addition. Stir in flour, vanilla, salt, and lemon extract. Spread batter evenly in pan.

Overlap about half the apple slices in a spiral pattern atop batter, covering batter completely; then add a second layer of apples, using remaining slices. Stir together nutmeg and remaining ¼ cup sugar; sprinkle evenly over apples.

Bake for 1 hour and 15 minutes or until a wooden pick inserted in center comes out clean. Transfer to a wire rack and let cool in pan for 5 minutes; then remove pan sides. Serve warm or at room temperature. Makes 6 servings.

Lemon Yogurt Cake

Greece

In the Middle East, yogurt is used in cooking and baking just as often as we might add cream or milk.

    3 **cups sifted cake flour**
    1 **teaspoon baking soda**
    ¼ **teaspoon salt**
    1 **cup (½ lb.) butter or margarine, softened**
    2 **cups sugar**
    6 **eggs, separated**
    2 **teaspoons grated lemon peel**
    ½ **teaspoon lemon extract**
    ½ **pint (1 cup) plain yogurt stirred together with 2 tablespoons brandy**

Preheat oven to 350°. Grease and flour-dust sides, tube, and bottom of a 10-inch tube pan; set aside. Stir together flour, baking soda, and salt; set aside.

In a large bowl, beat together butter and 1½ cups of the sugar with an electric mixer on high speed. Add egg yolks, lemon peel, and lemon extract; beat until thick and pale yellow. Stir in flour mixture alternately with yogurt-brandy mixture, starting and ending with flour.

Using clean, dry beaters, beat egg whites until soft peaks form. Beating constantly, gradually add remaining ½ cup sugar, 1 tablespoon at a time, until stiff, glossy peaks form. Fold into batter. Pour into pan. Bake for 55 to 60 minutes or until a wooden pick inserted in center comes out clean. Transfer to a wire rack and let cool in pan for 15 minutes; then turn out onto rack and let cool completely. Makes 12 servings.

Chocolate Sponge Cake

France

Classic *genoise* is a simple sponge cake that probably originated in the Italian city of Genoa.

    ⅔ **cup sifted cake flour**
    ¼ **cup sifted unsweetened cocoa**
    3 **eggs**
    ¾ **cup granulated sugar**
    ¼ **teaspoon** *each* **salt and vanilla**
    3 **tablespoons water**
    Sifted powdered sugar

Preheat oven to 375°. Lightly grease a 9-inch round baking pan and line bottom with wax paper; then grease paper and set pan aside. Stir together flour and cocoa; set aside.

Using an electric mixer on high speed, beat eggs in a medium-size bowl until frothy. Beating constantly, gradually add granulated sugar. Continue to beat, scraping bowl often, until mixture is thick and lemon colored and falls in a thick ribbon when beaters are lifted (no more than 5 minutes). Beat in salt, vanilla, and water.

Sprinkle flour mixture over eggs, ⅓ at a time, folding in each addition with a rubber spatula. Pour into pan; spread evenly.

Bake for 25 to 30 minutes or until top springs back when lightly pressed. Transfer to a wire rack and let cool in pan for 5 minutes, then turn out onto rack and let cool completely. Sprinkle with powdered sugar. Makes 8 servings.

Tortes

What's the richest and most delicate of European pastries? It might well be the torte—an exquisite cake made with lots of finely ground nuts, plenty of eggs, and little or no flour. Because these cakes are too delicate to withstand much handling, they're baked and cooled in a spring-form pan.

Chocolate Almond Torte

Switzerland

When you grind nuts for any torte, stop as soon as you achieve a fine, fluffy meal.

> 1½ **cups whole blanched almonds**
> ½ **cup all-purpose flour**
> 1 **teaspoon baking powder**
> ½ **teaspoon ground cinnamon**
> 6 **eggs, separated**
> ¾ **cup sugar**
> ⅓ **cup butter or margarine, melted and cooled**
> **Chocolate glaze (recipe follows)**

Preheat oven to 350°. Grease and flour-dust a 9-inch spring-form pan; set aside. In a food processor or blender, whirl almonds until ground to a fine, flourlike meal (overprocessing may turn nuts into butter). Pour almonds into a bowl and stir in flour, baking powder, and cinnamon. Set aside.

In a large bowl, beat egg whites with an electric mixer on high speed until foamy. Beating constantly, gradually add ¼ cup of the sugar, 1 tablespoon at a time, until stiff, glossy peaks form.

In another bowl, beat egg yolks with mixer on high speed until thick and lemon colored. Beating constantly, gradually add remaining ½ cup sugar; continue to beat until mixture falls in a thick ribbon when beaters are lifted. With a rubber spatula, fold in almond mixture, then butter. Fold in ⅓ of the beaten whites to lighten mixture, then fold in remaining whites. Pour into pan.

Bake for 40 minutes or until a wooden pick inserted in center comes out clean. Transfer to a wire rack and let cool completely in pan; remove pan sides. Meanwhile, prepare glaze. Spread glaze over top and sides of cake; refrigerate until set. Makes 8 to 10 servings.

Chocolate glaze. In top of a double boiler, melt 5 ounces **semisweet chocolate** with 2 tablespoons **butter** or margarine. Stir to blend. Remove pan from heat and let cool until thick enough to spread.

Viennese Nut Torte

Austria

Nowhere has the torte achieved such distinction and acclaim as in Vienna—and one taste of this rich, almondy treat explains why. You won't need a bit of flour to make it—but you will need zwieback crumbs. Look for zwieback toast in the cracker or baby food section of your supermarket; grind it into crumbs in a food processor or blender, or crush with a rolling pin.

> 2 **cups coarsely chopped walnuts or almonds**
> 5 **eggs, separated**
> 1 **cup granulated sugar**
> ⅔ **cup (¼ lb. plus 3 tablespoons) butter or margarine, softened**
> 1 **teaspoon vanilla or rum extract**
> ½ **cup finely crushed or ground zwieback toast crumbs**
> **Powdered sugar**
> **Walnut halves or whole almonds**
> **Sweetened whipped cream (optional)**

Preheat oven to 350°. Grease and flour-dust a 9-inch spring-form pan; set aside. In a food processor or blender, whirl walnuts until ground to a fine, flourlike meal (watch closely; overprocessing may turn nuts into butter). Set aside.

In a large bowl, beat egg whites with an electric mixer at high speed until foamy. Beating constantly, gradually add ½ cup of the granulated sugar, 1 tablespoon at a time, until stiff, glossy peaks form.

In another bowl, cream butter and remaining ½ cup granulated sugar. Add egg yolks and vanilla, beating until fluffy. Stir in walnuts and zwieback crumbs. Fold in ⅓ of the beaten whites to lighten mixture, then fold in remaining whites until blended. Pour into pan.

Bake for 45 to 55 minutes or until a wooden pick inserted in center comes out clean. Transfer to a wire rack and let cool completely in pan (cake will settle slightly). Remove pan sides. Lightly sift powdered sugar over top and garnish with walnut halves. Cut into wedges; top each piece with a dollop of sweetened whipped cream, if desired. Makes 8 to 10 servings.

Making a Mexican Flan (Recipe on facing page)

1 Shake and tilt pan to mix sugar as it begins to caramelize. As sugar melts, it turns straw colored, then quickly darkens to amber. Remove amber syrup from heat at once to prevent scorching.

2 Hold pan in one hand, baking dish in the other. Pour in caramel all at once, tilting dish to distribute syrup evenly over bottom and ½ inch up sides. Syrup cools quickly, so work fast.

3 Set caramel-coated dish in an 8 or 9-inch square baking pan. Quickly stir custard together; pour over caramel. Don't worry if caramel cracks—this won't harm the finished product.

4 Pour boiling water into pan to a depth of about 1 inch. This hot water bath insulates flan, preventing overcooking. Transfer pan to preheated oven, protecting hands with oven mitts.

5 When you chill baked flan, caramel liquefies into a glistening sweet sauce to spoon over each serving. Crunchy Mexican Teacakes (page 197) complement the custard's soft, silky texture.

Custards

Among the simplest of desserts, custards are nothing more than eggs, liquid (almost always milk), sugar, and flavoring. They're either baked to form a solid mold or stirred over simmering water to make a thick, soft, pourable cream. Either kind of custard makes a wonderfully satisfying dessert.

Flan

Mexico   (Pictured on facing page)

A classic dessert that's served from the Middle East to northern Europe and in former Spanish colonies everywhere, *flan* comes to the table crowned with caramel sauce. Undoubtedly, cooks discovered that the sweet sauce made the custard easier to unmold—as well as royally delicious.

⅓ **cup sugar**
6 **eggs**
6 **tablespoons sugar**
1 **teaspoon vanilla**
2 **cups whole milk**
  Boiling water

Preheat oven to 350°. In a small nonstick frying pan over medium heat, melt the ⅓ cup sugar, shaking and tilting pan to mix sugar as it begins to liquefy. Cook just until sugar is amber colored and completely melted. (If sugar turns darker or begins to bubble and foam, it's probably scorched. Discard it and start over with fresh sugar.) Immediately pour amber syrup, all at once, into a 1-quart baking dish, tilting dish to coat bottom and ½ inch of sides. Place dish in an 8 or 9-inch square baking pan; set aside.

In a bowl, beat eggs, the 6 tablespoons sugar, and vanilla until blended but not frothy. Add milk; stir well. Pour into caramel-coated dish. At once pour boiling water into baking pan to a depth of about 1 inch. Bake on center rack of oven for 40 minutes or until center of flan jiggles only slightly when dish is gently shaken.

Remove dish from water at once and let cool for 15 minutes on a wire rack; then refrigerate (caramel liquefies as flan cools). If made ahead, cover with plastic wrap when cooled, then refrigerate for up to 2 days.

To serve, run a knife between flan and dish. Cover dish with a rimmed serving plate; hold plate in place and quickly invert. Caramel will flow over flan. Cut into wedges; spoon caramel over each serving. Makes 6 servings.

FILIPINO LECHE FLAN

Follow directions for **Flan,** but add 3 **egg yolks,** decrease milk to ½ cup, and add 1 large can (13 oz.) **evaporated milk** and 1 teaspoon grated **lime or lemon peel.**

Zabaglione

Italy

Warm, rich, and velvety, this Sicilian stirred custard traditionally includes Marsala wine. Stretching tradition a bit, we've devised a nonalcoholic variation using orange juice.

Zabaglione needs last-minute attention. But don't panic—you can whisk the ingredients together in the top of a double boiler just before dinner, then set aside. You'll need only about 5 minutes (4 minutes for a half recipe) to complete the cooking. Serve the custard in stemmed glasses, and accompany it with crisp cookies.

6 **egg yolks**
¼ **cup sugar**
⅔ **cup sweet or dry Marsala**

Place egg yolks in top of a double boiler. Beat with a wire whisk to blend, then gradually whisk in sugar and Marsala. Pour hot water into bottom of double boiler, making sure water won't touch bottom of top pan. Bring to a boil over high heat, then reduce heat to keep water at a simmer.

Set top of double boiler in place. Whisk mixture until it's thick enough to hold a soft peak briefly when whisk is withdrawn (about 5 minutes; whisk constantly to prevent curdling). Pour into glasses; serve at once. Makes 4 to 6 servings.

ORANGE ZABAGLIONE

Follow directions for **Zabaglione,** but use **orange juice** instead of Marsala. Place 4 to 6 **orange segments** in each glass before pouring in custard.

Tarts

Generally speaking, tarts are simply topless pies, holding custard, fruit, or another sweet filling within a single buttery crust. This rich crust is thicker and sturdier than standard pie crust; once baked and cooled, it can stand on its own. To make our tarts, you can use a tart pan with removable sides (see page 6) or a pie pan.

Coconut Tart

Caribbean

Cooking on the island of Guadeloupe has a tempting French accent—especially noticeable in pastry treats like this coconut-custard delicacy.

>   **Orange flaky pastry (recipe follows)**
>   2   **eggs**
>   ½   **cup sugar**
>   ¼   **teaspoon salt**
>   ¼   **cup all-purpose flour**
>   2⅔ **cups (about 7 oz.) loosely packed sweetened flaked coconut**
>   ½   **cup orange juice**
>   ½   **cup (¼ lb.) butter or margarine, melted**
>   ¼   **cup apple or guava jelly**

Preheat oven to 325°. Prepare pastry. Reserve ⅓ of pastry for lattice top; press remaining pastry evenly over bottom and up sides of a 10-inch tart pan or pie pan. Trim off any excess dough to make edge of pastry flush with pan rim, then prick lightly all over with a fork. Bake for 8 minutes, then transfer pan to a wire rack.

Meanwhile, divide reserved pastry into 10 pieces; roll each into a 10-inch rope and set aside.

In a bowl, lightly beat eggs; then stir in sugar, salt, and flour. Add coconut, orange juice, and butter; stir to blend. Pour into crust. Crisscross dough ropes atop pie to make a lattice, as shown in illustrations below. Trim ends even with pan.

Return tart to oven and bake for 40 minutes or until pastry is golden brown. Transfer tart to a wire rack. Melt jelly in a small pan over low heat;

carefully brush over hot tart. Let cool for at least 12 hours, then remove sides of pan and cut tart into wedges. Makes 10 to 12 servings.

Orange flaky pastry. In a bowl, stir together 1⅔ cups **all-purpose flour,** ⅓ cup **sugar,** 1 teaspoon **baking powder,** and ¼ teaspoon **salt.** Then stir in 1 teaspoon grated **orange peel.** With your fingers, work in ½ cup (¼ lb.) **butter** or margarine, softened, until mixture is well blended. Add 1 **egg;** stir with a fork until dough holds together.

Dutch Magic Tart

Netherlands

You line a tart pan with a rich crust, pour in cake batter, then drizzle chocolate syrup atop—and like magic, the syrup sinks down during baking to form a dark, fudgy layer between cake and pastry.

>   **Short Pastry (recipe at right)**
>   1   **cup all-purpose flour**
>   1½ **teaspoons baking powder**
>   4   **tablespoons butter or margarine, softened**
>   1   **cup sugar**
>   1   **egg**
>   ½   **teaspoon vanilla**
>   ½   **cup milk**
>   **Chocolate syrup (recipe follows)**
>   **Sweetened whipped cream or ice cream**

Preheat oven to 350°. Prepare pastry and press evenly over bottom and up sides of a 10-inch tart pan or pie pan. Trim off any excess dough to make edge of pastry flush with pan rim. Set aside.

In a bowl, stir together flour and baking powder. In another bowl, beat butter and sugar until blended; beat in egg and vanilla. Add flour mixture alternately with milk, starting and ending with flour. Spoon mixture into crust. Prepare chocolate syrup; pour evenly over batter. Bake for 45 minutes or until cake is firm in center when lightly pressed. Transfer to a wire rack and let cool completely. Cut into wedges; top with whipped cream. Makes 6 servings.

Chocolate syrup. In a bowl, combine ½ cup **sugar** and ¼ cup sifted **unsweetened cocoa.** Add 6 tablespoons **water** and ½ teaspoon **vanilla;** stir until smooth.

HOW TO MAKE SHORT PASTRY

Unlike pie dough, this buttery press-in pastry benefits from plenty of handling. Stir together 1 cup **all-purpose flour** and 2 tablespoons **sugar.** With your fingers, work 6 tablespoons **butter** or margarine into flour mixture until well blended. Stir in 2 **egg yolks** or 1 whole egg with a fork; keep stirring until dough holds together. (Or whirl flour, sugar, and butter in a food processor until mixture resembles fine crumbs; add egg yolks and whirl just until dough holds together.)

Brandied Apricot Tart

France

Because this quick French tart uses canned rather than fresh apricots, you can enjoy it any time of year.

> **Short Pastry (recipe above)**
> ¾ **cup apricot jam**
> 2 **tablespoons apricot brandy or apricot-flavored liqueur**
> 4 **cans (17 oz. each) peeled whole apricots, drained well, cut in half, and pitted**
> 2 **tablespoons slivered almonds, toasted (page 87)**

Preheat oven to 350°. Prepare pastry and press evenly over bottom and sides of a 10-inch tart pan or pie pan. Trim off excess dough to make edge of pastry flush with pan rim, then prick lightly all over with a fork. Bake for 8 minutes; transfer to a wire rack.

In a small pan over low heat, combine jam and brandy; heat, stirring, until jam melts. Brush a thin layer of jam glaze over bottom of pastry. Then add a layer of apricots, cut side down; brush with more glaze. Decoratively arrange a second layer of apricots, cut side down, atop the first; brush generously with glaze. Sprinkle with almonds and brush with remaining glaze. Bake for 15 minutes or until crust is golden brown and apricots are heated through. Transfer to a wire rack and let cool. Cut into wedges. Makes 6 to 8 servings.

Linzertorte

Austria

When is a torte a tart? When it's a *Linzertorte.* A specialty of Linz, Austria, this lattice-topped tart features a rich, cookylike crust and a thick jam filling. Raspberry jam is the traditional choice, but you can use another fruit flavor if you prefer (you'll need about 2 cups). Or start with fresh berries and make the cooked fruit filling.

Though Linzertorte can be served the day it's made, it tastes best if allowed to stand for a day.

> 6 **cups hulled, halved strawberries (or whole blackberries, blueberries, boysenberries, olallieberries, or raspberries; or sliced pitted apricots, nectarines, plums, or peeled peaches)**
> ¾ **to 1¼ cups granulated sugar (depending on sweetness of fruit)**
> 1 **tablespoon lemon juice**
> 1 **cinnamon stick (optional; about 2 inches long)**
> **Short Pastry (recipe at left)**
> 3 **tablespoons granulated sugar**
> ⅔ **cup ground unblanched filberts or almonds**
> **Sifted powdered sugar**

In a 3-quart pan, combine strawberries, the ¾ to 1¼ cups granulated sugar, lemon juice, and cinnamon stick (if used); stir to mix. Bring to a boil over high heat. Reduce heat to medium-low and cook, stirring frequently to prevent sticking, until mixture is thickened and reduced to about 2 cups (45 minutes to 1 hour). Remove from heat, discard cinnamon stick, and let mixture cool to lukewarm.

Preheat oven to 350°. Prepare pastry, adding the 3 tablespoons granulated sugar and filberts to flour mixture. Reserve ⅓ of pastry for lattice top. Press remaining pastry evenly over bottom and sides of a 10-inch tart pan; trim off excess dough to make edge of pastry flush with pan rim, then prick lightly all over with a fork. Bake for 8 minutes, then transfer pan to a wire rack. Pour in filling.

Divide reserved pastry into 10 pieces. Roll each piece into a 10-inch rope; crisscross ropes atop filling to make a lattice (see illustrations on facing page). Trim ends even with pan. Return tart to oven and bake for 40 minutes or until crust is golden brown. Transfer to a wire rack and let cool completely; cover with foil and let stand at room temperature until next day. Just before serving, dust with powdered sugar. Cut into wedges. Makes 10 to 12 servings.

Fruit desserts

A perfectly ripe peach, a snappy-crisp apple, a wedge of chilled melon—these are simple, sublime desserts that need no embellishment. But you can always add a compatible cheese or offer a topping of tangy *crème fraîche* (page 212). Or serve several fruits in sweetly refreshing combination, as in our Chinese pear compote.

Sometimes, though, you'll really want to gild the lily. For those times, we offer a few extra-rich fruit treats: creamy Strawberries Romanoff, buttery Apple Crumble, caramel-sauced Blazing Bananas. And for dried-fruit lovers, there's a compote of mixed fruits plumped in a spicy honey-brandy syrup.

Fresh Berry Soup

Scandinavia

Sometimes thin as punch, sometimes thick as pudding, fruit soups are special favorites in Scandinavia—and in Germany, Poland, and parts of Asia. This vivid berry soup can be served hot or cold, at breakfast or for dessert (it thickens as it chills).

You can substitute frozen sweetened berries for fresh—but if you do, don't use sugar in the soup.

> 1 **cup water**
> ⅔ **cup sugar**
> 4 **cups fresh boysenberries, raspberries, olallieberries, or currants (or a combination)**
> 1½ **tablespoons cornstarch mixed with 2 tablespoons water**
> **Whipping cream or unsweetened whipped cream (optional)**

In a 2 to 3-quart pan, combine water and sugar. Bring to a boil over high heat; add berries. When mixture returns to a boil, cook for 1 minute, taking care that berries do not overcook, and fall apart. (If you want a smooth, seedless soup, force cooked berry-sugar mixture through a strainer, then return to pan and reheat to boiling.) Stir in cornstarch mixture; bring to a boil over high heat, stirring gently and constantly. Serve hot. Or let cool; then cover, refrigerate, and serve cold. If desired, pass cream at the table to spoon into soup. Makes 4 to 6 servings.

GETTING LIQUORS TO FLAME

Any liquor with an alcohol content of 20 percent or more (40 proof or higher) can be ignited. Brandy, kirsch, and rum fall into this category, as do sherries, vermouths, and many liqueurs. When heated, all release vapors that catch fire easily.

To flame liquor, measure it into a small, long-handled pan and heat *rapidly* over highest heat until bubbly. Strike a long-handled match and hold it close to the liquid's surface to ignite the vapors (be sure the exhaust fan is off). Pour the burning liquor all at once over the food to be flamed, then spoon it continuously over food until the flames die. For the most dramatic presentation, darken the room when you do this; the pale blue alcohol flame is hard to see otherwise.

CAUTION: Keep hands, face, and clothing away from food until flames die down completely.

Strawberries Romanoff

Russia

This Russian dessert is much like an English fruit fool—it's a simple but heavenly mixture of lightly crushed or chopped fresh fruit and cream.

> 4 **cups strawberries, hulled and quartered**
> ¼ **cup powdered sugar**
> 2 **tablespoons Cointreau or other orange-flavored liqueur**
> 1 **tablespoon brandy**
> ½ **pint (1 cup) whipping cream**

Place strawberries in a bowl; sprinkle on sugar, Cointreau, and brandy. Toss lightly to mix, then cover and refrigerate for at least 2 hours to blend flavors. Spoon out and reserve about ¼ cup of the berry mixture.

Beat cream until soft peaks form; fold in remaining strawberry mixture. Spoon into 6 dessert dishes and garnish with reserved strawberries. Serve immediately. Makes 6 servings.

Blazing Bananas

Brazil

Looking for a dramatic, extravagantly rich finale to a light meal? Try bananas in coffee-caramel sauce, first flamed with rum, then spooned over ice cream and topped with whipped cream and toasted nuts. You can make a Jamaican version of the same dessert simply by substituting citrus juice for coffee in the sauce.

⅓ **cup firmly packed brown sugar**
⅓ **cup butter or margarine**
1 **tablespoon powdered instant coffee**
4 **to 6 medium-size firm ripe bananas**
¼ **cup dark rum**
1 **quart vanilla or coffee ice cream (optional)**
 Sweetened whipped cream
6 **tablespoons sliced almonds, toasted (page 87)**

In a wide frying pan over medium heat, combine sugar, butter, and coffee; heat until bubbly. Meanwhile, peel bananas and cut diagonally into ½-inch slices. Add bananas to pan; turn to coat evenly with sauce. Flame rum as directed in "Getting Liquors to Flame" (facing page). After flame subsides, spoon bananas and sauce into dessert dishes (over scoops of ice cream, if desired). Top with whipped cream and almonds, and serve immediately. Makes 4 to 6 servings.

JAMAICAN HOT BANANAS

Follow directions for **Blazing Bananas,** but omit instant coffee. Instead, add ¼ cup **frozen orange juice concentrate** (thawed) and 1 tablespoon **lemon juice** to butter-sugar mixture.

Casablanca Oranges

Morocco

Morocco's citrus crop easily rivals that of the United States—and this simple dessert is equally welcome after an American or a Moroccan meal (you might offer it after a dinner of Bastilla, page 119). The fragrant orange flower water that flavors the fruit is sold in imported food shops and liquor stores.

4 **large navel oranges, peeled, white membranes removed**
2 **tablespoons *each* sugar and water**
1 **teaspoon orange flower water**
1 **tablespoon chopped pistachio nuts, almonds, or walnuts**

Holding fruit over a bowl to catch juice, cut between membranes of each orange and lift out segments; place in bowl. Stir together sugar, water, and orange flower water; drizzle over oranges, then cover and refrigerate for at least 2 hours. Evenly spoon oranges and juice into 4 dessert dishes; top with pistachio nuts. Makes 4 servings.

Apple Crumble

Australia

Like our own apple brown betty, Australian apple crumble is a spicy, homey dessert that's deliciously sweet and rich. To make it, you'll need firm, tart apples such as Granny Smith or Newtown pippin (or use Anjou or other firm pears).

3 **cups cubed day-old white bread (about 5 slices)**
⅓ **cup butter or margarine, melted**
6 **cups thinly sliced firm apples or pears**
1 **cup firmly packed brown sugar**
2 **tablespoons lemon juice**
½ **teaspoon *each* grated lemon peel and ground nutmeg**
1 **teaspoon *each* ground cinnamon and vanilla**
¾ **cup hot water**
 Whipping cream or ice cream (optional)

Butter a 2 quart casserole; set aside. In a bowl, toss together bread cubes and butter. In another bowl, stir together apples, sugar, lemon juice, lemon peel, nutmeg, cinnamon, and vanilla. Evenly spread ⅓ of the buttered bread cubes in casserole, then spoon on about half the apple mixture. Top with half the remaining bread cubes, then layer on remaining apple mixture and remaining bread cubes.

Pour hot water over top bread cubes, then cover and bake in a 350° oven for 45 minutes. Uncover and continue baking for 10 minutes or until top is golden brown. Serve warm or at room temperature; top with cream or ice cream, if desired. Makes 8 servings.

...Fruit desserts

Anise Pear Compote

China

Fresh Chinese snow or apple pears are the traditional stars of this lightly spiced compote. They're sold in Asian markets during autumn; if you can't find them, use Anjou or any other firm pears.

- ½ cup sugar
- ¾ cup water
- ¼ teaspoon anise seeds, crushed
- 1 teaspoon lemon juice
  Dash of salt
- 1½ pounds firm ripe pears
- 1 large orange, peeled, white membrane removed
- 1 grapefruit, peeled, white membrane removed
- ½ cup seedless grapes

In a 2-quart pan, bring sugar, water, anise seeds, lemon juice, and salt to a boil over high heat; then reduce heat to keep syrup at a simmer. Peel, quarter, and core pears. Place in hot syrup, cover, and simmer until barely tender when pierced (about 6 minutes); let cool.

Holding fruit over a bowl to catch juices, cut between membranes of orange and grapefruit; lift out segments. Add segments and juice to cooled pear mixture. Add grapes; mix gently. Cover; refrigerate until cold. Makes 4 servings.

Fresh Fruit with Crème Fraîche

France

With the richness of whipping cream and the consistency and tang of sour cream, *crème fraîche* offers an easy way to dress up any kind of fresh fruit—from peaches and berries in summer to pears and oranges in winter. By adding powdered sugar, you can make a sweeter, thinner topping that's essentially identical to Norwegian clabbered cream.

Making crème fraîche is simple. Just warm whipping cream, then add buttermilk. After about 12 hours at room temperature, the mixture will be thickened. Flavor depends on the brand of buttermilk you use, so select one you enjoy.

- Crème fraîche (recipe follows)
- 4 cups sliced fresh fruit of the season
  Sugar (optional)

Prepare crème fraîche.

Evenly divide fruit into 4 dishes and sprinkle with sugar, if desired. Top each portion with about 2 tablespoons crème fraîche. Makes 4 servings.

Crème fraîche. In a small pan over low heat, warm ½ pint (1 cup) **whipping cream** to between 90° and 100°. Stir in 1 tablespoon **buttermilk.** Pour into a glass or plastic container; cover and let stand at room temperature (68° to 72°) until mixture begins to thicken—12 to 16 hours. (Or use a yogurt maker—thickening time is about the same.) Refrigerate for at least 24 hours before using. During this time, the cream develops its characteristic acid flavor and thickens further, reaching an almost spreadable consistency. Store in the refrigerator for up to 2 weeks or as long as the taste is tangy but fresh. Makes 1 cup.

Brandied Fruit Compote

Jewish heritage

You might find a spicy, brandy-spiked compote like this one served in a Jewish home as part of a Hanukkah meal. Our recipe is just one version of a dish that's enjoyed all over the world—in Scandinavia and Peru, Russia and the Middle East. It's marvelous for dessert, and just as good as an accompaniment to baked chicken or roast goose.

- 3 cups water
- ⅓ cup honey
- 1 teaspoon grated orange peel
- 5 whole allspice, crushed
- ¼ teaspoon ground ginger
- 1 cinnamon stick (about 2 inches long)
- ½ cup raisins
- 2 packages (6 oz. each) mixed dried fruit
- 1 small apple (unpeeled), cored and diced
- ½ cup *each* orange juice and brandy, or 1 cup orange juice

In a 3-quart pan, combine water, honey, orange peel, allspice, ginger, cinnamon stick, raisins, and dried fruit. Bring to a boil over high heat; then cover, reduce heat, and simmer for 3 minutes. Remove pan from heat. Remove and discard cinnamon stick; stir in apple, orange juice, and brandy. Pour into a serving bowl and serve hot. Or let cool; then cover, refrigerate, and serve cold. Serve within 1 week. Makes 6 servings.

Fresh fruit ices

If you've traveled around Europe or taken a trip through Mexico, you've probably discovered the cooling refreshment of fruit ices: French *sorbets*, Italian *granitas*, and Mexican *paletas*. For authentically fresh-tasting results, use only *fresh* fruit juices in these recipes. If you don't, the ice won't have the pure fruit flavor it should.

Lemon Ice

Italy

Lemon zest and fresh lemon juice give *granita di limon* its refreshing tang.

> 1 **small lemon**
> **About ½ cup fresh lemon juice**
> 1 **cup sugar**
> 4 **cups water**
> **Dash of salt**

Using a vegetable peeler, pare zest (colored outer layer of peel) from lemon. Squeeze lemon, then strain juice and pour it into a 1-cup glass measure. Add enough additional lemon juice to make ⅔ cup liquid; cover and set aside.

Cut lemon zest into ½-inch pieces and place in a food processor; add sugar and process until zest is finely chopped. Place mixture in a 3-quart pan and add water and salt. Heat just until sugar is dissolved; let cool, then stir in lemon juice. Freeze as directed in "Freezing Fresh Fruit Ices" (below). Makes about 4½ cups (8 to 9 servings).

FREEZING FRESH FRUIT ICES

Prepare fruit purée as recipe directs; then pour it into a shallow metal pan, cover with foil, and freeze until solid (4 to 8 hours). Remove ice from freezer and let it stand at room temperature until you can break it into chunks with a spoon. Scoop into a food processor, about ⅓ at a time; use on-off bursts to break up ice, then run processor continuously until ice turns to velvety slush. Freeze until solid, process again.

Serve at once; or cover and freeze for up to 1 month. Before serving frozen ices, let them stand at room temperature for about 10 minutes to soften slightly.

Cranberry Ice

Mexico

In Mexico, you can enjoy fruit ices like this one in a juice bar—or buy them as "popsicles" from a street vendor.

> 1 **pound (4 cups) cranberries**
> 1½ **cups water**
> ⅔ **cup sugar (or to taste)**
> ½ **cup fresh orange juice (about 1 large orange)**
> ½ **teaspoon grated orange peel**
> 1 **tablespoon fresh lemon juice**

In a 2-quart pan, combine cranberries and water. Cook over medium heat, uncovered, until skins pop; stir often. Pour mixture through a wire strainer, pressing with the back of a spoon to force out as much liquid as possible. Discard residue. Combine strained cranberry mixture with sugar, orange juice, orange peel, and lemon juice; stir until sugar is dissolved. Let cool, then freeze as directed in "Freezing Fresh Fruit Ices" (at left). Makes about 3½ cups (6 or 7 servings).

Orange Ice

France

Orange peel steeped in a base of sugar and water gives this ice its fresh, natural flavor. For an extra-pretty presentation, freeze the ice in hollowed-out orange shells.

> 2 **tablespoons grated orange peel**
> 1¼ **cups sugar**
> 1 **cup water**
> 1½ **cups fresh orange juice (about 3 large oranges)**
> 2 **tablespoons fresh lemon juice**

In a medium-size bowl, combine orange peel, sugar, and water. Cover and let stand for at least 4 hours, stirring occasionally. Stir well, then pour through a fine wire strainer and discard peel. Add orange juice and lemon juice to orange mixture. Freeze as directed in "Freezing Fresh Fruit Ices" (at left). If desired, pour mixture into orange shells; cover filled shells and freeze until ice is solid. Serve at once, or package airtight and freeze for up to 1 month. Makes about 3 cups (about 6 servings).

Ice cream treats

Ice cream has been a popular dessert for centuries, and there's no indication that the situation is going to change. Diners around the world enjoy this rich, cool treat, either all by itself or dressed up with fruit, nuts, sauces, or other extras.

Any of the three make-ahead desserts on this page provides a refreshing finale to a robust or highly spiced meal.

Quick Tortoni

Italy

After a hearty Italian dinner, serve this easy version of *tortoni*: vanilla ice cream studded with cherries, chocolate, and almonds, frozen in individual paper cups.

- ½ **gallon vanilla ice cream, slightly softened**
- 1 **teaspoon *each* grated orange peel and grated lemon peel**
- 2 **tablespoons brandy**
- 1 **jar (8½ oz.) maraschino cherries (without stems), drained well**
- 4 **ounces semisweet chocolate or ¾ cup semisweet chocolate pieces, coarsely chopped**
- ¾ **cup slivered blanched almonds, toasted (page 87)**

Place ice cream in a large bowl. Stir in orange peel, lemon peel, and brandy. Reserve 8 to 10 cherries; coarsely chop remaining cherries. Add chopped cherries to ice cream along with chocolate and almonds; fold in until blended.

Spoon into 8 to 10 paper-lined muffin cups, or into 8 to 10 sherbet glasses. Top each cup with one of the reserved cherries.

Freeze until solid (about 4 hours). Serve, or wrap airtight and store in the freezer for up to 2 weeks. Let stand for 5 minutes before serving. Makes 8 to 10 servings.

Papaya-Lime Ice Cream

West Indies

Papaya and fresh lime add tropical flavor to this creamy summertime delight. Crisp cookies such as Mexican Teacakes (page 197) or Swedish Spritz (page 199) taste delicious alongside, offering a pleasantly crunchy contrast to the ice cream's smooth, velvety texture. (See page 46 for tips on seeding and chopping papaya.)

- 2 **cups (about 1 lb. *total*) peeled, seeded, chopped papaya**
- ¼ **cup fresh lime juice**
- ½ **pint (1 cup) whipping cream**
- 1 **cup half-and-half (light cream)**
- 1¼ **cups sugar**

In a blender or food processor, whirl papaya until puréed. Add lime juice, cream, half-and-half, and sugar; whirl until blended. Pour purée into a bowl and cover with plastic wrap. Freeze until mixture is hardened around edges (about 1½ hours), then beat with an electric mixer until smooth (or whirl in a food processor). Re-cover with plastic wrap, placing wrap directly on surface of mixture, and return to freezer until firm (several hours or until next day). Beat or whirl again until soft, then cover, return to freezer, and freeze until firm. Makes about 4 cups (about 8 servings).

Coffee Cream Sundae

Belgium

Combining coffee with ice cream for dessert is a continental custom well worth duplicating. In this Belgian creation, a sweet coffee-brandy sauce tops scoops of vanilla or coffee ice cream. You'll need to use a 4-quart pan to boil down the sugar-coffee mixture; it foams and bubbles vigorously as it boils down, and would overflow a smaller pan.

- 1 **cup firmly packed brown sugar**
- 1 **cup strong coffee**
- ¼ **teaspoon vanilla**
- 1 **tablespoon brandy**
- 1 **quart vanilla or coffee ice cream**
  Unsweetened whipped cream
- ⅓ **cup whole blanched almonds, toasted (page 87)**

In a 4-quart pan, combine brown sugar and coffee. Bring to a boil over high heat; boil, uncovered, stirring occasionally, until thickened (about 10 minutes). Remove from heat and stir in vanilla and brandy; let cool completely. Scoop ice cream into 6 serving dishes; top each portion with sauce, a dollop of whipped cream, and a sprinkling of almonds. Makes 6 servings.

Confections

When only the sweetest of sweets will do, try one of these candy-shop favorites: rich French truffles, chewy Indian *halva*, or crunchy peanut brittle from the United States.

Western Nut Brittle

United States

Baking soda is essential for producing the porous texture characteristic of nut brittles.

Butter
1½ **cups sugar**
¾ **cup light corn syrup**
¼ **cup water**
2 **cups coarsely chopped peanuts, almonds, filberts, pecans, or walnuts (or combination)**
1 **teaspoon baking soda**
½ **teaspoon salt**
1 **teaspoon vanilla**

Butter a rimmed baking pan; set aside. In a heavy 3-quart pan, stir together sugar, corn syrup, and water. Bring to a boil over high heat. Boil rapidly, stirring occasionally with a long-handled wooden spoon, until mixture begins to turn golden. Stir in 4 tablespoons butter. Continue to boil, stirring frequently to prevent burning, until temperature reaches 300° on a candy thermometer (hard crack stage), or until a teaspoon of syrup dropped into cold water separates into a hard, brittle thread.

Immediately remove from heat and stir in peanuts, soda, and salt (mixture will foam up). Stir in vanilla; pour at once into prepared pan and spread out. Let candy cool, then break into pieces. Store airtight. Makes about ¾ pound.

Chocolate Truffles

France

In France and Italy, these tiny sweets are served with strong coffee at the end of a meal.

4 **ounces semisweet chocolate, chopped**
2 **tablespoons whipping cream**
About 2 tablespoons ground chocolate or unsweetened cocoa

Place semisweet chocolate and cream in a small pan over low heat (if heat is too high, chocolate will separate). Heat, stirring constantly, until chocolate is melted and well blended with cream. Pour into a small bowl; cover and refrigerate just until mixture is firm enough to hold its shape (about 40 minutes).

Meanwhile, spread ground chocolate on a small plate. Using your fingers, quickly shape chocolate-cream mixture into balls, using about 1 teaspoon per ball. As each truffle is shaped, roll it in ground chocolate until completely coated. Arrange in a single layer in a shallow container; cover and refrigerate for up to 2 weeks. Let stand at room temperature for 5 to 10 minutes before serving. Makes about 1 dozen.

Halva

India

Unlike Middle Eastern sesame-seed *halvah*, Indian *halva* is based on a mixture of farina and milk cooked until thick. You can buy farina in the cereal section of your market.

Butter
2½ **cups slivered almonds, toasted (page 87)**
¼ **cup regular farina**
1½ **cups milk**
½ **teaspoon *each* salt and ground cardamom**
¼ **teaspoon ground cinnamon**
⅔ **cup sugar**
2 **tablespoons honey**
½ **cup raisins, coarsely chopped**

Butter an 8-inch square baking pan; set aside. Place 1 cup of the almonds in a blender or food processor and whirl until finely ground. Coarsely chop remaining 1½ cups almonds. Set nuts aside.

In a large pan over medium heat, melt 2 tablespoons butter. Add farina and cook, stirring, until lightly toasted. Gradually add milk, stirring until blended. Add salt, cardamom, cinnamon, sugar, honey, raisins, and ground almonds. Increase heat to medium-high. Cook, stirring constantly, until mixture is thick and stiff and pulls away from sides of pan (about 15 minutes). Stir in 2 more tablespoons butter and 1 cup of the chopped almonds. Spread evenly in prepared baking pan; sprinkle with remaining ½ cup chopped almonds.

Let candy cool, then cover and refrigerate until firm (about 2 hours). Cut into 1½-inch squares. Makes about 24 pieces.

Beverages: Coffee, tea, and hot chocolate

For soothing sipping any time of day, sample this tempting trayful of hot and cold beverages. The coffees and teas are good for afternoon or after dinner (you may want to serve *caffè granita* as a dessert). And to make breakfast extra special or warm up a chilly night, try a cup of Mexican chocolate or Norwegian hot cocoa.

Hot Thai Coffee

Thailand

To make coffee Thai style, you spice strongly brewed coffee with cardamom, then smooth and enrich it with sweetened condensed or evaporated milk. The result: an exotic-tasting beverage to serve hot or cold—almost as a dessert.

> ¾ **cup ground coffee**
> 2⅔ **cups water**
> **Ground cardamom**
> **About ½ cup sweetened condensed milk**

Brew coffee in a drip-style coffee maker or percolator, using amounts of coffee and water specified above. Pour into 4 cups. Add a dash of cardamom and about 2 tablespoons condensed milk to each cup; stir to blend. Makes 4 servings.

COLD THAI COFFEE

Brew coffee as directed for **Hot Thai Coffee;** let cool slightly. Fill four 10 to 12-ounce glasses to the rim with **ice cubes;** fill ⅔ full with coffee. Omit sweetened condensed milk; instead, stir 2 tablespoons **evaporated milk** into each serving. Sweeten to taste with **sugar.**

STORING COFFEE

Heat and moisture cause coffee to go stale quickly, so store both beans and ground coffee airtight in refrigerator or freezer. Glass containers with tight screw-on lids are your best choice. When you want to brew coffee, just remove the amount you need; there's no need to thaw or bring to room temperature before using. Buy coffee in small quantity; even if stored as directed above, it loses its freshness after a month.

Turkish Coffee

Turkey

"Turkish coffee" describes a certain grind of coffee and method of brewing (it doesn't mean the beans came from Turkey). You sweeten and boil a "powder" of pulverized coffee beans, then pour the strong, almost syrupy beverage into tiny cups without straining out the grounds.

> 1½ **cups cold water**
> 4 **teaspoons sugar**
> ¼ **cup pulverized medium or dark roast coffee beans**

In a small pan, combine the 1½ cups water and sugar. Cook over medium heat, stirring occasionally, until sugar is dissolved. Add coffee. Increase heat to medium-high; bring to a boil and let mixture froth, then remove from heat and let foam settle. Repeat this frothing process 2 more times. (For coffee that's less strong, allow mixture to froth only once.) Add a few drops of cold water to settle the grounds (don't stir). Spoon some of the foam into each of 4 demitasse cups, then pour in coffee. Makes 4 servings.

Caffè Granita

Italy

Fruit-flavored *granitas* (see page 213) aren't the only kind of water ices enjoyed in Italy; coffee granita is popular, too. Here, it's beaten to a soft slush and combined with ice cream to make a cool, bittersweet beverage.

> 2 **cups strong coffee, room temperature or cold**
> ½ **cup coffee, orange, or almond-flavored liqueur**
> **About 1 pint vanilla ice cream**
> **Sweetened whipped cream (optional)**
> 4 **chocolate-covered coffee beans (optional)**

In a medium-size bowl, stir together coffee and liqueur. Pour into 1 or 2 ice cube trays. Freeze until solid (about 4 hours); then remove cubes from trays. If made ahead, place in plastic bags and store in freezer for up to 1 month.

To serve, whirl coffee cubes in a blender or food processor until slushy (1 to 2 minutes), stopping occasionally to stir mixture down. Divide equally among four 8-ounce glasses. To each glass, add 1 or 2 scoops of ice cream; top with a dollop of whipped cream and a chocolate-covered coffee bean, if desired. Eat ice cream with a spoon; sip slush through a straw. Makes 4 servings.

Hot Chocolate

Mexico

Traditional Mexican hot chocolate is whipped to a froth with a wooden tool called a *molinillo*. Our recipe is authentic in flavor but modern in method: you grind chocolate, almonds, and sugar in the blender, then add hot milk and whirl until frothy.

> **4 cups whole milk**
> **3 cinnamon sticks (*each* about 3 inches long)**
> **6 ounces bittersweet or semisweet chocolate, broken into pieces**
> **⅓ cup slivered blanched almonds**
> **2 tablespoons sugar**

In a 2-quart pan, combine milk and cinnamon sticks. Warm over low heat, stirring occasionally. Meanwhile, place chocolate, almonds, and sugar in a blender; whirl into a coarse powder. Increase heat under milk to high; stir until milk begins to boil. Lift out cinnamon sticks and set aside. Pour half the milk into blender; whirl to blend. Add remaining milk and whirl until blended. Split cinnamon sticks in half lengthwise; put one piece in each of 6 mugs and fill with hot, foamy chocolate. Makes 6 servings.

Hot Cocoa

Norway

Norwegians consider hot cocoa properly made if a bit of butter is whisked in at the very last.

> **½ cup whipping cream**
> **2 tablespoons light rum**
> **6 cups whole milk**
> **2 tablespoons *each* sugar and unsweetened cocoa**
> **2 tablespoons butter**
> **Ground cinnamon**

Beat cream until it mounds softly; fold in rum. Set aside. In a 3-quart pan, warm milk over medium heat. In a small bowl, stir together sugar and co-

coa; then stir in a little of the hot milk to make a smooth paste. Stir cocoa mixture back into milk; increase heat to medium-high and cook, stirring, until milk just begins to boil. Immediately remove from heat and add butter; whisk (or stir) until melted. Pour into cups; top each with cream and a dusting of cinnamon. Makes 6 to 8 servings.

Spiced Tea

India

Sweet, spicy *masala chai* is an enjoyable finale to an Indian meal.

> **6 cups cold water**
> **12 whole cardamom pods**
> **3 cinnamon sticks (*each* 2½ to 3 inches long), broken into pieces**
> **3 tablespoons Ceylon tea**
> **¾ cup sugar**
> **2 cups milk**

In a 3-quart pan, combine water, cardamom pods, and cinnamon sticks. Bring to a boil over high heat; cover and boil for 10 minutes, then stir in tea. When mixture returns to a boil, cover, reduce heat, and simmer for 2 to 3 minutes. Add sugar and milk; stir until sugar is dissolved, then cover and simmer for 3 to 4 more minutes. Pour through a fine wire strainer; discard tea leaves and spices. Serve hot. Makes 6 servings.

Green Tea

Japan

To make authentic Japanese-style tea, use simmering water; the Japanese say that boiling water produces flat-tasting tea.

> **2 tablespoons green tea**
> **4 cups simmering water**

Fill an earthenware teapot with hot tap water. Let pot stand until heated through (about 5 minutes); pour out and discard water. Place tea in pot, then pour in the simmering water. Let steep for 2 to 4 minutes, depending on desired strength. Serve in small handleless teacups. Makes 8 to 10 servings.

General Index

...General Index

...General Index

Index to Countries & Regions

...Index to Countries & Regions